International Perspectives on Early Childhood Education and Care

Edited by Jan Georgeson and Jane Payler

Open University Press

Open University Press
McGraw-Hill Education
McGraw-Hill House
Shoppenhangers Road
Maidenhead
Berkshire
England
SL6 2QL

email: enquiries@openup.co.uk
world wide web: www.openup.co.uk

2011002616

and Two Penn Plaza, New York, NY 10121-2289, USA

First published 2013

Copyright © Jan Georgeson and Jane Payler 2013

A catalogue record of this book is available from the British Library

ISBN-13: 978-0-33-524591-8
ISBN-10: 0-33-524591-9
e-ISBN: 978-0-33-524592-5

Library of Congress Cataloging-in-Publication Data
CIP data applied for

Typeset by Aptara, Inc.
Printed in Great Britain by CPI Antony Rowe, Chippenham, Wiltshire.

The **McGraw·Hill** Companies

International Perspectives on Early
Childhood Education and Care

Contents

PART 1

Setting the scene

PART 2

How approaches have developed

Figures

Tables

Contributors

Verity Campbell-Barr is a Lecturer in Early Childhood Studies within the School of Education at Plymouth University. Before joining Plymouth University, she worked as a researcher conducting research on both national and local policy evaluations. Her research interests include the mixed economy of early childhood education and care provision, family decision-making on work–life balance, and multiple perspectives on the quality of early childhood education and care.

Federica Caruso is a Graduate Teaching Assistant at Newman University College where she teaches the course on 'Research Methods' on the 'Working with Children, Young People and Families' Programme. She is currently completing her PhD at the University of Leicester based on her extensive ethnographic inquiry on multi-professional practices in an urban children's centre in central England. Her research interests are in early childhood education, with a particular focus on the dilemmas and challenges faced by the different practitioners involved in children's services.

Carmen Dalli is Professor of Early Childhood Education and Director of the Institute for Early Childhood Studies at Victoria University of Wellington, New Zealand. Her research focuses on professionalism in early years practice and reveals the intersection of policy and pedagogy in children's and adults' experiences of group-based early childhood settings. Her recent book (with Linda Miller and Mathias Urban) *Early Childhood Grows Up: Towards a Critical Ecology of the Profession* published by Springer (2012) is based on a project that investigated *A Day in the Life of an Early Years Practitioner* in six countries.

Rebecca Carter Dillon is a Lecturer in Early Childhood Studies at the University of Plymouth, UK. She has a background in International Development in Sub-Saharan Africa and community development work in the UK. She has a particular interest in issues affecting disadvantaged children and families, such as refugee and asylum seeker communities, and her teaching focuses on social policy, social inequalities, child poverty, and childhood and wellbeing in the developing world.

Annie Davy is a freelance writer, facilitator of action learning, and a teacher with experience in early years, playwork, organizational and human development. She has an enduring interest in the natural world and the power of time spent with trees, sea, rivers, mountains, and plants for inspiration, creative renewal, and mental well-being. Annie was Head of Early Years for Oxfordshire County Council for 12 years and adviser to Learning through Landscapes (www.ltl.org.uk) for two years. She is now Director of The Nature Effect Community Interest Company (www.thenatureeffect.co.uk) and Barracks Lane Community Garden (www.barrackslanegarden. org.uk).

Chandrika Devarakonda is a Senior Lecturer in the Faculty of Education and Children's Services at the University of Chester. She has conducted research projects on several issues such as international perspectives in early childhood provision in India and the UK, inclusion, and diversity. There were several opportunities to share the research findings in different national and international conferences.

Alena Držalová has been teaching preschool children since 1992, and in 2002 she became headteacher of a split-site kindergarten for over 300 children in Pilsen, Czech Republic. She lectures on BA and professional development programmes for preschool teachers at the University of West Bohemia and her kindergarten provides seminars and block placement experiences for local students in training. Alena is also a preschool education consultant qualified in special needs and she teaches the special educational needs class within her kindergarten.

Hasina Banu Ebrahim is Discipline Coordinator/Leader of Early Childhood Development at the University of the Free State, South Africa. Her interest lies in deepening knowledge and practice in ECE, teacher education, and research from local realities. She is interested in alternative perspectives on enhancing practice, strengthening research capacity, and informing policy. She is Deputy President for the South Africa Research Association for ECE.

Susan Edwards is Associate Professor and Principal Research Fellow in the Faculty of Education at the Australian Catholic University. Research interests include examining how teachers perceive different dimensions of the early childhood curriculum, including their understandings of development, learning, and play. Susan is interested in examining how these dimensions of curriculum relate to teacher pedagogy and professional learning in early childhood contexts. She is also interested in examining the role of digital technologies in early learning and young children's play. Susan has published her work across a range of research and practitioner orientated journals, and has authored and edited several books, including the 2010 co-edited text *Engaging Play* (with Liz Brooker, published by McGraw-Hill).

Jan Georgeson is a Research Fellow in Early Education Development in the School of Education at Plymouth University, UK. After working as a teacher of children with special educational needs in a range of secondary, primary, and preschool settings, Jan developed a strong interest in the diversity of early years provision while working as an inspector of educational provision in the non-maintained sector. In 2006, she completed an EdD in Educational Disadvantage and Special Educational Needs at the University of Birmingham. Since then she has worked on research projects on disability and disadvantage from birth through school and into post-compulsory education, as well teaching candidates working towards Early Years Professional Status.

Dora Ho is Associate Professor of Early Childhood Education at the Hong Kong Institute of Education, Hong Kong SAR, China. Her research interests include school leadership, education policy, curriculum and pedagogy, and early childhood education. She has written extensively on issues of school leadership, curriculum change, policy of quality assurance, and teacher professionalism. She conducts research to identify the possibilities and difficulties encountered by local preschools in the change process. She has also worked as a consultant for school development projects. Two of her consultancy projects were awarded the Outstanding School Development Project by the Hong Kong Quality Education Funds.

Valerie Huggins is currently a Lecturer in Early Childhood Studies within the Faculty of Education at the University of Plymouth, with a lead role in Early Years teacher education and professional studies. She is an experienced Early Years teacher who has also worked as an Early Years consultant within a local authority. Valerie volunteered with VSO and took a role as a teacher educator in Ethiopia for a year, which has led to a keen interest in early childcare and education in the Majority World. She regularly supports students and teachers on study trips to The Gambia to promote development education, and is currently researching overseas field trips for a Doctorate in Education.

Anne Hunt is a member of the Early Childhood Research and Development Team at the Early Childhood Centre, University of New Brunswick. This team has developed the New Brunswick Curriculum for Early Learning and Childcare and continues to work with early childhood educators to develop curriculum support documents. Anne has had a long career as an entrance class teacher in public schools and has taught courses in early literacy, play, children's literature, and curriculum at both the Universities of New Brunswick and St. Thomas in Canada.

Kerstin Kööp has studied to be a kindergarten teacher. Her everyday work now is divided into two parts – one part is still in kindergarten with children and the other part is at Tallinn University, Estonia, as a lecturer for students who will become kindergarten teachers. She finished her master studies in 2006 and continues her student life in the Graduate School of Institute of Educational Sciences at Tallinn University.

Éva Kovácsné Bakosi is Dean and College Professor of the Faculty of Child and Adult Education at the University of Debrecen in Hungary, where she lectures on pedagogy. She has worked as a teacher in nursery school and primary school and with her late husband György Kovács has written several books on the pedagogy of play.

Caroline Leeson is Senior Lecturer and joint Progamme Leader on the BA(Hons) Early Childhood Studies degree at Plymouth University. She has particular interests in the welfare of looked after children, children's centre leadership, and reflective practice. Her PhD looked at the involvement of looked after children in decision-making processes. Before working in higher education, she worked as a social worker in child protection, fostering, and adoption.

Beth Marshall is the Director of Early Childhood at the HighScope Educational Research Foundation. She is the author of *HighScope Step by Step: Lesson Plans for the First 30 Days* and co-author of *Small-Group Times to Scaffold Early Learning*. She contributed to the development of the HighScope Preschool COR and PQA assessment instruments. She has written training materials for HighScope on a range of topics, including adult learning, art with young children, adult–child interactions, scaffolding children's maths learning, and the impact of brain research on early childhood practices. She has conducted training projects throughout the United States and internationally.

Nancy McDermott is a writer and editor based in New York, USA. She is best known for her role within *Park Slope Parents*, the nation's most influential parenting community where her compassionate, cool-headed counters to hyper-parenting culture have earned her the moniker of 'the voice of reason'. She is associated with the Centre for Parenting Culture Studies at the University of Kent at Canterbury.

Julia Morgan originally trained as a health professional and has worked for ten years in various NHS hospitals around the country. As well lecturing in Early Childhood Studies, she is currently the Strategic Lead for professional development for the Faculty of Health, Education and Society at Plymouth University. She has worked with children who live or work on the street in Mongolia, Southern Africa, and Romania, and is currently investigating support offered by schools to children with a father in prison. Her research interests include social policy, social justice, child development, children's health and wellbeing, children's perspectives, and cross-cultural studies of childhood.

Joce Nuttall is Associate Professor and Principal Research Fellow in the Faculty of Education at the Australian Catholic University and leads the faculty's Senior Proven Research Team. Her research interests focus on teachers' professional learning in early years settings, principally informed by cultural-historical activity theory, and early childhood curriculum and policy. Joce has recently co-authored (with Mindy Blaise) the text *Learning to Teach in the Early Years Classroom* (Oxford University Press, 2010).

Elin Eriksen Ødegaard, Associate Professor PHD, is a researcher at the Centre of Educational Research, Bergen University College, Norway, where she is leading the project *Kindergarten as an Arena for Cultural Formation* (Norwegian Research Council 2009–2013). In 2007, she received her PHD in Educational Science on the topic 'Narrative meaning-making in preschool' from the University of Gothenburg, Sweden. She is also the elected president of OMEP – Norway, 2009–2013, the Norwegian branch of the World Organization for Early Childhood Education. Her scholarly interests includes narrative, comparative and historical studies, as well as teacher professionalism, all within the field of early childhood.

Jane Payler, PhD is a Senior Lecturer in Early Years Education at the University of Winchester and Chair of TACTYC, Association for the Professional Development of Early Years Educators. Jane has taught, examined, researched, published, and practised in early years education and care for over twenty years. She has taught early years students from college vocational courses to university doctoral level. Prior to that, she worked in the NHS as a Health Education Officer. Since 2006, she has been closely involved in delivering and assessing the Early Years Professional Status, a graduate status for early years educators. Her publications and research interests include inter-professional practice, professional development, and young children's learning experiences.

Philip Selbie taught Reception children in English primary schools before moving overseas in 2000 to teach and lead early years provision at two international schools in Prague, Czech Republic. He now lectures in Early Childhood Studies on BA, BEd, and MA programmes at Plymouth University and is researching for a PhD on the contribution of Jan Amos Comenius (1592–1670) to early childhood care and education. Philip is a governor in a local nursery school and is active in promoting the importance of preschool education for young children's early development.

Paolo Sorzio (Venezia 1959) is lecturer in Education at the University of Trieste (Italy). His research interests are curriculum theory and teachers' professionalism. He is the author of *Dewey e l'educazione progressiva* [*Dewey and the Progressive Education*] (2009) and the editor of *Apprendimento e Istituzioni educative. Storia, contesti, soggetti* [*Learning and Educational Institutions: History, Contexts and Subjectivities*] (forthcoming).

Manabu Sumida is an Associate Professor of Science Education, Faculty of Education, Ehime University, Japan. He earned his PhD in Science Education from Hiroshima University, Japan. His research areas are culture studies in science education and science education for the early childhood years. He received the Young Scholars' Award from the Japan Society for Science Education in 1996, Young Scholars' Award from the Society of Japan Science Teaching in 1999, and Best Paper Presentation Award from the Japan Society for Science Education in 2007 and 2008.

Keang-ieng (Peggy) Vong has written papers on various topics in the field of early childhood education. Her early works include co-authored articles on young children's number concepts. Other publications cover topics of friendship across cultures, Chinese parents' beliefs and conceptions of children's creativity, the impact of different pedagogies on promoting children's creativity, and cognitive development in disparate learning contexts. She has also written about early childhood policies and practice in Macao, early childhood education in Macao, the manifestation of play in kindergartens in China, as well as the need for establishing kindergartens in rural areas of China. Currently, she is writing about teacher education, drawing on data from a comparative study about Chinese and Swedish teacher training systems for kindergarten teachers.

Karen Wickett is a Lecturer on Early Childhood Studies Degree courses at Plymouth University. She originally trained as a nursery nurse, established and managed a day nursery in Cornwall, and then trained as a teacher. Until recently, she was a children's centre teacher in Somerset, having previously been employed as the Sure Start Taunton Local Programme Early Years teacher. She is now researching informal learning in community contexts for a Doctorate in Education.

Acknowledgements

We would like to thank all those who have contributed to this book in many different ways: the children who gave their permission for their photographs to be included (and we must credit photographer, Bob Foran, for his photograph that appears as Figure 15.2) and the practitioners who have provided us with insights into their everyday experiences and allowed us to observe their practice.

Open University Press staff have been patient and supportive in helping us to shape the book in its final form as well as to publish it. We are also grateful to Taylor and Francis Publishers for their permission to reproduce in Chapter 14 an edited version of an article by Carmen Dalli that first appeared as Dalli, C. (2011) A curriculum of open possibilities: a New Zealand kindergarten teacher's view of professional practice, in *Early Years: An International Journal of Research and Development*, 31(3): 229–43. We would also like to thank Kind & Gezin for their permission to reproduce material from the SICS Well-being and Involvement in Care Settings: A Process-oriented Self-evaluation Instrument, Manual, which we reproduce as Figures 19.2 and 19.3, the SICS Scale for Well-being and the SICS Scale for Well-being respectively. We are also grateful to Routledge for allowing Manabu Sumida to reproduce a figure from *Debates on Early Childhood Policies and Practices: Global Snapshots of Pedagogical Thinking and Encounters* (2012), edited by Theodora Papatheodorou, reproduced here as Figure 21.2.

Finally, as editors, we want to thank our contributors from around the world who have put such effort into producing their chapters, sometimes under difficult personal circumstances, to share so vividly their experiences and knowledge of early childhood education and care.

PART 1
Setting the scene

1

THE IMPORTANCE OF INTERNATIONAL PERSPECTIVES

Jan Georgeson, Jane Payler and Verity Campbell-Barr

Those of us who work in the early years sector, wrapped up in the here-and-now triumphs and challenges of local provision, require a little nudge sometimes to take a broader view. The experience of immersing ourselves in provision in another country can make the familiarity of our own provision 'strange' and help us to examine and question why we do things the way we do. But there are other reasons for looking at international examples of early years education and care. Tobin et al., introducing their international study of preschools in three cultures, emphasize the important and revealing positions that early years settings hold in society:

> Preschools are sites where a variety of domains, interests, and social actors interact. Preschool is where child rearing meets education; where the world of parents and home first meets the world of teachers and schools and where the labor market's need for working women meets society's need for young children to be well cared for and prepared to be proactive in the future.
>
> (Tobin et al., 2009: 2)

They also draw attention to the global flow of ideas about early childhood education and care (ECEC), the borrowing and lending (perhaps leading towards global convergence), the rise and ebb on the tide of political expedience, as well as the selective stripping and moulding of imported ideas to suit local contexts (Tobin et al., 2009: 3–4). In this book, we offer examples of practice from countries whose ways of doing ECEC might be less familiar, as well as looking afresh at some of the established ideas in their local contexts. These established ideas can appear to offer attractive 'greener grass' from over the fence, but before replanting them in our own contexts, we need to consider *why* they developed as they did, *why* they work so well there, and whether we have the right conditions to transplant them into our own fields. Equally, we need to think carefully before assuming that our own approaches would automatically improve less familiar ways of providing ECEC.

Ideas about how young children should be cared for and educated have always been shared between countries and reflect the changing understandings of children and childhood over time (James and Prout, 1990); at present, however, there seems to be increasing interest in understanding how ECEC is organized and experienced internationally. At government level, the increasing interest in ECEC is based on a growing body of evidence that has demonstrated its social and economic benefits. Globally ECEC is seen as a social investment, albeit an investment that takes on different forms as to the level of investment and the weight given to the respective attributes listed under the social and economic advantages.

Yet, while there are many approaches to ECEC, the overarching social and economic benefits present some common trends. Internationally, there is recognition of the role of ECEC in expanding the human capital of a society. Knowledge and skills represent the 'stock' of human capital for any one country (OECD, 1998). With knowledge being key to economic growth (World Bank, 2003), governments are increasingly interested in ways in which they can upgrade their human capital. Historically, ECEC did not feature in the discussions on human capital (Heckman, 2000; Penn, 2010; Reynolds et al., 2010). As Carneiro and Heckman (2003) discuss, ECEC was largely ignored when Becker first developed the human capital model. However, it is now recognized that investment in early childhood education will provide the foundations for later learning and that investment in the young will yield greater economic returns than investment in the old (Heckman, 2000). Expenditure on ECEC is justified, as it can be presented as having a direct influence on reducing future socio-economic costs (see Piper, 2008).

There are undoubtedly criticisms of the human capital model. First, the research that provided the evidence for the economic contribution of ECEC had small sample sizes, was targeted at African American and Hispanic populations, and was conducted in the USA, with the latter two raising questions around the international relevance and applicability of the findings (see Penn, 2010). Second, the preoccupation with cognitive ability in human capital theory means that other important social skills are frequently lost in assessments of the outcomes of ECEC (Heckman, 2004: 1). While there are clear concerns that the focus on a narrow set of skills has implications for the way in which we view children, it also raises concerns for how we value children and ECEC. Children are valued on the skills obtained, for the people they will become, not the children that they are (Loreman, 2009). Sociological constructions of children as active social agents, children as being rather than becoming, challenge this (Piper, 2008). However, investment is predicated on ideas of economic returns and effectiveness of the investment. ECEC services are also valued against the outcomes that policy-makers deem to be important (Campbell-Barr, 2012). Social investment becomes social investment-profit (Babic, 2012).

The focus on how ECEC is valued is important in a book on international perspectives, as globally policy-makers seek to create a series of discursive truths (a correct reading) of what ECEC should look like. The desired outcomes of any government for ECEC services will shape the policy interventions that surround services. Different ECEC approaches have been developed in response to different political agendas; the social pedagogical tradition of Reggio Emilia was born out of the 'municipal socialism' of Reggio Emilia public life, seeking to promote the wellbeing of all children as part of community welfare (see Chapter 4), while the Head Start programmes in the USA were part of the War on Poverty (see Chapter 5). Where governments or local authorities are supplying money to support ECEC, they will want to see that it is helping to deliver outcomes in line with their policy objectives as a return on their investment. This can become an uncomfortable burden for practitioners if they do not share these objectives and, when governments change faster than training programmes for practitioners, practitioners can find themselves out-of-phase with government aims. With the subsequent sense of unease about the purpose of early years, looking out from beyond our own provision as Tobin suggests can help us to re-evaluate what we have constructed as education and care of our youngest children.

As systems for ECEC have developed, this has been accompanied by demands to increase the quality of provision, leading to growing emphasis on training for all those involved. In both established and newly developing early childhood services, this has often led to looking to other countries for models and approaches. Several approaches from across the world are widely admired (Reggio Emilia, Te Whariki, HighScope, Scandinavian approaches) and most practitioners will hear these mentioned in initial training or subsequent professional development. While many are inspired by a vision of another approach that seems to be getting it right, it is important for reflective practitioners to understand the motivation that gave rise to these influential approaches in their original context. Understanding the principles that underlie their form and content will enable students to engage with different approaches critically, with the confidence to incorporate and adjust what they have learned in a considered way, rather than concentrating on eye-catching resources or utopian ideals. It is also important that students are introduced to less well-known systems of ECEC to discover the challenges that practitioners in other countries have overcome, and encouraged to think critically about the complexities of providing ECEC.

International perspectives modules are becoming increasingly popular elements of initial and continuing professional development. In the UK in recent years there has been a concerted drive, initiated by the Labour government and supported by the current Coalition government, towards increasing the professional knowledge and educational qualifications of people employed in the care and education of young children. Included in this has been the drive for a graduate-led workforce in private, voluntary, and independent nursery provision with the introduction of Early Years Professional Status (see Chapter 22) and the move towards a master's level workforce in teaching. A workforce educated to such standards should have a good understanding of the international context of early years, the provenance of different early years approaches and principles, and the influences on their own country's provision.

This book aims to encourage critical thinking by both new and more experienced readers about global issues, influences and the complexities of providing ECEC, and promote critical reflection on their own provision and its current context. Local histories and priorities have led to provision for young children developing in different ways in different countries. Understanding this can help students to understand the varied experiences of children they might meet, contexts in which they might work and, more subtly, helps them to realize that the ECEC they encounter in their own country does not represent the only way of doing things.

Although we have divided the book into sections, there are recurrent themes throughout, such as 'child-centredness', the role of play, the purpose of pedagogy, the nature of staffing, and what a curriculum for early years should look like; we invite readers to pursue themes that interest them by using the index to find out about how these have played out in different countries. All the chapters consider the development of different approaches to provision in their socio-cultural contexts, and offer insight into daily life in short vignettes, longer case studies or comments from practitioners working in early years settings.

We adopted the term 'early childhood education and care' for the book to encompass the different aims and scope of provision in different countries, but of course the age range for which 'early childhood' provision is made differs between countries, and the balance between 'education' and 'care' also varies. In the UK, we have a wide variety of terms for different kinds of early years settings (preschool, day nursery, crèche, nursery school, children's centre) that do not match the ways in which provision is divided up in other countries, so finding the most appropriate English words to use has not been easy. We use 'day nursery' for an institution providing some element of day care, usually including the youngest children, and nursery school or kindergarten for settings where the emphasis is more on education and more often focused on children aged over two years. In the UK, we also use different terms to describe early years practitioners with different roles for whom there are different qualification routes and differences between the state-maintained and private/voluntary/independent sectors; readers should be aware that these differences do not translate exactly into terms used for practitioners in other countries, where the vocational/academic terrain might be different. It is also important not to make assumptions about which aspects of provision for children in other counties are universal, inclusive, targeted, segregated, free, subsidized or paid for by parents. Indeed, the process of locating oneself in another early childhood terrain brings into sharp focus the complexity of the situation in one's own country, as well as the difficulties new parents must experience as they seek to navigate their way through systems.

We have divided the book into four parts: the value of critically considering global approaches, why systems have developed as they have, emerging workforce issues, and how different approaches are realized in practice. Having adopted a socio-cultural approach to understanding practice (Hedegaard and Fleer, 2008), it is therefore not surprising to discover that there is considerable overlap between these topics, with authors offering some socio-historical context to help readers understand the 'why' of provision as well as the 'who' and 'how'. The different parts thus indicate the main emphases of chapters rather than clear-cut distinctions between content.

Here, in Part 1, we introduce the purpose of the book and flag up some important overarching themes. As well as the issue of ECEC's appeal for policy-makers and academics raised in this chapter, Chapter 2 considers the rationale behind studying international perspectives of ECEC and the value to be gained by critically considering approaches from around the world. Chapter 3 outlines children's rights issues, which underpin many aspects of such approaches.

Part 2 covers exploration of *why* approaches have developed as they have in different countries, with exemplars from Italy, USA, the Gambia, Estonia, Norway, and Sweden. Chapter 4 examines the conditions in which the ECEC discourse originated in Italy in the aftermath of the Second World War, focusing in particular on the example set by Loris Malaguzzi in Reggio Emilia. Chapter 5 critiques the way in which various explanations of poverty and disadvantage have influenced ECEC in the USA, culminating in the recent focus on brain development as the language of science has come to dominate discourse on social inequality. Chapter 6 speaks against euro-centric perspectives on ECEC and child wellbeing in the Gambia, calling instead for the perspectives of Gambian children, communities, and practitioners to be prioritized, and building on rather than dismissing indigenous thinking around ECEC. Chapters 7 and 8 trace the ways in which ECEC has been influenced by political and social history in Estonia, with its experience of both fascist and communist occupations, and in Norway and Sweden with regard to education for democracy.

Part 3 considers workforce issues in context from the perspectives of countries perhaps less often represented in texts on ECEC: South Africa and India. This section raises questions about who the people are who provide ECEC, who they work with, and where, inviting reflection on alternative models in challenging situations. Chapter 10 examines the role of quests for quality and leadership in supporting social and economic policy agendas in Hong Kong and England, while Chapter 12 explores the contribution of lifelong learning to the wellbeing of individuals in society and implications for quality in ECEC in the Czech Republic.

Part 4 addresses how approaches are played out in practice in relation to practical considerations of pedagogy and curriculum and related issues such as assessment and the environment. These are addressed through aspects of provision from nine countries, including Australia, Belgium, Canada, China, Hungary, Italy, Japan, New Zealand, and the USA. The final chapter returns to the development of ECEC in the four UK nations of England, Wales, Scotland, and Northern Ireland. It ends with a case study of a children's centre nursery in England, describing how international ideas were picked up by the staff team and assimilated into practice to meet local needs and priorities.

We hope you will find much to challenge your assumptions, stimulate your thinking, and refresh your enthusiasm for the global project of providing effectively for our youngest children.

Find Out More

- Consider the idea that ECEC contributes to 'human capital' and brings greater economic returns than investment in older people (see Carneiro and Heckman, 2003). What are the implications of this?
- Think critically about provision in a setting you are familiar with for glimpses of influence from other countries. What are the assumptions implied in the ways in which you and colleagues discuss approaches to ECEC from other countries?
- List some of the key issues and themes revealed in the current framework or approach to ECEC in your own country. How are these themes addressed in the countries represented in this book?

References and recommended reading

(Note: entries in bold are recommended reading here and throughout the book.)

Babic, N. (2012) *Contemporary Childhood: Ideals and Reality. Social Science Studies IV. Integration, Inclusion, Multiculturalism (Társadalomtudományi tanulmányok IV. Integráció-Inklúzió-Multikulturalitás)*. Debrecen: University of Debrecen Press.

Campbell-Barr, V. (2010) *Providing a Context for Looking at Quality and Value in Early Years Education: Report to the Office for National Statistics Measuring Outcomes for Public*. **Newport: Office for National Statistics.**

Campbell-Barr, V. (2012) Early years education and the value for money folklore, *European Early Childhood Education Research Journal*. **20(3):423-37.**

Carneiro, P. and Heckman, J.J. (2003) *Human Capital Policy*, Working Paper 9495. Cambridge: National Bureau of Economic Research. Available online at: http://www.nber.org/papers/w9495 (accessed 9 June 2012).

Heckman, J.J. (2000) *Invest in the Very Young*. Chicago, IL: Ounce of Prevention Fund and the University of Chicago Harris School of Public Policy Studies.

Heckman, J.J. (2004) Invest in the very young, in R.E. Tremblay, R.G. Barr and R.DeV. Peters (eds.) *Encyclopaedia on Early Childhood Development* [online]. Montreal, Quebec: Centre of Excellence for Early Childhood Development. Available online at: http://child-encyclopedia.com/pages/PDF/Importance-early-childhood-development.pdf.

Hedegaard, M. and Fleer, M. (2008) *Studying Children: A Cultural-Historical Approach*. Maidenhead: Open University Press.

James, A. and Prout, A. (1990) *Constructing and Reconstructing Childhood: Contemporary Issues in the Sociological Study of Childhood*. London: Falmer Press.

Loreman, T. (2009) *Respecting Childhood*. London: Continuum.

Organization for Economic Cooperation and Development (OECD) (1998) *Human Capital Investment: An International Comparison*. Paris: OECD.

Penn, H. (2010) Shaping the future: how human capital arguments about investment in early childhood are being (mis)used in poor countries, in N. Yelland (ed.) *Contemporary Perspectives on Early Childhood Education*. Maidenhead: Open University Press.

Piper, C. (2008) *Investing in Children: Policy, Law and Practice in Context*. Cullompton: Willan Publishing.

Reynolds, A., Rolnick, A., Englund, M. and Temple, J. (eds.) (2010) *Childhood Programs and Practices in the First Decade of Life: A Human Capital Integration*. Cambridge: Cambridge University Press.

Tobin, J., Hsueh, Y. and Karasawa, M. (2009) *Preschool in Three Cultures Revisited: China, Japan, and the United States*. Chicago, IL: University of Chicago Press.

Waller, T. (2005) International perspectives, in T. Waller (ed.) *An Introduction to Early Childhood: A Multidisciplinary Approach*. **London: Paul Chapman.**

World Bank (2003) *Lifelong Learning in the Global Knowledge Economy: Challenges for Developing Countries*. Washington, DC: World Bank.

2

WIDENING AWARENESS OF INTERNATIONAL APPROACHES: AN IMPERATIVE FOR TWENTY-FIRST-CENTURY EARLY YEARS PRACTITIONERS?

Valerie Huggins

Summary

In this chapter, I argue that early years practitioners, embarking upon a career that may span thirty years or more, must widen and develop their perspectives upon patterns of education and care internationally. If such awareness stays limited, they will remain bound by taken-for-granted views of what constitutes appropriate early years education and of such core concepts as 'child', 'play', and 'family', views that are based on very narrow beliefs and values drawn from their own culture and experiences. They may find it difficult to learn from positive developments and initiatives elsewhere in the world. This could compromise their ability to act as critically reflexive professionals and to undertake leadership roles in this rapidly changing global context. I use several theoretical models to explain and justify this position and to suggest ways forward.

Introduction

It is essential that, as early years practitioners, we open up our minds to a range of international perspectives on early childhood education and care (ECEC) for three key reasons.

First, it is very easy for us to get caught up in the everyday 'busyness' of our settings, doing things the way they have always been done, and so become very limited not only in our practice but also in our thinking. As Penn (2008) argues, many practitioners become stuck in the time warp of their initial training, acquiring what Bourdieu termed a 'habitus', which is a set of socially learnt dispositions that shape and guide the way we behave and think in a taken-for-granted way (Bourdieu and Wacquart, 1992). This leads us professionally to invest in certain limited forms of knowledge about ECEC and in certain ways of acting as an early years practitioner.

Looking at our familiar behaviour from international perspectives enables us to appreciate its 'strangeness' (Holliday, 2010), and that it is merely one way among many in which different societies look to care for and educate their young. Becoming aware of systems, practices, and approaches from elsewhere in the world will sometimes help challenge the validity of our own ways of working; at other times it will confirm them as good practice. This process will make us better practitioners.

Case Study

Tom, a 4-year-old child born in August of a British father and an Estonian mother, is offered a full-time reception class place in September at the local primary school. His parents are unhappy because he is small for his age, shy, and has only recently settled in the UK. The response of the school's headteacher to this is: 'This is what happens in England; it is good for children and gives them an academic head start; if you do not take up the place now, it will not be available for Tom later in the year'.

We should consider how the headteacher might have come to hold such rigid views and what might be the historical, political, and social factors preserving the UK's continuation of this pattern. It is important to examine the evidence for and against a statutory school starting age of 5, in contrast to many other Minority World countries (see, for example, Sharp, 2002).

Second, in recent decades there has been a huge expansion in ECEC across the globe, in response to research and the prevailing international discourses, such as from the United Nations, that children need to be given the best start in life in order to be successful in the future. But all too often this expansion has been shaped by a particular Minority World model of early years education, based on the notion of 'developmentally appropriate practice' (Smidt, 2006). Our Western ideas about what constitutes effective practice and provision have been allowed to dominate the discourses because of our current and historical political and economic dominance over the Majority World (Holliday, 2010). This dominance has been strengthened by our tendency to believe, without any clear evidence or justification, that our approaches are superior and so see ourselves as having a 'civilizing mission' (Andreotti, 2006: 41) in our educational work in international contexts. This can lead us to define alternative approaches as deficient, needing an input of Western expertise and resources to bring them up to an acceptable standard.

There are several concerns about this view. One is that it contributes to the image of the child and of childhood becoming increasingly uniform and homogenized and thus the diversity of childhoods in different cultures being eroded (Pence and Nsamenang, 2008). A second is that, while the view is often justified by the argument, based on human capital theory (Schultz, 1971; see also Chapter 1, p. 4), investment in early childhood education of this type will bring greater returns than investment in any other stage of education (Naudeau et al., 2011), though there is little evidence that this argument is valid internationally (Penn, 2008). A third concern is over basing early childhood education upon Minority World models of developmentally appropriate practice. While extensive research has identified and confirmed certain patterns of child learning and development, many of them valid across cultures, the presumption that these will define what will be necessary educational provision in all parts of the world is much weaker (Penn, 2010).

Underlying these concerns is that they all depend to a greater or lesser degree upon a positivistic view of knowledge as objective, scientifically based, and so applicable everywhere. What this ignores is that, in a highly complex area of human behaviour such as early education and care, a socio-cultural model of the construction and validation of what each community considers worthwhile and useful is much more effective in explaining how patterns of behaviour and provision are arrived at (Rogoff, 2003). For example, the powerful emphasis upon the development in 4-year-olds of *sagesse* (good behaviour) in a French école maternelle, upon full engagement in the outdoors in a Norwegian kindergarten, upon cooperative rather than individual construction activities in a Chinese setting, upon the achievement of specific academic goals in a UK reception class – these goals are all socially constructed rather than being the inevitable result of developmental imperatives. Knowing about such international differences, and understanding something of how they have come about, enables us to reflect more critically upon the effectiveness of our own provision and, as Pence and Nsamenang (2008) argue, creates the space for us to consider other ideas, patterns, and perspectives.

Case Study

Abiyatou, aged 4 years, together with her friends and older sister, walks and runs 3 kilometres from her home to the local school outside Brufut, in rural Gambia. Her windowless classroom is bare, with no displays and no 'play' equipment, and has fifty desks and benches in rows facing a blackboard and desk, from which the teacher directs highly formal learning activities. At the end of the school day at 1 pm, the children run the 3 kilometres home, where they play outside their homes, often with earth, sand, stones and water, engage in elaborate social and collaborative role-play, singing and dancing, and help their parents tend their crops and livestock.

A feature of UK early years practice has been the taken-for-granted view that certain types of preschool provision – such as sand, water, role-play opportunities, vigorous play and exercise, learning from and about the outdoor environment – are crucial in an early years setting. Narrow adherence to this view through the lens of standard UK practice might lead us to consider that provision in this school in rural Gambia for young children is 'deficient'. If, however, early years patterns of provision are seen not as 'given' but as responding to the needs of the children, this might lead us to consider modifications as a result of the significant changes in many UK children's lifestyles and experiences (see Chapter 6 for a full discussion of euro-centric responses to early education in the Gambia).

Such consideration constantly brings us back to our own culture and our own settings. An appreciation of the wider socio-economic conditions of early childhood in poorer countries in the world and the effect of poverty (Smidt, 2006) helps us to understand the impact of poverty on children's lives in the UK. Poor nutrition, poor health, neglect, abuse, and a lack of resources are by no means confined to the Majority World; indeed, they are increasingly part of the experience of children living in Minority World countries such as the USA and the UK. Moreover, gaining international perspectives sensitizes us to diversity, which is crucial if we are to respond positively to the many children and families we will encounter whose ways of life, beliefs, attitudes, and circumstances will differ significantly from our own; this can be as significant an issue in the 'monocultural' areas of rural communities in the UK as in the more obviously multicultural contexts of inner cities (Carter Dillon and Huggins, 2010). We are working today in a world of growing social mobility (Goodwin, 2010) where, as Perry and Southwell (2011) remind us, changes in communication and travel mean that early years practitioners can be exposed to much greater ethnic, cultural, and social diversity without necessarily recognizing it:

Case Study

Ching Lan is the 4-year-old child of a Chinese family running a restaurant in a small English town's 'Takeaway Alley'. She lives in a small flat above the restaurant and when at home is expected to play quietly and sensibly on the carpet or at the table, to watch TV, to play simple games on a Nintendo DS, and to help look after a younger sibling. Both parents work full-time in the restaurant and cannot spend much time interacting with her.

She attends the local primary school and is in a reception class of thirty children and two members of staff. The curriculum in the mornings is highly focused on literacy and numeracy and play activities are usually only offered to children who have finished their 'work'. A small outside playground space is used for short periods in the afternoon, provided the weather is good. The teacher's view of Ching Lan is that 'she is doing very well – such a polite, well-behaved girl. She doesn't speak much in class, only when she is asked a question. And it's a pity that we don't ever see her parents – she's brought and collected by a friend – and they don't come to Open Evening or parents' meetings.'

What difference would it make if the teacher got to know more about Ching Lan's family and the cultural and social patterns of Chinese families working in the restaurant trade? Would it help her to adapt this pattern of educational provision to meet Ching Lan's needs at this stage and so respond to her as an individual?

Looking to the future, there is a third powerful reason for practitioners to develop international perspectives on their work. With the growth of globalization, practitioners are increasingly required to incorporate a global dimension into their curricula and their approaches. At national policy level in the UK there is a now a requirement from the Department for International Development (DfID, 2012) for schools to make links with a setting in the Majority World in order to exchange ideas and experiences, both to increase the awareness and understanding of all participants and to offer support to the Majority World setting. There is also a growing expectation by the Department for Education and Skills (DfES, 2005) that practitioners should be prepared and able to teach their pupils about global issues. There are increasing opportunities for study visits, volunteering activities abroad, and teacher secondments and exchanges, as well as the growing possibility of employment in early years education in another country. All this means that some international understanding and experience is likely to become an important aspect of a practitioner's career trajectory and an increasingly vital qualification for undertaking leadership roles, even if confined to their own country.

This analysis of the value of international perspectives offers reasons for us as practitioners to widen our views and visions for ECEC, and many UK teachers and students in training are showing great interest and willingness to engage in this new aspect of work. However, both theory and experience warn us that doing so is not a simple matter of getting to know more about other approaches in other countries, nor even of making visits to see them in action (Martin, 2008). Even those who, like Walters et al. (2009), believe that international study visits can be immensely beneficial to participants often acknowledge that 'for some, the experience created or reinforced negative stereotypes about the host culture, educational system and people' (p. 513). How can this be?

In the first place, we have to acknowledge the powerful psychological advantages to us of feeling competent, knowledgeable, and secure in an existing professional identity, developed over time, and of holding a strong and clear (if often unacknowledged) sense of the superiority of our own model of ECEC. It is not uncommon for British practitioners to view 'nursery education' as yet another of the UK's gifts to the world. This can make us unconsciously unwilling to accept that other models we encounter may have much to offer us, and may even be superior in many respects.

Second, as Holliday (2010) forcefully argues, we have grown up with views about the rest of the world developed over centuries and based upon ideologies of world aggression, colonization, and a sense of having an improving mission to peoples we have always considered inferior and less developed. To understand and appreciate that there are other equally valid approaches to our own, we first need to become aware of how what we believe and do has been shaped by our own historical, cultural, social, political, and economic context (Trahar, 2011) rather than being self-evidently 'right'.

The French social theorist Michel Foucault asserts that power, knowledge, and truth operate within certain dominant discourses that he terms 'regimes of truth', which favour certain kinds of knowledge and so shape our behaviours and professional practice (Mac Naughton, 2005). All this means that we are not automatically open to new ideas and experiences, but are prone to assimilate these into our existing schemas and to interpret them in light of our established beliefs and values. As Stromquist (2002) argues, for us to recognize and appreciate the 'other' it is necessary to recognize and understand ourselves, in particular those aspects of which we may not be fully aware.

Third, we have to be prepared for this process to be both difficult and uncomfortable. Turniansky et al. (2009) acknowledge that it involves extra effort and may introduce an element of risk to professional 'complacency'; it challenges us and so creates disequilibrium. It involves a need to acknowledge our own part in perpetuating the inequalities between ourselves and the people in the Majority World, as well as unlearning our own privilege, in order to engage with them ethically and with understanding. Kapoor (2004) stresses that this involves us in having to 'retrace the itinerary of our prejudices and learning habits . . . stopping oneself from always wanting to correct, teach, theorize, develop, colonize, appropriate, use, record, inscribe, enlighten' (pp. 641–2). Moreover, taking such steps and acknowledging our favoured position in the world may even result in us experiencing 'guilt, internal conflict and paralysis, critical disengagement, a feeling of helplessness' (Andreotti, 2006: 48).

All this explains our resistances and emphasizes that what we need is not simply to know more but to develop what Walters et al. (2009) term 'intercultural capabilities', such as a sensitivity to cultural differences, a questioning of our own beliefs and values about cultures, and a recognition that our own world views are not universally held. Again this is not a simple matter of acquiring new ideas. Andreotti and de Souza (2008a: 28–9) put forward a clear model and conceptual framework for engaging in such a transformative process. They argue that such a process must take us through four stages:

1. Significantly, the first stage is *learning to unlearn*. This involves looking critically at the taken-for-granted ways of doing things around here, which Bourdieu terms 'habitus' (Bourdieu and Wacquart, 1992). This stage involves us in making connections with the socio-historical processes that have shaped our contexts and cultures, and the constructions of our knowledges and identities, so that we can understand that ours is only one perspective among many and not necessarily superior.

2. The second stage is *learning to listen*. As we recognize the limitations and potentially disturbing effects of our established perspectives, we can begin to accept other perspectives and voices as being as legitimate, valid, and powerful as our own. The ideas of Reggio Emilia, Te Whariki, and Steiner-Waldorf, for example, are increasingly introduced in training courses and professional texts on ECEC (e.g. Miller and Pound, 2011) to provide examples of difference. These can draw our attention to how certain 'regimes of truth' have come to dominate our UK way of thinking, such as the neo-liberal focus on the child as an autonomous individual whose needs must be met by the practitioner, in contrast to the socio-collective approach of Reggio Emilia, where much learning happens in group projects.

3. This leads to the third stage, which opens up the possibility of us *learning to learn* from the practice of others. This involves not only hearing and taking on board such new perspectives, but engaging with the new concepts to rearrange our cultural baggage and renegotiate our existing understandings. Then we can adapt and change our practice in light of these new understandings, but in ways that reflect and respect our own context. This empowers us to resist attempts to impose inappropriate approaches and techniques from outside because we are aware of their cultural, historical, and political context, what has been used to measure their effectiveness, and so what they may offer us.

4. In the final stage, *learning to reach out*, we gain the confidence to try out, explore, and initiate new possible ways of being, of relating to others, becoming willing to engage in that potentially insecure and uncomfortable space where identities, power, and ideas are renegotiated, and coming to see conflict as a productive component of

learning. We have become informed and critically reflective practitioners, willing to engage in 'risky' teaching (Blaise, 2005), innovative and challenging, responsive to the diverse needs of the children and the families with whom we work – all assisted by our knowledge and understanding of different international approaches.

Andreotti and de Souza (2008b) stress that following the process through these stages will potentially enable our narratives, representations, and framings to move from an egocentric stance, through an ethnocentric one (within one's own social group) and a humancentric one (within other social groups) to arrive at a world-centric view from which we can engage in a persistent and ongoing critique of the hegemonic discourses and representations that we are engaged in.

This book on international perspectives cannot in itself take you through these stages of learning. But it may offer you a stimulus and a space where you are, in the words of Andreotti (2006: 49), 'safe to analyse and experiment with other forms of seeing/thinking and being/relating to one another', which will enable you to learn from difference and reconstruct your worldview and identity based on 'an ethical relationship to the other'.

Find Out More

- Your school is linked to one in a town in rural Ethiopia. You are planning to visit as part of the Global Schools Partnership initiative. The headteacher of the Ethiopian school gets in touch and asks you, as part of the visit, to provide some advice and professional development for the teacher who is teaching the newly introduced Zero Grade class for children aged 3–6 years. What steps would you think it necessary to take to be in a position to offer ethical, appropriate, and practicable advice?
- Many Asian countries are achieving higher scores on international tests of achievements in science and mathematics than the UK, whose levels appear to be dropping. Undertake a critical assessment of this statement. You may wish to research and consider:
  - The nature of the tests – what do they measure?
  - Why are such achievements seen to be important by the countries involved?
  - How do educational settings prepare students to do well in such 'tests'?
  - What in terms of 'wider' educational objectives might be lost in such preparation?
  - Does this demonstrate that UK teaching is of a lower standard?
  - What political, social, and cultural factors might be pertinent in explaining your findings?
- What patterns of ethnic and cultural diversity are there in your local community?
  - Are there 'monocultural areas'? Does the term have any meaning?
  - What might be 'invisible' diversity in your class/setting/area? How might you find out?

References and recommended reading

Andreotti, V. (2006) Soft versus critical global citizenship education, *Policy and Practice: A Development Education Review*, 3(Autumn): 40–51.

Andreotti, V. and de Souza, M. (2008a) Translating theory into practice and walking mine-fields: lessons from the project 'Through Other Eyes', *International Journal of Development Education and Global Learning*, 1(1): 23–36.

Andreotti, V. and De Souza, M. (2008b) *Through Other Eyes: Conceptual Framework*. Derby: Global Education. Available online at: www.throughothereyes.org.uk (accessed 3 June 2012).

Andreotti, V. and Warwick, P. (2007) *Engaging Students with Controversial Issues through a Dialogue Based Approach*. Produced by citizED. Available at: http://www.citized.info/?strand=3&r_menu=res (accessed 3 June 2012).

Blaise, M. (2005) *Playing it Straight: Uncovering Gender Discourses in the Early Childhood Classroom*. Abingdon: Routledge.

Bourdieu, P. and Wacquart, L.J.D. (1992) *An Invitation to Reflexive Sociology*. Cambridge: Polity Press.

Carter Dillon, R. and Huggins, V. (2010) Children's well-being in the developing world, in R. Parker-Rees and C. Leeson (eds.) *Early Childhood Studies*. Exeter: Learning Matters.

Department for Education and Skills (DfES) (2005) *Developing the Global Dimension in the School Curriculum*. London: DfES.

Department for International Development (DfID) (2012) *Global Schools Partnership*. Available online at: http://www.dfid.gov.uk/Get-Involved/In-your-school/global-school-partnerships/ (accessed 3 June 2012).

Goodwin, A.L. (2010) Globalization and the preparation of quality teachers: rethinking knowledge domains for teaching, *Teaching Education*, 21(1): 19–32.

Holliday, A. (2010) Submission, emergence, and personal knowledge: new takes and principles for validity in decentred quality research, in F. Shamin and R. Qureshi (eds.) *Perils, Pitfalls and Reflexivity in Qualitative Research in Education*. Oxford: Oxford University Press.

Kapoor, I. (2004) Hyper-self-reflexive development? Spivak on representing the Third World 'Other', *Third World Quarterly*, 4: 627–47.

Mac Naughton, G. (2005) *Doing Foucault in Early Childhood Studies*. London: Routledge.

Martin, F. (2008) Mutual learning: the impact of a study visit course on UK teachers' knowledge and understanding of global partnerships, *Critical Literacy: Theories and Practices*, 2(1): 60–75.

Miller, L. and Pound, L. (2011) *Theories and Approaches to Learning in the Early Years*. London: Sage.

Naudeau, S., Kataoka, N., Valerio, A., Neuman, M.J. and Elder, L.K. (2011) *Investing in Young Children: An Early Childhood Development Guide for Policy Dialogue and Project Preparation*. Washington, DC: World Bank.

Pence, A. and Nsamenang, B.A. (2008) *A Case for Early Development in Sub-Saharan Africa*, Working Paper No. 51. The Hague, Netherlands: Bernard Van Leer Foundation.

Penn, H. (2008) *Understanding Early Childhood: Issues and Controversies*. Maidenhead: Open University Press.

Penn, H. (2010) Does it matter what country you are in?, in S. Smidt (ed.) *Key Issues in Early Years Education*. London: Routledge.

Perry, L.B. and Southwell, L. (2011) Developing intercultural understandings and skills: models and approaches, *Intercultural Education*, 22(6): 453–66.

Rogoff, B. (2003) *The Cultural Nature of Human Development*. New York: Oxford University Press.

Schultz, T. (1971) *Investment in Human Capital.* New York: Free Press.

Sharp, C. (2002) School starting age: European policy and recent research. Paper presented at the LGA Seminar 'When Should Our Children Start School?', LGA Conference Centre, London, 1 November. Available at: http://www.nfer.ac.uk/nfer/publications/44410/44410. pdf (accessed 3 June 2012).

Smidt, S. (2006) *The Developing Child in the 21st Century: A Global Perspective on Child Development.* London: Routledge.

Stromquist, N. (2002) Globalization, the I and the Other, *Current Issues in Comparative Education*, 4(2): 87–94.

Trahar, S. (2011) *Developing Cultural Capability in International Higher Education.* Abingdon: Routledge.

Turniansky, B., Tuval, S., Mansur, R., Barak, J. and Gidron, A. (2009) From the inside out: learning to understand and appreciate multiple voices through telling identities, *New Directions for Teaching and Learning*, 118: 39–47.

Walters, L.M., Garii, B. and Walters, T. (2009) Learning globally, teaching locally: incorporating international exchange and intercultural learning into preservice teacher training, *Intercultural Education*, 20(suppl. 1): S151–8.

3

INTERNATIONAL RECOGNITION OF CHILDREN'S RIGHTS AND ITS INFLUENCE ON EARLY CHILDHOOD EDUCATION AND CARE: THE CASE OF ZAMBIA

Julia Morgan

Summary

This chapter explores the concept of children's rights. Reference is made to the United Nations Convention on the Rights of the Child (United Nations, 1989), the African Charter on the Rights and Welfare of the Child (Organization of African Unity, 1990), and the sociology of childhood, which positions the child as an active agent (Jenks, 1982; Prout and James, 1990). After discussing children's rights in some depth and problematizing the concept of children's rights in the international context, the chapter ends by briefly examining how the recognition of children's right to education has influenced the provision of early childhood education and care in Zambia.

Introduction

Over the last two decades, there has been increasing international interest in children's rights. This can be seen in the publication of the United Nations Convention on the Rights of the Child in 1989, which attempted to universalize the concept of children's rights; in the publication of the African Charter on the Rights and Welfare of the Child in 1990; the publication of the Declaration of the Rights and Care of the Child in Islam in 1994; and the publication of the Rabat Declaration on Child Issues in 2005. Alongside the publication of these documents there has also been a focus in the academic literature, especially literature influenced by the sociology of childhood, on children as competent, active social agents who are not only knowledgeable about their world but also have an impact on their world (Jenks, 1982). As a result, children have increasingly been positioned in international policy, practice, and research as holders of rights who have much to say about issues that affect their lives. This positioning of children as knowledgeable agents has led to an increase in research and consultation aimed at understanding the perspectives of children. However, while the importance of children's rights cannot be underestimated, it is also necessary to critically examine the concept so as to 'unpick' a discourse that is often used in both a national and international context but not always reflected upon.

What do we mean by children's rights?

The term 'children's rights' can be understood in a number of ways and despite universal decrees like the United Nations Convention on the Rights of the Child (United Nations, 1989), this does not mean that all cultures, communities, and societies interpret the concept in the same way (Jones and Welch, 2010). One definition of children's rights is as follows:

> children's rights are about treating children with the equality, respect and dignity to which they are entitled, not because they are the 'adults of tomorrow', but because they are human beings today.
>
> (Children's Rights International Network, 2012)

This definition focuses on children as human beings in the here and now, and it is evident that it is influenced by the sociology of childhood, which views children as human beings as opposed to human becomings (Qvortrup, 1994; Kjørholt, 2004). The latter view – children as becomings – is said to be influenced by developmental psychology, which views childhood as a process of development; the child is in a process of 'becoming' or 'developing'. As a result, children, it is said, are more likely to be viewed as passive and less capable due to reasons of developmental immaturity and competence (see Burman, 1994a). Those influenced by the sociology of childhood, on the other hand, position children as active, knowledgeable social agents who have an impact on the world around them and have expert knowledge of their life because of their agency (Hardman, 1973; Prout and James, 1990; Prout, 2005; Christensen and James, 2008). This knowledge and agency means that children, like adults, should be viewed as holders of rights who are entitled to participate in all matters that concern them.

Another definition of children's rights taken from the African Charter on the Rights and Welfare of the Child focuses not only on the child's rights but also the child's responsibility and duty:

> every child shall have responsibility towards his family and society, the State and other legally recognized communities and the international community . . . The child . . . shall have the duty . . . to respect his parents, superiors and elders at all times and to assist them in case of need.
>
> (Organization of African Unity, 1990: Article 31)

This emphasis on the responsibility and duty of the child to others is not really a focus of many other definitions of children's rights, such as those contained within the United Nations Convention on the Rights of the Child (UNCRC). Instead, what we see in the UNCRC and many similar children's rights initiatives in the West, for example, is an emphasis on the rights of children and the responsibilities of States and caregivers to children with little or no mention of the child's responsibilities to others. It is therefore evident from briefly examining the African Charter and the Children's Rights International Network's definition above that how children's rights are conceptualized differs.

Generally speaking, children's rights can be said to fall into two (often opposing) areas (Franklin and Franklin, 1996). First, children's rights can be viewed as relating to welfare rights, including the right to protection (for example, from exploitation), the right to provision (for example, education), and the right to prevention (for example, the right to life) (Freeman, 1983; Franklin and Franklin, 1996). Welfare rights are in most cases not something that the children have themselves or provide for themselves, as usually it is adults who provide the right to welfare – that is, education, health, and protection (Wyness, 2012). Second, children's rights can be seen as relating to liberty rights, including participation, self-determination, and power. It is often the relationship of liberty rights and children that causes most concern for some adults, whereas welfare rights for children are more likely to fit ideas of what adults do for children and thus are more readily acceptable.

As stated above, there are differing conceptualizations of children's rights and this may be a result of one aspect of children's rights (welfare vs. liberty) being privileged over the other. For example, countries, States or groups which privilege children's welfare rights may view childhood as a stage during which adults protect and provide services for children and cultural representations of childhood may depict children as more vulnerable or less knowledgeable than adults. As a result, less importance may be given to gaining the views of the child and to liberty rights. This may be complicated further by the socio-economic and public health situation in many countries and among many groups where the emphasis may be on the survival of children as opposed to participation and other liberty rights (Skelton, 2007). This point is made to some extent in the African Charter on the Rights and Welfare of the Child (ratified by 45 of 53 African countries), which focuses on the need for a Charter because of the many cultural and social aspects that are particular to Africa.

> NOTING WITH CONCERN [sic] that the situation of most African children, remains critical due to the unique factors of their socio-economic, cultural, traditional and developmental circumstances, natural disasters, armed conflicts, exploitation and hunger and on account of the child's physical and mental immaturity he/she needs special safeguards and care.
> (Organization of African Unity, 1990: Preamble)

Murray (2004) also makes the same point and highlights how many countries in Africa are more concerned with the welfare rights of children than their liberty rights.

Woodhead (2010), on the other hand, has highlighted how many children's rights organizations, mostly in the West, have tended to privilege liberty rights and have equated children's participation with children's rights *per se*; this, as Woodhead states, can lead to protection, provision, and prevention being overlooked as an aspect of children's rights. The UNCRC makes it clear, however, that children's rights are not just about participation or liberty rights, but that welfare rights and liberty rights go hand in hand and that the realization of welfare rights can lead to liberty rights and vice versa. Although this may be the case, there is a tension between welfare rights and liberty rights and they can often be seen to be in opposition. For example, liberty rights imply that a child may make decisions that the adult does not think are in their best interests (Wyness, 2012), while welfare rights imply that an adult may make a decision that the child does not think is in their best interests. This is complicated further in the UK, for example, because of concepts of parental responsibility and the parent being held responsible for the actions of the child. This tension, which often positions adults in opposition to children, has led to a recent focus on the relational aspects of children's rights and the importance of looking at children's rights within a framework that acknowledges the reciprocal negotiated relationship that exists between adults and children as well as between welfare and liberty rights (Kjørholt, 2008; Mannion, 2010).

United Nations Convention on the Rights of the Child (UNCRC) and children's participation

The United Nations Convention on the Rights of the Child (United Nations, 1989) is often held up as the authoritative document on children's rights. Passed in 1989, to date it has been ratified by 194 countries, including all members of the United Nations (UN) except the United States, South Sudan, and Somalia. The UNCRC contains 54 articles and two optional protocols (a third optional protocol is to be introduced in 2012, see http://www.unicef.org/crc/), which set out the requirements of State signatories to implement the UNCRC recommendations in their countries' laws and policies (United Nations, 1989: Article 4). The articles and optional protocols that make up the UNCRC apply to all children and young people under the age of 18 years (United Nations, 1989: Article 1) and puts responsibility on governments ('State Parties' in the words of the UNCRC) to provide 'special care and assistance' (United Nations, 1989: Preamble) to children because of their status as children to ensure that their best interests are upheld (United Nations, 1989: Article 3). Children's Rights within the UNCRC can be understood in terms of the 'three p's' (Franklin, 2002): the right to protection (against sexual abuse, neglect, exploitation), the right to provision (right to life, shelter, education, clean water, adequate health care, food), and the right to participation (right to privacy, freedom of association, expression, and thought). The first two rights, the right to protection and provision, can be seen to relate to welfare rights as discussed above, while the latter right relates to liberty rights.

The publication of the UNCRC in 1989 reconfirmed the child's right to welfare as set out in the previous children's rights document, the Declaration of the Rights of the Child (UN General Assembly, 1959). What was new about the UNCRC was the emphasis placed upon liberty rights for children – the rights of the child to participate and the right to self-determination (United Nations, 1989: Articles 12.1 to 15.1). The UNCRC emphasized that 'the child who is capable of forming his or her views, [has] the right to express those views freely in all matters affecting the child, the views of the child being given due weight in accordance with the age and maturity of the child' (United Nations, 1989: Article 12.1).

This decree led to a marked increase in the number of children's participation projects that aimed to enable children to give their views on a number of issues, including being consulted on services being provided for them. However, as can be seen from the definition above, the UNCRC appears to link participation in decision-making to competency; the more competent the child is judged to be, usually by an adult, the more right the child has to express their view. This is problematic, as children with particular disabilities as well as very young children may be judged as less competent and thus not seen as being able to make decisions about their lives. This appears to be the case for early childhood and it has been stated that the UNCRC has had little impact on the participation of young children in decision-making because 'it fails to recognize or value the voices of children under five years of age' (Mac Naughton et al., 2007: 163). In recognizing this, the United Nations introduced more guidance on implementing children's rights in early childhood, as it was felt that young children were often not given the same rights as older children due to issues around competency (Office for the High Commission of Human Rights, 2005). General Comment No. 7 states that young children's feelings and views should be taken into account in 'the development of policies and services, including through research and consultations' (OHCHR, 2005: 7).

General Comment No. 7 then continues to outline how early childhood is important for children's rights, as it is lays the foundations for children's rights to be realized both in terms of welfare rights and liberty rights. However, the majority of children's participation projects still focus on older children, and young children are still excluded from participating in decision-making because of their age and ideas about competency.

Although the UNCRC has been operating for more than twenty years and has put the subject of children's rights on the map, it is open to debate how much change has been brought about in terms of how children experience their day-to-day lives. For example, in many signatory countries, including the UK, the articles are not always upheld or put into practice in any meaningful way (Moorehead, 1997, cited in Alston and Tobin, 2005). It is apparent, therefore, that practice does not always follow well-meaning rhetoric and many children's participation initiatives, for example, are often tokenistic or manipulated to fit adult agendas (Percy-Smith and Thomas, 2010). Jones and Welch (2010: 26) refer to the 'veneer of children's rights' and discuss how agencies and individuals can give the impression of engaging with a rights-based agenda and yet at the same time not fully engage. This performing of child's rights may or may not be something which the adult is aware of but may often reflect long-standing attitudes and judgements about children's competencies and the relationship between adults and children (Jones and Welch, 2010).

Problematizing children's rights in the international context

The UNCRC can be seen as a ground-breaking document. However, there are a number of critiques of it, as well as more general critiques of the concept of children's rights and children's participation, especially in relation to their application in countries in the majority non-Western world and this is what I will focus on in the following section.

First, it is argued that the discourse of children's rights, as influenced by the UNCRC and human rights legislation in general, reflects Western neo-liberal thinking, which emphasizes the importance of the autonomous individual, democracy, consumerism, and user involvement (Stephens, 1995; White and Choudhury, 2007; Kjørholt, 2008). To be a citizen in Western market-driven societies, it is claimed, is to be an individual who makes consumer choices, upholds democratic principles, has rights to services, and the right to free speech. Childhood and the discourse of children's rights, therefore, becomes an important arena for the transmission of these ideas about what it is to be a democratic citizen (Stephens, 1995; Skelton, 2007), and offers an opportunity in which children can practise the application and understanding of their rights, including participation rights, so that they will become the 'right' type of democratic citizen who is actively involved in decision-making. These Western 'truths' about what it is to be human and understandings of what 'rights' are, are then exported to non-Western majority world countries which do not necessarily recognize children as having individual rights outside of their kin, clan or community group (Aitken, 2001; Pupavac, 2001; Burr, 2004). Instead of individual rights, children may be seen as having a responsibility and duty towards their kin-group or elders and may talk about their rights in relation to their family or group or their duty to their religion or community; this can be seen, to some extent, in the African Charter on the Rights and Welfare of the Child and in the case of religion in the Declaration of the Rights and Care of the Child in Islam.

Second, it is argued that many children's rights initiatives including the UNCRC are based on Western middle-class notions of childhood, which places emphasis on childhood as a time of innocence, parental support, education, and play (Boyden, 1990; Pupavac, 2001). Children in this discourse tend to be positioned both as vulnerable and in need of protection (normally provided by both parents and the State) but also as competent and able to express their views on matters that concern them (Boyden, 1990). This view of childhood, which very often informs Western-led or -funded children's rights delivery in the Majority World, may not be a reality on the ground and in many cases children may be engaged in hazardous work, be the head of the household due to the death of their parents or be excluded from schooling because of war, illness, homelessness or poverty (Wells, 2009). Coupled with this, many children live in communities that emphasize deference to elders, and this may make it difficult for children to participate in decision-making or have their views taken seriously (Twum-Danso, 2009). The notion of childhood, therefore, implicit in much of the children's rights discourse, may not be culturally meaningful or achievable in many Majority World countries and has been critiqued for being paternalistic, portraying local representations of childhood as deficit models that need intervention by the West to become the 'right' kind of childhood (Burman, 1994b; Stephens, 1995; Pupavac, 2001).

Third, there is an ethically based critique of children's participation projects and children's rights initiatives that aims to empower children in Majority World countries and, as a result, challenge community norms and values. Concerns have been raised, for example, about the effect that these programmes can have on the relationship between children, their families, and their communities (Skelton, 2007). This is an important consideration, as in many countries child protection systems are often non-existent or poorly funded and this may lead to children relying heavily on their families and communities for support. Any fractures within this relationship, as a result of children acting in non-culturally acceptable ways, may mean that the children lose the support of their family and community. As Skelton (2007) states, this can have terrible consequences. Furthermore, questions have been raised as to how ethical it is to talk to children about rights that they may not ever be able to use (White, 2007), and rights-based initiatives have been criticized for not taking into account the impact of the local context in terms of the economic and political resources available as well as issues such as war and HIV/AIDS on the ability of children to achieve their rights (Hart, 2006).

Children's rights and early childhood education and care: the case of Zambia

The right to education for all children is enshrined in Article 28 of the UNCRC (United Nations, 1989) with early childhood education being the particular focus of General Comment No. 7, which states that 'the committee interprets the right to education during early childhood as beginning at birth' (OHCHR, 2005: 13). Since the ratification of the UNCRC and the UNESCO World Conference on Education for All held in Jomtien in 1990 and Dakar in 2000, which identified the provision of early childhood care and education as an important part of 'basic' education, there has been much focus on the goal of 'expanding and improving early childhood care and education, especially for the most vulnerable and disadvantaged children' (UNESCO, 2000: 8). The subsequent publication, by the World Bank, of *Early Childhood Development: Investing in the Future* (Young, 1996) plus a series of loans for ECEC development in Majority World countries cemented the importance of the area, leading to ECEC becoming a priority for international development.

Zambia, in Sub-Saharan Africa, is a signatory to the UNCRC, the Millennium Development Goals, and the Education for All framework, and the importance of ECEC is discussed in Zambia's education policy 'Educating our Future' (Ministry of Education, 1996) plus other documents such as the 6th National Development Plan (Republic of Zambia, 2011). However, although ECEC has been recognized as being important by both the Zambian Government and the Ministry of Education (a national policy has been developed and has been awaiting cabinet approval since 2010), this has not really translated into practice and Zambia is off-course to meet the Education for All goal of expanding and improving ECEC by 2015. Currently, only a minority of Zambian children aged 3–6 years have access to early childhood education and care provision and there are very few, if any, government-funded centres. As the comments from the headteacher below show, government support for ECEC is directed at training preschool teachers, providing a curriculum, and inspecting provision. The actual provision and funding of ECEC is left to private individuals and non-governmental organizations (NGOs) including church groups, leading to variations in terms of provision and quality with many rural areas and very young children (0–3 years old) not being catered for.

Case Study

The Government in Zambia trains preschool teachers but these teachers do not go into government schools, they go into private settings. The government thinks that preschool education is important but provides no money or resources for it, only training for preschool teachers. Preschool education is provided privately, by charities, churches, and non-governmental organizations. Some preschools charge high fees; some are reasonable. Quality is important; many of the preschools will not be of high quality and will have low ratios of staff to children; they will not be monitored and the children will not learn much. Rural preschools, if they exist, do not have facilities; there is no government infrastructure, very few schools open in rural areas, and there are no professionals to run the preschools in rural areas.

To work with young children you need a good heart for young ones and like to work with young children. The remuneration is not good; those with a good heart have motivation and will not move on. Some do not have motivation and do it for the money – they do not have a good heart for children – and will move onto primary and secondary with more money and qualifications. Those without heart do not uphold children's rights and manhandle them or do not listen to them. The children will not want to go to school. Our children want to come to school even in the holiday – our preschool is very popular.

Children have a right to education. Preschool education lays down the foundation of a child's right to education; by not providing preschool education we infringe on their right. Children also have the right to association and many young children are alone in the family and not allowed to go out. Going to preschool allows young children to associate with their peers, to play and to learn.

We do not give them rules, we encourage our students in their orientation to make their own rules – we may want them to do this or that but they need to tell us; if they decide the rules, they will follow them. We have workshops to remind teachers about this – that children are part of the school rules. If we tell them then we are like their mum – telling them. If they understand and make the rules they will follow them. The rules in the school involve the children.

(Preschool headteacher, Zambia)

To understand why Zambia may not meet the Education for All goal of expanding ECEC, it is important to look at the local context. Zambia is a low-income country with 59% of people being on less than US$1 a day (the international poverty rate). It has a high rate of orphans and child-headed households, and an HIV/AIDS prevalence rate of 13.5%, which has impacted on the workforce (World Bank, 2012). Although free basic primary education was introduced in Zambia in 2002, the quality of primary education can be poor, including a lack of qualified teachers, poor learning environments, and a high pupil–teacher ratio especially in rural areas. There are, therefore, a number of challenges that the Zambian Government faces in terms of balancing development priorities and how it will allocate often limited financial resources. The right to ECEC provision, therefore, may not currently be a reality for many Zambian children and it has been argued that a focus on ECEC may be 'damaging to an already tenuous education system' (Thomas and Thomas, 2009: 6).

Conclusions

The ratification of the UNCRC was an important milestone in the history of children's rights and put the concept of children's rights on the international agenda. However, children's rights, as put forward by the UNCRC and by many aid agencies and organizations, has been critiqued for promoting Western ideals as well as 'global childhood', based on European and North American models, which, it is said, can be achieved by all societies. This is problematic, as structural inequalities and local living conditions may mean that many children are unable to realize their rights as defined by the UNCRC and many countries may be unable to meet the commitments that they have signed up to. Furthermore, cultural and local representations of childhood may mean that there are a variety of understandings as to what children's rights are. It is important, therefore, to take into account the local context on the ground and the meanings attributed to children's rights by children, caregivers, and communities so as to ensure that rights-based initiatives have local relevance.

Find Out More

- Examine the United Nations Convention on the Rights of the Child (www. unicef.org/crc). While doing this, reflect on your own views about children's rights and children's participation. What has influenced your views on children's rights?
- Explore the Child Rights International Website (http://www.crin.org) and research in more detail a children's rights issue that is of interest to you.
- Examine a key policy document relating to ECEC in your own country and explore how children's rights have (or have not) been incorporated into this document. Compare and contrast the key policy document that you have identified with an ECEC policy document from another country (the country chosen should ideally be a country different from your own). What are the similarities and what are the differences between the two policy documents in relation to children's rights? Reflect on what could explain these similarities and differences.

References and recommended reading

Aitken, S.C. (2001) Global crisis of childhood: rights, justice and the unchildlike child, *Area*, 33(2): 119–27.

Alston, P. and Tobin, J. (2005) *Laying the Foundation for Children's Rights*. Florence: UNICEF Innocenti Research Centre.

Boyden, J. (1990) Childhood and the policy makers: a comparative perspective on the globalisation of childhood, in A. James and A. Prout (eds.) *Constructing and Reconstructing Childhood: Contemporary Issues in the Sociology of Childhood*. London: Falmer Press.

Burman, E. (1994a) *Deconstructing Developmental Psychology*. London: Routledge.

Burman, E. (1994b) Innocents abroad: Western fantasies of childhood and the iconography of emergencies, *Disasters*, 18(3): 238–53.

Burr, R. (2004) Children's rights: international policy and lived practice, in M.J. Kehily (ed.) *An Introduction to Childhood Studies*. Maidenhead: Open University Press.

Children's Rights International Network (CRIN) (2012) About Children's Rights. Available online at: http://www.crin.org/themes/ViewTheme.asp?id=2 (accessed 5 June 2012).

Christensen, P. and James, A. (2008) *Research with Children: Perspectives and Practices* (2nd edn). London: Falmer Press.

Franklin, A. and Franklin, B. (1996) Growing pains: the developing children's rights movement in the UK, in J. Pilcher and S. Wagg (eds.) *Thatcher's Children?* London: Falmer Press.

Franklin, B. (2002) *The New Handbook of Children's Rights*. London: Routledge.

Freeman, M. (1983) *The Rights and Wrongs of Children*. London: Francis Pinter.

Hardman, C. (1973) Can there be an anthropology of children?, *Journal of the Anthropology Society of Oxford*, 4(1): 85–99.

Hart, R. (2006) Putting children in the picture, *Forced Migration Review*, July (suppl.): 9–10.

Jenks, C. (1982) *The Sociology of Childhood: Essential Readings*. London: Batsford.

Jones, P. and Welch, S. (2010) *Rethinking Children's Rights: Attitudes in Contemporary Society*. London: Continuum Books.

Kjørholt, A.T. (2004) *Childhood as a Social and Symbolic Space: Discourses on Children as Social Participants in Society*. Trondheim: Department of Education/Norwegian Centre for Child Research.

Kjørholt, A.T. (2008) Children as new citizens: in the best interests of the child?, in A. James and A.L. James (eds.) *European Childhoods: Cultures, Politics and Childhoods in Europe*. Chippenham: Palgrave Macmillan.

Mac Naughton, G., Hughes, P. and Smith, K. (2007) Early childhood professionals and children's rights: tensions and possibilities around the United Nations General Comment No. 7 on Children's Rights, *International Journal of Early Years Education*, 15(2): 161–70.

Mannion, G. (2010) After participation, the socio-spatial performance of intergenerational becoming, in B. Percy-Smith and N. Thomas (eds.) *A Handbook of Children and Young People's Participation: Perspectives from Theory and Practice*. London: Routledge.

Ministry of Education (1996) *Educating our Future: National Policy on Education*. Lusaka: Zambia Educational Publishing House.

Murray, R. (2004) *Human Rights in Africa: From the OAU to the African Union*. Cambridge: Cambridge University Press.

Office for the High Commission of Human Rights (OHCHR) (2005) *General Comment No. 7: Implementing Child Rights in Early Childhood*. Geneva: United Nations. Available at: http://www2.ohchr.org/english/bodies/crc/docs/AdvanceVersions/ GeneralComment7Rev1.pdf (accessed 10 June 2012).

Organization of African Unity (1990) *African Charter on the Rights and Welfare of the Child.* Available at: http://www.unhcr.org/refworld/docid/3ae6b38c18.html (accessed 10 June 2012).

Percy-Smith, B. and Thomas, N. (2010) *A Handbook of Children and Young People's Participation: Perspectives from Theory and Practice.* **London: Routledge.**

Prout, A. (2005) *The Future of Childhood.* London: RoutledgeFalmer.

Prout, A. and James, A. (eds.) (1990) *Constructing and Reconstructing Childhood: Contemporary Issues in the Sociology of Childhood.* London: Falmer Press.

Pupavac, V. (2001) Misanthropy without border: the international children's rights regime, *Disasters,* 25(2): 95–112.

Qvortrup, J. (1994) *Childhood Matters: Social Theory, Practice and Politics.* Aldershot: Avebury.

Republic of Zambia (2011) *Sixth National Development Plan 2011–2015: Sustained Economic Growth and Poverty Reduction.* Available at: http://siteresources.worldbank.org/INTZAM-BIA/Resources/SNDP_Final_Draft_20_01_2011.pdf (accessed 10 June 2012).

Skelton, T. (2007) Children, young people, UNICEF and participation, *Children's Geographies,* 5(1/2): 165–81.

Stephens, S. (1995) Introduction: children and the politics of culture in 'Late Capitalism', in S. Stephens (ed.) *Children and the Politics of Culture.* Princeton, NJ: Princeton University Press.

Thomas, C.M. and Thomas, M.A.M. (2009) Early childhood care and education in Zambia: an integral part of education provision? *Current Issues in Comparative Education,* 11: 6–14.

Twum-Danso, A. (2009) Situating participatory methodologies in context: the impact of culture on adult–child interactions in research and other projects, *Children's Geographies,* 7(4): 379–89.

UNESCO (2000) *The Dakar Framework for Action. Education for All: Meeting Our Collective Commitments.* Available at: http://unesdoc.unesco.org/images/0012/001211/121147e.pdf (accessed 5 June 2012).

UN General Assembly (1959) *Declaration of the Rights of the Child.* Available at: http://www.unhcr.org/refworld/docid/3ae6b38e3.html (accessed 10 June 2012).

United Nations (1989) *United Nations Convention on the Rights of the Child.* **Geneva: United Nations.**

Wells, K. (2009) *Childhood in a Global Perspective.* Cambridge: Polity Press.

White, S.C. (2007) Children's rights and the imagination of community in Bangladesh, *Childhood,* 14(4): 505–20.

White, S.C. and Choudhury, S.A. (2007) The politics of child participation in international development: the dilemma of agency, *European Journal of Development Research,* 19(4): 529–50.

Woodhead, M. (2010) Foreword, in B. Percy-Smith and N. Thomas (eds.) *A Handbook of Children and Young People's Participation: Perspectives from Theory and Practice.* London: Routledge.

World Bank (2012) *Zambia Data and Statistics.* Available at: http://web.worldbank.org/WBSITE/EXTERNAL/COUNTRIES/AFRICAEXT/ZAMBIAEXTN/0,,menuPK:375700~pagePK:141132~piPK:141109~theSitePK:375589,00.html (accessed 7 June 2012).

Wyness, M. (2012) *Childhood and Society* (2nd edn.). Basingstoke: Palgrave Macmillan.

Young, M.E. (1996) *Early Childhood Development: Investing in the Future.* Washington, DC: World Bank.

PART 2

How approaches have developed

4

EMBEDDING EARLY CHILDHOOD EDUCATION AND CARE IN THE SOCIO-CULTURAL CONTEXT: THE CASE OF ITALY

Federica Caruso

Summary

The aim of this chapter is to present an overview of the socio-cultural conditions in which the ECEC discourse originated in Italy in the aftermath of the Second World War, focusing in particular on the example set by Loris Malaguzzi in Reggio Emilia. In highlighting the distinctive vision from which the Reggio Emilia system has been developed, I critically analyse how it has influenced and transformed the pedagogical discourse and the curriculum for children aged 3–6 years throughout Italy. The main idea of the chapter is that innovative processes, such as the Reggio Emilia approach, emerge in relation to stimulating environments, in connection with other experiences and by unifying a variety of practices into a consistent vision.

Historical context

The unification of Italy as a nation-state in 1861 presented deep-rooted discrepancies in economic, institutional, and social organizations throughout its territory. These can be ascribed to the different lines of development, over the centuries, of the formerly independent local States. Since the medieval period, Emilia Romagna, the region to which Reggio Emilia belongs, has always had a tradition of 'civic community', characterized by social solidarity, citizens' active participation in public life and their involvement in deliberations related to the institutional activities of the local communities.

During the first two decades of the twentieth century, a culture of 'municipal socialism' structured Reggio Emilia public life. In particular, women had more opportunities to work outside the family than in other Italian regions. Thus they asked for community provision of welfare services as well as for the recognition of the proactive civic role that education can have for the community itself.

During Fascism (1922–1943), children's education was subordinated to the values of the 'ethical Nation-State of Fascism'. It is evident that this model did not leave space for the development of citizenship and participation in the community based on critical thinking, access to information, and pluralism of views.

The fight against Nazi-fascist rule in Italy (1943–1945) represented a turning point in the culture of education as well as in gender and generational relations (Allemann-Ghionda, 2000). The Allies introduced the idea of progressive education whereby a generation of young teachers started to think of schooling as an engine for the development of intellectual, moral, and democratic attitudes in children. Women had a very important and recognized role in the Resistance Movement and, particularly in Emilia-Romagna, had a voice in the development of the welfare system. This is one grounding element of the innovative conception of ECEC in terms of the promotion of children's personal development, rather than in terms of assistance and reproduction of family roles.

Origins of the Reggio Emilia innovative approach

Immediately after the end of the Second World War in the spring of 1945, Malaguzzi, a young teacher, was involved in the reconstruction of democratic education. He joined a group of parents who built a school in the neighbourhood of Reggio Emilia and also worked in a public mental health centre for children. His sensitivity led him to recognize children's potential and capabilities, in order to develop effective educational programmes. Malaguzzi developed his innovative educational perspective through constant dialogue with colleagues in the Movement of Educational Cooperation (MEC), an association of teachers founded in 1951 to introduce an educational method based on children actively exploring their environment. Furthermore, throughout his life, Malaguzzi promoted debates on educational issues in early childhood among practitioners as well as researchers through distinguished journals for teacher in-service education, such as *Zerosei* ('Zero-Six') and *Bambini* ('Children'). He encouraged the publication of papers on educational theories and their potential application in school settings.

In 1963, the first Reggio Emilia Municipality-run pre-primary school was established with sixty children in two classrooms. In 1970, the first nursery school (for children from 7 months to 3 years) was established, as a service for both mothers and children. In Italy, the system of pre-primary schools was somewhat fragmentary, and the lion's share of early childhood education outside the family was provided by religious associations. The Reggio Emilia Town Council set up an integrated system of pre-primary schools to promote the wellbeing of all children and community welfare. This organization was directed by Malaguzzi, who introduced a new culture in ECEC provision and encouraged the integration of advanced theories about child development and everyday practice in educational settings.

Defining the Reggio Emilia approach: vision, organization, curriculum, and documentation

Vision: the child as 'rich in potentialities'

As Moss et al. (2000) point out, educational discourses are never neutral or self-evident: they embody social values, historical trends, and pedagogical priorities.

Educators should be aware of the impact that the use of specific visions of childhood have on their practice. Not only are specific concepts produced by social discourses, they also produce a consistent approach to real children in practice. In the recent British ECEC context, the concept of the 'child in need' is still rather powerful (see Chapter 22). By referring to children as 'in need', both policy discourse and practice tend to concentrate on what children lack, what they are not able to think or perform; the role of the teacher becomes a directive and corrective one.

The Reggio Emilia approach has rejected this idea. Instead, it has developed both an explicitly different vision of childhood and a considerably distinctive understanding of educational practice with children. The focal idea in the Reggio Emilia discourse is that 'childhood is rich': any child is endowed at birth with 'a potential for growth', a set of personal resources that can be developed into competences through meaningful interaction with a stimulating educational environment. Through meaningful experiences, the child will master a 'hundred languages' to express and share ideas and to appreciate artefacts of cultural value (Edwards et al., 1998). As Malaguzzi (1993: 10) maintained, 'our image of the child is rich in potential, strong, powerful, competent and most of all connected to adults and other children'.

The core concepts of the Reggio Emilia approach are adult support for children's exploration of their environment and constant encouragement to develop their identity through 'all of their available "expressive, communicative, and cognitive languages"', whether these be words, movement, drawing, painting, building, sculpture, shadow play, collage, dramatic play, or music, to name a few . . . Classrooms are organized to support a highly collaborative problem-solving approach to learning' (Edwards et al., 1998: 7).

By considering children as the subject of their own learning, some consequences follow:

- Learning consists of a constant process of personal transformation of one's own resources through meaningful experiences. Furthermore, learning is contextualized in social, symbolic, and natural environments, which structure the conditions for children's experiences and learning processes.
- It is the whole system of interactions that supports the children's development; designing complex learning environments is an integral part of the educational process, since they offer the learners exciting experiences with narratives, sounds, colours, tools, and daily objects.
- Dialogue is a pivotal tool of development, since children enhance their understanding by engaging in joint activity with adults and peers, based on mutual respect.

In this sense, the perspective espoused in Reggio Emilia recognizes that human development and social interactions are profoundly intertwined: a child constructs new understanding of the world by being engaged in activities situated in social environments. Different aspects of experience encourage new questions to be raised and ideas to be formulated, expressed, and compared with others. Different points of view are recognized; in turn, dialogue promotes human development, since children use language and other symbolic systems to integrate their ideas in public and recognizable artefacts. By connecting what they already know to new experiences, learners extend their understanding of themselves and of the world.

This approach represents a radical departure from the traditional educational model in which teaching was considered a directing, modelling, and controlling process, and learning was seen as rather mechanical, repetitive, and imitative.

Spaces

One of the characteristics that make Reggio Emilia different and valuable is the importance of the school environment as an evolving system (Filippini, 2009). Educational settings are not considered static elements that simply surround the educational activities, but conditions that support children's learning – thus they are objects of reflection and continuing innovation.

As Gandini (1998: 161) points out, 'space is an essential element' of the Reggio Emilia educational approach, as it is thought to shape the children's affective, cognitive, and linguistic acquisitions. Spaces are designed to promote learners' interactions during their activities, thus teachers and families co-design settings with the architects. As a result, the learning environment incorporates the Reggio Emilia educational perspective and supports children's active exploration and movements. At the centre of each school building is an open and large common space called the 'piazza' (square), which is used for public events such as everyday assemblies. The classroom spaces are subdivided into small areas. Pieces of documentation of children's activities and projects are displayed in the school space, in order to make their feelings, ideas, and actions visible and recognizable as part of the public culture of the school.

Typically, each school has an atelier: a workshop or a studio where children work out their ideas, manipulate materials, and construct objects. As will be explained in the following section, the atelierista has a unique professional role that supports the teaching team. As an expert in art, the atelierista collaborates with the teachers and offers a new perspective on the children's representations and ideas. Close to each classroom there is a mini-atelier to conduct extended project work. Given the support of the atelierista, the children learn to master the symbolic language of art to express themselves to others and develop their potential.

The teaching team

At the beginning of the 1970s, Loris Malaguzzi introduced a teaching team of two teachers for each class, who could support different activities at the same time. This model was eventually adopted by the recently developed national system of pre-primary and primary schools, from 1990 to 2008. The teachers have many opportunities to discuss as a team and work out projects. They continuously document everyday activities through audio- and video-recordings, structured observations, and by gathering what children have produced. They organize documentation in portfolios so as to reflect on their teaching activities and to introduce changes in educational settings.

Unique to the Reggio Emilia municipal educational system are two more professional roles: the 'atelierista' and the 'pedagogist'. The atelierista is an art teacher, who offers new insights to children when they are working on some projects, by making them aware of new relationships between objects, new narratives, and new points of view that can be further developed in unexpected ways by the children themselves. The Reggio Emilia model values the atelierista as a member of the teaching staff who supports the children's inquiry into language. For example, the children can introduce changes in well-known fairy tales and create new ones; reflect on spontaneous movements and develop a dance; observe simple recovered objects from a new perspective and use them to construct an artwork or puppets, or the material representation of an animal (Project Zero and Reggio Children, 2001). As a matter of principle, it is maintained that by acquiring a material form, learners' ideas become more structured and precise.

The 'pedagogist' is the coordinator who promotes the social and cultural development of the Reggio Emilia system as a whole. The pedagogist supervises the consistency of the educational activities over time among the different schools; they discuss with politicians and families about organizational issues, work with the teaching teams to develop new projects, and support teachers' professional development through supervision or in-service training programmes.

The curriculum

At the outset, the teachers do not plan the educational activities as a sequence of structured procedures that the children are asked to perform in order to produce expected outcomes. Rather, they formulate hypotheses on topics that could be of interest to children and have the potential to enhance their learning; they formulate flexible plans and open activities, and discuss them with the atelierista, the pedagogist, and the children's families.

One of the most groundbreaking educational ideas developed in the Reggio Emilia schools is 'project-work' (*progettazione* in Italian) as a prolonged activity that creates the conditions for children to make meaningful experiences about an area of interest. From the educational point of view, the importance of project-work is that it is an open activity, without an expected outcome. Therefore, the children are not asked to conform to the teachers' expectations, but are engaged in authentic activities, whose outcomes depend on the nature of the topic, the interests of the children, and the strategies that are adopted. Children have multiple opportunities to realize ideas, test hypotheses, exercise their creativity, and propose narratives. By using different symbolic codes, such as verbal, figurative, and kinaesthetic languages, they can express themselves, materialize their ideas, discuss them with others, develop collaborative inquiries, and work out more elaborated representations of their reality. The projects evolve according to the children's interests and evolving experiences. By achieving some relevant, visible outcomes of their activity (a dramatic play, an object, a documentation of their thoughts and feelings), they increase their disposition to learn (Katz, 1998). As Malaguzzi (1998: 88) aptly stated: 'the teachers follow the children, not the plans'.

Rather than cultivating the talented children, all activities are intended to promote the full development of the rich potentialities in each child. Teachers take note of children's activities and progress in daily journals, as elements of further professional reflection and as a reference point for communication with their families. Teachers' field notes are organized in different formats according to their objectives and the nature of the activities: the gathered data are subsequently analysed to help understand the implication of specific patterns of activity for the process of learning.

Documentation

The outcomes of project-work activities are displayed on notice boards or in exhibitions, along with photographs and teachers' reflections and evaluations. This procedure is called 'pedagogical documentation' and gives children the sense that adults value their products as the outcomes of their engagement in the project-work; this in turn promotes learners' self-confidence, as children begin to view themselves as contributors to the educational activities. Through the documentation of children's purposeful activity, parents become aware of their children's learning outside the family environment, and thus their engagement with the school system is enhanced.

It is important to point out that pedagogical documentation is not a form of early assessment of children's achievements, but instead focuses on a more encompassing area of competence, such as cooperative learning and communication in different symbolic codes. Therefore, in documenting all the activities children are engaged in, pedagogical documentation does not assess the products of the children according to standardized measures. It is a tool to deepen adults' as well as children's understanding of the development of ideas in material objects, the emerging patterns of interaction, and children's complex paths towards learning (Dahlberg et al., 1999).

The circulation of ideas and the reform of pre-primary education in Italy

It is important to recognize that groundbreaking experiences do not emerge from the originality of a single, isolated mind, but through the interaction between fertile ideas and stimulating environments. This is the case with the Reggio Emilia experience, which is characterized by the fruitful combination of good ideas and a 'culture of citizenship' (Ginsborg, 2003: xi) that puts forward the vision of children as naturally and universally endowed with resources and competences, as well as bearers of human and social rights to develop to their full potential, rather than of needs to be addressed (Moss et al., 2000). According to these principles, the educational system during childhood is expected to offer stimulating environments to enable children to have meaningful experiences and develop their potentialities. By engaging the learners in relevant human relationships, pre-primary education sustains the development of mutual respect and cooperative activities. In a sense, early childhood education becomes the grounding experience for future personal development.

Through the journals he edited and in dialogue with other prominent educators, Loris Malaguzzi promoted pedagogical debate and the circulation of innovative ideas that connected to other cultural initiatives with a progressive education perspective. Together, they inspired an innovative approach in the Pre-Primary School Curriculum Guidelines (Department of Education, 1991; revised and integrated into the Compulsory School Curriculum in 2007: Department of Education, 2007). In these official documents, it is explicitly stated that the pre-primary school should promote the full development of children, including:

- learning to achieve personal wellbeing, to feel secure in exploring the environment, and to have new educational experiences;
- learning to recognize one's own emotions, being able to express them, to integrate them with cognitive and social competences;
- learning to feel able to participate in social activities by creatively contributing to their development;
- learning to reflect on one's own experience and change one's own cognitive schemes;
- learning to recognize and understand peers' different points of view and to solve social conflicts peacefully as they emerge during interactions.

One central tenet of the Italian progressive movement in early childhood education is the idea that pre-primary education is part of the larger system of schooling, and therefore it should promote equal access to the cultural system on the basis of social class, gender, ethnicity, and ability. Furthermore, the instructional practice should be built upon and extend the children's experiences. To make visible the content and method of the curriculum in the pre-primary school, the 1991 Guidelines introduce the concept of 'experiential fields', defined as 'spaces of children's engagement, guided by the teachers, and mediated by the use of the symbolic system of the culture' (Department of Education, 1991). They characterize five areas of child development: 'the self and others', 'the body and movement', 'expression, creativity, and art', 'language, communication, and culture', and 'knowing the world'. The term 'experiential fields' refers to areas of goal-oriented activity, devised by the teachers, who establish the educational goals; however, its realization requires the creative and innovative participation of the children, through their own imagination and understanding, in a caring and stimulating environment.

A major contribution of the Reggio Emilia approach to Italian ECEC culture is the idea that all children can contribute to the school environment, since all of them have potentialities and rights that can be developed through meaningful experiences in collaboration with others. When a child with severe learning difficulties is integrated into the mainstream classroom, a specialized teacher joins the teaching team. However, support is not exclusively given to the child alone, but to the whole class so as to facilitate the child's participation in educational activities. To make sense of this inclusive policy, the following illustrative vignette is presented from the daily activities in a pre-primary class.

Inclusive dramatic play

> ### Case Study
>
> A 4-year-old child with severe learning difficulties is encouraged and assisted in his participation in educational activities with his peers. A drama play is devised with the educational goal of improving the children's sensory-motor competences; therefore, they are asked to imitate the characteristic movements of different animals. The child participates with the others in the play, and he is helped to make the correct movements when jumping and running, in an attempt to move beyond his actual abilities. He is expected to respect the two most fundamental rules of the school, as his peers do: do not harm oneself or others, and do not break down the activities of others. Therefore, whenever he misbehaves, the teacher makes him understand that his behaviour is detrimental to his classmates.

A teacher explains the school vision about the inclusion of children with severe learning difficulties: 'They do not need a special environment, but sensitive assistance to participate with the others in real, complex activities. Therefore, vulnerable children experience all the obstacles, the rules, the engagement, the success, the joy, the encouragements and the reprisals that their peers do'.

Why is Reggio Emilia still ahead of other experiences in ECEC?

Although there is a dissemination of innovative ideas in the public system of ECEC in Italy, the Reggio Emilia system is still the most advanced in pre-primary school provision. Reasons for this include:

1. It is part of a system of childhood education that values children's expression and participation in community life. The municipality holds in high regard the quality of the school system, encourages innovation, supports the work of teaching teams, and offers financial support to maintain the high level of commitment to childhood welfare. The culture of pre-primary schools is present all over the town of Reggio Emilia and the children's artefacts are shown in dedicated public exhibitions. A Documentation and Conference Centre was recently established to support in-service education programmes for teachers from different countries. This approach is seldom present in other locations, since financial cuts have reduced the quality of school settings.

2. It is systematically oriented to innovation and change. Reggio Emilia schools are connected with Italian and foreign universities, as a way to develop models and theories and to work out new research techniques to document daily practice. Becoming an explicit object of reflection, school activities can be jointly analysed and improved.

3. All the participants in the educational system have a voice in working out the settings and the activities: the teachers, the children and their families co-participate in developing project-work and in restructuring educational spaces.

4. The teaching teams present a wide range of expertise; in particular, the atelier-ists and the pedagogist offer insightful perspectives about the development of children's activities and support the construction of artefacts that cannot be con-sidered merely as examples of school tasks, but objects with an intrinsic value.

Not all the conditions present in Reggio Emilia are part of the educational system elsewhere in Italy: quite often, the teachers adapt pre-existing architecture to their educational goals and activities. Teaching teams do not have the atelierista and the pedagogist; furthermore, the teaching staff are at risk of redundancy, given the financial crisis; and in-service teacher education is expensive and often considered not worth it. As a result, schools are not oriented to a systematic culture of innova-tion. In many cases, teachers try to introduce some changes, but they do not rely on systematic documentation, or on an encompassing conception of change. There-fore, some aspects of the educational setting are identified as objects of change, while others remain untouched.

On the other hand, it is important to note that in many difficult circumstances, teachers try to create stimulating and effective environments by adapting limited settings with passion and creativity, as exemplified in Chapter 13. They challenge institutional obstacles in an attempt to promote children's active engagement in meaningful experiences, and offer a democratic learning environment in spite of social differences in class, ethnicity, and gender.

Find Out More

- What implications do different concepts of childhood have for educational practice?
- Identify the social conditions that might constrain the diffusion of the Reggio Emilia approach in your own context.
- Explain why the environment is considered of pivotal importance for chil-dren's learning. What characteristics of the environment might hinder the children's learning?

The best introduction to the Reggio educational vision is *The Hundred Languages of Children* (Edwards et al., 1998). In this book, some of the most significant charac-teristics of the Reggio approach, such as the environment as an integral part of the educational activity, the project-work, and the teaching team are explained in terms of the concept of the child as 'rich' in competences and potentialities. Mercillott-Hewett (2001) is a clear and essential introduction to the main aspects of the Reggio Emilia approach and Hall et al. (2003) also adds a longitudinal perspective. A docu-mentary film narrating the social history of the Reggio Emilia Municipal School System is *Not Just Anyplace* directed by Fasano (2002). Some personal accounts of their experiences of the Reggio approach by British scholars and practitioners are to be found in *Experiencing Reggio Emilia: Implications for Pre-school Provision* (Abbott and Nutbrown, 2001). The book offers some implications for extending the Reggio ideas in other situations. New (1999) analyses the different micro-cultures that structure some of the most advanced Italian experiences in ECEC.

A useful application of the documentation model developed at the Reggio Emilia school is Moss and Dahlberg (2008). The paper criticizes the managerialist approach to evaluate the quality of ECEC provision and proposes an alternative perspective based on the Reggio Emilia vision.

References and recommended reading

Abbott, L. and Nutbrown, C. (eds.) (2001) *Experiencing Reggio Emilia: Implications for Pre-school Provision*. Buckingham: Open University Press.

Allemann-Ghionda, C. (2000) Dewey in post-war Italy: the case of re-education, *Studies in Philosophy and Education*, 19(1): 53–67.

Dahlberg, G., Moss, P. and Pence, A. (1999) *Beyond Quality in Early Childhood Education and Care: Postmodern Perspectives*. London: Falmer Press.

Department of Education (1991) *Orientamenti dell'attività educative nelle scuole materne statali*, D.M. 3 giugno 1991 [*National Guidelines for the Educational Activities in Pre-primary Schools*]. Available at: http://www.edscuola.it/archivio/norme/decreti/dm3691.html (accessed 27 September 2011).

Department of Education (2007) *Indicazioni nazionali per il curricolo per la scuola dell'infanzia e per il primo ciclo di istruzione*, D.M. 3 Agosto 2007, n. 68 [*National Guidelines for Pre-primary and for Primary and Middle Schools*]. Available at: http://www.edscuola.it/archivio/norme/programmi/indicazioni_nazionali.pdf (accessed 28 September 2011).

Edwards, C., Gandini, L. and Forman, G. (1998) *The Hundred Languages of Children: The Reggio Emilia Approach. Advanced Reflections* (2nd edn.). Westport, CT: Ablex.

Fasano, M. (Director) (2002) *Not Just Anyplace* (DVD). Reggio Emilia, Italy: Reggio Children Publisher.

Filippini, T. (2009) Sulla natura dell'organizzazione [On the nature of the organization], in I. Cavallini, C. Giudici, M. Bendotti and L. Trancossi (eds.) *Rendere visibile l'apprendimento. Bambini che apprendono individualmente e in gruppo* [*Making Learning Visible: Children Who Learn Individually and in Groups*]. Reggio Emilia, Italy: Reggio Children Publisher.

Gandini, L. (1998) Educational and caring spaces, in C. Edwards, L. Gandini and G. Forman (eds.) *The Hundred Languages of Children: The Reggio Emilia Approach. Advanced Reflections* (2nd edn.). Westport, CT: Ablex.

Ginsborg, P. (2003) *Italy and its Discontents: Family, Civil Society, State*. New York: Palgrave Macmillan.

Hall, K., Horgan, M., Ridgway, A., Murphy, R., Cunneen, M. and Cunningham, D. (eds.) (2003) *Loris Malaguzzi and the Reggio Emilia Experience*. London: Continuum Books.

Katz, L.G. (1998) What can we learn from Reggio Emilia?, in C. Edwards, L. Gandini and G. Forman (eds.) *The Hundred Languages of Children: The Reggio Emilia Approach. Advanced Reflections* (2nd edn.). Westport, CT: Ablex.

Malaguzzi, L. (1993) For an education based on relationship, *Young Children*, 49(1): 9–12.

Malaguzzi, L. (1998) History, ideas, and basic philosophy: an interview with Lella Gandini, in C. Edwards, L. Gandini and G. Forman (eds.) *The Hundred Languages of Children: The Reggio Emilia Approach. Advanced Reflections* (2nd edn.). Westport, CT: Ablex.

Mercillott-Hewett, V. (2001) Examining the Reggio Emilia approach to early child-hood education, *Early Childhood Education Journal*, 29(2): 95–100.

Moss, P. and Dahlberg, G. (2008) Beyond quality in early childhood education and care – languages of evaluation, *New Zealand Journal of Teachers' Work,* 5(1). *Available at: http://www.teacherswork.ac.nz/journal/volume5_issue1/moss.pdf* (accessed 7 June 2012).

Moss, P., Dillon, J. and Statham, J. (2000) The 'child in need' and 'the rich child': discourses, constructions and practice, *Critical Social Policy*, 20(2): 233–54.

New, R.S. (1999) What should children learn? Making choices and taking chances, *Early Childhood Research and Practice,* 1(2). Available at: http://ecrp.uiuc.edu/v1n2/new.html (accessed 7 January 2012).

Project Zero and Reggio Children (2001) *Making Learning Visible: Children as Individual and Group Learners.* Reggio Emilia, Italy: Reggio Children Publisher.

5

THE NEW FACE OF EARLY CHILDHOOD IN THE UNITED STATES
Nancy McDermott

Summary

The Obama administration's emphasis on early childhood in the United States is the product of more than forty years of anti-poverty initiatives. In that time, the origins of social and economic deprivation have been variously explained as resulting from historical and political factors, family structure, culture, and finally as the interactions between individual parents and children and their effects on brain development. On closer examination this shift in emphasis, especially with regard to brain development, has less to do with neuroscience itself than the degree to which the language of science has come to dominate discourse on social inequality.

Introduction

> If your child has jelly on her list, then you can talk about whether the jar is big or small, whether the jar is round, if the surface is smooth, and then you're talking about the bread, and look, this loaf of bread is soft, but this roll is hard. When you get to a bag of sugar, understanding what's heavy and what's light.
>
> (Tough, 2008: 203)

These are instructions offered to participants in the Harlem Children's Zone's Three-Year-Old Journey programme. Instructors are coaching parents in preparation for a visit to the local supermarket where, it is hoped, they will use the opportunity to build their children's language skills. The Three-Year-Old Journey is just one of a number of very early childhood programmes offered by the Harlem Children's Zone (HCZ), a non-profit organization providing services to impoverished children in a 97-block area of Harlem, New York. Hailed as the 'Harlem Miracle' for its innovative programmes and good academic results, it has become the leading model for education and child policy.

The HCZ brings together early childhood intervention, social services, and a rigorous charter school under the auspices of a public/private partnership. The philosophy, that for children to be successful a critical mass of the adults around them need to be 'well versed in the techniques of effective parenting, and engaged in local educational, social, and religious activities with their children', relies on 'early and progressive intervention', ideally beginning before birth and continuing through college (HCZ, 2003: i).

The HCZ early childhood offering consists of three parts: Baby College, a prenatal parent training programme with 'at home: follow up'; The Three-Old-Year Journey, a training programme for the parents of very young children; and the Harlem Gems preschool, analogous to Head Start. Although the components are not unique, their incorporation into a larger scientized framework reflects the latest thinking in child development and social policy. In that sense, Head Start's major objectives are somewhat different today than they were in the past in that the interventions are self-consciously presented as grounded in science and managed for 'outcomes', return on investment, and sustainability.

It's an approach the Obama administration has strongly embraced. Indeed, it was at an HCZ conference in November of 2009 that Education Secretary, Arne Duncan, announced plans for the Promise Neighborhoods, the most radical shake up of early childhood education since the Head Start programme of 1965. Like the HCZ, the Promise Neighborhoods would 'build a seamless continuum of support and services for low-income children from birth to career to parenthood' capable of 'breaking the cradle-to-prison pipeline that plagues so many poverty-stricken neighborhoods' (Duncan, 2009). Duncan went on to announce US$10 million in planning grants to organizations interested in setting up these HCZ-like initiatives.

This chapter traces the development of early childhood intervention programmes in the United States from their origins as a political expedient in the War on Poverty to their present position as the centrepiece of a science-driven social policy agenda. In particular, we will critically consider the role of neuroscience in shaping child policy more generally. To do this we must start with the question of poverty.

Poverty: from morality to return on investment

What are the roots of poverty? In the United States, this question has been answered in a variety of different ways: as a matter of social equality, as a cultural issue or even as an inevitable consequence of natural differences. Today it is framed as a question of child development, specifically one of deficits of cognitive (IQ) and non-cognitive abilities (impulse control, social skills, etc.). These deficiencies are said to arise from the quality of children's interactions early in life and the way in which these shape brain development. They are, in many ways, seen as deficits in parenting.

Though early childhood has featured in the discussions of poverty since the 1960s, it has done so for very different reasons. In the early days of the Johnson administration (1963–1968), reformers believed that poverty could be overcome by bringing the resources of the State to bear on correcting historical inequalities between rich and poor and especially African Americans. Lyndon Johnson's so-called War on Poverty[1] saw a series of anti-poverty initiatives and civil rights reforms with the ambitious aim of eradicating poverty once and for all.

The focus on children also comes to us from that era; however, it was not, like today, primarily motivated by the belief that interventions at a young age might be more successful. At the time, anti-poverty interventions targeted a variety of age groups. Rather, politicians emphasized and promoted early childhood programmes as a matter of political expediency.

In an interview with Jeanette Valentine, Sargent Shriver, the then Director of the Office of Economic Opportunity and champion of the Head Start programme, recalled:

> I suddenly realized then that there was another advantage to doing something about children – particularly from a racial point of view . . . In our society there is a bias against helping adults. The prevalent idea is: 'By God there's plenty of work to be done, and if poor people had any get-up-and-go they'd go out and get jobs for themselves.' But there's a contrary bias in favour of helping children. Even in the black belt of the deepest South, there's always been a prejudice in favour of little black children. The old-time term of 'pickaninny' was one of endearment. It wasn't until blacks grew up that white people began to feel animosity or show actual violence toward them. I hoped we would overcome a lot of hostility in our society against the poor in general and specifically against black people who are poor, by aiming for the children.
>
> (Valentine and Zigler, 1979: 52)

The War on Poverty was short-lived, losing most of its funding to the Vietnam War but its legacy in the form of civil rights legislation and the framework it created for welfare and social services made a lasting impact on America's poor and minority communities. Though it helped to improve prospects for middle-class African Americans, mainly through civil rights legislation, it soon became apparent that for a significant number of poor and minority people conditions remained the same or had become significantly worse. As poverty increased and became concentrated in inner-city black and minority neighbourhoods, policy-makers began to re-examine the questions of race, poverty, and inequality.

Two landmark government reports, the Moynihan Report of 1965 and the Coleman Report of 1966, both suggested that poverty endured, not through a lack of equal opportunities or structural changes to the economy but because of factors in the backgrounds of minority families.

In his report, sociologist Daniel Patrick Moynihan singled out black families headed by women as a major contributing factor to poverty. In particular, he argued that 'a national effort is required that will give a unity of purpose to the many activities of the Federal government in this area, directed to a new kind of national goal: the establishment of a stable Negro family structure' (US Department of Labor, 1965). Similarly, James Coleman's Equality of Opportunity Study found that even when black schools and white schools received equal resources, the family background of poor individuals left them ill-equipped to take advantage of new opportunities (Coleman, 1966).

In other words, the barriers to overcoming poverty were no longer seen primarily as a problem of resources, racism, and historic inequalities but as arising from the culture of the poor themselves. But where did these perceived cultural deficits come from? The two most influential voices in the discussion were Charles Murray and William Julius Wilson.

Writing in 1984, Charles Murray, a fellow at the Manhattan Institute, argued that the culture of poverty was rooted in anti-poverty programmes themselves. In his book, *Losing Ground: American Social Policy 1950–1980*, Murray used data collected by various federal agencies to make the case that welfare programmes, like food stamps and Medicaid from the Johnson era, had the unintended consequence of trapping poor families in a cycle of poverty and dependence. Making the poor dependent on the state for basic necessities, he argued, created a culture of low expectations, and a lack of personal responsibility that served to perpetuate poverty. He suggested reforms to the existing system, in particular an end to income support of people of working age (Murray, 1984: 227–8).

William Julius Wilson, at the University of Chicago, countered that the persistence of poverty in inner-city neighbourhoods was primarily structural, rooted in the exodus of the black middle class from places like Harlem to jobs in and neighbourhoods in other places and segments of the economy. These structural changes worked to demoralize entire communities and to deprive them of any sense of upward mobility. For young people, it created an expectation of joblessness as a way of life. Wilson's policy recommendations, which focused on job creation and the establishment of a robust safety net, drew favour from the Clinton administration.

In the course of the two decades after the War on Poverty, the emphasis of anti-poverty programmes began to shift. Where once reformers focused on political and social inequalities, a new consensus emerged that the more pressing problem was the culture of dependency itself, especially when a sustained economic recovery in the 1990s made little impact on the poorest neighbourhoods. Without addressing aspects of this culture, it was believed, anti-poverty initiatives were doomed to fail. It was in this context that the period of early childhood was to become a focus again.

The Bell Curve

In 1994, Richard Herrnstein and Charles Murray published their book, *The Bell Curve: Intelligence and Class Structure in American Life*. Though wildly controversial and widely criticized, it would change the discussion of race and poverty forever.

Building on the data-intensive approach in *Losing Ground* (Murray, 1984), Murray and Herrnstein turned their focus to the origins of inequality. They analysed data from the Armed Forces Qualifications Test (AFQT), a diagnostic tool used by the military to channel recruits into their various training schools combined with data from the National Longitudinal Study of Youth in an attempt to isolate factors that correlated with long-term success.[2] It emerged that intelligence quotient (IQ) was the single most effective predictor of an individual's prospects. Men with lower IQs were more likely to drop out of school, lose their jobs or become long-term welfare recipients than those with higher IQs. Furthermore, these lower test scores were more closely associated with future failure than family background or socio-economic status.

IQ scores, they argued, could account for inequalities between blacks and whites, rich and poor. Since intelligence was believed to be largely inherited or at least fixed at a young age, it made little sense to invest heavily in education or training programmes or especially welfare programmes that might, in effect, subsidize the pregnancies of women with low IQs who were likely to have children of similarly low intelligence. They warned of the potential for society to become divided with permanent substrata of individuals dependent on the state. It was far better and more realistic, they argued, to find ways for people of lower intelligence to make a contribution to society in jobs suited to their abilities.

The book was controversial both for its reliance on IQ and because it suggested a link between race, poverty, and intelligence. Though its methodology and conclusions have been widely disputed, it changed the terms of the discussion of poverty in two important ways. First, by placing data from psychometric testing front and centre, it helped to scientize the question of poverty. Success became 'optimal outcomes', human potential a matter of 'cognitive and non-cognitive skills', and the imperative to combat poverty a question of return on investment. After the Bell Curve it became virtually impossible to discuss poverty in any other terms. The use of psychometric testing also codified the idea that success must, in a teleological way, be determined by factors in the past rather than factors or circumstances at any other time.

Economist James Heckman's critique of *The Bell Curve* is instructive. Not only is Heckman uncritical of the book's approach, he is actually quite complementary. His argument is not with its data-driven approach, but with aspects of the book's methodology and conclusions. In particular, he argues that what appears as an intractable difference in IQ in the Bell Curve's data is really more of a function of the age group of the people taking the AFQT (15–23 years) (Heckman, 1995).

Heckman argues that while education and training initiatives might not improve prospects for older teens and young adults, longitudinal studies of children who participated in early childhood programmes like the Perry Preschool Project or the Abecedarian programmes (precursors of Head Start) show that early intervention made a lasting positive impact above and beyond IQ (Heckman, 2008: 20). Participants held down jobs, earned more, owned homes, and were less likely to go on welfare or to spend time in prison than their peers. Even if early childhood programmes did not significantly raise IQ, they seemed to play a role in improving non-cognitive skills such as motivation, sociability, focus, and impulse control.

Over the next two decades, early childhood was to become a subject of intense interest to researchers in a variety of fields. In particular, psychologists and sociologists wished to understand the differences in early experience and environments between middle-class homes and the homes of the poor. Hart and Risley (1995), both psychologists, focused on the numbers and the tone of words children heard in the first years; others focused on the interactions between children and their caregivers (Brady-Smith et al., 1999; Totsika and Sylva, 2004). Annette Lareau, in her book *Unequal Childhoods* (2003), brought out a number of subtle cultural differences in the way families of different classes relate to one another and to institutions. This explosion of research yielded new insights into the forces that shape young children's development, but the discoveries that would finally position early childhood as the key period for intervention would not come from the study of children's lives, but from the study of their brains.

Discovering the brain

Neuroscience first became prominent in the discussion of child policy in the 1990s. Though scientists had been aware of rapid brain development in young children for some time, new magnetic resonance imaging (MRI) techniques made the rapid formation of synapses and their subsequent 'pruning back' around age 3 more concrete. The significance of these changes was far from clear, but they were widely interpreted to mean that children could be 'hardwired' for success or failure early in life. John Bruer, author of the book *The Myth of the First Three Years*, sums up the popular (mis)conceptions and understanding of neuroscience this way:

> The age from birth to three is the period of peak synaptic density... in the human brain, during which more synapses are formed than are eliminated. Synaptic densities peak during early childhood at levels exceeding adult densities. By puberty synaptic elimination reduces these densities to adult levels. The Myth uses these neuroscientific findings to claim that the period of high synaptic density is the critical period for brain development, during which children learn most easily and efficiently and during which experience results in largely irreversible neural changes. These irreversible changes determine life-long behavior. During this period enriched environments cause more synapses to be formed and thus more synapses to be retained after synaptic pruning occurs at puberty. Conversely, deprivation, neglect, or abuse during this period results in fewer synapses being formed and thus fewer being retained into adulthood.
>
> (Bruer, 2011: 4)

In fact, as Bruer demonstrates in his book, none of these claims about the effects of environment on the developing brain are true. Nevertheless, they command a powerful hold on the public imagination.

By the mid-1990s, the country had fallen into to a sort of 'brain fever'. Parents invested in 'brain-building' toys and crib mobiles in black, red, and white. The so-called 'Mozart Effect' spawned a craze for playing classical music for babies in hopes of increasing their IQs. Politicians, too, bought into the promise of the young brain. Zell Miller, the Governor of Georgia, pledged 'to deliver the first cassettes and CDs of classical music . . . to every newborn' in the belief that research had shown it would enhance their brain development (Sack, 1998).

Film director Rob Reiner was so enthused that he set up the *I am Your Child* foundation to raise public awareness of the importance of early brain development. Reiner produced a number of documentaries on the subject featuring celebrities and politicians including the likes of the Clintons, Mel Brooks, Tom Hanks, and Jamie Lee Curtis. Speaking to the National Governor's Association in February 1997,

Reiner perfectly articulated the popular misunderstanding of early brain development as follows: 'We now know through science that the first three years of life is the
most critical time period. It is the time period when the brain develops at a greater
rate than any time during the course of a person's life . . . But by age 10 your brain
is cooked and there's nothing much you can do' (Reiner, 1997).

Many members of the scientific community (Kagen, 1998; Bruer, 1999; Spelke,
1999; Rutter, 2002) rallied to challenge the highly exaggerated and misleading representations of neuroscience with the result that campaigns like *I Am Your Child*
quietly shut down or toned down their rhetoric. Nevertheless, the claims for neuroscience, albeit in a more mediated form, have not gone away. They persist because
posing child development in terms of physical changes to the brain becomes an
effective of way describing the more abstract mental experiences that are the stuff of
sociology and developmental psychology.

From neurons to neighbourhoods

In 1998, The Institute of Medicine, the Board on Children, Youth and Families,
and the National Research Council formed The Committee on Integrating the Science of Early Childhood Development. Two years later, they published their landmark report *From Neurons to Neighborhoods: The Science of Early Child Development*
(Shonkoff and Phillips, 2000).

The report was groundbreaking in a number of respects. It represented the first
attempt to integrate the findings from different scientific fields into one overarching
'science' of child development. It also self-consciously sought to move the question
of child policy out of the realm of politics and into the realm of science. The authors
write: 'In this context and based on the evidence gleaned from a rich and rapidly
growing knowledge base, we feel an urgent need to call for a new national dialogue
focused on rethinking the meaning of both shared responsibility for children and
strategic investment in their future' (Shonkoff and Phillips, 2000: 15). They called
for an end to 'blaming parents, communities, business, and government' and for the
creation of a new shared agenda (based on science) for ensuring the welfare and
future of children.

It was also striking that the report was not commissioned by the state but by
extra-governmental organizations. This reflected the new reality of state intervention.
After forty years of failed anti-poverty programmes and in the face of pressure to cut
public spending, policy-makers had become reluctant to invest in initiatives without
some guarantee of their effectiveness. It would fall on advocates to provide a vision
for social policy that would combine a scientific rationale with the rigorous reporting
and evaluation necessary to make investing in early childhood programmes attractive.
It was a vision powerful enough to inspire private foundations and philanthropists as
well, thus creating an important new source of support for early childhood initiatives.

A science-driven agenda

Early childhood policy today combines both the data-driven approach of Murray
and Heckman and scientific framing of child development pioneered by Shonkoff

and Phillips (2000) (best exemplified today by the Center on the Developing Child at Harvard). But what looks to be an effective strategy in advocating for early childhood programmes may ultimately prove problematic. In reality, the impact of early childhood programmes is not well understood and may not yield the promised results.

For instance, in a 2009 study of the HCZ commissioned by the National Bureau of Economic Research (NBER), researchers found no connection between early childhood programmes and academic achievement. Though the report credited the HCZ middle school for 'closing the black–white achievement gap in mathematics' and 'reducing it by nearly half in English Language arts' in the middle school and completely eliminating it at the elementary level (Dobbie and Fryer, 2009: 8–9), there was no difference in the academic performance of children who participated in HCZ early childhood programmes and those who did not. It appears, at least superficially, that the effect of the HCZ early childhood programmes, like other similar programmes, tend to fade out by third-grade (Dobbie and Fryer, 2009). These results echo studies of other early childhood programmes such as the Nurse–Family partnership (Olds et al., 2007), Head Start (US Department of Health and Human Services, Administration for Children and Families, 2010) and Start programmes that found no measurable impact on academic achievement (Ricciuti et al., 2004).

Another study published in 2010 by the Brookings Institute comparing the HCZ with other charter schools in New York City found no relationship between the programmes offered in the HCZ and performance. Indeed, more than half of New York City's charter schools performed as well or better than the HCZ. The top performer, a Knowledge Is Power Program (KIPP) school, offers no community or social services at all (Croft and Whitehurst, 2010).

When it comes to academic achievement, there appears to be little evidence for a positive relationship with early childhood education or social interventions. Though longitudinal studies show a measurable difference in success later in life (Heckman, 2008), how this works is unclear. It begs ethical questions about the degree to which the focus on early childhood negatively impacts investments in programmes for older children or whether parenting interventions are really necessary or appropriate. The danger, as the Promise Neighborhoods roll out across the country, is that the science-based, data-driven focus on child development may ultimately blind us to more complex social and political factors shaping the lives of America's poor.

Conclusions

In the nearly fifty years between the Johnson and Obama administrations, the understanding of the problem of poverty has changed considerably and with it the rationale for addressing the problem. Lyndon Johnson motivated the War on Poverty on the basis that inequality was incompatible with the 'demands of morality and the needs of the spirit'. In contrast, Barack Obama asserts that 'every dollar that we spend on these [early childhood] programs "saves" as much as $10 in reduced health care costs, crime, and welfare later on' (Obama, 2008: 249). Combating poverty is no longer a moral imperative but a pragmatic one in which experts employ scientific data to determine which activities will likely lead to desired 'outcomes'.

But science as a source of cultural authority may be a double-edged sword. What appears scientific may, in fact, be a pragmatic prioritization designed to appeal to policy-makers. It may not so much enlighten as endorse a particular set of views about childrearing and poverty while dismissing the potential of adults and older children. Worst of all, it may serve to blind us to more subtle reasons for the success of programmes like the HCZ.

It may be that the success of the HCZ has nothing to do with parenting classes or the effects of early childhood programmes on brain development. It may simply be the case that HCZ provides an anchor of stability for impoverished families with young children or that it makes it easier for parents to work and ensures that their children will have access to basic necessities, nutritious meals, and health care. It may be that it simply fosters a culture of achievement among children and families. Whatever the reason, as important as early childhood is, the experience of the older children involved with the HCZ and programmes like KIPP should remind us that the human potential of poor students does not end after kindergarten, and that good quality teaching, hard work, and ambition have the potential to turn the most careful scientific analysis on its head.

Find Out More

- Why do you think neuroscience has become such a popular way to discuss early childhood?
- Are there limitations to the scientific, data-driven approach?
- What are the consequences of the focus on outcomes for children, parents, and educators?

Notes

1   'The War on Poverty' is the popular name given to the series of ambitious policy initiatives outlined in President Lyndon Johnson's State of the Union address on 8 January 1964. Johnson's 'unconditional war against poverty' aimed to 'prove the success of our system; to disprove those cynics and critics at home and abroad who question our purpose and our competence'. The administration managed, especially in its first two years, to push through an unprecedented number of anti-poverty and civil rights initiatives and shaped policy initiatives for years to come. Its most enduring institutional legacy is in the delivery of social services at the local level and in particular, the Head Start programme.

2   The National Longitudinal Study of Youth is an on-going set of surveys carried out by the United States Department of Labor's Bureau of Labor and Statistics. The surveys are designed to gather information at multiple points in time on the labour market activities and other significant life events of several groups of men and women. The first surveys began in 1966 for 5225 young men, aged 14–24 years. Interviews with this cohort, referenced in *Losing Ground*, ceased in 1981. Current surveys and historical data are available online at: http://www.bls.gov/nls/overview.htm.

References and recommended reading

Brady-Smith, C., O'Brien, C., Berlin, L. and Ware, A.M. (1999) *Early Head Start Research and Evaluation Project: 24-Month Child–Parent Interaction Rating Scales for the Three-Bag Assessment*. New York: National Center for Children and Families, Teachers College, Columbia University.

Bruer, J.T. (1999) *The Myth of the First Three Years: A New Understanding of Early Brain Development and Lifelong Learning*. New York: Free Press.

Bruer, J.T. (2011) Revisiting the myth of the first three years. Paper at the conference on *Monitoring Parents: Science, Evidence, Experts and the New Parenting Culture*, Centre for Parenting Culture Studies, University of Kent, Canterbury, UK, 13–14 September.

Coleman, J.S. (1966) *Equality of Educational Opportunity Study* (EEOS). Washington, DC: US Department of Health, Education and Welfare.

Croft, M. and Whitehurst, G.J. (2010) *The Harlem Children's Zone, Promise Neighborhoods, and the Broader, Bolder Approach to Education*. Washington, DC: The Brookings Institution. Available at: http://www.brookings.edu/reports/2010/0720_hcz_whitehurst.aspx (accessed 12 May 2012).

Dobbie, W. and Fryer, R. (2009) *Are High Quality Schools Enough to Close the Achievement Gap? Evidence from a Social Experiment in Harlem*. NBER Working Paper No. 15473. Cambridge, MA: National Bureau of Economic Research.

Duncan, A. (2009) *The Promise of Promise Neighborhoods: Beyond Good Intentions*. Remarks of US Secretary Arne Duncan to the Harlem Children's Zone Conference, 10 November.

Ellsworth, J. and Ames, L.J. (eds.) (1998) *Critical Perspectives on Project Head Start: Revisioning the Hope and Challenge*. Albany, NY: State University of New York Press.

Harlem Children's Zone (HCZ) (2003) *Growth Plan FY 2001 – FY 2009*. New York: Harlem Children's Zone, Inc.

Hart, B. and Risley, R.T. (1995) *Meaningful Differences in the Everyday Experience of Young American Children*. Baltimore, MD: Paul Brooks.

Heckman, J.J. (1995) 'Cracked Bell', *Reason Magazine*, March.

Heckman, J.J. (2008) *Schools, Skills, and Synapses*. DP 3515. Bonn, Germany: Institute for the Study of Labor.

Herrnstein, R.J. and Murray, C. (1994) *The Bell Curve: Intelligence and Class Structure in American Life*. New York: Free Press.

Kagen, J. (1998) *Three Seductive Ideas*. Cambridge, MA: Harvard University Press.

Lareau, A. (2003) *Unequal Childhoods: Class, Race and Family Life*. Berkeley, CA: University of California Press.

Murray, C.A. (1984) *Losing Ground: American Social Policy 1950–1980*. New York: Basic Books.

Obama, B. (2008) *Change We Can Believe In: Barack Obama's Plan to Renew America*. New York: Three Rivers Press.

Olds, D.L., Kitzman, H., Hanks, C., Cole, R., Anson, E., Sidora-Arcelo, K., Luckey, D.W., Henderson, C.R., Holmberg, J., Tutt, R.A., Stevenson, A.J. and Bondy, J. (2007) Effects of nurse home visiting on maternal and child functioning: age-9 follow-up of a randomized trial, *Pediatrics*, 120(4): e832–45.

Rauscher, F., Shaw, G. and Ky, K. (1993) Music and spatial task performance, *Nature*, 365 (6447): 611.

Reiner, R. (1997) Speech to the National Governors' Association. Available at: http://www.nga.org/files/live/sites/NGA/files/pdf/1997NGAWinterMeeting.pdf (accessed 12 May 2012).

Ricciuti, A.E., St. Pierre, R.G., Lee, W., Parsad, A. and Rimdzius, T. (2004) *Third National Even Start Evaluation: Follow-Up Findings From the Experimental Design Study.* Washington, DC: US Department of Education, Institute of Education Sciences, National Center for Education Evaluation and Regional Assistance. Available at: http://ies.ed.gov/ncee/pdf/20053002.pdf (accessed 12 May 2012).

Rutter, M. (2002) Nature, nurture, and development: from evangelism through science toward policy and practice, *Child Development*, 73(1): 1–2.

Sack, K. (1998) Georgia's governor seeks musical start for babies, *New York Times*, 15 January.

Shonkoff, J.P. and Phillips, D.A. (eds.) (2000) *From Neurons to Neighborhoods: The Science of Early Childhood Development.* Washington, DC: National Academy Press.

Spelke, E. (1999) The myth of the first three years: a new understanding of brain development and lifelong learning, *Nature*, 401(6754): 643–4.

Tallis, R. (2011) *Aping Mankind: Neuromania, Darwinitis and the Misrepresentation of Humanity*. Durham: Acumen Publishing.

Totsika, V. and Sylva, K. (2004) The Home Observation for Measurement of the Environment revisited, *Child and Adolescent Mental Health*, 9(1): 25–35.

Tough, P. (2008) *Whatever it Takes: Geoffrey Canada's Quest to Change Harlem and America*. New York: Houghton Mifflin.

US Department of Health and Human Services, Administration for Children and Families (2010) *Head Start Impact Study: Final Report.* Washington, DC: US Department of Health and Human Services, Administration for Children and Families.

US Department of Labor (1965) *The Negro Family: The Case for National Action.* Washington, DC: US Department of Labor.

Valentine, J. and Zigler, E. (eds.) (1979) *Project Head Start: A Legacy of the War on Poverty.* New York: Free Press.

6

A CRITIQUE OF EURO-CENTRIC PERSPECTIVES ON EARLY CHILDHOOD EDUCATION AND CARE IN THE GAMBIA

Rebecca Carter Dillon

Summary

This chapter looks at developments in the provision of early childhood education and care (ECEC) in The Gambia, West Africa, a country that ranks very low on the United Nations Human Development Index and is characterized by high levels of poverty and social inequality. It seeks to acknowledge the challenges and opportunities for developing contextually appropriate provision. ECEC and education more widely are seen as central to addressing poverty in sub-Saharan Africa and other parts of the Majority World, yet there are on-going challenges associated with delivering a quality ECEC experience for children, especially given the economic circumstances in many contexts. It is important to acknowledge and critique euro-centric perspectives on ECEC and child wellbeing in The Gambia. By prioritizing the perspectives of Gambian children, communities, and practitioners, and building on rather than dismissing indigenous thinking around ECEC, provision is more likely to be contextually appropriate and lead to better outcomes. Indeed, in recognition that a Western model of English-medium schooling is not catering adequately for many children, the Government of The Gambia is now in the process of rolling out a programme of mother-tongue ECEC and lower basic education and locally produced teaching and learning resources, the aim of which is to enhance community support for formal schooling, improve outcomes for Gambian children, and celebrate rather than dislocate them from their cultural heritage.

Introduction

As discussed by Huggins (Chapter 2), the UK Coalition government has made a continuing commitment to the Global Schools Partnership Programme (DfID, 2012) and there is an expectation that every UK teacher will be able to deliver an education that is mindful of global issues and to link their schools with those in other global contexts; it is therefore imperative that students on teacher training programmes at UK universities are enabled to develop a well-informed global perspective as part of their degree studies. Plymouth University has for many years run study trips to The Gambia in West Africa as part of this endeavour, and these trips give our students the opportunity to consider ECEC provision and lower basic education (equivalent to UK primary schooling) in this context.

The challenge for UK students is to see the approach taken to ECEC in The Gambia not as deficient as judged by Western standards and notions of 'developmentally appropriate practice' (Penn, 2008) but as a product of a very particular historical, political, economic, social, and cultural context. A great deal of infrastructure and community development work is being funded by Western and Middle Eastern non-governmental organizations (NGOs) and bilateral aid in The Gambia, and when students see the well-resourced and familiar environments of nursery schools in The Gambia that are funded by organizations such as the British charity the Gambian Schools Trust (2012), their response to the resource-poor state schools they visit is often that they are inadequate in comparison, as I will illustrate. The challenge is to engage students in debates about post-colonial ways of seeing and knowing about the world and move away from seeing UK and other Western approaches to ECEC and education in general as necessarily superior and universal, and other perspectives and approaches as inferior.

This chapter seeks to illustrate the role ECEC has in addressing poverty in the Majority World, and to highlight the particular context in which Gambian ECEC and educational settings are functioning and the challenges they face. In considering the developments currently being rolled out by the Government of The Gambia, it is important to consider what constitutes quality ECEC provision and what form this should take to best meet the needs of marginalized children and communities (see Chapter 10 for further discussion of quality and context).

The importance of ECEC and education in alleviating poverty in the Majority World

In 2001, the Organization for African Unity (OAU) reiterated that investment in children and young people is crucial for the socio-economic transformation of the continent, and that this investment needed to be holistic in its approach, taking into account health, nutrition, water and sanitation, community empowerment, as well as the care and educational needs of African children (Aidoo, 2008) (see Chapter 9 on how a holistic approach is being adopted in South Africa). Education from birth to adulthood is seen as being key to reducing infant mortality and fertility rates, increasing life expectancy, improving democracy and political stability, and reducing inequalities and poverty; economic growth and improved life chances are reliant on a combination of factors, and education is certainly seen as central to any efforts (Appiah and McMahon, 2002; Desai and Potter, 2008).

Many African governments and NGOs have worked since independence to develop ECEC activities (often termed Early Child Development (ECD) in sub-Saharan Africa) and many countries, including The Gambia, are now working on specific national policies. It has been acknowledged that the lack of national ECEC policies in countries including Kenya, Rwanda, and Zambia constrains political and public support for and the requisite financing of adequate provision (Aidoo, 2008). The African Charter on the Rights and Welfare of the Child (ACRWC) also calls on nation-states to 'eliminate harmful social and cultural practices affecting the welfare, dignity, normal growth and development of the child' (OAU, 1999). These include practices such as child marriage and female genital mutilation – significant health, social, and gender issues affecting many children across Africa (see Chapter 3 for further discussion of children's rights in an African context).

A commitment to universal access and gender equity in educational opportunities was a key aspect of the Millennium Development Goals (MDG), agreed in 2000 (United Nations, 2012). The goals build on the internationally championed 'Education for All' agenda (UNESCO, 2012) that was enshrined in Gambian legislation in 1997, and efforts have been made to address gender disparities in school enrolment and attendance by offering girl children reduced cost or free education for the first few years of schooling in The Gambia and elsewhere in Africa, to good effect (DfID, 2011). However, despite improvements in many contexts, it remains very unlikely that the majority of poor countries in sub-Saharan Africa and elsewhere will meet the MDG targets by 2015, as was the aim, and the Education for All agenda continues to face many challenges (Lewin, 2007). Rural girls are most likely to be denied access to education, or may not stay on to completion – a pattern that is repeated across much of Africa (Shabaya and Konadu-Agyemang, 2004).

Taking a child rights or child welfare perspective as the starting point, with the aim of breaking the cycle of poor children becoming poor adults, provides a very useful approach to poverty alleviation for communities as a whole (Jaramillo and Mingat, 2008: 52); the financial resources and stakeholder commitment needed to achieve this social and economic transformation is of course a key issue, as the Gambian example illustrates. As in other parts of the continent, a disproportionally large child population and high proportion of children affected by HIV/AIDS in the Gambia, put a real strain on financial and human resources available to affected communities. The link between economic growth and human development is well documented – the latter being any efforts made to 'improve the choices of individuals so as to enable them to lead longer, healthier and fuller lives' (Suri et al., 2011: 506). In a Majority World context with very limited access to free or low-cost welfare services, what determines the choices available to people is often the financial resources available to individual families.

The Gambian context

The Gambia is a country of stark contrasts. Under British colonial rule, its location on the West Coast of Africa was strategic in terms of trade in an otherwise francophone region, but its limited economic worth meant it received little colonial investment before independence in 1965. At the time, the Gambian population stood at 300,000 and the economy was largely reliant on fishing and subsistence agriculture; by 2010 the population had risen to 1.7 million and while traditional economic pursuits remained significant, particularly in rural areas, the service industry had developed considerably based largely around tourism on the Atlantic coast (UNDP,

2011). The UN estimates that undernourishment runs at 30% and while the country has experienced economic growth over the past decade, levels of income poverty and inequality in The Gambia are very high, with close to 60% of the population living below the internationally recognized poverty line of US$1 per day (IMF, 2011; UNDP, 2011). There are structures in place that help to maintain and perpetuate income inequalities in the country; for example, civil servants are able to borrow money to buy property, in the form of a government employee mortgage, which therefore enables them to build capital assets that are beyond the reach of the majority of the population.

Formal education in lower basic school starts at age 7 in The Gambia, but enrolment and retention drops with age. The UN Human Development Index (HDI) estimates that a Gambian child under the age of 7 years will on average experience 9 years of schooling, compared with 5.9 years in 1980 (UNDP, 2011). This has certainly improved over time, as the average number of years of formal education received by Gambians over the age of 25 is just 2.8 years. In addition, the number of students enrolled in primary, secondary, and tertiary education, regardless of age, as a percentage of the population is 57%, up from 30% in 1995 (UNDP, 2011). Figures from 2008 do indicate that ECEC provision in The Gambia at 28% coverage does compare favourably with that in neighbouring Senegal, at 3% (Jaramillo and Mingat, 2008: 56); however, these figures mask some stark inequalities in The Gambia. The administrative centre of Banjul and the Atlantic Coast region enjoy far better infrastructure, ECEC and school provision than communities in the interior, and therefore rural communities in the eastern region of the country, of Basse and beyond, have far lower school enrolment and retention rates.

In addition, the official figures do not include the numbers of children that attend Madrassa. It is acknowledged that Madrassa provide an important function, not just for religious instruction, but also for literacy, numeracy, and life skills for many children, particularly in isolated communities. Many Gambians, as Muslims, value the Madrassa and are concerned that so-called 'European'-type schools may be seeking to teach Christianity to Gambian children. Madrassa existed in the Gambia long before the imposition of Western modes of schooling under British colonial rule, and still exist alongside the formal system; many children attend both. However, the statistics that are recognized by the UN and other international agencies are only concerned with formal schooling; this devalues the Madrassa's contribution to children's learning and development and the status they enjoy in communities.

Cost and attendance: the challenges facing teachers and ECEC practitioners

Schooling in The Gambia is certainly very cheap by Western standards. In 2012, this stood at an average of 35 Dalasi per term at lower basic level, the equivalent of approximately US$1, but this is in a country where GDP per capita is just over US$500 (IMF, 2012) and school teachers in the state system are paid on average 90 Dalasi (US$2.50) a month. Many schools manage with a combination of trainee and qualified teachers and the Gambian Government is increasing the availability of ECEC/ECD training. Nevertheless, the training and development opportunities available to teachers, and certainly the very poor remuneration, mean that the profession struggles to recruit and retain staff. The medium of instruction is English, a hangover from the colonial era, and many children come into school aged 7 with very little or no experience of ECEC and are expected to learn this new language and new concepts in tandem, which is of course very challenging for teacher and learner alike.

As well as gender and cost issues, undernourishment and other health and wellbeing concerns affect attendance and children's ability to achieve while in school. A de-worming programme for children in disadvantaged communities in Kenya demonstrated that addressing such problems can be instrumental in improving children's access to and experience of schooling; untreated parasitic worms can lead to serious illness and hamper cognitive development in young children (Innovations for Poverty Action, 2012). Again, a holistic community-based approach is needed to ensure that parents understand the value of engaging with efforts to reduce children's vulnerability to such infections, because of the negative implications for their learning and development.

Case Study: The challenge of providing 'Education for All'

Mandinari Lower Basic School, a state school catering for more than 900 pupils in a rural community on the River Gambia south of the capital Banjul, is an example of the challenges facing educators in The Gambia. Mandinari proudly states its mission to meet the personal and learning needs of all children in the community, by means of a statement painted on the wall as you enter the grounds. This reflects the notion of access to education as a fundamental right for all children, as proposed by the Education for All agenda.

The school occupies a large compound but the number of classrooms and teachers available means that the school day must be organized so that four grades attend in the morning, and two in the afternoon. Even so, there are upwards of 50 pupils per class, and the windowless classrooms are organized in rows of tables facing a blackboard, with children sharing chairs, books and pencils, and very little evidence of any additional resources.

The cost is 15 Dalasi, three times a year, but the headteacher finds that many families cannot afford these fees and also struggle to cover the cost of uniforms and schoolbooks for their children. The government only provides new textbooks every five years, so many children do not have access to adequate learning resources. She estimates that some 80% of the local children attend school, but less than half are able to pay the fees regularly. The community is predominantly Mandinka, with fewer Wolof and Fula and children from minority ethnic backgrounds. There are a very small number of Christian children in what is a largely Muslim community.

Teachers therefore often buy teaching resources themselves and rely on donations of cash or resources from contacts, often UK or other European visitors to the school. Mandinari has been able to install five water taps, a library, toilets, and a school garden thanks to external donations and the World Food Programme (WFP) provides a school lunch for each child. In an effort to ensure the sustainability of the lunch provision, a very small fee is charged, which is saved for such a time as the WFP support ends. Children are able to pay in kind if their family are not able to pay the fee, and we witnessed a young girl bringing a small bag of tomatoes from her family farm as payment for her week's lunches. The headteacher was clear that all children will eat regardless of their ability to pay, and recognizes the need for children to be adequately nourished so that they can achieve while in school.

The community is closely involved with the school and the Mothers Club is active in income-generation activities that enable the school to provide uniforms for children whose families cannot afford them. The school library is well stocked, but almost exclusively with UK textbooks, many of which are very outdated. The school has very little access to Gambian language resources, as there is limited availability and they are very expensive; most children do not speak, read or write any English before coming to school.

Mother tongue education

There is a strong argument that mother tongue education is not only a practical means of improving children's educational engagement and attainment, but also sends an important message about the value a government places on indigenous culture and capabilities. Ideally, education should celebrate rather than dislocate a child from their cultural heritage. Indeed, as a strong cultural identifier, the championing of minority and indigenous languages is an important aspect of wider efforts to champion the rights of minorities (Watson, 2007), particularly in The Gambia where the dominance of the colonial language prevails. Mother tongue educational endeavours elsewhere in Africa have been well received by communities who wish to see their identities and priorities reflected in the education system (Trudell, 2005). Indigenous experiences of and attitudes towards a Western formal model of schooling, and people's willingness and ability to engage with this, is a key issue; it is understandable that individuals and communities may reject any model that does not acknowledge or value local languages or, for example, local perspectives around childrearing, child wellbeing, and approaches to education.

Research with indigenous peoples around the world who are being subjected to the imposition of an alien educational model has indicated that working with rather than dismissing locally specific cultural skills and perspectives, and imbedding these within the new system, allows for the development of meaningful educational opportunities that enjoy the support of local communities (Barnhardt and Kawagley, 2005). However, there is also a perception that formal education needs to be conducted in a 'proper' – that is, European – language that enables children to access well-paid employment opportunities in the future (Trudell, 2007). European languages have the benefit of being in standardized form, whereas in many parts of the Majority World languages may be oral without a standardized written form, which makes the development of mother tongue resources challenging. Diversity in language reflects local cultural quirks and geographical dislocation, and the variety within Mandinka, for example, serves to illustrate the rich diversity and wide geographical spread of the people who speak the language (Juffermans, 2011). The Government of The Gambia now sees the need for both mother tongue and English language proficiency, with the second being reliant on a good grasp of the former, and this has required the need to produce standardized versions of the main indigenous languages so that teaching resources can be developed.

As elsewhere in the Majority World, children in The Gambia face the challenge of needing to grasp the written word in different scripts: those who attend Madrassa will learn to read the Koran in Arabic and to follow the text from right to left. In an English-medium school, suddenly there is an expectation that they can pick up the Roman script and understand that reading can also be from left to right! Innovative solutions are therefore imperative; there is evidence in Eritrea of educational practitioners adapting Western modes of teaching literacy to fit the local context, with the development of a phonics programme that uses symbols and sounds embedded in the cultural norms of the local Tigrinya language (Asfaha and Kroon, 2011).

The future for ECEC in The Gambia

In recent years, the Government of The Gambia has prioritized ECEC development, and the Ministry of Education is currently piloting a new approach up to 2013, financed by the Japan Social Development Fund through the World Bank. The aim is to increase ECEC provision, attached to lower basic schools, as it is currently concentrated in the private and to a lesser extent NGO sectors. The pilot is running in two regions, the urban West Coast Region 2 and the rural Upper River Region 6, in order to ascertain what is suitable in different contexts. The Ministry acknowledges that the early years curriculum that came out in 2008 was too complex for implementation in settings with significant staff training and resource needs, and has been looking to good practice in other English-speaking African countries, including Uganda and South Africa, to feed into the development of a context-appropriate programme.

Infrastructural support for the implementation of the programme comes in the form of an e-learning pilot, also supported by the World Bank, which is enabling 3000 teachers to access training opportunities through six regional centres located around the country. Clusters of schools are being furnished with the hardware and broadband access to enable teachers who cannot travel to the Teacher Training Institute in Brikama in the West Coast region to access these professional development opportunities, so that they can be skilled up to deliver this new ECEC programme and feel part of the new agenda. Broadband internet connectivity has been very significant for many poor and small states globally, who are increasingly able to participate in the global knowledge economy and develop such innovative approaches as this e-learning programme to reach isolated communities and practitioners (Crossley et al., 2009: 732).

The pilot involves introducing mother tongue instruction in settings such as nurseries, and up to and including Grade 4 in lower basic schools where, unless they have had gaps in their schooling, children are generally aged 10–11 years. The mother tongue agenda is supported by the development of resources in the main indigenous Gambian languages of Mandinka, Wolof, Fula, and Jola; the Ministry is working with Macmillan Publishers, who have a history of publishing a range of English language 'Africa Books for Schools' (Macmillan, 2012), to produce story books and other resources in these languages, challenging the dominance of English language resources. There is scope to develop resources that can also be used in neighbouring Senegal, which shares many of the same languages, which would possibly reduce the costs. This approach has been proposed by the World Bank as a useful response to budgetary concerns about the prohibitive costs of rolling out the programme (Vawda and Patrinos, 1999).

In addition, locally produced teaching materials such as wooden counting blocks are being used to support learning in the pilot areas. The ECEC provision (taken as 0–6 years in this context) is split into a 0–3 programme run by the National Nutrition Agency, which focuses on supporting parents' understanding of feeding and nutrition, immunizations, and other health- and wellbeing-related issues, and a 3–6 syllabus that aims to support young children in their transition to lower basic schooling. The aim is to develop a contextually appropriate standardized curriculum, and the Ministry is working to assess the impact of this provision by tracking the learning and development of the children in the pilot areas. Priority is being given to communities without formal schools or Madrassa, and the Ministry reports that communities and teachers have responded well to the mother tongue approach, which enables children to engage with and celebrate their own cultural heritage as part of their formal learning experience.

Priority is given to community participation in education, a theme that is certainly transferable to the UK context, as there is a recognition that children do well when their parents are engaged in their education, and also when the experience of schooling in terms of the curricula and the mode of delivery makes sense in the local context (Bray, 2003). There are significant financial challenges associated with rolling out the pilot nationally, but the Ministry is keen to improve access to ECEC provision, to ensure that this is of high quality and meaningful for children, and to regulate provision, ensuring that all ECEC settings are registered and available for inspection.

Euro-centric perceptions of Gambian ECEC provision and schooling

On a recent visit to The Gambia, it was interesting to engage in personal reflection and to capture UK early years students' perceptions of the teaching approach and use of resources in a Gambian lower basic school and a UK-funded nursery school. In both contexts, the teaching observed was generally by rote, and to the Western eye it appeared repetitive and overly formal, with little evidence of individualized or group work, or any on-going assessment. However, students were impressed by the children's obvious enthusiasm for learning, and saw some inspiring teaching in very challenging circumstances. They questioned how they would manage with no or minimal teaching resources to support their activities, and acknowledged that an effective teacher should be able to inspire without a reliance on resources.

At Mandinari, British-authored textbooks about the Gambia were available, but nothing was produced locally, and certainly nothing in any Gambian languages. It surprised the British students that children in both settings were familiar with British nursery rhymes and were singing the phonics songs that are used in UK schools to support literacy, complete with reference to unfamiliar concepts that they are unlikely to have little understanding of, such as 't . . . t . . . t for tennis'! There was a sense, therefore, that donations of English language resources for school libraries, along with UK educational toys and second-hand school uniforms, and the imposition of euro-centric approaches such as the use of phonics, are well-meaning but do nothing to enhance the children's sense of their own history or cultural heritage.

On visiting another nursery school supported by the British NGO The Gambian Schools Trust, students were shocked to see the poverty in the village in which the school was located, and questioned whether NGO intervention should take a whole-community approach, rather than providing one resource which highlighted the marked inequalities in the community. It was noted that there were young children in the village who were evidently not able to access the nursery. In keeping with existing research into study trips to The Gambia (see, for example, McGillivray, 2009), students were unsettled by the poverty they witnessed and struggled to reconcile this with a perception that many Gambian children appeared to be happy and enjoyed freedoms that British children do not, such as unsupervised play outside the home.

Exploring their environment and having time with children and teachers in the various settings enabled the British students to see beyond stereotypes and to view the children as individual personalities; there was appreciation that the role that high-quality and enjoyable ECEC and schooling has for improving the longer-term prospects for children in the Gambian context is very much influenced by wider socio-economic realities. Students reported that they felt the experience would put them in a stronger position to teach UK children about global issues from a critical and now better-informed standpoint.

Conclusions

Although high-quality ECEC and schooling is valuable *per se*, its long-term impact on Gambian children's life chances cannot be predicted without a good understanding of the complex political and socio-economic context. In a country with entrenched social inequalities such as The Gambia, an uneven distribution of knowledge and skills makes the need for wide coverage of quality, context-appropriate ECEC and school provision all the more crucial (Lewin, 2007). The mother tongue developments currently being piloted are encouraging, and there is potential to take approaches such as phonics and adapt them to the local context, as has been the case elsewhere (Asfaha and Kroon, 2011). The MDGs targets and EFA agenda that govern the Gambian approach are useful, but much needs to be done to address the socio-economic, geographic, and infrastructure challenges that remain. Certainly for UK trainee teachers embarking on efforts to engage UK children in understanding issues pertinent to the Majority World, making sense of the complexities requires much in the way of reflecting on their experience and continuing to take up opportunities to develop a well-informed critical perspective (see Chapter 2). For many of our students, the Gambian trip served only to raise more questions, and many are motivated to return in an effort to find answers.

Find Out More

- Consider the Mandinari Lower Basic School case study, and the Gambian context as a whole. What are the challenges associated with providing an innovative, stimulating, and enjoyable learning experience for young children in this context?
- Do you consider it to be a universal phenomenon that, for marginalized children, educational success requires a dislocation from one's cultural heritage and an engagement with dominant ways of being and knowing?
- How useful is it for UK student teachers to experience ECEC in a completely different context? What might it mean in terms of their practice in the UK?
- Do UK university study trips to the developing world constitute 'development tourism'? Who benefits and how from such activities, and what are the potential pitfalls?
- If you didn't have any resources to draw on, how would you teach?

References and recommended reading

Aidoo, A.A. (2008) Positioning ECD nationally: trends in selected African countries, in M. Garcia, A. Pence and J. Evans (eds.) *Africa's Future, Africa's Challenge: Early Childhood Care and Development in Sub-Saharan Africa*. Washington, DC: The World Bank.

Appiah, E.N. and McMahon, W.W. (2002) The social outcomes of education and feedbacks on economic growth in Africa, *Journal of Development Studies*, 38(4): 27–68.

Asfaha, Y.M. and Kroon, S. (2011) Multilingual education policy in practice: classroom literacy instruction in different scripts in Eritrea, *Compare: A Journal of Comparative and International Education*, 41(2): 229–46.

Barnhardt, R. and Kawagley, A.O. (2005) Indigenous knowledge systems and Alaska native ways of knowing, *Anthropology and Education Quarterly*, 36(1): 8–23.

Bray, M. (2003) Community initiatives in education: goals, dimensions and linkages with governments, *Compare: A Journal of Comparative and International Education*, 33(1): 31–45.

Crossley, M., Bray, M. and Packer, S. (2009) Education in the small states of the Commonwealth: towards and beyond global goals and targets, *The Round Table: The Commonwealth Journal of International Affairs*, 98(405): 731–51.

Department for International Development (DfID) (2011) *Education for All in The Gambia*. Available at: http://www.dfid.gov.uk/stories/case-studies/2011/mdg-3-education-for-all-in-the-gambia/ (accessed 4 June 2012).

Department for International Development (DfID) (2012) *Global Schools Partnership*. Available at: http://www.dfid.gov.uk/Get-Involved/In-your-school/global-school-partnerships/ (accessed 11 June 2012).

Desai, V. and Potter, R.B. (2008) *The Companion to Development Studies* (2nd edn.). London: Hodder Education.

Gambian Schools Trust (2012) *The Gambian Schools Trust*. Available at: http://www.gambianschools.org/Gambian_Schools_Trust/welcome.html (accessed 4 June 2012).

Garcia, M., Pence, A. and Evans, J. (eds.) (2008) *Africa's Future, Africa's Challenge: Early Childhood Care and Development in Sub-Saharan Africa*. Washington, DC: The World Bank.

Innovations for Poverty Action (IPA) (2012) *Primary School De-worming in Kenya*. Available at: http://poverty-action.org/project/0067 (accessed 4 June 2012).

International Monetary Fund (IMF) (2011) *The Gambia: Poverty Reduction Strategy Paper—Progress Report*. Washington, DC: IMF.

International Monetary Fund (IMF) (2012) *World Economic Outlook Database*. Available at: http://www.imf.org/external/ns/cs.aspx?id=28 (accessed 4 June 2012).

Jaramillo, A. and Mingat, A. (2008) Early childhood care and education in Sub-Saharan Africa: what would it take to meet the Millennium Development Goals?, in M. Garcia, A. Pence and J. Evans (eds.) *Africa's Future, Africa's Challenge: Early Childhood Care and Development in Sub-Saharan Africa*. Washington, DC: The World Bank.

Juffermans, K. (2011) 'Do you want me to translate this in English or in a better Mandinka language?' Unequal literacy regimes and grassroots spelling practices in peri-urban Gambia, *International Journal of Educational Development*, 31: 643–53.

Lewin, K. (2007) Diversity in convergence: access to education for all, *Compare: A Journal of Comparative and International Education*, 37(5): 577–99.

Macmillan Publishers (2012) *Africa Books for Schools*. Available at: http://www.macmillaneducation.com/Default.aspx (accessed 4 June 2012).

McGillivray, G. (2009) Constructs of childhood: enduring or open to change? Early years students' reflections on first hand experiences of childhood and early years education in a different country and culture, *European Early Childhood Education Research Journal*, 17(3): 271–82.

Organization of African Unity (OAU) (1999) *African Charter on the Welfare and Rights of Children*. Available at: http://www.au.int/en/content/african-charter-rights-and-welfare-child (accessed 4 June 2012).

Penn, H. (2008) *Understanding Early Childhood: Issues and Controversies*. Maidenhead: Open University Press.

Shabaya, J. and Konadu-Agyemang, K. (2004) Unequal access, unequal participation: some spatial and socio-economic dimensions of the gender gap in education in Africa with special reference to Ghana, Zimbabwe and Kenya, *Compare: A Journal of Comparative and International Education*, 34(4): 395–424.

Suri, T., Boozer, M., Ranis, G. and Stewart, F. (2011) Paths to success: the relationship between human development and economic growth, *World Development*, 39(4): 506–22.

Trudell, B. (2005) Language choice, education and community identity, *International Journal of Educational Development*, 25: 237–51.

Trudell, B. (2007) Local community perspectives and language of education in sub-Saharan African communities, *International Journal of Educational Development*, 27: 552–63.

United Nations (UN) (2012) *The Millennium Development Goals*. Available at: http://www.un.org/millenniumgoals/index.shtml (accessed 4 June 2012).

United Nations Development Programme (UNDP) (2011) *Human Development Report 2011*. Available at: http://hdr.undp.org/en/statistics/hdi/ (accessed 4 June 2012).

United Nations Educational, Scientific and Cultural Organisation (UNESCO) (2012) *Education for All*. Available at: http://www.unesco.org/new/en/education/themes/leading-the-international-agenda/education-for-all/ (accessed 4 June 2012).

Vawda, A.Y. and Patrinos, H.A. (1999) Producing educational materials in local languages: costs from Guatemala and Senegal, *International Journal of Educational Development*, 19: 287–99.

Watson, K. (2007) Language, education and ethnicity: whose rights prevail in an age of globalisation?, *International Journal of Educational Development*, 27: 252–65.

7

ESTONIA: SOCIO-HISTORIC AND POLITICAL INFLUENCES ON THE EARLY CHILDHOOD EDUCATION AND CARE SYSTEM

Kerstin Kööp

Summary

This chapter gives an overview of the development of Estonian early childhood education within the general educational and cultural context of Europe. The roots of the kindergarten system in Estonia lead back over 170 years. This can be a short period historically speaking, but during that time many different foreign powers and governments have ruled Estonia and its educational system, with the main influence coming from Germany and Russia. However, Estonians didn't embrace all new rules and regulations completely, such as those of the Soviet Union, as commonly thought. Estonian teachers developed their own programmes and kept their nationalism even during the many years of occupation.

Case Study: A day in the life of a child in an Estonian kindergarten

Kindergartens in Estonia are usually open from seven in the morning until seven at night, but with variation among areas. In the countryside, kindergartens may be open longer so that parents who work in the city can collect their children after work. Not all of the groups or classes in any one kindergarten are open for the whole period; some run from 7.30 am to 6 pm or from 8 am to 6 pm, depending on the teachers' workload and management role in the kindergarten. Children who need to start early or finish late join together in one group. Between 8.30 am and 9.30 am, it is time for breakfast. All food is provided by the kindergarten, which parents pay for. Educational activities including music lessons and physical education take place from about 9 am to 11 am. From 11 am to 12.30 pm, children usually play outside and lunch is served from 12.30 pm to 1 pm. Between 1 pm and 3 pm, it is time for the silent hour, during which the younger children sleep and the older children take part in quiet activities. But as the kindergarten day is so long, almost all children fall asleep even if they do not want to. Children wake at around 3 pm, beds are made, and between 3.15 pm and 3.45 pm a small meal is served. After that, educational activities and free play continue until the children's parents collect them, usually between 5 pm and 7 pm.

The history of Estonian early childhood education

The first early childhood institution in Estonia was a so-called infants' day-care centre founded in 1840 in Tallinn, the capital of Estonia. Established as a private institution by Baroness Elisabeth von Uexküll, it catered for boys and girls aged 2–7 years from poor families. The first institution in Estonia to be called 'a kindergarten' was founded in 1862. Early kindergarten founders and also kindergarten teacher trainers were German private individuals or German societies. The kindergartens' main task was to look after children. The main activities included handicraft, religious education, and learning to read. Initially, children's play was considered a waste of time, but gradually the importance of play was understood and play activities were introduced. Teaching in kindergartens was carried out partly in German, but also in Russian and Estonian (Torm, 2000: 56; Torm, 2011: 83). At the end of the nineteenth century, childcare institutions were established mainly for workers' children. The educational work of kindergartens mainly followed Christian foundations and aims. Landlords were also interested in using mothers as workers, so 'playschools' were organized near bigger manors. 'Playschool' was operational throughout the whole year, open from 8 am to 7 pm and children up to 10 years of age were accepted. The main focus was on handicraft: crocheting, knitting, and sewing (Järvekülg, 1940: 231–2). The first Estonian language kindergarten was opened in Tartu in 1905, established by the Tartu Estonian Kindergarten Society. It was considered necessary to teach children in their mother tongue and in the national spirit (Torm, 2000: 56; Jürimäe and Treier, 2008: 149).

According to Järvekülg (1940), the growth and development of kindergartens suffered a setback during the First World War. After Estonian independence in 1918, group care for preschool age children emerged. Local municipalities started to run kindergartens and also provided support to organizations and private individuals to do so (Järvekülg, 1940: 234). C.H. Niggol (1851–1927) was a pioneer of early childhood education in Estonia. His 1921 book *Kasvatus enne kooli* (*Preschool Education*) provided an overview of preschool children's intellectual development, game theories, toys and their use, and game organizing methodology (Niggol, 1921). The book became a practical handbook for the first professional kindergarten teachers in Estonia. Niggol was a proponent of Fröbel's educational ideas and so Fröbel's pedagogic principles formed a part of Estonian kindergarten working practice (Torm, 1998). At the beginning of the twentieth century, discussions about the 'new child and new pedagogy' emerged, with Maria Montessori among the innovators, whose ideas were revolutionary in the light of pedagogical ideas of the time (Hirsjärvi and Huttunen, 1998: 32). Thanks to Niggol and Montessori, ideas on early years pedagogy reached Estonia in the first decades of the twentieth century. For example, in the 1926–1927 academic year, the Tallinn city government provided five of Tallinn's kindergartens with Montessori means of instruction, illustrating how the principles of Montessori's pedagogy influenced educational practice in Estonian kindergartens. Three different kinds of activities stand out in the kindergartens' work plans: play, singing, and work. Pedagogical activities took a new direction based on nationalistic ideals and, in choosing educational methods and working practices, a more Estonia-centred approach was adopted. It was considered important that the educational methods used in kindergartens would develop in accordance with the needs of real life and would be based on the Estonian mentality and conditions (Torm, 1998).

By 1923, there were 34 kindergartens in Estonia, catering to a total of 1600 children aged 3–7 years. All kindergartens, whether municipally or privately owned, were located in towns or townships. Kindergartens of the time lacked a general framework and there was no state regulation of early childhood education (Ugaste and Õun, 2007: 3; Jürimäe and Treier, 2008: 149–50). According to Jürimäe and Treier (2008), Estonia lagged behind many other countries that had by that time passed laws regulating childcare institutions (Jürimäe and Treier, 2008: 153) and kindergarten managers still compiled their own annual and daily plans (Haas, 1940: 227). Initially, the Ministry of Education of the Republic of Estonia did not involve itself in the running of kindergartens; this was the jurisdiction of the School Councillor. During the last years of the Republic of Estonia, when there were 78 kindergartens, their social importance was understood and work began to draft a law for kindergartens (Elango, 1940: 210). This process was cut short by the occupation of Estonia by Soviet Russia in 1940.

The pre-war Republic of Estonia (1918–1940) was a highly developed country in the fields of education and science, in that it had taken the opportunity to design its own educational politics and to communicate freely with other countries. During that period, the need for kindergartens was high, but owing to a lack of funding, such as in Tallinn, the number of kindergartens did not meet that need. Solutions to the problem were sought with private institutions, but costs were prohibitive; it was for economic reasons that parents did not enrol their children in private kindergartens (Andreas, 2003: 11–16).

First Soviet occupation, 1940–1941

On 6 August 1940, the Republic of Estonia was annexed to the Soviet Union. After occupation by the Soviet Army, educational activities were subject to the principles of Soviet pedagogy. Early childhood education formed the basis of the system of national education in the former Soviet Union. Its aim and task was communist education of children and their preparation for successful studies at school (Fljorina, 1949). According to Jürimäe and Treier (2008), increasing the number of kindergartens was made a national priority in 1940, mainly as a means to increase women's employment (Jürimäe and Treier, 2008: 153). However, because of the changed political situation, private persons, churches, and organizations were no longer allowed to open kindergartens. From August 1940, a committee for compiling lists of forbidden publications began working alongside the Department of Education. In the same year, it was decreed that all print matter had to be scrutinized by the Head Office of Literary and Publishing Matters. Textbooks and children's literature formed a large part of the forbidden publications and faced destruction. To replace them, new educational materials that suited the new ideology were introduced. The Soviets also began to re-educate teachers, since their worldview, which was considered inappropriate, did not fit the Soviet ideology. Throughout the whole country, compulsory teachers' days, training courses, and congresses were organized. Foundations were laid for publishing Soviet pedagogical materials. By the beginning of 1941, the Soviets had destroyed all the structures of the Republic of Estonia. This also had its effects on the activities of kindergartens. The German occupation later in 1941 brought all Soviet structures to a halt, including the work of educational institutions in the territory of Estonia (Andreas, 2003: 18–19).

German occupation, 1941–1944

On 15 September 1941, Estonia's Local Government (*die Estnische Verwaltung*) was established. It was to be a local governing body overseeing management boards. The work of the Local Government was managed and controlled by the local General Commissariat. Educational, cultural, and recruitment matters, as well as those of propaganda and the courts, fell under the jurisdiction of the Director of Education and Courts (Keskasutused (Centralized Establishments) 1987: 10, cited in Andreas, 2003: 42). It became compulsory to maintain kindergartens and playgrounds in all cities and industrial areas, where at least fifteen 3- to 7-year-old children lived and whose parents wished to enrol them in the kindergarten at the beginning of the school year. Children's studies and other activities were to be established in accordance with the systems created by Fröbel and Montessori. From the age of 6, children were required to receive elementary primer studies in reading, writing, and arithmetic (Määrus lasteaedade korraldamise kohta [Decree for Organizing Kindergartens], 1942: 31, cited in Andreas, 2003: 42). The aim of kindergartens and playgrounds was to take care of the children's health, physical and mental development, in the children's native tongue and free of charge, and to prepare them for primary school. In accordance with the new decree, it was compulsory for a child above the age of 6 to attend a kindergarten. Rural and City School Governments had the right to exempt such families from this obligation if the children were guaranteed home schooling or some other upbringing and educational activities equivalent to the level intended for kindergartens or preschools. Private persons and groups of parents were allowed to establish and run kindergartens and playgrounds, but they had to apply for a permit from the local City or Rural School Government (Andreas, 2003: 43).

As during the first Soviet occupation, the new powers started removing ideologically unsuitable literature from shops, libraries, and warehouses, including school textbooks. However, during the German occupation, the lists of forbidden publications were not directed against the Estonian national culture, but against Soviet occupation (Andreas, 2003: 46).

Second Soviet occupation, 1944–1991

From the late autumn of 1944, Estonia again came under Red Army control and the country became part of the Union of Soviet Socialist Republics. Soviet authority and corresponding authorities were re-established. Once again, the Soviets began to control curriculum and pedagogy in Estonia, with education coming under Soviet propaganda. Unlike many other Soviet Republics, the school system preserved an Estonian language education at all levels and ideas of progressive and democratic education survived (Andreas, 2003: 55–6; Ruus et al., 2008: 15). The main task for teachers was to raise dignified citizens fit for socialist society and teachers themselves were expected to embrace communist beliefs in full. However, the traditions of the former republic silently continued. Kindergarten teachers with an education from the Republic of Estonia were still following and developing Fröbel's educational ideas and this influenced the pedagogical development of preschool education, even under the ideological pressure of Soviet power (Jürimäe and Treier, 2008: 153).

The aim of the communist education was to raise children for communist society, children who combined spiritual wealth, moral purity, and physical perfection. Special attention was paid to raising children's communist morale, which in turn involved two important components: collective education and labour education. Moral education was at the centre of the curriculum at all stages of education during the Soviet period (Tudge, 1991: 128). Common features of all educational levels characterizing the Soviet period were as follows (Tudge, 1991: 125):

- With few exceptions, all students at the same level of education throughout the Soviet Union used the same materials and methods of teaching.
- There were no private educational establishments or schools.
- The staff of an educational institution lacked the right to develop or change curricula.

It should be emphasized that because foreign researchers are hindered in their study of the original materials due to language barriers and a lack of knowledge of local peculiarities, generalizations about the Soviet educational system are difficult to make. Although all teachers were ostensibly working to the curricula and guidance of the Soviet system in Estonia, Kinos and Pukk (2010) note just how important the teachers' own cultural beliefs and inner motivation were in maintaining the Estonian culture in their approaches to early years education (Kinos and Pukk, 2010: 13).

In accordance with the post-war statute for kindergartens of the Estonian Soviet Socialist Republic (ESSR), the kindergarten became a national institution with the goal of giving a Soviet social education to children aged 3–7 years and to ensure their overall versatile development. As an organization, kindergartens also allowed mothers/women to take part in economic, national, cultural, and social-political life (Andreas, 2003: 62). From 1950, preschool education was regulated at the state level through legislation and curriculum planning (Jürimäe and Treier, 2008: 153).

All kindergartens, regardless of which organization or institution they functioned under, had to work in accordance with the Kindergartens' Statute and the

ESSR Ministry of Education's programme-methodical instructions. This statute established that kindergartens were to be responsible for children's health, intellectual and physical development, as well as developing habits of work and organization. Naturally the statutes included an emphasis on the kindergarten's obligation to teach children, in accordance with age-specific cohorts, to love their social-ist homeland, its leaders, the Soviet Army, heroes, Stakhanovites of factories and socialist farms (Guide for kindergarten educator: kindergarten statute [*Juhend lasteaia kasvatajale: lasteaia põhikiri*], 1950: 5–15). Whereas before the Second World War there was a blurred distinction between kindergartens and crèches, the two were considered separate under the Soviet regime, although crèches for children aged 1–3 years could belong to a kindergarten. During the academic year of 1958–1959, a new type of institution – the day care centre – joined kindergar-tens and crèches. During the Soviet era, kindergartens became an essential part of society because they maximized the employment of women. From the end of the 1960s, especially in rural areas, round-the-clock and all-week groups for chil-dren of all ages were also established as preschool institutions (Jürimäe and Treier, 2008: 153–4).

Kindergartens were mostly opened in larger towns, on collective farms and industrial centres with the transport of children from rural areas organized by the local economic unit/municipality. The positive aspects were that they enjoyed quite good spatial and material conditions, but the drawbacks were that there were too many children in the groups (25–30) and the activities in the kindergarten were organized according to a unified programme, which did not consider children's individual characteristics. During the Soviet period, mothers had the right to paid maternity leave until the child was 2 months old and unpaid leave until the child was a year old, during which time the mother's job remained open to her. Some mothers, however, returned to work earlier, either hiring a babysitter or, more often, taking the child to a nursery, as there was a well-functioning state childcare system (Ugaste and Õun, 2007: 6–8; Õun, 2011: 18).

Ferdinand Eisen (1914–2000) became Minister of Education in 1960. He emphasized that education in Estonia should be conducted according to a local Estonian programme and a group of Estonian authors was gathered. A locally compiled programme called *About Preschool Education in a Child Care Establish-ment: Programme and Instructions* (*Koolieelsest kasvatusest lasteasutuses. Programm ja juhend*) was published by Estonian educationalists in 1968. It became a source doc-ument for teachers' routine work and included fields, themes, and learning content based on the ages of the children. For each age group, exemplary learning materials and a methodical guide were provided in the programme. It emphasized getting to know each child and taking account of their individuality. This programme intro-duced learning to read and write from the age of 6 years to kindergartens (Jürimäe and Treier, 2008: 157). The compulsory programme was implemented at once in all Estonian language kindergartens and those Russian language kindergartens that had Estonian groups (Selg, 1968) and was amended and supplemented in 1972 and 1979. In 1987, a new programme called *About Preschool Education in a Child Care Establishment* [*Koolieelsest kasvatusest lasteasutuses. Programm*] was completed; however, this programme was not implemented in full.

By the 1980s, there was a well-functioning network of early childhood institutions in Estonia. By the end of the Soviet period in 1989, there were 747 preschool establishments with 83,693 children (Jürimäe and Treier, 2008: 160).

The Republic of Estonia

After regaining independence in 1991, the Republic of Estonia initiated reform of the education system to once more value democratic principles. Changes were implemented in the content of learning (proceeding from the concept of lifelong learning), the system of educational institutions (the restructuring of the school network, new types of educational institutions), and educational provision (from centralized management and financing to decentralized provision). Regarding the organization of educational activities, the overriding principle was based on individual child development, a move away from the Soviet period approach in which studies were directed and controlled by the teacher. Basically, there was a transition from an adult-orientated system to a child-oriented one, taking account of the needs and interests of the children. The value of children of the same age to be together was recognized and, in addition to the social needs of the child, attention was paid to individual needs. Instead of subjects, free play was emphasized.

The network of early childhood institutions that had opened during the Soviet time was almost unchanged. The administration and financing of the institutions, however, was now under the jurisdiction of the local municipalities (Sarv, 1999; Ugaste and Õun, 2007: 7; Kinos and Pukk, 2010: 15). In connection with the educational reforms in the 1990s, people in Estonia were open to educational innovations. Educational scientists and practitioners were interested in alternative pedagogical trends, such as those of Waldorf, Freinet, Reggio Emilia, Montessori, and the 'Step-by-Step' approach (Ugaste and Õun, 2007: 8; Jürimäe and Treier, 2008: 160).

After the regaining of independence, Soviet laws and programmes were no longer valid. Creating new ones took time and as a result kindergartens had to fend for themselves. Previous programmes, lessons from other countries, and new initiatives were adopted. In 1993, the activities of preschool institutions were regulated by the Law on Preschool Child Institutions (*Koolieelse lasteasutuse seadus*). This was just the second law to be passed after regaining independence. The Law on Preschool Child Institutions was adopted in 1999 and remains valid today. The basis for learning and upbringing was the Framework Curriculum of Preschool Education [*Alushariduse raamõppekava*] (1999). As it became clear from implementation surveys that the objectives, content, and approaches required change, the old programme was updated and in 2008 the new National Curriculum for Pre-School Child Care Institutions [*Koolieelse lasteasutuse riiklik õppekava*] became effective. The document's structure was generally similar to the skeleton syllabus, but the objectives, approach, educational and raising principles and information on child development were changed. Over time, Estonia's main objective had been to favour children's development and maintain and improve children's health. Since 1999, the main difference has been that it is possible for the personnel of children's educational establishments to draw up their own curricula to reflect each individual educational establishment. Nowadays, the educational and raising activities aren't merely oriented to academic knowledge and preparation for schools, but to every-day life in general (Õun, 2011: 18).

One of the main methodologies now in use in kindergartens across Estonia – 'Step-by-Step'

The educational programme 'Step-by-Step' was introduced in Estonia in 1994. The programme increased its number of participants and its scope to the extent that, in January 2007, about 250 kindergarten groups in Estonia applied the Step-by-Step methodology in full (Ugaste et al., 2008: 159). Step-by-Step was created as a response to the marked changes in post-Soviet society in an attempt to prepare children to cope with a new democratic way of life. The goals of the programme were to increase the role of families in bringing up children, and to support individualized teaching in kindergartens, which would help the children to make their own choices and democratic decisions (Õun, 2011: 19). Changes in society (for example, unemployment of parents, privatization, economic inequality, changes in the ownership of educational establishments) created the need for changes in education. With these new circumstances came the realization that it was important to support children and families by offering a model of integrated care that linked educational, medical, and social services (Ugaste et al., 2008: 158).

The Step-by-Step programme is based on integrated methods for children from birth to age 10 years. The theoretical basis of the programme comes from Vygotsky's and Piaget's approaches to child development, which emphasized the need to consider a child's individual development. The basics of the programme also include the principles of democratic education (Hansen et al., 1997: 14).

Implementation of the Step-by-Step programme in Estonian kindergartens exercised a substantial influence on the teaching and educational activity of the childcare institutions, where more attention was paid to children's individuality, group work, child-centred design of the learning space, enabling of opportunities, and application of democratic teaching methods (Ugaste and Õun, 2007: 9). Having worked for eight years in a kindergarten using the Step-by-Step methodology, I can say that it has supported the consideration of the child's individuality and increased the teacher's cooperation with parents. It is gratifying to see that many of the Step-by-Step principles have also been implemented in the 2008 National Curriculum for Pre-School Child Care Institutions.

The current educational system in Estonia

Preschool childcare institutions now include crèches (up to age 3 years) and nursery schools (3–7 years), which are maintained either publicly or privately. Preschool education is followed by 9 years of basic schooling, divided into three stages: first stage (7 to 9–10 years), second stage (10 to 12–13 years), and third stage (13 to 15–16 years). The first two stages are often referred to as primary school. Schooling is free for all who study in state-financed or municipal schools. There are also private schools and private vocational schools, which are fee-paying, and special schools and classes for children with special educational needs (Kikas and Lerkkanen, 2011: 34–5). The Estonian educational system is described in Eurydice (undated).

Kindergartens are divided into municipal and private childcare institutions. Parents are responsible for a child's preschool education, and are supported by local government in maintaining the preschool institutions. Because preschool education establishments receive funding from different sources, the cost to parents varies. Usually, the number of children in crèches can be up to 14 children and in kindergarten groups up to 20 children, though in some cases these numbers can reach 16 and 24–26 respectively, depending on the local government and opportunities in the kindergarten. Classrooms are usually supervised by two teachers, working in shifts, and one assistant teacher, so that one teacher and assistant teacher are present in the classroom (the child-to-adult ratio is about 20–24 to 2) (Kikas and Lerkkanen, 2011: 35). Assistant teachers are usually responsible for serving meals and cleaning, but a teacher may use the assistant's help also in teaching activities. In Estonia, kindergarten teachers are university graduates in early years education. It is also possible to work while studying. There are no qualification requirements for assistant teachers, but they usually receive special training from the preshool or local government. According to the Ministry of Education and Sciences (undated), there were 643 child care institutions with 66,207 children in Estonia in 2011.

Problems and bottlenecks in Estonia's early childhood education

In Estonia, preparation for school and the promotion of children's learning abilities is a part of preschool education before entering formal schooling. The availability of preschool education for all children has not yet been regulated at the state level. From the 1990s, the birth rate decreased and mothers could remain home with their children until the child was 3 years old (with a maternal salary for 18 months), so many kindergartens closed. Now, there are insufficient kindergarten places, especially for children between the ages of 18 months and 3 years.

In addition to kindergartens, there are also private preschool groups in Estonia providing preschool education for children. Very often, a so-called double system exists where a child who receives preschool education at the kindergarten also joins a preschool group at school (Kööp, 2011: 415). Preschool groups follow the same National Curriculum for Pre-School Child Care Institutions (2008) as kindergartens and should be available for children who do not attend kindergarten. But in reality about 50% of children in Tallinn, for example, participate in preschool groups *in addition* to kindergarten (Kööp, 2011: 421). It is said that a smooth transition from kindergarten to school is emphasized in Estonia, but in reality training for school entry exams is taking place. The reason for this is that the most popular schools in Tallinn and Tartu, the two largest cities in the country, have school admission trials and many parents want to prepare their children as well as possible to achieve high grades (Kööp, 2006: 9–10). More and more parents are emphasizing the intellectual part of school readiness – the skills of reading, writing, and calculating, with the physical and social aspects remaining in the background. Parents of school-age children notice the lack of emphasis on social development once they can see how their child is coping in school (Kööp, 2011: 420).

Other current issues in early years education relate to a lack of appreciation of the work done by kindergarten teachers and other kindergarten personnel. Regionally, there are wide variations in salaries, the number of children in one group, and working conditions.

Conclusions

There has been extensive change to Estonia's educational landscape to which the local population, including teachers, have had to become accustomed. Our pedagogical thoughts and methods have been influenced by the traditions of different cultures and educationalists from different countries. We have picked the best from the options available to us and are striving towards perfection. Issues remain, but that is where we need to extend our learning.

Find Out More

- Compare Estonia's and Britain's historical background and the development of preschool education based on their different histories.
- Consider the approaches to and meaning of school preparedness in different countries.
- Consider the pros and cons of a Soviet kindergarten's daily routine compared with a contemporary European kindergarten.

References and recommended reading

About Preschool Education in a Child Care Establishment: Programme and Instructions [Koolieelsest kasvatusest lasteasutuses. Programm ja juhend] (1968) (1974, 1979). Eesti NSV Haridusministeerium. Tallinn: Valgus.

About Preschool Education in a Child Care Establishment [Koolieelsest kasvatusest lasteasutuses. Programm] (1987) Tallinn: Eesti NSV Haridusministeerium.

Andreas, T. (2003) Lasteaedade võrgu areng Tallinnas aastail 1940–1950 [The development of kindergarten network in Tallinn during 1940–1950]. Bachelor's thesis. Tallinn: Tallinn Pedagogical University.

Coughlin, P.A. and Walsh, K.B. (1996) *Ühelt astmelt teisele. Hea Alguse algklasside programm lastele ja nende vanematele [From one Step to Another: Step-by-Step Programme for Elementary School Children and Their Families]*. Tallinn: Avatud Eesti Fond.

Crèches and Kindergartens in Collective Farms and State Farms [Lastesõimed ja lasteaiad kolhoosides ja sovhoosides] (1950) Tallinn: Eesti Riiklik Kirjastus.

Elango, A. (1940) 10 aastat lasteaia arengut [10 years of kindergarten development], *Eesti Kool*, 4: 204–11.

Eurydice (undated) *Eurybase, the Database of Education Systems in Europe*. Estonia. Available at: https://webgate.ec.europa.eu/fpfis/mwikis/eurydice/index.php/Estonia:Overview (accessed 5 February 2012).

Fljorina, J.A. (1949) *Eelkoolipedagoogika [Early Childhood Education]*. Tallinn: Pedagoogiline Kirjastus.

Framework Curriculum of Preschool Education [Alushariduse raamõppekava]. (1999) RTI, 28.10.1999, 80, 737. Available at: https://www.riigiteataja.ee/akt/77809 (accessed 11 January 2012).

Haas, M. (1940) Tänapäeva lasteaed kasvatustegurina [Today's kindergarten as a growing factor], *Eesti kool*, 4: 225–9.

Hansen, K., Kaufmann, A. and Walsh, R.K. (1997) *'Hea Alguse' lasteaedade programm. [Step-by-Step Kindergarten Programme]*. Tallinn: Avatud Ühikonna Instituut.

Hirsjärvi, J. and Huttunen, H. (1998) *Sissejuhatus kasvatusteadusesse [Introduction to Educational Science]*. Tallinn: Arendusabi, Tallinn Pedagogical University.

Järvekülg, E. (1940) Lasteaiad ja lastepäevakodud Eestis. Nende areng ja praegune seisukord. [Kindergartens and day care establishments in Estonia: their development and status today], *Eesti Kool*, 4: 229–35.

Jürimäe, M. and Treier, J. (2008) *Õppekavad ja lasteaed [Curriculums and Kindergarten]*. Tartu: Tartu Ülikooli kirjastus.

Kikas, E. and Lerkkanen, M.-K. (2011) Education in Estonia and Finland, in M. Veisson, E. Hujala, P.K. Smith, M. Waniganayake and E. Kikas (eds.) *Global Perspectives in Early Childhood Education: Diversity, Challenges and Possibilities*. Frankfurt am Main: Peter Lang Verlag.

Kinos, J. and Pukk, M. (2010) *Lapsest lähtuv kasvatus [Child-based Education]*. Tea ja toimeta. Tallinn: Tea kirjastus.

Kööp, K. (2006) Lapse üleminek lasteaiast kooli – lapsevanema nägemus [Child's transition from kindergarten to school – parental view]. Master's thesis. Tallinn: Tallinn University.

Kööp, K. (2011) Children's transition from kindergarten to school in Estonia—the parental viewpoint, in M. Veisson, E. Hujala, P.K. Smith, M. Waniganayake and E. Kikas (eds.) *Global Perspectives in Early Childhood Education: Diversity, Challenges and Possibilities*. Frankfurt am Main: Peter Lang Verlag.

Law of Pre-School Child Institutions [Koolieelse lasteasutuse seadus] (1999) *Riigi Teataja, I*, 27, 387. Available at: https://www.riigiteataja.ee/akt/754369 (accessed 12 January 2012).

National Curriculum for Pre-School Child Care Institutions [Koolieelse lasteasutuse riiklik õppekava] (2008) *Riigi Teataja, I*, 23, 152. Available at: https://www.riigiteataja.ee/akt/12970917 (accessed 1 February 2012).

Niggol, C.H. (1921) *Kasvatus enne kooli [Preschool Education]*. Tallinn: Tallinna Eesti Kirjastus-Ühisus.

Õun, T. (2011) Koolieelse lasteasutuse kvaliteet lapsekeskse kasvatuse aspektist [The quality of preschool from the aspect of child-centred education]. Dissertation on Social Sciences. Tallinn: Tallinn University.

Ruus, V.-R., Henno, I., Eisenschmidt, E., Loogma, K., Noorväli, H., Reiska, P. and Rekkor, S. (2008) Reforms, developments and trends in Estonian education during recent decades, in J. Mikk, M. Veisson and P. Luik (eds.) *Reforms and Innovations in Estonian Education*. Frankfurt am Main: Peter Lang Verlag.

Sarv, E.S. (1999) Analysis in the Estonian context, in H. Niemi (ed.) *Moving Horizons in Education: International Transformations and Challenges of Democracy*. Helsinki: University of Helsinki.

Selg, R. (1968) Uus kasvatustöö programm [New upbringing programme]. *Nõukogude õpetaja*, 39 (28 September).

Torm, M. (1998) Lasteaednike koolitus kuni 1949 a. ja selle mõju koolieelse kasvatuse arengule Eestis [The training of kindergarten teachers until 1949 and its influence on development of preschool education in Estonia]. Master's thesis. Tallinn: Tallinn Pedagogical University.

Torm, M. (2000) Mõnda Tallinna lasteaedade ajaloost [Some things about the history of kindergartens in Tallinn], *Haridus*, 1: 56–9.

Torm, M. (2011) 170 years of development in Estonian preschool institutions: historical trends in preschool education, in M. Veisson, E. Hujala, P.K. Smith, M. Waniganayake and E. Kikas (eds.) *Global Perspectives in Early Childhood Education: Diversity, Challenges and Possibilities*. Frankfurt am Main: Peter Lang Verlag.

Tudge, J. (1991) Education of young children in the Soviet Union: current practice in historical perspective, *Elementary School Journal*, 92: 121–33.

Ugaste, A. and Õun, T. (2007) History and current situation in Estonian early childhood education, in U. Härkonen and E. Savolainen (eds.) *International Views on Early Childhood Education*. Joensuu: University of Joensuu. E-book. Available at: http://sokl.joensuu.fi/verkkojulkaisut/varhais/ (accessed 3 February 2012).

Ugaste, A., Õun, T. and Tuul, M. (2008) Implementation of a child-centered approach in post-socialist society, in J. Mikk, M. Veisson and P. Luik (eds.) *Reforms and Innovations in Estonian Education*. Frankfurt am Main: Peter Lang Verlag.

8

EARLY CHILDHOOD EDUCATION IN NORWAY AND SWEDEN TODAY: EDUCATION FOR DEMOCRACY

Elin Ødegaard

Summary

The aim of this chapter is to illuminate a cultural-historical understanding of a relatively stable and dominant educational idea in Norway and Sweden: education for democracy. The chapter examines *why* approaches associated with education for democracy have taken the direction they have. An argument will be made that education *for* democracy and *through* democratic approaches has developed in close relation with political events and philosophical ideas active in Sweden and Norway. Ideological conditions have formed a habitus of folksiness that corresponds to democratic values. Through a description and analysis of *what* the national curricula articulate in terms of democratic values, the logic of current early childhood education practice can be understood. *How* democratic ideas circulate in everyday practice will be illustrated by a case study taken from a recent kindergarten study called *Circles of Participation*.[1]

Case Study

When Inna was 4 years old, her parents moved to Norway to work and Inna began attending a kindergarten near their new home. Nobody there spoke her mother tongue and many of her first weeks were spent reluctantly and silently observing the other children and adults. The day usually began with a quiet cry when her parents dropped her off. Nevertheless, she took the hand of an adult and went into the play area to eat breakfast. When Vanja, also 4 years of age, arrived half an hour later, they would start playing in the family corner. If Vanja left the family corner or if some of the other children wanted to join in, Inna's eyes would fill with fresh tears. This became a daily event. The adults usually tried to talk her into welcoming more children or persuade her to go with Vanja or another child to engage in new activities. Inna resisted these attempts. She demonstrated her reluctance by remaining as long as she could in the family corner, silently hiding behind the corner walls or playing alone at the small table there with the cups and plates. She also demonstrated this by ignoring the adults' initiatives, refusing to take their hand as encouragement to try a new activity. This pattern changed one particular day and allowed us to see what approaches were made and how she responded to them.

Twice a week, Inna's group spent half a day in the woods near the kindergarten. She had reluctantly come on these trips with Vanja holding her hand. She had seen the other children take photos for several weeks now, but this was the first time she had held a camera in her hands, and she held it tight. She liked to take photos. This was evident in her smiling face when she realized that she would be in charge of the camera that particular day. This was equally evident as she began to take lots of photos as the children wandered towards a steep rock. They had brought climbing ropes to climb the rock. They had done this before and everyone knew the procedure. Everyone stood in line and came forwards one by one as they were attached for safety. When it was Inna's turn, Harald, the preschool teacher, said that he would take care of the camera while she was climbing up the hill. She immediately decided *not* to climb. She made her decision clear by stepping back while keeping a tight grasp on the camera. Harald asked if she would rather walk around the rock with Anne (an assistant), Vanja, and Peter and Odin (a couple of 1-year-olds in a pushchair). Harald and Inna agreed and Harald asked in a friendly voice if she could take some more photos on the way round so that everyone could look at them later. On their walk, Inna took time to study a variety of flowers through the camera lens. She also took pictures of Vanja and the assistant. This led to many smiles and humorous dialogue in which Inna participated; she also let Vanja keep the camera for a while.

Returning to kindergarten, there were another three hours before Inna's parents were due to come and fetch her. Harald sensed a possible turning point and so dropped what he was doing. Instead, he invited Inna and Vanja straight into the media room and the three of them started to look at the pictures on a digital interactive board. Vanja and Inna explored the digital colour board and pencilled on some more pink. Vanja had done this before and Inna had watched others making collages with Picasa some days earlier; now she took the initiative to make a collage from her flower pictures. When Harald asked her who the collage was for, she promptly replied that it was for her mum and dad. So, as soon as the collage was finished, it was sent to them by e-mail. Her dad spotted the e-mail before he came to fetch Inna and that day the mood in the hallway was the lightest it had ever been.[2]

Introduction

Historical socio-cultural contexts are conditioning the way kindergartens act institutionally and organize practice. Several researchers have pointed to the connection between nation building, local culture, social values, and political ideas (Hultqvist, 1990; Allen, 2000; Wollons, 2000; Strand, 2006; Folke-Fichtelius, 2008). The epistemology of a country's ECE programme and practice is closely related in a complex way to its demographic situation, political ideas, and national historical events. Texts as well as practice from a range of people, from political actors to kindergarten pioneers, circulate across national and institutional borders. From this perspective, a national curriculum is not only a question of implementation, it is discursive and negotiated over time.

Norway and Sweden: a habitus of folksiness

Bourdieu's cultural sociology informs the chapter in the form of the concept of 'habitus', a set of dispositions that generate culturally based practice (Bourdieu, 1977, 2006). ECE practice can, from a cultural perspective, be understood as practice formed by historical remembrance, language, constitutions, and embodiment. Personal and local practice will also be socio-historical and habitual practices. To understand democratic practice as it has been negotiated in Norway and Sweden, we will first turn to historical descriptions.

Norway and Sweden share more than just a long border. In 1814, the two countries agreed to the union of two sovereign states, each with its own laws, parliament, government, currency, church, and army, yet sharing a king, foreign affairs, and diplomatic representation. Industrialization and growing democratic ideas, according to the historian Frances Sejersted, represent two sides of the coin (Sejersted, 2005). A division between the public and private economy followed modernization, yet it was political democratization addressing the issue of universal suffrage that came first. In fact, such processes can be traced back to early 1800. Economic democratic issues were addressed later with the construction of the welfare state after the Second World War.

Movements outside the established governance such as religious-spirited, pietistic, and temperance movements had a large impact on the dissemination of democratic values. Such local activities were dominant in both countries in the nineteenth and twentieth centuries. In addition to these movements, local initiatives arose in Norway opposing the colonization of the Norwegian language by Danish during the period 1380–1814. A new movement organized a restoration of the (New) Norwegian language.

Swedish-Norwegian democratic folksiness was in this respect different from that which arose, for example, in Germany, where a glorification of dictatorship was cultivated. At a local level, Sweden developed an organized civil society with gatherings of local labour unions, whereas Norway was organized in municipalities with political authority. This difference is conceptualized as a Norwegian 'municipality socialism' and a Swedish 'labour municipality' (Sejersted, 2005: 63). In Norway, this way of organizing society resulted in an early version of local welfare municipalities, while in Sweden local labour unions and individuals cooperated in socio-democratic aims outside the official governing institutions. Active politicians were recruited from these oppositional folk movements; they were trained in organizing and fighting problems. These have distinctly different historical roots from those of countries that historically have recruited politicians from the educated or economic elite.

Another difference between history connected to democracy in Sweden and Norway is worth mentioning. Sweden has historically had closer links with the European aristocracy, although this influence has gradually diminished. They retained the use of hereditary noble titles until 1902. Norway has historically been under the governance of Denmark, Sweden, and Germany and therefore Norwegian society in a European context has always had a weak upper class. Boarding schools for the upper class, as in England, have never existed. The Norwegian Royal Family has, in contrast, chosen open and public kindergartens and schools for their children and can be seen as an image of folksiness; they mirror the identity of their people and gain popularity and credit in return. Democratic ideas, as I have stated, are not new ideas. Educational philosophy has taken the values incorporated in the political idea and suggested reflections on its powerfulness, the dilemmas that come with it, and ideas on implementation, methods, and didactics in educational settings.

Ellen Key, a Swedish woman known for her feminist critical voice on social and societal issues, sought to identify contextual barriers and conditions for the individual human being. In her book *Century of the Child*, her special concern was conditions for children. She argued radically and rhetorically that:

> Time cries for 'personality', this cry is however in vain until we let our children live and learn as personalities; let them have free will, let them think personal thoughts, experience the achievement of knowledge, build their own reputation.[3]

> (Stavseng, 2000: 20)

Ideas circulate through dissemination, but also through personal relationships and debate. Ellen Key had a personal relationship with two internationally known Norwegian authors: Bjørnstjerne Bjørnson[4] and Henrik Ibsen,[5] both well known for their social commitment to human rights, democracy, and peace. Ellen Key was also a contemporary of John Dewey. She does not take the same position as the educational philosopher, but nevertheless a close intellectual relationship existed between the two (Lange, 2010). Both Dewey and Key were forward thinking with regards the view that children should be considered the focal point for political reform and education, promoting holistic and child-centred approaches to education.

While Dewey's thoughts on experimental education, children's inquiry, and school as an extension of civil society were systematically and distinctly disseminated, Key's thoughts can be identified in anonymous intertextualities by Elsa Köhler and Charlotte Bühler (Stavseng, 2000). Her thoughts were thereby disseminated back to Sweden and the Nordic countries as they were read in both Sweden and Norway.

Let us examine how *The Century of the Child* points the way forward by taking Norway as an example. In 1915, the Norwegian Castberg Laws were enacted.

Women's movements and the labour movement had for many years argued that illegitimate children should not be stigmatized. Now, a father's responsibility for his biological child was enacted by the child's right to the name and legacy of his father and the mother's right to economic support from the state if the father failed to fulfil his responsibilities. Vulnerable children were now made secure in a way that made a difference. Internationally, these laws were seen as progressive, since similar reforms were passed in many other Western countries much later. In 1956, the law was reformed, but it was not until 1981 that every child born in or outside of wedlock, rich or poor, would be covered by a single law on equality: the Child Law. Following this law, the Ombudsman for Children was established in Norway in 1981. This is an official government office and representative appointed by the government's Minister of Children and Inclusion. The United Nations Convention on the Right of the Child was first adopted in 1989. During the century of the child, we can therefore see a change in the public view from the child as 'submissive' to a view of the child as 'in need for protection' (Thuen, 2008).

From this historical backdrop, we can understand that ideas of opposition as a constructive force can grow. Ideas grounded in folksiness would naturally impact on the formation of the educational system. In Sweden, the concept of 'Folkbildning' and in Norway the concept of 'Folkedannelse' arose (Sejersted, 2005). The meaning behind these concepts was closely linked as both 'bildning' and 'dannelse' have the same etymological root; the German concept of 'Bildung' in the nineteenth century meant the formation of man related to education. During the 1800s, an understanding of this concept brought together civil social education and the ideal of the responsible individual's self-formative process, seen in labour and craftsmanship as well as in learning cultural knowledge and customs rather than bourgeoisie etiquette (Kosseleck, 2007). All major folk movements saw education from the perspective (Qvarsell, 2003) of both teaching about local and international issues as well as encouraging self-improvement and governance related to being a human democratic subject. The dissemination of these ideas was conducted in local study groups arranged by labour unions, religious and secular organizations, and the language movement (Sejersted, 2005). With these examples, we can see that a widespread localization of power, freedom, and self-realization created a habitus of folksiness as an ideal and how, from early on, this included women and children as equal human beings in thoughts and ideas.

Democratic education as a powerful but ambiguous core concept

Although this chapter is subtitled 'education for democracy' and talks about Norwegian and Swedish ECE as arenas for democratic curricula, the *concept* of 'democracy' was first seen in the Swedish Curriculum in 1998 (Swedish Ministry of Education and Science, 1998) and in the Norwegian Kindergarten Act of 2005 (Kunnskapsdepartement, 2005). This means that the concept of democracy has only recently become related to ECE programmes even if we have identified cultural undercurrents.

The concept of democracy can be understood and articulated in many ways, such as a way of governing and as a way of living (Dewey, 1966; Biesta, 2006, 2007;

Held, 2006; Karlsson, 2009; Grindheim, 2011; Jansen et al., 2011). In everyday discourse, it is often associated with governance in Western countries. In educational contexts, democracy is viewed as two distinct discourses: teaching specific values about democracy and living democratically by following values often identified with democracy (Emilsson, 2011).

Tracing the etymology, we find that 'demos' means people and 'kratos' means strength, power, rule or govern. In an ECE context, the concept must be associated with children: the people are the community of children and the children are given the strength and power to rule or govern. Put in this way, the concept of democracy is obviously a radical and therefore also ambiguous concept when it comes to young people and education. Education following political aims is not necessarily in children's best interests, as they understand it here and now. Questions that intrude include: are young children skilled, mature, knowledgeable and wise enough to rule? Can they understand the situation of self and others so that they can make informed choices and take responsibility of self and others? These questions were also addressed in the 1920s in the Lippmann-Dewey debate. Dewey responded to Lippmann's (1925) argument stated in his book *The Phantom Public* that the crowd of citizens must be ruled by specialists whose interests go beyond the individual and local interest. The reason for Lippmann's argument was the fact that the world was a complex and multifaceted stage and the idea that the ordinary man could have the information needed to make informed choices was a mistaken one. He meant that the idea of the 'omnipotent citizen' was an impossible one (Wipple, 2005).

Nevertheless, this discussion keeps resurfacing when democracy is connected to the uneducated, the illiterate, youth, and children. Understandings of democracy can be functionalistic or normative. A functionalistic understanding relates to control through political parties, public opinion, and general voting systems. To participate in democracy based on a functionalist understanding, it is necessary to have obtained certain relevant knowledge. Specific knowledge is not necessary based on a normative understanding of democracy since the aim is to participate. Everyone can participate in realizing democracy based on a normative understanding. This understanding suits kindergarten practice; the idea is that when children participate in a local community such as a school or kindergarten they experience and live democracy, which eventually leads to an habituation of participation and the competence to understand and learn more about functionalistic democracy. We can find a combination of these understandings of democracy in both the Norwegian Framework Plan for Kindergarten and in the Swedish Curriculum Plan. Democracy is connected to the learning of language in the Norwegian Framework Plan: in the long run, development of language is crucial to be able to participate in a modern democracy and in a knowledge society (Norwegian Ministry of Education, 2011: 5).

Several researchers have tried to solve the problem of children and democracy. The UNCRC had a huge impact on policies and practices in both Norway and Sweden (United Nations, 1990). Together with the discussions following implementation, thinkers like Antonio Gramsci and Paulo Freire were also heard in the Swedish and Norwegian educational debate. They argued that everyone has enough intellectual capacity to participate in society, but not everyone is given the opportunity.

Some researchers have tried to solve the problem by suggesting levels of democracy. Roger A. Hart developed *The Ladder of Participation* in response to a request from UNICEF and has inspired many local projects worldwide (Hart, 1979). Pateman's levels of pseudoparticipation—part participation and full participation – have been productive in analysing and evaluating children's participation (Børhaug, 2010). In such analyses, even small steps up the ladder or from one stage to another are seen as significant. This level analysis can be criticized for its static view of children's potential participation. We can see an increasing interest in Norway and Sweden from the 1990s onwards where children's perspectives, children's culture, inclusion, and meaning-making are analysed and discussed in relation to democracy (Samuelsson and Lindahl, 1999; Johansson, 2003; Karlsson, 2009; Emilsson, 2011; Jansen et al., 2011; Bae, 2012).

In these studies, it is not the functionalistic understanding or the level understanding that is dominant, but a Deweyian idea of democracy as a way of life, where values associated with sharing, exchanging, and negotiating perspectives and opinions are presented. Some of these studies from the 1990s to the present day also describe and strive to come to grips with a complex picture and do so by pointing to links and correspondence between global economies, international curriculum transitions, and a cultural historical blend, as does this chapter.

Ideas related to democracy appear in the literature under a variety of names and are also associated with and articulated as, for example, the 'holistic approach', 'participatory learning curriculum', 'play-based curriculum' or 'child-centred approach'. In some studies, values connected to relationships and the child viewed as a subject are dominant approaches.

In the Swedish context, democratic 'fostran', which is often translated as to foster, raise, bring up or nurture, is a concept with a history. Democratic education is seen as coming close to children's perspectives and living democratic *values* (Karlsson, 2009). The values associated with empirical studies are children's opportunities to make their own choices, take initiatives, solve problems, think divergently, and take risks. Emilsson and Johansson found three related values often communicated in teacher–child interactions, namely participation, influence, and negotiation.

To illustrate these points further, a Swedish-based analysis of 102 co-narratives between toddlers and teachers during mealtimes in a Norwegian kindergarten showed that cultural values were inscribed in teacher practices. Practices unfolded in which adults and children participated in negotiations regarding what was worth talking about. The study revealed how teachers adjusted to the contributions they anticipated from the children. Even if the teachers appeared to start with a specific agenda, they followed up on the children's contributions. The main discourse they lived by seemed to be that children have a right to be listened to. Democracy and empowering children to talk about their experiences were values inscribed in the teachers' agendas. Thus, in accordance with this practice of negotiation, two of the boys in the group set the cultural agenda and influenced everyday practice. The rest of the children in the group did not position themselves in ways that led to any influence observed by the researcher (Ødegaard, 2006, 2007, 2012).

In a recent Norwegian ECE project, the concept of democratic 'danning' was also explored. This Norwegian concept embraces the thinking of a human cultural and dialogical individual, an active subject that shapes inner meaning, character, and self-identity. The historical translation here associated with the Latin word 'formatio' provides an analytic concept to explore, among other issues, beyond children's participation. With a socio-spatial approach, we can go beyond relating democratic education to merely listening to children's voices. Children's voices can easily be ignored. As the critical event narrative (Webster and Mertova, 2007) described in the case study at the beginning of this chapter reveals, education for democracy can move in *circles of participation* (Knudsen and Ødegaard, 2011). 'Spatio' means that the curriculum is open to children's expressions, initiatives, and play. To be considered democratic, however, there must also be social action; someone must pick up on the initiatives and expressions, understand them to be suitable, and invite or take actions accordingly. I will now present the norms and values found in the Norwegian and Swedish national curricula, framework plans, and policy documents.

Norms and values found in policy documents and framework plans

How are democratic values articulated in the latest national curriculum documents? 'Democracy forms the basis of preschool' – this is the first sentence in the Swedish *Läroplan for förskolan – 98* [*Curriculum for Preschool – 98*] (revised in 2010). The main aim is formulated as follows: 'Preschool shall actively and consciously influence and stimulate children to develop an understanding of our society's common democratic values and subsequently include them'. In the Norwegian Kindergarten Act §1 and in Framework Plan for Kindergarten in Norway (revised in 2011), it is stated that: 'Kindergarten will promote democracy and equality and combat all forms of discrimination'.

In these key articulations, formal political norms are understood as rules of behaviour and expectations that are devised politically. Democracy is articulated in the first sentence in the most recent documents in both countries. In the Swedish curriculum, it is further stated: 'Preschool should actively and consciously influence and stimulate children into developing their understanding and acceptance of our society's shared democratic values'.

There are variations and nuances regarding the concept of democracy in Norwegian and Swedish ECE (see Table 8.1). Historically, Sweden was the first of the two countries to develop national plans for preschools. With an official White Paper, 'Barnstugeutredningen' (The Child Care Survey) (SOU, 1972: 26, 27), Sweden proposed education based on communication and dialogue. Until this time, curriculum literature for the education of preschool teachers consisted of philosophical extracts from Fröbel, Pestalozzi, Comenius, and Rousseau. According to the Swedish curriculum researcher Ann-Christin Vallberg Roth, the period from around 1900 until the post-war era was characterized by 'The curriculum of the good home and the native district', which meant that children should both play and do household work (Roth, 2006). Even if ideas and thoughts about the century of the child had been circulated, obedience and an asymmetric relationship between children and teachers still dominated. A change in ideology was seen in politics; a shift from social conservatism and social liberalism to social democracy and socialism rein-

Table 8.1 Concepts of democracy in Norwegian and Swedish ECEC

	Norway	Sweden
Attendance (statistics)	2009–2010[a] 89% aged 1–5 years attend 97.3% aged 3–5 years attend	2009–2010[b] 83% aged 1–5 years attend 94.5% aged 5 years attend
Curriculum	Framework plan, 2006 – revised 2011	Curriculum plan, 1998 – revised 2010
Foundation	Christianity and religions with joint values and beliefs Human rights and Convention on the Right of the Child.	Human rights and Convention on the Right of the Child
'Democracy' – how is the concept articulated in the main aim in the official Framework and Curriculum plans?	Kindergarten shall promote democracy and equality and combat all forms of discrimination	Democracy forms the basis of preschool education
What are the specific values articulated in the plans?	Charity, forgiveness, equality, and solidarity Respect for human dignity and the nature of intellectual freedom	Openness, respect, solidarity, responsibility, empathy, helpfulness, and ethical behaviour *All persons have equal value* independent of social background and regardless of gender, ethnic affiliation, religion or other belief, sexual orientation or functional impairment *Respect for all forms of life,* as well as care for the immediate environment
How is the dominant formal norm articulated?	Kindergartens shall promote democracy and equality and combat all forms of discrimination	Preschool education should actively and consciously influence and stimulate children into developing their understanding and acceptance of our society's shared democratic values
How is democracy to be implemented?	By influence according to age and maturity Considering children's views both in verbal and bodily expressions Supporting children in taking into account other people's views	By influence through working methods and content Developing children's responsibility for their own actions and compassion for others Preparing children to participate and share responsibilities, rights, and obligations that apply in a democratic society

	Norway	Sweden
Similarities and differences	The Norwegian plan is grounded in both a human rights tradition and Christianity, while the Swedish one is grounded solely in a human rights tradition. The Swedish plan places slightly more emphasis on 'the responsibility for others' aspect, while the Norwegian one is weighted slightly more towards 'freedom of voice'	

[a]Statistics Norway (www.ssb.no/utdanning_tema_en/; accessed 18 January 2012).
[b]Skolverket (www.skolverket.se/polopoly_fs/1.26652!Menu/article/attachment/; accessed 18 January 2012).

forced the second period rooted in 1930s politics (by Alva Myrdal[6] in Sweden, among others) and especially after the Second World War and up to 1980, a period she labels as the 'curriculum of the welfare state' (Roth, 2006: 87). From the 1950s, there was prosperous economic development and a strong consensus for solidarity and equal opportunities for all people, where the welfare state focused on individual collectivism and politics systematically sought to narrow the gaps between social classes and genders (Roth, 2006: 89).

The Child Care Survey (SOU, 1972: 26, 27) was used in both Norway and Sweden. In 1982, the Norwegian Ministry of Family and Administration Affairs developed a handbook called 'Goal Directed Work in Day Care Centres' (FAD, 1982).[7] This handbook was the first Norwegian public document for people working with young children in which the purpose of ECE and the social mandate was articulated.

In Norway, the first 'Framework Plan for Day Care Institutions' was implemented in January 1996 (Q-0903, 1996; Q-0917E, 1996). In elaborative ways, this plan articulated government policy intentions, formulated values and norms, and how these were to be implemented in daily work with children and staff, as well as in organizational plans. Sweden's new curriculum, 'Curriculum for Preschool' (Utbildningsdepartementet, 1998), was implemented in 1998; this is the year ECE became part of the education system in Sweden.

In both countries, the United Nations Declaration of the Rights of the Child provides a basis for this first generation of national plans. In the Norwegian plan, values such as 'respect for life, equality, tolerance and respect for people from other cultures, tolerance and respect for people with disabilities, equality of the sexes, altruism and solidarity, justice, truth and honesty, peace and understanding, responsibility for conservation of nature and culture, and responsibility for others' are central to children's development in ECE.

Alvestad and Samuelsson (1999) find one crucial difference in values in their comparative analysis of the Swedish and Norwegian first-generation framework plans. Norwegian ECE is built upon ethical values deeply rooted in Christianity, grounded in the supposition that Christianity has a broad acceptance among the public at large. The framework plan states that neutrality in values is neither possible nor desirable. Preschools have to work with ethical questions, concretized through cultural traditions and major Christian festivals. In the Swedish plan, however, the ethical code is directly founded in the concept of democracy, as pointed out earlier.

Swedish ECE is not founded in religion as the church and the state are separate, while in Norway public churches are state-funded and administered. In Sweden, activities and ways of being and acting in preschool were set in accordance with fundamental democratic values. Care of and respect for other human beings in the form of justice and equality should form the basis for activities.

We can see that now democracy appears as the first and foremost value. This is a strong political signal and a *ethico-political* label may be proposed (Mac Naughton, 2003). Democratic practice is further articulated as children's influence. It is understood as children's right to express their views on daily activities. Children shall also have the opportunity to be active participants in planning and evaluating institutional life. It is stated that children's views are to be considered according to their age and maturity. Bodily and emotional expressions are to be taken as children's views and it is noted that children are to be supported in understanding the views of others and taking these into account.

Conclusions

The kindergarten idea is globally disseminated, as noted throughout this book. In the kindergarten micro-cosmos, teachers and children engage in relational practices whereby ideas are embodied and locally situated, exchanged, disputed, and carried out. This chapter has examined *why* approaches associated with education for democracy have taken the direction they have and argued that education *for* democracy and *through* democratic approaches developed in close relation with political events and philosophical ideas active in Sweden and Norway. Such ideological conditions can be seen as forming a 'habitus' of folksiness that corresponds to democratic values. Through a description and analysis of *what* the national curricula articulate in terms of democratic values, the logic of current ECE practice can be understood. Although Sweden and Norway share common ground with regard to the socio-historical background of ECE, there are nonetheless some discrepancies, as described.

Find Out More

- Are young children skilled, mature, knowledgeable, and wise enough to rule?
- Can they understand the situation of self and others so that they can make informed choices and take responsibilities?
- What are the critical and beneficial points of democratic approaches?

Notes

1 This is a sub-project to a larger project entitled *Kindergarten as an Arena for Cultural Formation*. The project was founded by the Norwegian Research Council 2009–2013 and led by Elin Eriksen Ødegaard).

2   This vignette is a decomposed story from field notes from the *Circles of Participation* project conducted by Ida M. Knudsen and Elin Eriksen Ødegaard.

3   My translated paraphrase.

4   Awarded the Nobel Prize in Literature in 1903.

5   Known as the father of modern drama.

6   A Swedish politician in the Social Democratic Party who fought for equal rights for men and woman, held the first top positions by a woman at the UN and UNESCO (1949–1955) and, together with Alfonso Gracia Robles, received the Nobel Peace Prize in 1982.

7   A more detailed historical overview of official documents and their general functions may be found in Alvestad and Samuelsson (1999).

References and recommended reading

Allen, A.T. (2000) Children between public and private worlds: the kindergarten and public policy in Germany 1840 – present, in R. Wollon (ed.) *Kindergartens and Cultures: The Global Diffusion of an Idea.* New Haven, CT: Yale University Press.

Alvestad, M. and Samuelsson, I.P. (1999) A comparison of the national preschool curricula in Norway and Sweden, *Early Childhood Research and Practice*, 1(2). Available at: http://www.ecrp.uiuc.edu/v1n2/alvestad.html (accessed 5 June 2012).

Bae, B. (2010) Realizing children's right to participation in early childhood settings – some critical issues in a Norwegian context, *Early Years: An International Journal of Research and Development*, 30(3): 205–18.

Bae, B. (ed.) (2012) *Medvirkning i barnehagen – Potensialer i det uforutsette [Participation in Kindergarten – Potentials of the Unexpected].* Bergen: Fagbokforlaget (in Norwegian).

Biesta, G. (2006) *Beyond Learning: Democratic Education for a Human Future.* Boulder, CO: Paradigm.

Biesta, G. (2007) 'Don't count me in': democracy, education and the question of inclusion, *Nordisk pedagogik*, 27(1): 18–31.

Børhaug, K. (2010) Medverknad for barn i barnehagen – meir påverknad?, *Tidsskriftet FoU i praksis*, 4(2): 9–23.

Bourdieu, P. (1977) *Outline of a Theory of Practice.* Cambridge: Cambridge University Press.

Bourdieu, P. (2006) Habitus og livsstilenes rom [Habitus and lifestyle], *Agora*, 24(1/2): 74–112.

Dewey, J. (1966) *Democracy and Education: An Introduction to the Philosophy of Education.* New York: Macmillan/Free Press.

Emilsson, A. (2011) Democracy learning in a preschool context, in N.P.I.P. Samuelsson (ed.) *Educational Encounters: Nordic Studies in Early Childhood Didactics.* Dordrecht: Springer.

FAD (1982) *Målrettet arbeid i barnehagen. En håndbok [Goal-directed Work in Day Care Centres: A Handbook].* Ministry of Family and Administration Affairs. Oslo: Universitetsforlaget.

Folke-Fichtelius, M. (2008) *Förskolans formande: statlig reglering 1944–2008 [Preschool Formation: Regulation by the State].* Uppsala Studies in Education 119. Uppsala: Acta Universitatis Upsaliensis.

Grindheim, L.T. (2011) Barnefellesskap som demokratisk danningsarena [Preschool as an arena for cultural formation] – Kva kan gje hove til medverknad i leik i barnehagen? *Nordisk barnehageforskning*, 4(2): 91–102.

Hart, R. (1979) *Children's Participation from Tokenism to Citizenship*. Innocenti Essays No. 4. Florence: UNICEF. Available at: http://www.unicef-irc.org/publications/pdf/childrens_ (accessed 28 May 2012).

Held, D. (2006) *Models of Democracy*. Cambridge: Polity.

Hultqvist, K. (1990) *Förskolebarnet: en konstruktion för gemenskapen och den individuella frigörelsen: en nutidshistorisk studie om makt och kunskap i bilden av barnet i statliga utredningar om förskolan* [*Preschool Children: A Design for the Community and Individual Liberation: A Contemporary Historical Study of Power and Knowledge in the Image of the Child in Government Studies on Preschool*]. Stockholm: Symposion Publishing.

Jansen, K., Johansson, E.M. and Ødegaard, E.E. (2011) På jakt etter demokrati begrep i barnehagen [On the track of concepts for democracy in kindergarten], *Nordisk Barnehageforskning*, 4(2): 61–4.

Johansson, E. (2003) Att närma sig barns perspektiv – Forskares och pedagogers möten med barns perspektiv [Approaching the child's perspective: researchers' and teachers' meetings with the child's perspective], *Pedagogisk Forskning i Sverige*, 8(1/2): 42–57.

Karlsson, R. (2009) *Demokratiska värden i förskolebarns vardag* [*Democratic Values in Preschool Children's Everyday Lives*]. Göteborg Studies in Educational Sciences 279. Göteborg: Acta Universitatis Gothoburgensis.

Knudsen, I.M. and Ødegaard, E.E. (2011) Fotofloker – vilkår for deltakelse når digitale bilder tas i bruk i barnehagen [Photo tangles – conditions for participation when digital images are used in the nursery], *Nordisk barnehageforskning*, 4(2): 115–28.

Kosseleck, R. (2007) Dannelsens antropologiske og semantiske struktur [Anthropological and semantic structure], *Slagmark*, 48: 11–48.

Kunnskapsdepartement, D.K.N. (2005) Lov om barnehager [Day Care Institutions Act], in Kunnskapsdepartementet (ed.). Available at: http://www.lovdata.no/all/nl-20050617-064.html (accessed 5 June 2012).

Lange, M.D. (2010) Keys to the classroom and educational reform, in M.I.C. Studies (ed.) *A Collection of Papers*. Linköping: Linköping University.

Lippmann, W. (1925) *The Phantom Public*. New York: Harcourt Brace.

Mac Naughton, G. (2003) *Shaping Early Childhood*. Buckingham: Open University Press.

Norwegian Ministry of Education (2011) *Framework Plan for the Content and Task of Kindergarten*, No. 51. Oslo: UDIR.

Ødegaard, E.E. (2006) What's worth talking about? Meaning-making in toddler-initiated co-narratives in preschool, *Early Years: An International Journal of Research and Development*, 26(1): 79–92.

Ødegaard, E.E. (2007) What's on the teachers agenda?, *International Journal of Early Childhood*, 39(2): 45–65.

Ødegaard, E.E. (2012) Piracy in policy – children influencing curriculum in kindergartens in Norway, in T. Papatheodorou (ed.) *Early Childhood in the 21st Century: International Perspectives on Policy Curriculum and Pedagogy*. London: Routledge.

Qvarsell, B. (2003) Barns perspektiv och mänskliga rättigheter – Godhetsmaximering eller kunskapsbildning?, *Pedagogisk Forskning i Sverige*, 8(1/2): 101–13.

Roth, A.-C.V. (2006) Early childhood curricula in Sweden – from the 1850s to the present, *International Journal of Early Childhood*, 38(1): 77–98.

Samuelsson, I.P. and Lindahl, M. (1999) *Att förstå det lilla barnets värld med videons hjälp* [*To Understand the Little Child's World – with the Help of a Video Camera*]. Stockholm: Liber.

Sejersted, F. (2005) *Sosialdemokratiets tidsalder – Norge og Sverige i det 20. Århundre.* [*Social Democratic Era – Norway and Sweden in the 20th Century*]. Oslo: Pax Forlag.

Statens Offentliga Utredningar (SOU) (1972) *Barnstugeutredningen* (*The Child Care Survey*). Stockholm: Socialdepartementet.

Stavseng, O. (2000) Ellen Key – en introduksjon [Ellen Key – an introduction], in E. Hauglund (ed.) *Barnets århundre og Ellen Key – 8 nøkler til en låst tid* [*The Child's Century – Ellen Key – 8 Keys to a Locked Time*]. Oslo: Akribe.

Strand, T. (2006) The social game of early childhood education – the case of Norway, in E. Johanna and J. Wagner (eds.) *Nordic Childhoods and Early Education.* Greenwich, CT: Information Age Publishing.

Swedish Ministry of Education and Science (1998) *Läroplan för förskolan* [*Curriculum for Preschool*]. Regeringskansliet. Stockholm: Skolverket.

Thuen, H. (2008) *Om barnet – Oppdragelse, opplæring og omsorg gjennom historien* [*About the Child – Upbringing, Education and Care through History*]. Oslo: Abstrakt forlag.

United Nations (1990) *Convention on the Rights of the Child.* Available at: http://www2.ohchr. org/english/law/crc.htm (accessed 5 June 2012).

Utbildningsdepartementet (1998). *Lpfö 98. Läroplan för förskolan* [*Curriculum for Preschool*]. Stockholm: Fritzes.

Webster, L. and Mertova, P. (2007) *Using Narrative Inquiry as a Research Method: An Introduction to Using Critical Event Narrative Analysis in Research on Learning and Teaching.* London: Routledge.

Wipple, M. (2005) The Dewey-Lippmann debate today: communication, distortions, reflective agency and participatory democracy, *Sociological Theory*, 23(2): 156–78.

Wollons, R. (ed.) (2000) *Kindergartens and Cultures: The Global Diffusion of an Idea.* New Haven, CT: Yale University Press.

PART 3

Workforce issues

9

SOUTH AFRICA: WHO ARE THE EARLY YEARS PRACTITIONERS AND WHERE DO THEY WORK?

Hasina Banu Ebrahim

Summary

This chapter focuses on practitioners involved in early childhood care and education, in particular those involved in innovative family- and community-based models being developed in the provinces of KwaZulu-Natal and Free State in South Africa. These models provide alternatives to centre-based provision in contexts where primary caregivers are living in poor socio-economic conditions. The practitioners, known as community development practitioners and family facilitators, are responsible for implementing comprehensive programmes for vulnerable children and their families in homes and communities. For this demanding work, practitioners receive basic training and irregular stipends. The adoption of alternative models to centre-based provision and the inclusion of the new practitioners in the early childhood workforce pose challenges regarding qualifications, career path, community involvement, and issues of quality.

Introduction

In examining the question posed in the title of this chapter, it is imperative to understand the context that gave rise to the need for particular types of practitioners and certain ways of doing early childhood work. In this chapter, two models that are aimed at family support and community development for birth to 4 years are used to shed light on the new early childhood practitioners and the nature of their work.

In South Africa, provison from birth to 4 years is included within a broader definition of early childhood development (ECD). ECD is defined as 'an umbrella term, which applies to the processes by which children from birth to 9 years, grow and thrive, physically, mentally, emotionally, morally and socially' (Department of Education, 1995: 33). Birth to 4 years is the preschool phase. Historically, the caregiving arrangements for this phase were the responsibility of parents. However, in South Africa the public service response became necessary in the light of women's employment outside the home, the inequities created by apartheid, current levels of poverty, unemployment, and the vulnerabilities that poor socio-economic conditions create in young children's lives.

The dominant public response to early care and education is centre-based provision. In South Africa, this type of provision is problematic for several reasons – lack of demand due to unemployment and poverty, lack of access due to geographical constraints, unsuitability of settings for babies and toddlers, and variable quality. Practitioners that work in these centres, most of whom are women, are untrained and not highly qualified. Basic levels of training to improve qualifications are in place. Practitioners are keen to improve their qualifications but are discouraged by the limited ECD career options. This is currently being attended to (Department of Social Development, 2012).

In light of the limitations of the centre-based model, alternatives supporting an integrated approach to early care and education for birth to 4 years are emerging. The National Integrated Plan (NIP) for ECD (Departments of Education, Social Development and Health, 2005) promotes an approach whereby basic services aimed at childcare – early stimulation, learning, health, nutrition, pre-natal and post-natal care, and community development – are merged into comprehensive programmes. Taking into account how the history of apartheid affected ECD services in South Africa (Ebrahim, 2010), the current inequalities, and childhood adversities, comprehensive programmes are needed to intervene in the lives of children and families living in poor socio-economic conditions. ECD centres are not the only sites for intervention. The NIP also acknowledges the value of homes, communities, and institutions for child care in early childhood interventions.

Due to competing priorities, financial constraints, and the positioning of the South African Government as a facilitative state, there is heavy reliance on nongovernmental organizations (NGOs) for innovations in early childhood. The ECD NGOs have been at the forefront of developing models to deliver comprehensive early childhood programmes. This is giving rise to new hybrid workers who are not confined to ECD centres (Ebrahim et al., 2010: 395). The nature of work is more in line with the social services professions.

This chapter describes the Community Development and Family Support (CDFSP) programme of Lesedi Educare in the Free State Province and the Family Support Programme (FSP) of the Little Elephant Training Centre for Early Education (LETCEE) in KwaZulu-Natal in South Africa. The roles and responsibilities of the new workers form an integral part of the discussion. This is followed by a discussion of the challenges related to family and community support programmes.

The Community Development and Family Support Programme

The CDFSP extends the idea of the ECD centre as a critical node for community outreach in urban areas in the Free State (see Figure 9.1). The programme was developed to meet the needs of children living in poor socio-economic conditions

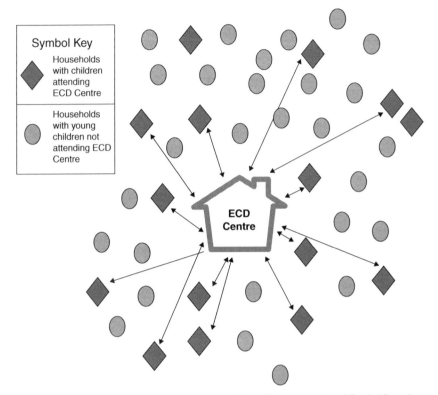

Figure 9.1 An ECD centre reaching out to households (Departments of Social Development and Education, 2006)

near an ECD centre. The programme is directed both at children who experience vulnerabilities and those whose caregivers cannot afford the fees for centre-based early education.

The managers of the centres, who normally live in the area, play a key role in selecting the community development practitioners (CDPs). Each manager in consultation with the community develops criteria for the selection of volunteers to serve as CDPs. The criteria broadly relate to personal qualities and promising skills to support early education and aspects of community development. Once the CDPs are identified, they work with the managers to identify the needs of families in the area. Each CDP receives training with Lesedi.

The CDPs receive basic training in topics related to self-improvement, early childhood education, community development and, depending on their choices for the community project, training for entrepreneurship and fundraising are also included. It is envisaged that this basic training will lead to a Level 4 qualification in Community Development with a focus on ECD. The registration of this qualification, however, has been problematic. The career path is therefore uncertain. The CDPs are paid a stipend of R400 (about £30) a month when external funding is available. The training is viewed as having value in itself.

In the home-visiting component, the CDPs develop early stimulation activities. This is approached with sensitivity to existing cultural practices of parents and other primary caregivers. Parent education is also approached in a strengths-based way. Based on their understanding and needs, parents are advised on health, nutrition, and access to services. Due to the high illiteracy rate among adults in the communities, the CDPs assist with interpretation of documentation. Where older siblings are literate, they are enabled to perform this function. Where families are at risk, the CDPs make referrals to the managers in the centres who forward these to the relevant authorities.

Each CDP also plays a facilitative role in one or two community development projects – playgroups, support groups, income-generation and aftercare clubs at ECD centres for orphans at schools. Neighbourhood playgroups are run on an informal basis. On a weekly basis, CDPs encourage caregivers (mothers, grandmothers, aunts) to join the children for play sessions. This is sometimes undertaken in a toy library bus. Caregivers get the opportunity to learn about different ways to interact with children. This is important, taking into account how stress in family life reduces the amount of time caregivers can devote to children. The CDPs also run support groups to help caregivers to deal with the problems they encounter. Due to the high rates of poverty and especially child poverty, income-generation projects are encouraged. The CDPs also work with orphans after school. They help them with homework and computer literacy, and create platforms to enable their talents (music, dance, drama).

The work of the CDPs is directly monitored by the managers on a regular basis. The community support structure is responsible for the overall running and sustainability of the programme. This structure is made up of the managers, the CDPs, local councillors, and members of the community. They are responsible for the monitoring of the activities of the CDPs, the managers, community development workers, and how the NGOs are involved. The councillors and the community development workers are tasked with raising issues at a higher level (municipality/local authority forums).

The Family Support Programme

This FSP was developed specifically for a rural context. It recognizes the importance of the family as the first line of intervention in a context where multiple problems affect children's lives. The home is valued as an important space for nurturing young children. The entire community is mobilized to rally around children.

The FSP begins with raising awareness in the community of early care and education. One of the first structures to be engaged in this process was the traditional leadership. Traditional leaders are recognized structures that are responsible for community governance in South Africa. All projects must gain their approval before implementation.

The *Siyabantwana Abantwana* ('We love the children') programme began in March 2008, facilitated by LETCEE and with the assistance of the members of the community and the traditional leadership. A community committee was formed of members from the traditional and political leadership and from the community.

The task of this structure was to monitor the project and ensure sustainability. In the initial stage of the programme, the community committee was also responsible for conducting a needs survey. This provided information on the problems that families experienced and the type of interventions that were needed.

The family facilitators are appointed by the community committee to work in close collaboration with them and structures in the community. They are selected based on their personal qualities and commitment to make a difference in children's lives. When available, they receive a stipend of R300 to R400 (about £23 to £30) a month. Their training is basic with possibilities for learnerships towards a Level 4 qualification in ECD.

Once appointed, the family facilitators are allocated ten families. The poorest of the poor are prioritized. The family facilitators' duties include home visiting, parent education, nutrition and health advice, early stimulation, giving logistical support to the elderly, and moral support to those with HIV/AIDs. There are many orphans in the area. The family facilitators assist caregivers in obtaining, completing, and forwarding documentation to the social development services. Since many caregivers cannot afford centre-based early education, children are taught in neighbourhood playgroups that sometimes draw on the cultural practices of the families and the community.

The family facilitators are also responsible for coordinating a Buddy Programme. This child-to-child programme includes children aged 8–13 years intervening in the lives of young children (James and Ebrahim, 2012). The buddies conduct playgroup activities with young children after school and during weekends.

Case Study: A day in the life of a family facilitator

Margaret Cele [not her real name] is 37 years old. She is married with three children of school-going age. Her husband is a policeman in Durban, KwaZulu-Natal. She was selected by the community to be a family facilitator in Busane, Matimatolo.

It is a very cold day in July in Matimatolo. Margaret takes her bag of toys which she received from the LETCEE toy library and leaves home at 9.30. She walks to neighbouring homesteads to fetch the children in her group. She lives in a hilly area and walks some way down into the valley to the homesteads. Poorer homesteads are normally further away from the main road.

She collects six children between the ages of 2 and 6. Four of them are not wearing shoes. She takes them to a homestead where two more children join the group. These children are orphans who live with their grandparents. The elder of the two has not been sent to school because his ailing grandparents could not afford to buy a uniform at the beginning of the year. The entire family depends on the grandmother's pension. Margaret approached LETCEE to help the grandmother to obtain the documentation required to apply for a pension. Margaret speaks to the grandfather. She asks him how his garden is developing. She encourages caregivers to grow food gardens so that they can supplement their diets and save money. He says he has some spinach that is ready and he has planted carrots.

Margaret takes the children to a space behind the house. She greets them, where they sing and pray. They recite a rhyme about a frog and jump around to get warm. They recite a number rhymes and count on their fingers. Margaret asks them about their activities when they do not come to the play-group. A child responds by saying that he goes to church and Sunday School. Margaret takes a skipping rope out of her bag and the children skip. Margaret reminds them about turn-taking. They also play with a ball.

Margaret notices a sore on a child's head. She calls the child and tells her to ask her aunt to take her to the clinic. The child then joins the game. Margaret allows the children to play freely. As they play, she notices a child with a burn on her face. She asks the child how she got burnt. The child replies that she was playing with a stick from the fire. Margaret tells her not to play with fire as it can hurt her.

Margaret then calls the children together and they go into a small ron-davel. Margaret takes sheets of paper and paints out of her bag. The children paint their houses. They are very pleased with their paintings. The children tell Margaret about people who live with them. They then take the paintings outside to dry.

Later, when the children have gone home, Margaret visits another home-stead in the valley. There are dirty blankets and clothes lying on the grass. Three children aged 3–4 years run around the house. They do not have jer-seys or shoes. Margaret calls the children and takes them inside. Their grand-mother is inside the house. When she sees Margaret, she cries and says that she is sick. She has no food and her pension is not due until next week. Her 18-year-old daughter has taken a sick child to the clinic. Margaret comforts her. She dresses the children in warm clothes and arranges them around the fire, telling them not to touch the fire and instructing the eldest child to watch them.

(adapted from Rule et al., 2008)

Challenges facing the scaling up of family and community support programmes

The models presented here have potential for improving children and family outcomes in disadvantaged contexts. There are, however, many challenges that arise from these programmes in that they are largely in the hands of NGOs who rely on external funding to sustain them. The following is a discussion of three issues confronting these programmes in their current implementation efforts.

Practitioner training, career path, and recognition

In the ECD family and community support programmes, high demands are made on practitioners. They are expected to be knowledgeable about early childhood care, education, family dynamics, social and community development. The work is also physically and emotionally draining. To be truly effective, the practitioners would require regular training based on inter- and multi-disciplinary knowledge for the work they do and for their self-development. They would also need skills development through carefully monitored work-based experience. This will only occur if the government takes full responsibility for training and the career development for practitioners working with children from birth to 4 years.

At present, the problems experienced relate to the *ad hoc* nature of training, lack of capacity and expertise for monitoring in the family and community context, lack of a clear career path, problems with registration of qualifications and volunteerism. In evaluating the CDFSP, Milstein (2010: 10) notes how *ad hoc* training and the failure to materialize of a Level 1 qualification in Community Development with the focus on ECD as a nationally recognized qualification led to practitioners leaving the programme. Ebrahim et al. (2010: 394) noted how practitioners were considering career prospects in schooling, which was better structured in terms of qualifications, career path, and salaries.

Another challenge that is surfacing at present relates to whether the practitioners in the alternative models are adequately catered for in the Children's Act 38 of 2005 (date of commencement: 1 April 2010). This Act regulates the work of the social services professions. The ECD Working Group (2011) notes how the Act is not clear about the role of the new ECD practitioners as workers who are meeting the objectives of the developmental model of social development as proposed by the Act. There is strong support for the formal recognition of ECD practice as an occupation within the social services professions. The ECD Working Group argues that ECD practice as an occupation must be included in the Act to strengthen the child services workforce.

Working with communities

Both the above models rely heavily on community cohesion as a concept to sustain them, and make the assumption that a community is a group of people who share a lot in common and therefore can unite for action towards a specific aspect affecting its members. Ideas of active citizenship and civic-driven change are used to mobilize communities to volunteer their services.

However, the reality is quite different. This is especially the case when people have to operate in a monetized environment. The commitment, dedication, and responsibility of members in a community becomes complicated when money is introduced. The stipends, even though small, create a hierarchy in an environment where most people are unemployed. For example, in a focus group interview with family facilitators in the FSP, the respondents spoke about how even the meagre amount they received created tensions with unemployed members of the community.

Individuals acting in their own interest is also a powerful feature that has not been given adequate attention in the alternative models to centre-based provision. For example, in the FSP, the highly respected traditional leader whose actions were critical in starting the FSP became involved in personal power struggles, which led to a lack of trust of community members in his leadership. This affected the roll out of the programme.

The true extent of the community's potential to serve as a resource for early care and education in poor socio-economic circumstances must be acknowledged. People experience high levels of stress and live in oppressive circumstances. They do find it difficult to cooperate unless they can see an immediate tangible benefit that helps them to improve their circumstances. The CDPs and family facilitators may not always deliver in these ways, especially if the shift is towards social development rather than social welfare.

Quality of programmes

The expansion of early childhood programmes to include family and community support has resulted in access to opportunities for ECD. However, the expansion has not given sufficient thought to quality. Conceptualizations of quality for family and community support programmes are poor. This is also complicated by the absence of a clear regulatory environment. In two evaluations in 2008 and 2009 of the CDFSP and the FSP, it was evident that the focus was on short-term impacts on individual children and their families (Rule et al., 2008; Ebrahim et al., 2009). Where quality indicators exist, they are drawn from centre-based provision, which does not adequately address the range of services included in comprehensive programmes. There is also a lack of measurement tools that are sufficiently adapted to the socio-cultural context of South Africa, the settings, and types of interventions (see also Chapter 10 for a discussion of the development of quality indicators appropriate for the Hong Kong context, and Chapter 16 for Chinese kindergartens).

Another factor creating cause for concern is how the notion of quality is only grounded in the local context. Britto et al. (2011) argue that developing world contexts need to pay greater attention to quality at the broader regional and national level. They offer a conceptualization of quality that uses an ecological systems perspective that pays attention to children and adults as targets of change and the setting and systems that are implicated in the change. They also offer cross-cutting dimensions of quality that are helpful to consider, notably alignment with community and societal values and principles, resource levels and distribution; physical and spatial characteristics; leadership and management; and interactions and communications. This new conceptualization of quality needs to be explored and developed further.

Conclusions

The inclusion of family and community support programmes in the ECD landscape in South Africa is seen as broadening the scope of intervention in the lives of children and families living in vulnerable circumstances. In a country that is seeking solutions to unemployment, the new childcare work is welcomed. However, the current challenges related to government involvement, regulation, practitioner development, community cohesion, and attention to the quality issues are complicating the adoption of the alternatives to centre-based provision. It is imperative that the complexities of the new models and the new workforce be teased out and addressed at different tiers that affect children and families in both the near and far environments.

Find Out More

- How do history and inequalities shape models of early care and education in resource-poor countries?
- How does the absence of regulation and qualifications affect the early childhood workforce?
- How does the quality of preschool early childhood services affect children's outcomes?

References and recommended reading

Britto, P.R., Yoshikawa, H. and Boller, K. (2011) Quality of early childhood development programs in global context: rationale for investment, conceptual framework and implications for equity, *Social Policy Report*, 25(2): 1–31.

Department of Education (1995) *White Paper on Education and Training*. Pretoria: Government Printers.

Departments of Education, Social Development and Health (2005) *National Integrated Plan for Early Childhood Development in South Africa*, 2005–2010. New York: UNICEF. Available at: http://www.unicef.org/southafrica/SAF_resources_nip.pdf (accessed 29 May 2012).

Departments of Social Development and Education (2006) *Conceptual Framework – Early Childhood Development Centres as Resources for Care and Support for Poor and Vulnerable Children, their Families, including Orphans and Vulnerable Children*. New York: UNICEF.

Department of Social Development (2012) First draft towards a national plan for early childhood development conference 2012–2017. Unpublished.

Ebrahim, H.B. (2010) Tracing historical shifts in early care and education in South Africa, *Journal of Education*, 48: 119–35.

Ebrahim, H.B., Killian, B. and Rule, P. (2009) *Report on Practice, Principles, Methodologies, Core Interventions, Networking, Stakeholder Analysis, Outcomes and Benefits* – Lesedi Family Support and Community Development Programme – Free State. Unpublished Research Report. New York: UNICEF.

Ebrahim, H.B., Killian, B. and Rule, P. (2010) Practice of early childhood practitioners for poor and vulnerable children from birth to four years in South African, *Early Child Development and Care*, 181(3): 387–96.

ECD (Early Childhood Development) Working Group (2011) Discussion Paper: Early Childhood Development (ECD) and the Social Service Professions Bill. Unpublished submission for registration of ECD practitioners.

James, M. and Ebrahim, H.B. (2012) Pedagogic activities for early education in a child to child programme in South Africa, in T. Papatheodorou (ed.) *Debates on Early Childhood Policies and Practices: Global Snapshots of Pedagogical Thinking and Encounters*. London: Routledge.

Milstein, S. (2010) External evaluation of Lesedi's community development and family support programme, 2007–2010. Unpublished report.

Penn, H. and Maynard, T. (2010) *Siyabonana: We All See Each Other*. **Edinburgh: Children of Scotland.**

Republic of South Africa (2005) Children's Act, No. 38 of 2005 as amended by Children's Amendment Act, No. 41 of 2007; Child Justice Act, No. 75 of 2008. Available at: www.ci.org.za. (accessed 18 February 2012).

Rule, P., Ebrahim, H.B. and Killian, B. (2008) *Report on the Practice, Principles, Cost Drivers, Interventions, Methodologies and Stakeholder Analysis of the Project Based on the Concept of ECD Programmes as Resources for the Care and Support of Poor and Vulnerable Young Children – LETCEE: Siyabathanda Abantwana and Sikhulakahle interventions*. Unpublished Research Report. New York: UNICEF.

Swift, A. and Maher, S. (2008) *Growing Pains: How Poverty and AIDS are Challenging Childhood*. **London: Panos.**

10

THE QUEST FOR QUALITY EARLY CHILDHOOD EDUCATION AND CARE: LEADERSHIP IN A CHANGING POLITICAL CONTEXT IN ENGLAND AND HONG KONG

Verity Campbell-Barr, Caroline Leeson and Dora Ho

Summary

Internationally policy-makers are looking at the role that quality ECEC services can have in supporting social and economic policy agendas. In particular, a number of countries (including England and Hong Kong) have recognized the role that ECEC can play in developing the human capital of a country. Building on evidence that ECEC can enhance children's social and cognitive development, both England and Hong Kong are now investing in the provision of services. However, both countries are reliant on a mixed economy of provision to fulfil policy objectives. The result is that those leading ECEC are expected to respond both to the quality criteria of policy-makers and consumers raising questions about how best to achieve this.

Introduction

Internationally, there is recognition of the social and economic benefits of early childhood education and care (ECEC) (OECD, 2006; Penn, 2010a). Socially, ECEC contributes to child development, child wellbeing, and equality of access to services, while economically it facilitates parental employment, with an inevitable interplay between these two areas (see Bertram and Pascal, 2002; Calman and Tarr-Whelan, 2005; White, 2011). However, it is clear that it is not just the provision of ECEC, but of quality ECEC that is important. Here we look at two examples of the drive for quality in ECEC: England and Hong Kong.

It is important to bear in mind the motivation for governments' interest in ECEC as a means of upgrading their human capital (see Chapter 1), because this helps to illuminate how policy seeks to create a correct reading of ECEC as a series of discursive truths of what quality within ECEC looks like. Both England and Hong Kong (along with other neo-liberal economies) are, however, reliant on a mixed market to provide ECEC services. The result is that those leading ECEC provision are expected to respond to quality criteria as laid out by governments, but also to respond to the needs of their consumers – that is, parents. We conclude by looking at existing and emerging models of leadership and ask questions about their capacity to enable providers to meet both policy and consumer objectives.

Funding ECEC

Both England and Hong Kong, together with many other countries, have invested in the provision of ECEC. For both countries, there was relatively little political interest in the provision of ECEC services before the late 1990s (see Opper, 1992; Ho et al., 2010). In England, the National Childcare Strategy (DfEE, 1998) focused on the quality, affordability, and accessibility of ECEC, with the addition of flexibility following the Ten Year Plan in 2004 (see Lloyd, 2008; Campbell-Barr and Garnham, 2010). There were initiatives to support the cost of childcare services through means-tested tax credits; the introduction of free early years education places for 3- and 4-year-olds and later 2-year-olds in deprived areas; capital funding to support the expansion of provision; and a number of initiatives that looked at addressing the quality of provision, such as the upskilling and professionalization of the workforce and reviews of the Early Years Curriculum Framework (see OECD, 2006; Lloyd, 2008; see also Chapter 22).

In Hong Kong, policy initiatives have included 'upgrading teacher qualifications, harmonizing pre-primary education services, implementing a quality assurance framework, and introducing new curriculum guidelines' (Ho et al., 2010: 248). The Pre-primary Education Voucher Scheme (PEVS) introduced in 2007 aimed to develop the efficiency of preschools and increase parental choice. Rather than a free entitlement, as early years education is in England, parents of children aged 3–6 years are provided with a (non-means-tested) voucher to contribute to the cost of ECEC (Li et al., 2008).

Ensuring quality

In England and Hong Kong, what constitutes good-quality ECEC has been elaborated in a curriculum framework (i.e. Early Years Foundation Stage in England and Guide to Pre-primary Curriculum in Hong Kong) and a set of regulatory guidelines (i.e. Office for Standards in Education (Ofsted) criteria in England and performance indicators in Hong Kong). To improve preschool effectiveness, the Hong Kong Government has used performance indicators to evaluate preschools on different aspects of their performance, including children's development, management and organization, learning and teaching, support to children, and school culture. Quality criteria for learning and teaching are built on age appropriateness, individual uniqueness, and responsive practice. These three basic tenets were originally drawn from developmentally appropriate practice of the National Association for the Education of Young Children (NAEYC) (Wien, 1996). There are questions surrounding the relevancy of these Western educational ideologies for ECEC in Hong Kong, which historically has been influenced by Chinese culture. For example, a traditional instruction approach focused on rote learning and memorization has long been perceived by local teachers as effective for good teaching despite the upgrading of professional qualifications in recent years (Li, 2003; see also Chapter 12).

To further enhance the quality of ECEC in Hong Kong, the Quality Review Framework was formally implemented in 2007. Under the framework, all local preschools are required to develop internal mechanisms for continuous self-improvement, whereby they are responsible for their own development and planning, as well as self-evaluation (Wong and Li, 2010). The Quality Assurance Inspectorate conducts a follow-up inspection to provide an external review on the preschool performance. The school self-evaluation adopts a 'bottom-up approach' that attempts to enhance quality through the joint efforts and commitment of the school community. It aims to establish and strengthen collaboration among school stakeholders and to build their ownership of quality improvement.

In England, minimum standards as set out by Ofsted in the Early Years Foundation Stage (EYFS) are required for all ECEC sectors. Similar to Hong Kong, ECEC services are graded on their quality on a four-point scale ranging from poor to outstanding. Each ECEC provider is required to complete a Self-Evaluation Form (SEF) to fulfil the inspection. On this form, service providers have to provide evidence of how they have met the quality criteria set out in the EYFS. They also need to consult with parents as a demonstration that they consider their needs when improving quality. The inspectors then verify whether the comments in the SEF are consistent with the actual service performance. Policy-makers assume that this inspection process will result in 'improvement through inspection' (Ehren and Visscher, 2006). How effective this inspection is will depend on several factors, including the relationship between the inspector and the school, communication during the inspection, the characteristics of feedback from inspection, the school's reactions, and the availability of external support (Ehren and Visscher, 2006). That is, inspections do not necessarily lead to quality improvement in the English context. Indeed, the inspection system has been viewed and interpreted by service providers as being problematic (Matthews and Sammons, 2004; Campbell-Barr, 2010).

In addition to monitoring the minimum standards of ECEC, both the governments of England and Hong Kong offer systems of funding to support the provision and consumption of services. Closely coupled with the Quality Review Framework, the introduction of the Pre-primary Education Voucher Scheme (PEVS) by the Hong Kong Government was designed to speed up the pace of quality improvement in 2007. All local preschools are private and driven by market forces. Hence the schools rely on funding from fees for their survival. Therefore, it is essential for most service providers to join the PEVS to secure funding. The condition of getting PEVS is that the preschools have to meet the prescribed minimum standards of performance indicators and to conduct school self-evaluation. In England, for parents to be eligible for subsidized tax credits for the cost of childcare, providers must be registered with Ofsted. The registration requirement also applies to being able to draw down funding to provide the free early years education entitlement.

However, as Cheng (2009) pointed out in the case of Hong Kong, pre-schools improve the quality of their provision for the purpose of attracting parents to 'spend' their vouchers with them. This is consistent with the findings of Ho's (2008) study on leading for quality – parents as consumers have significant influence on the operation of preschools. School principals have to work hard for formulating strategies to satisfy parental demands. There is, therefore, a strong implication that quality improvement in ECEC in Hong Kong is predominantly market driven. However, in England Penn has questioned the effectiveness of the market in securing quality because parents' choice of ECEC provision is subjective, often based on word of mouth, constrained by what people can afford, what is available in the locality, and what is most convenient for their own circumstances (Penn, 2010a, 2010b).

Nevertheless, to a greater or lesser extent, the views of consumers cannot be ignored and as a leader of an ECEC setting in England and Hong Kong, you are expected to meet the subjective quality criteria of parents alongside those set out by policy-makers.

Case Study: England

My experience as a private ECEC provider has indicated that parents select a setting based on location, cost, service, and 'feel'. It is a provider-led market driven by availability. Improvements in information sharing mean that some parents do access Ofsted reports in advance of a first visit, but in my experience these parents do not represent the majority and are generally middle-class. However, in an area with excessive choice, parents will consider inspection outcomes and make comparisons. This is especially noticeable between the large nursery chains. This does not take away from the fact that in a parent's eyes the indicators of quality are interpreted by how their child is cared for, if they are happy to be left at the setting, and if the practitioners are supportive of their needs and confident in their demeanour. Outstanding grades may be a good marketing tool to attract new business but from the point of view of a parent, this is not the overruling factor. As providers we have to wrestle the demands for accountability with Ofsted inspections, quality indicators (such as ECERS [Early Childhood Environmental Rating Scale]), prescriptive curricula (EYFS), and workforce reforms. We have to balance all this with the expectations of our parents wanting good-quality flexible childcare in an increasingly competitive market. It is important to remember the child in all this!

(Nursery owner of two settings in England)

Case Study: Hong Kong

The ecology of early childhood education in Hong Kong is complex and has many paradoxical aspects. Free competition among schools promotes parental choice and diversity of service provision. The advantage of this situation is that schools have autonomy in making decisions on curriculum design and its implementation. On the other hand, schools also have to consider parental preferences and adjust the curriculum to attract pupils in order to ensure that schools are viable. For a principal, it is an inescapable responsibility to keep improving the school. To some extent, the new quality assurance system raises public confidence that established standards are being maintained and schools are providing quality services. In the new system, external inspectors provide advice on quality improvement, but if these inspectors are not well-informed, or if they do not have contextual understandings of the complexity of teaching and learning and are not sympathetic to the developments in the schools, they will simply act as external critics of the schools and judge the performance of schools in the traditional, top-down way. If that happens, the whole thrust of the current reforms will be undermined, and the validity and reliability of inspection outcomes will be called into question. On the other hand, if the school principals do not have the professional confidence to communicate their concerns and queries about inspection reports openly with inspectors, or if they remain silent in order to maintain good relationships between the inspectorate and the school, the quality improvement efforts advocated by local government will be dissipated and become mere personal interpretations.

(Kindergarten principal in Hong Kong)

So what about leadership?

In England and Hong Kong, quality criteria have included standards for ECEC settings to be led by a graduate. Policy drivers in both England and Hong Kong have used the proven link between quality outcomes and highly qualified staff (e.g. Sylva et al., 2004) to make explicit demands on new and existing staff to upskill and thereby improve their professional status. Models of leadership from business and education have been used as a starting point to develop a new body of knowledge and understanding for the leadership of these new, well-qualified teams. Theoretical perspectives and understandings of the practical nature of ECEC leadership have gradually developed within the field involving practitioners and academics but have yet to become sufficiently embedded in the social culture, leaving it vulnerable. The influence of policy drivers and initiatives in the development of ECEC leadership in England has been limited, although the development in 2003 of the National Professional Qualification (NPQICL) by the National College of School Leadership (NCSL), and the publication of the National Standards for Leaders of Sure Start Children's Centres (DfES, 2007) are indicative of a growing interest from politicians in how leadership could/should be manifest in ECEC. Most recently, however, it could be argued that the development of distinct models of ECEC leadership has been seriously affected by changes in policy direction towards a more overt human capital agenda and a reduction of public spending (National College and C4EO, 2011).

Those engaged in the debate surrounding the development of ECEC leadership in England have taken a particular interest in the new leadership paradigms (Northouse, 2010), searching for possible models that focus in particular on the importance of good relationships between adults and children, between communities and community services. The inception of Sure Start children centres and an improved ECEC provision (DfEE, 1998) were designed to address the social justice issues of community engagement, empowerment, and self-determination, as well as engaging with the rhetoric of human capital. As a result, children's centres reflect the dual aims of policy-makers in trying to meet both social and economic objectives (see Campbell-Barr et al., 2011). These important issues were central to the development of the NPQICL (NCSL, 2004; Whalley, 2006) and the National Standards for Children Centre Leaders (DfES, 2007), where an ECEC leader was seen as crucial to developing community relationships and empowering their local communities. This desire for bottom-up models of leadership has taken ECEC away from the top-down business approach involving hierarchies and the central importance of the leader as someone within whom all the essential qualities are manifest (Simkins, 2005, cited in Garvey and Lancaster, 2010) – in other words, a superstar (Quinn Mills, 2005) – towards transformational or distributed leadership (Leeson, 2010) where the leader may be found in the background, as an enabler rather than a director. Thus, ECEC leadership could be regarded as a property of the social context or system (Simkins, 2005, cited in Garvey and Lancaster, 2010) and therefore collaborative and socially constructed by those engaged in the processes. Certainly, the role of the market in shaping the quality of provision would appear to sit comfortably with the notion of a socially constructed and locally situated understanding of quality. The question then becomes, what style of leadership will best achieve this?

In Hong Kong, we have seen a similar, although more recent, shift from a top-down highly bureaucratic style of leadership towards more collaborative, participative models (Ho, 2012; Leeson et al., 2012). The powerful policy driver of the voucher scheme (PEVS), where settings can only register their participation provided they can demonstrate their work towards improving leadership practice, has helped significantly in making that shift, but the tensions between centralization and decentralization still exists, hindering the process. Further problems lie in the strong consumerist influence of parental preference, which has also curtailed some of the actions that might have been taken. Nevertheless, a distributive practice of leadership appears to be gradually emerging in ECEC in Hong Kong.

Both distributed and transformational models of leadership have a core belief that leadership can be transformative through concentrating on developing relationships. Transformational leadership encourages the leader to develop the workforce through empowerment (Burns, 1978; Bass, 1985; Van Maurik, 2001; Goleman et al., 2002), whereas distributed leadership extends this principle to include leadership itself – anyone can be a leader at any level of the organization (Owen, 2000; Gronn, 2002; Hartley, 2007). Distributed leadership acknowledges that the superstar leader is unlikely and undesirable, and that the tasks of leaders are too complex and multi-variant for one person or a small team of people to do. Using the skills and attributes of everyone within the organization enables completion of tasks as well as encouraging the collaboration and interdependence that is required to develop sustainable learning communities, usually created within a non-hierarchical collaborative network, separated from the managerial power (Aubrey, 2007). Distributed leadership requires a shift towards adaptability, expecting settings to share decision-making or delegate responsibilities for decision-making, which, in a structure that previously valued top-down approaches, may be difficult to embrace.

Influenced by work coming from Australasia (Macpherson, 2009) and the United States (Goleman et al., 2002; Avolio and Gardner, 2005), both models have been embraced by ECEC leaders and have begun to have a significant impact upon the more established discourse of educational leadership, challenging previously held models of headteacher leadership (National Professional Qualification for Headship; DfEE, 1999) to make a shift towards more egalitarian, shared practices.

However, as we have seen, leadership is not just about responding to the needs of a given community, it is also about meeting policy objectives. Meeting quality criteria as laid out by governments is one aspect of this policy context, but it goes further. The policy context is also about recognizing the role that ECEC has in meeting objectives around child development, child wellbeing, parental employment, and so on. As stated earlier, quality criteria will be those that best ensure that the policy objectives for investing in ECEC are being met; human capital models highlight that effective provision is that which will ensure economic returns. The current financial climate suggests that this will become more prevalent.

Discussion

The financial difficulties of the last two to three years in England have the potential to derail recent leadership developments. The new ECEC leadership models are insufficiently embedded, and their merits and aspirations are poorly understood by the wider community outside of ECEC settings, especially politicians and policy-makers. We now see virtual leaders with jurisdiction over several settings with an inevitable move away from the relatively flat hierarchy required by transformational or distributed leadership towards a hierarchical structure involving senior management teams and task orientations. One might argue that this could still fit within a distributed leadership framework, but what might also be argued is that this is a clear example of the theory being corrupted to allow an arm's length leadership to take place; where the structure is hierarchical and the core business is task-oriented and performance related, this permits outcome-driven work to take precedence (Hartley, 2007) and loses the culture of collaborative work (Aubrey, 2007) that was and is important to the identity of ECEC leaders. The current requirement seems to be for a leader who is able to make extremely hard decisions in tough economic times to maintain some level of service (National College and C4EO, 2011). In other words, what is required is a chief executive, something that has already been evidenced where private businesses have taken over 'failing' schools and hospitals, even when they have no knowledge or expertise in that line of work.

One of the core difficulties that keeps resurfacing is a lack of clarity over what is meant by leadership of ECEC settings – are we looking at models of leadership or styles of management? Certainly in England at the present time, we could argue that we are operating in a space where management practices are preferred – balancing the books, identifying business opportunities, and minimizing risky decisions (Leeson, 2010). The role of the chief executive seems to have corrupted the role of leader with demands to be frugal, to limit vision and aspiration – to do more with less. If this is the situation, then a model of transformative leadership will be seriously threatened, even rendered impossible. The rise of distributed leadership seems, therefore, inevitable if we accept the criticisms of Hartley (2007) and Harris (2007) that it can be manipulated to 'fit' any situation and can become a diaspora rather than a reality.

Conclusions

We strongly believe that quality ECEC is fundamentally important for children, families, and society, but we wish to question the way in which ECEC has been valued politically and the consequences of this for ECEC leaders. The link between what is an assessable outcome and what is regarded as quality provision runs the risk of undermining the full range of outcomes that ECEC contributes towards (see Chapter 1, p. 4). The human capital framework means that priority is given to educational attainment over and above social competencies. Yet the interplay of the market, the role of Self-Evaluation Forms in both England and Hong Kong, along with the move to a bottom-up approach to quality improvement in Hong Kong suggest that there is scope for ECEC to reclaim the social in developing the quality of their services. In responding to the needs of consumers and the communities in which they live, there is the potential to broaden understandings of what is important in ECEC beyond human capital perspectives.

Find Out More

- Both England and Hong Kong have adopted self-evaluation as a part of the ongoing commitment to improve quality. Do you complete a self-evaluation? If so, do you do this as a team? Who leads the process? Can you relate the leadership of the self-evaluation to any of the above models?
- We have discussed that quality criteria reflect the policy objectives of a country, particularly in relation to economic aspirations. What quality criteria exist in your own context? Do you feel they reflect social or economic objectives or both?
- We have explored current models of ECEC leadership that place importance on the development of sustainable learning communities. What styles of leadership are you aware of in ECEC settings in your own context? How does the leadership impact upon the quality of education and care that the children experience?

References and recommended reading

Aubrey, C. (2007) *Leading and Managing in the Early Years*. London: Sage.

Avolio, B.J. and Gardner, W.L. (2005) Authentic leadership development: getting to the roots of positive forms of leadership, *Leadership Quarterly*, 16: 315–38.

Bass, B. (1985) *Leadership and Performance Beyond Expectation*. New York: Free Press.

Bertram, T. and Pascal, C. (2002) *Early Years Education: An International Perspective*. London: Qualifications and Curriculum Authority.

Burns, J. (1978) *Leadership*. New York: Harper & Row.

Cable, C. and Miller, L. (2011) *Professionalization, Leadership and Management in the Early Years*. London: Sage.

Calman, L. and Tarr-Whelan, L. (2005) *Early Childhood Education for All: A Wise Investment*. New York: Legal Momentum.

Campbell-Barr, V. (2010) The research, policy and practice triangle in early childhood education and care, in R. Parker-Rees, C. Leeson, J. Willan and J. Savage (eds.) *Early Childhood Studies: An Introduction to the Study of Children's Lives and Worlds*. Exeter: Learning Matters.

Campbell-Barr, V. and Garnham, A. (2010) *What Parents Want: Parents and Childcare – A Literature Review*. Manchester: Equality and Human Rights Commission. Available at: http://www.equalityhumanrights.com/advice-and-guidance/here-for-everyone-here-for-business/working-better/ (accessed 7 June 2012).

Campbell-Barr, V.J.G., Lavelle, M. and Wickett, K. (2011) Exploring alternative approaches to child outcome assessments in Children's Centres, *Early Child Development and Care*, 182(7): 859–74.

Cheng, Y.C. (2009) Educational reforms in Hong Kong in the last decade: reform syndrome and new developments, *International Journal of Educational Management*, 23(1): 65–86.

Department for Education and Employment (DfEE) (1998) *Meeting the Childcare Challenge* (Green Paper). London: HMSO.

Department for Education and Employment (DfEE) (1999) *National College for School Leadership: A Prospectus*. London: DfEE.

Department for Education and Skills (DfES) (2007) *National Standards for Leaders of SureStart Children's Centres*. London: HMSO.

Ehren, M. and Visscher, A. (2006) Towards a theory on the impact of school inspections, *British Journal of Educational Studies*, 54(1): 51–72.

Garvey, D. and Lancaster, A. (2010) *Leadership for Quality in Early Years and Playwork*. London: NCB.

Goleman, D., Boyatzis, R. and McKee, A. (2002) *The New Leaders*. London: Little Brown.

Gronn, P. (2002) Distributed leadership as a unit of analysis, *Leadership Quarterly*, 13(4): 423–51.

Harris, A. (2007) Distributed leadership: conceptual confusion and empirical reticence, *International Journal of Leadership in Education*, 10(3): 315–25.

Hartley, D. (2007) The emergence of distributed leadership in education: why now?, *British Journal of Educational Studies*, 55(2): 202–14.

Heckman, J.J. (2000) *Invest in the Very Young*. Chicago, IL: Ounce of Prevention Fund and the University of Chicago Harris School of Public Policy Studies.

Ho, C.W.D. (2008) Exploring the definitions of quality early childhood programmes in a market-driven context: case studies of two Hong Kong preschools, *International Journal of Early Years Education*, 16(3): 223–36.

Ho, D. (2012) The paradox of power in leadership in early childhood education, *Peabody Journal of Education*, 87(2): 253–66.

Ho, D., Campbell-Barr, V. and Leeson, C. (2010) Quality improvement in early years settings in Hong Kong and England, *International Journal of Early Years Education*, 18(3): 241–56.

Leeson, C. (2010) Leadership in early childhood settings, R. Parker-Rees, C. Leeson, J. Willan and J. Savage (eds.) *Early Childhood Studies: An Introduction to the Study of Children's Lives and Worlds*. Exeter: Learning Matters.

Leeson, C., Campbell-Barr, V. and Ho, D. (2012) Leading for quality improvement: a comparative research agenda in early childhood education in England and Hong Kong, *International Journal of School Leadership*, 15(2): 221–36.

Li, H., Wong, J.M.S. and Wang, C.X. (2008) Chinese views of Early Childhood Education Voucher: an Internet study of Hong Kong case, *International Journal of Early Childhood*, 40(2): 49–63.

Li, Y.L. (2003) What makes a good kindergarten teacher? A pilot interview study in Hong Kong, *Early Child Development and Care*, 173(1): 19–31.

Lloyd, E. (2008) The interface between childcare, family support and child poverty strategies under New Labour: tensions and contradictions, *Social Policy and Society*, 7(4): 479–94.

Macpherson, R. (2009) The professionalisation of educational leadership: implications of recent international policy research in leadership development for Australasian education systems, *Journal of Educational Leadership, Policy and Practice*, 24(1): 53–117.

Matthews, P. and Sammons, P. (2004) *Improvement through Inspection: An Evaluation of the Impact of Ofsted's Work*. London: Ofsted.

National College and C4EO (2011) *Resourceful Leadership: Leading for Outcomes in a Time of Shock*. Nottingham: National College for Leadership of Schools and Children's Services. Available at: http://www.c4eo.org.uk/themes/files/leading_for_outcomes_in_a_time_of_shock.pdf (accessed 7 June 2012).

National College of School Leadership (NCSL) (2004) *National Professional Qualification in Integrated Centre Leadership (NPQICL)*. Nottingham: NCSL.

Northouse, P.G. (2010) *Leadership: Theory and Practice* (5th edn.). London: Sage.

Organization for Economic Cooperation and Development (OECD) (2006) *Starting Strong II: Early Childhood Education and Care*. Paris: OECD Publications.

Opper, S. (1992) *Hong Kong's Young Children: Their Preschools and Families*. Hong Kong: University of Hong Kong Press.

Owen, H. (2000) *In Search of Leaders*. London: Wiley.

Penn, H. (2010a) Shaping the future: how human capital arguments about investment in early childhood are being (mis)used in poor countries, in N. Yelland (ed.) *Contemporary Perspective on Early Childhood Education*. Maidenhead: Open University Press.

Penn, H. (2010b) *The Debate about Quality in the Private For-profit Childcare Market*, Social Policy Association Conference, Lincoln, 6 July. Available at: http://www.social-policy.org. uk/lincoln/Penn.pdf (Quick view accessed 7 June 2012).

Quinn Mills, D. (2005) Asian and American leadership styles: how are they unique?, *Harvard Business School Working Knowledge*. Available at: http://hbswk.hbs.edu/item/4869. html (accessed 7 June 2012).

Sylva, K., Melhuish, E., Sammons, P., Siraj-Blatchford, I. and Taggart, B. (2004) *The Effective Provision of Pre-School Education (EPPE) Project: Final Report – A Longitudinal Study Funded by the DfES 1997–2004*, Sure Start Research Report, SSU/FR/2004/01. Nottingham: DCSF.

Van Maurik, J. (2001) *Writers on Leadership*. London: Penguin.

Whalley, M. (2006) Leadership in integrated centres and services for children and families – a community development approach: engaging with the struggle, *Children's Issues*, 10(2): 8–13.

White, L.A. (2011) The internationalization of early childhood education and care issues: framing gender justice and child well-being, *Governance: An International Journal of Policy Administration and Institutions*, 24(2): 285–309.

Wien, C.A. (1996) Time, work, and developmentally appropriate practice, *Early Childhood Research Quarterly*, 11(3): 377–403.

Wong, M.N.C. and Li, H. (2010) From external inspection to self-evaluation: a study of quality assurance in Hong Kong kindergartens, *Early Education and Development*, 21(2): 205–33.

11

INDIA: EARLY CHILDHOOD EDUCATORS IN CHANGING PATTERNS OF EARLY CHILDHOOD EDUCATION AND CARE

Chandrika Devarakonda

Summary

This chapter focuses on early childhood provision from an Indian perspective. It explores a range of key issues around early childhood provision prevalent in India. Reference is made to significant research studies, legislation, and government initiatives, as well as the role of non-governmental organizations in early childhood provision. Traditional morals and values, and changing constructions of childhood in contemporary Indian society with an influence on early childhood provision will be discussed.

Key terms

ICDS: Integrated Child Development Services – a government-initiated programme providing a wide range of services to children and their families from disadvantaged communities.

Anganwadi: a community-based centre, where all the activities related to ICDS are coordinated and delivered to children and their families from disadvantaged communities.

Anganwadi worker: a person from the community who is responsible for implementing the ICDS programme of the anganwadi, which is located on the doorstep of the community.

Balwadi: a balwadi provides preschool education to children aged 3–5 years in urban areas where children from poor families cannot access preschool provision provided by government (Anganwadi), private sources or non-governmental organizations.

Case Study: A day in the life of a child in India

A child might start attending a preschool after his or her third birthday. Depending on the age of the child, the type of setting or the circumstances of the parents (if both parents are working), a child will spend from three hours to a full day in the setting. The compulsory age at which a child starts school is 6 years.

Preschool children aged 3–5 years attend an early childhood setting usually referred to as a nursery, crèche, play group, kindergarten or Montessori school, depending on the age of the child or the location of the setting – rural, urban or tribal area. A child's day can run from 8.30 am to 10.30 am, 11 am to 1 pm, 8.30 am to 3 pm or 8.30 am to 6 pm. Most children are sent to a setting close to home unless it is a nursery attached to a popular school in a large city. The child is usually dropped off by one of the parents around 8.30 am. The child may finish at 12 noon, 3.30 pm or even 6.30 pm. The routine, curriculum, and resources provided may differ from one setting to another.

For Maya, aged 2 years, the activities are informal. The day usually starts with registration and prayer followed by playtime, both indoors and outdoors, and then story time and home time. There will also be a wide range of activities stimulating all-round development. If Maya stays longer than three hours in the setting, lunch, sleep time, and snack time are also included.

For a child between 3 and 6 years, the activities focus on formal and basic education emphasizing reading and writing. The typical day for Karan, a 4-year-old child attending lower kindergarten, might focus on activities related to reading, writing, and numbers, preparing her for primary school. Children may be expected to know alphabets, be aware of a wide range of concepts, shapes, colours, numbers, and objects, as well as listen to stories, sing nursery rhymes, and play both indoors and outdoors. Karan returns home around 4 pm and might have homework to do.

Introduction

Early childhood programmes are a priority for many governments to ensure children are healthier and develop well in all areas. Provision of early childhood care and education is one of the six Education for All (EFA) goals. Governments have been urged to expand access and improve quality of early childhood care and education (ECCE) services. The Dakar Framework for Action prioritized early childhood as, 'Goal 1: Expanding and improving comprehensive early childhood care and education, especially for the most vulnerable and disadvantaged children' (UNESCO, 2000).

According to figures of the Ministry of Home Affairs, Government of India (2011), India has the largest population of children in the world, totalling 158 million aged from birth to 6 years. Early childhood education and care is provided mainly by three distinct means: public, private, and non-governmental organizations (NGOs). The Government of India provides early childhood provision under the preschool component of Integrated Child Development Services (ICDS), mainly for children from disadvantaged families. The ICDS includes a package of integrated services for children aged from birth to 6 years and their families, which includes not only preschool education, but also the provision of supplementary nutrition and health education to members of the community, immunization and referral services to pregnant and lactating mothers and their children to break the vicious cycle of malnutrition, morbidity, and mortality of children.

In government schools, a child attends a pre-primary class for one year before Class 1 in primary school, whereas in many of the private schools, pre-primary consists of two or even three years, variously known as lower kindergarten, upper kindergarten, pre-nursery, nursery, and preparatory. In addition, 'crèche' is a common term used to indicate informal care as well as the pre-primary education some schools offer. There are also 'play schools', which are exclusively for younger children and usually run for two to three years. Parents prepare to send their 2- to 2½-year-old children to preschool.

Preschool provision offered by the private sector was initially available for children from wealthy and elite families and in urban areas based on affordability. However, they are increasingly popular with children from underprivileged families as well those of the privileged rich, middle class. In the current context, nurseries have been extended to small towns and villages, semi-urban and urban slums, attracting children and their families of different socio-economic status in addition to the statutory crèches. Parents seem to be attracted by 'quality' provision proclaimed by the settings as well as English medium teaching in contrast to the regional languages used in government settings. Some children from disadvantaged families are able to access these services, funded by international and national NGOs.

Constitutional provision

India is a vast country and is a union of 28 states and seven Union territories. India follows a parliamentary system of government with the nation as a whole governed centrally and the states each having their own state government.

Historically, early childhood provision in India has been accessed by a small percentage of children due to the nature of the extended family involved in the care of young children. However, in the past few years, the structure of families has changed dramatically due to the movement of families seeking better jobs, leaving parents with little support for childcare. Furthermore, there has been an increase in female employment, resulting in a need for quality childcare provision.

Families that choose not to use preschool provision provided by the government, perhaps due to perceptions of the poor quality of the preschool component, prefer to use private fee-paying nurseries, some of which are part of primary schools. Preschool provision is referred to as kindergarten and is divided into two stages: children aged 3–4 years begin in lower kindergarten (LKG) and children aged

4–5 years are in upper kindergarten (UKG). After finishing upper kindergarten, a child enters Class 1 of primary school.

Legislation and policy influencing early childhood in India has changed dramatically over the last few decades, with an emphasis now on ECCE. Article 21 of the Indian Constitution recommends free and compulsory education for children up to 14 years; the 86th Amendment to the Constitution divides the 0–14 age group into two cohorts: birth to 6 years and 6 to 14 years. Article 45 notes that the 'state shall endeavour to provide ECCE for all children until they complete the age of six years'. In 1968, the Education Commission emphasized preschool education. The National Policy on Education (NPE) (Government of India, 1986) addressed the role of ECCE to prepare children for primary education as well as to support working women, leading to an expansion of ECCE. This was followed in 2005 by a national plan of action for children, resulting in increased enrolment of children into preschool provision.

ECCE was an essential part of India's first 'five-year plan', five-year plans being the country-wide economic development plans devised by the government. The preschool sector was dominated by voluntary and private provision during the first three five-year plans. This resulted in preschool provision being available to elite families mainly in urban areas. The fourth five-year plan was significant in extending provision of comprehensive welfare services to rural areas, enabling other families to be become involved. The fifth five-year plan initiated ICDS focusing on holistic development of the child. ICDS is a central government programme with state governments supporting its implementation. The tenth five-year plan reiterated strengthening of the preschool education aspect of ICDS by improving the training of anganwadi workers (early childhood practitioners).

Most government-initiated programmes that can be accessed are either free or heavily subsidized for families from disadvantaged areas. In 2002, the Ministry of Women and Child Development launched a new crèche scheme called Rajiv Gandhi National Crèche scheme for working mothers, providing preschool as well as care of children. There are 22,038 crèches accessed by 0.55 million children across the country. This programme is mainly accessible in rural and tribal areas where there is a lack of other services. It provides services to children aged from birth to 6 years, including supplementary nutrition, emergency medicines, and contingency services.

Sarva Shiksha Abhiyaan (SSA) is a government initiative introduced in 2000–2001 in response to the universalization of elementary education to provide good-quality education in collaboration with community settings. This initiative supports the opening of new early childhood provision in areas not covered by ICDS. Sarva Shiksha Abhiyaan is also involved in strengthening the preschool education component of ICDS as well as the setting up of balwadis (child gardens) as innovative early childhood interventions.

The last few decades saw an unprecedented expansion of private early childhood initiatives, usually providing child care for a wide range of young children aged 1–3 years. Some preschools and nurseries are part of private schools. These are fee-charging and profit-making initiatives and include family and day care

Table 11.1 Coverage under various ECEC initiatives

Programmes	Number of centres	Coverage
ICDS	767,680[a]	24 million
Rajiv Gandhi National Crèche Scheme for the Children of Working Mothers	22,038[b]	0.55 million, with 25 children per crèche
Pre-primary school	38,533	(1, 94,000) ~0.02 million[c]
NGO services for ECCE		Varies from 3 to 20 million
Private initiatives		~10 million (2005)[d]

[a]Ministry of Women and Child Development (as of 31 December 2005).
[b]Ministry of Women and Child Development website (www.wcd.nic.in).
[c]Early Childhood Care and Education – An Overview (Ministry of Human Resource Development, 2003).
[d]Report of the National Focus Group on ECE appointed by NCERT under the initiative of the National Curriculum Framework Review, 2005.
Source: Ministry of Women and Child Development (2007).

centres, nurseries, kindergartens, and pre-primary classes in private primary schools. Although found mainly in urban areas, they have been extended more recently to semi-urban and rural areas.

A range of voluntary and corporate initiatives also exists. These include those funded by national and international aid agencies, trusts in socially and economically backward areas, as well as special communities in different and difficult circumstances such as mobile crèches for construction workers. Several international organizations, including Action Aid, the World Bank, Save the Children, Oxfam, CARE, and Plan International have been involved in a range of activities promoting holistic care and education of children, especially those from disadvantaged families. Organizations such as the Bernard Van Leer Foundation, the Oxford Department for International Development (DfID), and British Council have encouraged research into ECCE by sponsoring collaboration and networking between individuals and organizations in different countries to share good practice and engage in joint research projects. Save the Children sponsors *Young Lives*, a longitudinal research study on childhood poverty across four countries tracking 12,000 children. Coverage of ECEC under these different initiatives is summarized in Table 11.1.

History of early childhood education in India

Early childhood education in India has been widely influenced by Maria Montessori and her principles. One of the first kindergartens was established in the 1890s and Gijubhai Badheka and Tarabai Modak pioneered several early childhood settings and teacher training centres in Gujarat, a state in Western India. However, these early childhood settings were mainly in urban areas and in specific regions where parents could afford to pay for their children to attend.

The Central Social Welfare Board, created in 1953, sponsored voluntary organizations in setting up early childhood settings for children from disadvantaged families known as balwadis. The main objective of this programme was to shift the focus from preschool education to the all-round development of the child. A need for trained workers who were able to foster the growth and holistic development of children from disadvantaged families in rural areas was realized. This resulted in the term 'balsevika' (one who serves the child), with the Bal Sevika Training (BST) programme being launched in 1961 by the Indian Council for Child Welfare. The BST focused on health and nutrition, preschool education, and community organization. Although the effectiveness of this initiative was significant, the size of the country limited its impact. One of the major criticisms of this programme is that the balwadis were located mainly in urban or semi-urban areas and were accessed by affluent families and not children from disadvantaged families. Furthermore, the emphasis was mainly on basic formal education rather than on the all-round development of the child.

The launch of ICDS in 1974 provided a major breakthrough in the provision of a range of services to disadvantaged families. The initiative started with 33 projects reaching about 150,000 young children. It has expanded to nearly 7015 projects reaching 35,502,137 children aged 3–6 years provided by nearly one and a quarter million anganwadi centres (anganwadi is translated as courtyard garden, a term borrowed from the local language) (Ministry of Women and Child Development, 2010). The programmes concentrate on urban slums, tribal areas, and the more remote and backward rural regions of the country.

The main objective of ICDS is to provide opportunities for children to develop holistically. The ICDS package consists of the following basic services:

- supplementary nutrition;
- immunization;
- health check-ups and referrals;
- preschool education for children aged 3–6 years;
- health and nutrition for women.

The focal point for the delivery of these services is the anganwadi. An anganwadi centre is likely to be located in the courtyard of a village home and serves a population of one thousand people. Its working hours are from 9 am to 4 pm on all working days. However, several anganwadi workers tend to be flexible and maintain an open door policy. On average, 120 children access services from a single anganwadi centre. The age distribution of children accessing the services of an anganwadi centre is roughly as follows: age from birth to 6 months, five children; age 1–2 years, fifteen children; age 2–3 years, twenty children; and age 3–6 years, forty children.

Staffing

An anganwadi worker is usually a woman familiar with the local community and is the key worker responsible for all the services provided in the centre. She is considered to be a paraprofessional who is a committed agent of social change, able to mobilize support from the community to provide services. Anganwadi workers usually have basic qualifications and are knowledgeable about the needs of the community. This enables anganwadi workers to empathize with families and have a good understanding of the issues impacting them. Due to her close relationship with the families, the majority of the local community trust the anganwadi worker, including men and community leaders, who are able to confide in and share their problems with her. She coordinates and collaborates with professionals and agencies in the community to provide appropriate services to the children and their families. The anganwadi worker is also expected to make home visits to identify children, and to review and monitor the needs of children and families (NIPCCD, 2006). She is also responsible for recording all the activities in relation to the package of services. A supervisor monitors the anganwadi worker and helps resolve issues related to the running of the anganwadi. Each anganwadi worker receives support from a helper and on some occasions by women (adolescent girls and mothers) from the community.

The Department of Women and Child Welfare provides thorough training to every anganwadi worker and helper for one month at training centres in different states of the country. The centres provide training in early childhood care and development, nutrition and health, communication, advocacy and community participation, and management of an anganwadi. The practice of anganwadi workers is also supervised when on placement. There are opportunities for anganwadi workers to attend refresher training courses every two years for two weeks.

Legislation

The Right of Children to Free and Compulsory Education Act 2009 or Right to Education Act (RTE) legalized the right to education for 6- to 14-year-olds, paving the way for children above the age of 3 years to be prepared for elementary education. The Act, which came into force on 1 April 2010, made it mandatory for private educational institutions to reserve 25% of places for children from disadvantaged families.

However, as pre-primary education is not yet covered by legislation, it is not monitored by any regulatory body. Private nurseries are driven mainly by profit, so the quality of the provision is inconsistent. In their report entitled *Report of the Committee on Pre-primary and Preschool Education in Delhi*, Chona et al. (2007) state that it is not just the preschools that are responsible for the inconsistent quality, parents are as well. They note:

> It appears that many parents feel that their children should get a head start in the rat race of academic success and expect the pre-primary class to make their children adept in reading, writing and arithmetic. There are also parents who send their 3-year-old children for private tuition after their 'regular' school hours!

(Chona et al., 2007: 6)

Curriculum

An ideal preschool curriculum emphasizes providing young children with opportunities to develop in a holistic and integrated way. However, it is common in preschools to find children learning by rote without understanding the concepts. Furthermore, children are assessed on their ability to remember the information memorized and to recite mechanically. The Yashpal Committee, in its report entitled *Learning without Burden* (NCERT, 1993), states that 'deeply harmful practices in preschools and primary schools such as early emphasis on shapely drawing, writing and memorizing information' (NCERT, 1993: 11) result in a lot of stress and anxiety for the children. 'A curriculum policy that takes away the elements of joy and inquiry from learning obviously contributes to the rate at which children leave school in the early years' (Chona et al., 2007: 11).

The Yashpal Committee recommended an activity-oriented and play-based curriculum, including play activities, physical activities, group activities, physical training including simple exercises and dance, manual activities, sensorial education, handwork and artistic activities including finger skills, drawing, painting, music, personal hygiene, and self service. The spirit of the recommendations lies in providing informal, activity-rich, and interesting learning experiences for the children. Some schools are influenced by ideas from other countries, such as the Montessori movement, which emphasizes child-initiated learning as well enabling a child to learn through play in a stress-free environment. In contrast, the committee on ECE appointed by the Government of India in 2004 reported that parents expected their children to be proficient in academic subjects, especially English – speaking, reading, and writing. The economic and social progress made by many families has enabled them to access private English medium schools rather than the government initiatives. The private sector has capitalized on this awareness of the importance of preschool education, and this has resulted in a rising number of preschool and English medium schools.

Debates and controversies

Few schools offer a holistic and healthy developmental environment for children of pre-primary age. The increased focus on formal learning in the early years has resulted in some schools and parents perceiving that young children need an academic, teacher-directed curriculum, thus demonstrating little understanding of and sensitivity to the needs of children. There is wide variation in the quality and interpretation of services provided by different early childhood settings in the country. Very often, physical comforts such as temperature regulation and the display of colourful resources are equated with high-quality settings. Relationships between practitioners and parents are very formal. Some preschool settings are as structured as a primary school, with formal methods of teaching and sometimes the environment may contribute little to the holistic development of young children. Several preschools use a range of strategies in the admission process that are not reflective of the setting's philosophy and vision; some private nurseries follow rigorous admission procedures, with the parents and their child being interviewed by a panel of experts. In admission tests, young children are tested on their academic skills – reading, writing, and numeracy – and at interview, they are assessed for their general knowledge and asked to perform specific tasks which they will be expected to perform in the year following admission. Furthermore, the parents may be interviewed on their commitment and ability to support their child with homework. Most nurseries follow this practice in spite of the government's warning not to put pressure on children and their parents. Parents, however, endeavour to gain admission for their child to a preschool that will confirm a place in a popular primary school, especially in big cities (Chona et al., 2007).

Most private nurseries do not expect their staff to possess any relevant qualifications or experience, and there are limited opportunities for regular training and to share good practice. The quality of care and education provided by settings to children are not monitored by any authorities. Training for the nursery workforce is inconsistent, and sometimes non-existent in some settings. Some of the key concerns around early childhood education relate to formal learning and the homework involved, assessments that children have to undertake before admission into a nursery, and formative and summative examinations on a regular basis.

Globalization has raised awareness of diverse and popular international perspectives of early childhood education, including Reggio Emilia, Montessori, and HighScope. Some private nurseries are influenced by these philosophies, but their implementation is diluted and often influenced by local values and practices. Montessori schools are popular in the major cities in India with some organizations, such as the Indian Montessori Foundation, Indian Montessori Centre, engaged in propagating the principles of Montessori education.

Research evidence

A significant international research project engaged in longitudinal research (from 2000 to 2015) is the Young Lives Project. This is an international study of childhood poverty in four countries – Ethiopia, India, Peru, and Vietnam – involving 12,000 children. In India, the Young Lives Project is based in Andhra Pradesh, the fifth largest state in the country. India is characterized by wide disparities between regions and social groups in relation to poverty, access to welfare programmes and education. The findings indicate that to improve outcomes for children in the long term, more efficient resourcing and effective regulation are needed to strengthen existing services, both public and private.

Some of the findings indicate superficial positive impacts, such as access to early childhood provision as well as improved attendance in primary schools. Qualitative data indicate that parents' priorities have shifted from sending their children to a free preschool that provides a package of services free of cost to a private nursery offering better quality provision and enabling their children to be better prepared for primary school. Furthermore, it is noted that schools expect children to fit into their existing system, and do little to make the school ready for the children's needs. One of the key recommendations of this long-term project is the need to review policies and programmes to ensure the quality of programmes are enhanced and provide equality of access to all children, including those from disadvantaged families (Vennam et al., 2009).

Research indicates a positive impact of early childhood initiatives, especially on the psycho-social and cognitive competencies of children. Several studies conducted by research-active institutions, including the National Institute for Public Cooperation and Child Development (NIPCCD), National Council of Applied Economic Research (NCAER), and National Council for Educational Research and Training (NCERT) report that anganwadi workers have been successful in enabling children to access preschool education-related activities (Datta, 2001).

The excessive workloads of anganwadi workers as well as the emphasis on the nutritional status of children have affected the quality of the preschool education component of the ICDS programme. Mid-term evaluation of the tenth five-year plan suggests the preschool education component of ICDS to be weak, and that the health and nutritional aspects of the programme are the main focus (Government of India, 2007).

Find Out More

- Discuss the major influences on ECCE in India. Compare and contrast these with another country.
- How would you compare these with your own country?
- Critically evaluate the way in which policies have influenced ECCE in India.

References and recommended reading

Bandyopadhyay, M. and Behera, J. (2010) *Pre-primary Education in India*. Create India Policy Brief. Available at: http://www.create-rpc.org/pdf_documents/India_Policy_Brief_1.pdf (accessed 1 December 2011).

Chona, S., Kumar, K., Ganguly, A., Kunnunkal, T.V. and Vyas, V. (2007) *Report of the Committee on Pre-primary and Preschool Education in Delhi*. Available at: www.cbse.nic.in (accessed 20 May 2012).

Cleghorn, A. and Prochner, L. (2003) Contrasting visions of early childhood education: examples from rural and urban settings in Zimbabwe and India, *Journal of Early Childhood Research*, 1(2): 131–53.

Datta, V. (2001) *Job Performance of Anganwadi Workers in Three Districts in Maharashtra: A Project Sponsored by UNICEF*. Mumbai: Tata Institute of Social Sciences (TISS).

Datta, V. (2003) Child care in India: emerging issues and challenges for the 21st century, in *Proceedings of the 7th Early Childhood Convention*, Vol. 2, Nelson, New Zealand.

Galab, S., Kumar, S.V., Reddy, P.R., Singh, R. and Vennam, U. (2011) *The Impact on Childhood Poverty in Andhra Pradesh: Initial Findings from India, Round Three Survey Report*. Delhi: Young Lives.

Government of India (1949) *Constitution of India*. New Delhi: Government of India.

Government of India (1986) *National Policy on Education 1986*. New Delhi: Ministry of Human Resource Development.

Government of India (2007) *Early Childhood Education in the Eleventh Five Year Plan (2007–2012) – Subgroup Report.* New Delhi: Ministry of Women and Child Development.

Gupta, A. (2004) Working with large class size: dispositions of early childhood teachers in India, *Contemporary Issues in Early Childhood*, 5(3): 361–77.

Leghorn, A. and Prochner, L. (2010) *Shades of Globalization in Three Early Childhood Settings: Views from India, South Africa, and Canada.* Rotterdam: Sense Publishers.

Manhas, S. and Qadiri, F. (2010) Comparative study of preschool education in early childhood education centres in India, *Contemporary Issues in Early Childhood*, 11(4): 443–7.

Ministry of Home Affairs (Government of India) (2011) *Provisional Population Totals.* Paper 1 of 2011 India Series 1. Available at: https://staffmail.winchester.ac.uk/owa/UrlBlockedError.aspx>http://www.censusindia.gov.in/2011-prov-results/prov_results_paper1_india.html (accessed 22 January 2012).

Ministry of Women and Child Development (2007) *Working Group on Development of Children for the Eleventh Five Year Plan (2007–2012) – A Report.* Available at: http://wcd.nic.in/wgearlychild.pdf. (accessed 24 May 2012).

Ministry of Women and Child Development (2010) *Integrated Child Development Services Scheme Data Tables.* Available at: http://wcd.nic.in/icdsdatatables.htm. (accessed 11 April 2012).

National Council of Applied Economic Research (NCAER) (2001) *Concurrent Evaluation of ICDS: National Reports.* New Delhi: NCAER.

National Council of Educational Research and Training (NCERT) (1993) *Learning without Burden: Report of the Yashpal Committee.* New Delhi: NCERT.

National Council of Educational Research and Training (NCERT) (2005) *Seventh All India Educational Survey: Provisional Statistics as on September 30, 2002.* New Delhi: NCERT.

National Institute for Public Cooperation and Child Development (NIPCCD) (2006) *Three Decades of ICDS: An Appraisal.* Bangalore: NIPCCD.

National University of Educational Planning and Administration (NUEPA) (2008) *Status of Education in India: National Report.* New Delhi: NUEPA and Department of Higher Education, Ministry of Human Resource Development.

Streuli, N., Vennam, U. and Woodhead, M. (2011) *Increasing Choice or Inequality? Pathways through Early Education in Andhra Pradesh, India.* Working Papers in Early Childhood Development 58. The Hague: Bernard van Leer Foundation.

Vennam, U., Komanduri, A., Cooper, E., Crivello, G. and Woodhead, M. (2009) *Early Childhood Education Trajectories and Transitions: A Study of the Experiences and Perspectives of Parents and Children in Andhra Pradesh, India.* Young Lives Working Paper 52. Oxford: Young Lives, University of Oxford, Department of International Development.

UNESCO (2000) *The Dakar Framework for Action: Education for All – Meeting Our Collective Commitments.* Paris: UNESCO.

UNESCO (2006) *Strong Foundations: Early Childhood Education and Care.* EFA Global Monitoring Report. Paris: UNESCO.

Useful websites

Bernard Van Leer Foundation: http://www.bernardvanleer.org
NIPCCD: http://nipccd.nic.in/
Young Lives: http://www.younglives.org.uk/

12

EARLY CHILDHOOD EDUCATION AND CARE IN THE CZECH REPUBLIC: RECENT DEVELOPMENTS WITHIN A CHANGING SOCIETY

Philip Selbie and Alena Držalová

Summary

Many aspects of preschool provision in the Czech Republic have undergone significant change in recent times. This is due in part to the changes affecting areas of public policy in the most recent European Union states. However, it is also the result of changing perceptions about the role of early education and the contribution of lifelong learning to the wellbeing of individuals in society. This chapter places these changes within the context of recent historical and political events in the country and discusses the developments in practice for those working with very young children. More significantly, the chapter explores the implications for quality within the sector and considers how such changes are likely to affect Czech early childhood education and care in the future.

Introduction

On 1 May 2004, the Czech Republic gained full accession to the European Union (EU) and joined 24 other member countries representing 450 million people in one political and economic arena. Five years earlier, this small nation of about 10.5 million people sharing borders with Germany, Poland, Austria, and Slovakia had also joined NATO (North Atlantic Treaty Organization). Ever since the Czech Velvet Revolution in November 1989 and the subsequent collapse of Communism, the country had been seeking deeper integration with the West and so joining the EU was another important milestone on the journey back into the heart of Europe. The referendum on joining the EU held the previous year showed overwhelming support for the move among the relatively high turnout of 55% with 77% of votes in favour of accession (Lazarová, 2003). There was little in the way of opposition among the mainstream political parties and the public clearly felt that after more than a generation of painful isolation, greater political freedom and the promise of economic prosperity lay ahead.

The Lisbon Strategy adopted by the European Council in 2000 aimed to make the EU 'the most competitive and dynamic knowledge-based economy in the world capable of sustainable economic growth with more and better jobs and greater social cohesion' (European Council, 2000: para. 5). Part of the strategy was to devise a long-term work plan for education, which was eventually finalized and published four years later as *Education and Training 2010* (Council of the European Union, 2004). A year later a progress report was published by the Czech Ministry of Education, Youth and Sports, *Ministerstvo školství, mládeže a tělovýchovy* (MEYS), reporting on the country's implementation of the work plan which made reference to the objectives of *Education and Training 2010* and reform as part of the country's new membership responsibilities: 'accession of the Czech Republic to the European Union means not only a commitment to the pursuit of the objective of long-term development of the European Union, but also a requirement to change the education system as one of the principal preconditions for economic and social development' (MEYS, 2005: 7).

The report endorsed the country's progress in its first year of EU membership and emphasized the compatibility between the objectives of the country's own education policy and those of the EU. Specific attention was drawn to recent national legislation that had sought to reverse some of the poor conditions and low status afforded to those working in education as a result of the previous political and social system. Furthermore, significant changes had begun in relation to curriculum reform so that it was less prescriptive and teaching methods were encouraged to be more learner-centred and less based upon rote memorization. The term 'lifelong learning' began to feature in policy documents and there was also an emphasis on the need for learners to be equipped to take their place within an emerging market economy and a liberal democracy.

One such document was the National Programme for the Development of Education in the Czech Republic (MEYS, 2001) (commonly referred to as the White Paper, *Bílá kniha*), which contained many far-reaching changes to the entire education system, including regulation of compulsory preschool, primary, secondary, as well as tertiary education. The White Paper set out the basis for the Education Act No. 561 of the Czech Republic, which enshrined in law several general goals for all levels of education, the first being 'the personal development of a human being who shall possess knowledge and social competencies, ethical and spiritual values for their personal and civil life, for the execution of a profession or working activities, and for acquiring information and learning in the course of life' (Section 2.2.a). It may be difficult to grasp the significance of this for a nation that had endured such a tightly controlled education system for so long and under which many Czechs had been denied access to post-compulsory education on purely discriminatory grounds.

Some historical background

Early childhood education has a long tradition in the country, dating back to the influential writings of the Moravian bishop and reformer Comenius, *Jan Amos Komenský* (1592–1670). Often referred to as the 'father of modern education', Comenius lived in exile for most of his life and conceived a form of education in complete contrast to the rigid authoritarian system imposed by the ruling Habsburgs. In 1623, Comenius wrote *The School of Infancy* in which he proposed that education for the under 6s was best provided by mothers in the home environment. Outlining in some detail how this should take place, Comenius placed great emphasis on beginning with the child's interests, the importance of language and play, together with the need for young children to learn about the world through practical activity. History is often said to repeat itself and it is perhaps ironic that the concept of 'lifelong learning' was recognized by Comenius when over three centuries earlier he stated in another of his great writings: 'Seneca is therefore right when he says: "Life is long, if we know how to use it. It suffices for the completion of the greatest undertakings, if it be properly employed". It is consequently of importance that we understand the art of making the very best use of our lives' (Comenius, 1638: 110).

Specific reforms to preschool provision were introduced through legislation at the beginning of 2005, although the details were first discussed in a review commissioned by the MEYS almost fifteen years earlier. Not long after the momentous events of 1989, a group of experts in the field of early childhood education met to consider the design of a system of preschool education suitable for a post-communist society. The resulting report (Opravilová et al., 1993) led to several important proposals for preschool provision published eight years later as part of the White Paper.

The impetus for change to early childhood education and care (ECEC) had also gathered momentum after the country joined the Organization for Economic Cooperation and Development (OECD) in 1995. The OECD's Thematic Review of ECEC Policy in the Czech Republic had highlighted certain issues that needed to be addressed at the level of preschool provision in order to support the OECD's long-term aims at the beginning of the twenty-first century. Developing young children's natural disposition towards curiosity and independence was seen as prerequisite for a system of education dedicated to the promotion of lifelong learning, sustainable economic growth, and a rising standard of living. Specifically, the OECD review stated there was a need to 'search for framework solutions to a number of specific ECEC issues', implement 'innovative policy into the present political and pedagogical practice', and 'acquire new insights into addressing issues associated with the rapidly developing preschool context' (MEYS, 2000a: 6).

Provision for 3- to 6-year-olds

Preschool in the Czech Republic is for children between 3 and 6 years and although not compulsory, it is considered a valuable and important part of state provision designed to complement and support a child's natural development within the family. It is governed by the MEYS and classified as Level 0 according to the

International Standard Classification of Education (ISCED). Preschool provision takes place in a kindergarten, *mateřská škola*, which is generally established by the town or municipality in which it is situated and take up is generally high with 79.2% of 3-year-olds, 92.6% of 4-year-olds, and 95.8% of 5-year-olds attending in 2007 (EACEA, 2009: 166). In the major cities especially, private individuals, churches, and businesses may also be granted the authority to establish kindergartens.

The financial resources necessary for the running of the school buildings and purchase of teaching materials are allocated by the founding entity, provided the school is registered with one of the fourteen autonomous regional authorities. Major expenditure such as staff salaries is met through the state budget for education, although this is controlled through the appropriate regional authority provided that the standard of education meets the criteria set down in the appropriate legislation. In addition, it is generally the case that municipal and state funding is supplemented by a small amount of additional income derived from fees paid by parents unless they are receiving social benefits. The headteacher is responsible for calculating the parental contribution, which must not exceed 50% of the running costs and be the same for each child. However, preschools may not levy parents directly for any income in the child's last year before entering compulsory education, since it is legislated that this must remain free (EACEA, 2012).

Provision for under-3s

State-funded crèches, *jesle*, were originally established at the end of the nineteenth century to look after the very youngest children in society and especially those of socially disadvantaged families. Soon after the end of the Second World War, the number of crèches grew significantly as mothers were encouraged to work in state-run agricultural or industrial enterprises. Provision for the under-3s is based around care rather than education and responsibility for crèches has remained with the Ministry of Health since 1960. A common curriculum for both crèches and kindergartens was introduced the year after the Warsaw Pact invasion in 1968, although initially this was a recommendation only for the under-threes; however, as part of tightening political control, ten years later a compulsory curriculum was introduced for the under-3s as well as preschool children (Oberhuemer et al., 2010).

Crèches were a thriving part of the state system and during the height of their popularity around 20% of the very youngest children in society were enrolled in crèches, although this fell to nearer 13% by 1989 and continued to decline rapidly with only 0.6% attending in 2003. Demand fell away after the fall of Communism as many Czechs felt able to turn their backs on an idea that they were never particularly comfortable with and especially as institutionalized care for the very young had become synonymous with the hated political and social system. The subsequent decline in the birth rate in the early 1990s compounded this drop in demand and rendered the need for state-run crèches virtually obsolete (Rabušicová, 2008).

A generous state family policy also helped maintain the low demand for crèches within a society that has traditionally identified early childcare with motherhood. Maternity leave gives a new mother 68% of her previous salary for 28 weeks after the birth of her child followed by the option of a period of parental leave set at 20%

of her previous salary up until the child is 3 years old. In addition, previous employ-
ers are obliged to offer a returning employee a position of a similar status and salary up until the child's third birthday. Should that position not be taken up by the
mother, she may continue her parental leave and financial support from the state
until the child is 4 years old (Oberhuemer et al., 2010). Such a decline in demand is
borne out by statistics which show that while in 1989 there were over 1300 state-run
crèches catering for well over 52,000 children, less than twenty years later only 58
remained with a capacity of 1674, which were mostly used by low-income families
seeking work (Rabušicová, 2008).

Similarly, the demand for preschool provision also declined immediately after
1989; however, the number of kindergartens has remained fairly constant ever since
with figures for 2010–2011 listing around 4800 (MEYS, 2011). While preschool
provision remains healthy in that respect, a noticeable rise in the birth rate in recent
years is now putting pressure on some municipalities where state-run kindergartens
no longer have enough places to cater for the demand. Some kindergartens are
beginning to face pressure to accept children under three as a new generation of
working parents find they are in need of crèche facilities, which are no longer provided in sufficient numbers by the state. This issue is considered further later in the
chapter.

Preschool teaching and learning

While the White Paper introduced the concept of a new teaching and learning
framework to kindergartens in 2001, this was initially on a non-statutory basis until
the final version was published three years later and became law at the beginning
of 2005. The Framework Educational Program for Preschool Education (FEP PE)
(Research Institute of Education, 2004) required kindergartens to work within relatively minimal national guidelines while the detail of teaching and learning was
devolved to the kindergartens themselves.

To support the concept of lifelong learning, the overarching goal of the FEP PE
has three aims: the development of a child's early learning, the acquisition of values
upon which interpersonal relations are based and, finally, the promotion of a sense of
self together with growing personal independence. It is noticeable that the aims and
principles underlying the FEP PE reflect the recommendations of the report from
preschool experts and originally commissioned by the MEYS in the early 1990s.
'The personality-oriented model of preschool education' (Opravilová et al., 1993)
advocated a much more child-centred approach to learning than had previously
been the case and the final version of the FEP PE endorses this as follows:

> Education should run in integrated blocks across 'education areas' or 'folders',
> in which a child is offered educational content in its natural context, links and
> relations. The content of the blocks should be based on the child's life, so that it
> makes sense, is interesting and useful for them. Implementation of these blocks
> provides the child with a wide variety of activities and offers him a deeper expe-
> rience.
>
> (Research Institute of Education, 2004: 7)

The FEP PE also encourages kindergarten teachers to work in close partnership with families so as to deepen the teachers' knowledge of children and adopt the use of practical activities in their teaching. Many of these ideas, including the importance of learning though play, had been considered universal standard practice in early learning for several centuries, although had not been a feature of Czech ECEC for at least a generation. The FEP PE also states that the teacher 'should guide the child on their way to knowledge, stimulate their active interest and desire to look around, listen and discover, instead of assigning tasks and controlling their completion' (Research Institute of Education, 2004: 7).

In keeping with greater freedom within educational policy, the authorities also recognized the potential contribution of 'alternative' forms of education to the development of young children. Provided they met the statutory requirements of the FEP PE, a number of Montessori and Steiner Waldorf kindergartens were established after 1989 and were able to draw funding from municipal and state budgets.

Preschool planning

The FEP PE also introduced a high degree of curricular autonomy for kindergartens to design a School Education Programme (SEP), *Školní vzdělávací program*, which defines the content and form of learning experiences. The responsibility for the SEP lies with the headteacher and must take account of the characteristics of the locality, the expertise of the staff, and the nature of the catchment area from which the children come. Learning experiences must be planned in five interrelated areas of learning: biological, psychological, interpersonal, socio-cultural, and environmental. At the time of planning as well as at the point of teaching, kindergarten teachers are required to ensure the children develop an appropriate level of ability in five key competencies. It is anticipated that by the end of kindergarten each child will be able to demonstrate an appropriate level of competence in Learning, Problem-solving, Communication, Personal and Social affairs, as well as Civics. For example, a child should be able to 'apply his/her experience in practical situations and further learning' (Learning competency), 'communicate with gestures and words, distinguish some symbols, understand their meaning and function' (Communication competency), and 'understand that s/he is allowed to make decisions but can be held responsible for them' (Civic competency). Great significance is placed upon these key competencies, which run throughout compulsory education and represent important prerequisites for lifelong learning.

The interrelationship between the statutory National Educational Framework, the FEP PE, and the local responsibility of the school to design and provide curricular content is illustrated in Figure 12.1. As an example, topics might be planned on a two- or three-year cycle so that each class receives similar input over the period. Each term's topic ensures that the five interrelated areas of learning are covered in a way that will engage the children and support their progress in the key competences. Additional all-year themes such as Physical Education and Environmental Education might complement each term's topics and reflect something of the nature of the school and its location. In an increasing number of Czech kindergartens, the older children receive some early English language tuition and they generally take part in

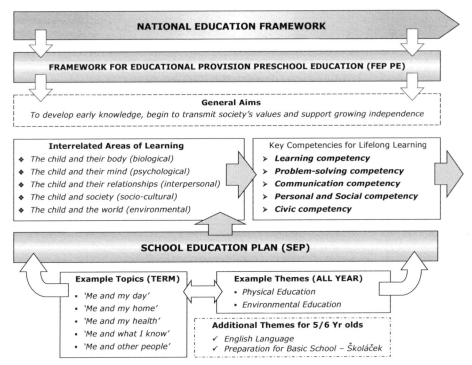

Figure 12.1 A kindergarten's education plan is guided by statutory frameworks in its development of key competencies

a special programme of activities (*Školáček*) designed to help them make the transition to primary school (*Základní škola*).

Preschool and the daily routine

Kindergartens often open as early as 6.00 am, when many take preschool children of working parents who start work at 7.00 am. Depending upon the age of the children, the daily routine is a mixture of planned and spontaneous learning activities based upon the topics and themes set out in the SEP. An example of a typical daily routine is set out in Figure 12.2. Together with plenty of time for outdoor activities such as free play or walks in the neighbourhood, children receive a mid-morning snack and a cooked meal at around midday. Eating food together is considered to be an important opportunity for learning and a time when young children develop their independence as well as their identity as part of a group. Teacher-led learning experiences tend to focus on personal and social development, verbal language skills, creative activities involving music and art, as well as physical activities both indoors and outside. While practical resources in kindergartens include books and early mathematical apparatus, there is no attempt to develop formal reading, writing or mathematical recording skills, because this is not considered an appropriate part of preschool provision.

06:00–07:00	Relaxation and free play for early arriving children
	Morning games, activities and discussions with duty teacher
07:00–08:00	Formal school starts with free play and games with class teacher
	Additional programme - Školáček
08:00–10:00	**Snack**
	Physical activities (including changing into special clothes once a week)
	Teacher-directed activities (in large or small groups or as individuals)
10:00–12:00	Outdoor activities in the school grounds or locality
12:00–12:30	**Lunch**
12:30–14:00	Rest time (according to individual needs)
	Quiet alternative activities for children who do not need sleep
	Additional programme - Školáček
14:00–16:00	Afternoon games and activities
	Teacher-directed activities (in large or small groups or as individuals)

Figure 12.2 Example of a daily programme for preschool children aged 5–6 years

Afternoon sessions always begin with a period of relaxation when children change into their pyjamas before settling down on to prepared beds. Depending upon the age of the class, all the children either listen quietly to a traditional story or fairytale told by their teacher or are encouraged to sleep for at least an hour if they are tired (see Figure 12.3). Sleep is considered to be a necessary and important part of a young child's daily routine to provide rest for the mind and the body as well as giving time for food to digest before the afternoon activities. The FEP PE highlights the importance of this by stating that the daily programme offered by the kindergarten should ensure 'individual children's needs for activity, sleep and rest are respected' (Research Institute of Education, 2004: 31).

Preschool provision and special needs

Significant changes in special needs education at preschool have also taken place alongside the social and political changes of the last twenty years. Prior to 1989 all children with special needs were provided for in special institutions and separated from those in the mainstream. More recently, educational policy has sought to integrate children with special needs into regular preschool provision through the establishing of special needs classes. The FEP PE specifically states that kindergarten teachers with responsibility for children with special needs should

Figure 12.3 Sleep and rest during the early afternoon is an important part of the daily routine

be trained in the field of special education and that the framework 'encourages the integration of children wherever possible with respect to the kind and degree of their disability or handicap' (Research Institute of Education, 2004: 37).

Provision for special needs is based around the principles of strong advisory support from specialists such as speech therapists, cooperation with other special needs classes from other kindergartens, and structured support for parents using self-help groups and specialist advice centres. Early intervention and close partnership with families, including home visits and flexible attendance patterns, are advocated to ensure that the child benefits from the care of the family at home as long as possible. In 2000, there were 593 special needs kindergarten classes and of these 37 were organized by private institutions or churches (MEYS, 2000b). In support of greater integration, it is possible for a child in his or her last year of preschool to remain in a kindergarten environment if it is considered to be in their best interest. This decision is subject to discussion and agreement between the kindergarten and the child's parents and must be supplemented by a report issued by the school nurse. Often as many as 20% of children in their last year of preschool have their transition to primary school deferred by twelve months and do not enter the first year of compulsory education until they reach the age of 7 years. Responsibility for the final decision about any possible deferment ultimately rests with the parents of the child and is evidence of the close cooperation that generally exists between kindergartens and families.

Preschool staff and qualifications

Preschool children are taught by teachers who have graduated from secondary schools specializing in preschool pedagogy. During the four-year programme, nearly half of the time is spent on general education and a third is given over to a vocational part focusing on pedagogical and psychological disciplines and special and social pedagogy. Particular importance is placed on developing skills and knowledge in art, music and sports, which traditionally have been seen as very important in the training of preschool teachers. During the programme, students are also required to complete over 800 hours of supervised practice in the field to gain personal experiences of working with children (MEYS, 2000b).

Since the passing of legislation in 2005, continuing professional development (CPD) opportunities are now possible for staff wishing to deepen their knowledge, with the fees paid either by the kindergarten (at the discretion of the headteacher) or from the state education budget provided the course is accredited by the MEYS. In addition, kindergarten teachers are entitled to twelve days paid study leave per year for the purpose of increasing or deepening their qualifications. In the case of newly qualified staff, these days may be used to address some areas of professional practice identified by a more experienced teacher with the responsibility for mentoring them. Some preschool teachers have gained a three-year Bachelor's degree (Bc.) or continue for a further two years to complete a Master's degree (Mgr.) in preschool pedagogy.

Kindergarten teachers work a forty-hour week (thirty-one hours contact time) and are entitled to eight weeks of annual holiday; however, their salary is generally not sufficient to meet their individual monthly living costs. The average monthly salary for a newly qualified preschool teacher is 20,000 Kč (about £660) before tax rising very minimally on an annual basis thereafter. Staff work on a shift basis (generally 7.00 to 12.30 pm or 9.00 to 4.00 pm), meaning that there are two adults per class during the middle period of the day providing a higher adult-to-child ratio and an opportunity for a greater variety of learning activities. Class sizes are generally between thirteen and twenty-four children and may be of a single or a mixed age group according to the discretion of the headteacher.

ECEC and the future

This chapter began by stating that accession to the EU seven years ago was generally considered to be a positive step by the Czech people; however, today the public mood towards the EU is not so enthusiastic. A recent survey revealed that only 41% are satisfied with the country's membership and in a hypothetical referendum 57% of respondents said they would now vote against joining the EU (Falvey, 2012). Despite this recent pessimism, there is little doubt that the country has benefited in many ways since accession. The nation is now well integrated among the liberal democracies of Western Europe, citizens can travel freely within member states, and the prospect of domination by powerful military neighbours to the east seems increasingly remote. The security afforded by NATO membership and EU accession has encouraged financial investment and contributed to a stronger economy and new infrastructure networks. Improved employment prospects and higher living standards for many of the younger generation have followed and, although not everyone is optimistic, until very recently confidence in the future remained relatively high.

So, what is the outlook for young children and their families in a nation naturally wishing to protect the gains made as the result of such a successful political and economic transformation in the last two decades? More significantly, what changes are there likely to be in ECEC policy and practice as the government seeks to maintain public confidence in the face of the current economic downturn?

First of all, a combination of factors is currently leading to a high demand for preschool provision that the state is unable to provide. The economic prosperity brought about in recent years for some sections of society has coincided with a rising birth rate and a desire for a higher standard of living, especially among the younger generation. To service this lifestyle, many young couples as well as older families with young children have begun to abandon the traditional role model of mothers remaining at home. It is increasingly common, especially in urban areas, for both parents to be working and therefore in need of crèche or preschool provision for their children. This 'gap in the market' is beginning to be occupied by private companies or individuals who have identified a growing business opportunity. To date, this is inevitably concentrated in the bigger towns and cities but preschool provision from early morning until late afternoon can cost as much as 9000 K (about £300) per month. Despite such costs representing a significant proportion of an average monthly income, it is very likely that the private sector rather than the state will increasingly be in a position to meet the demand for scarce kindergarten places. The EU has also recently funded an innovative project in one of the main cities to address the needs of professional parents who may not live near their own parents due to work commitments. Known informally as 'rent-a-granny', the project's real title of 'Clover' symbolizes the intention to encourage a bond between the three generations: seniors, young parents, and children (Lazarová, 2012).

The second factor likely to play a part in shaping the future of ECEC in the country is the likelihood of reform resulting from closer scrutiny of assessment procedures within kindergartens. Teachers carry out continuous self-evaluation of their own teaching in order to improve upon their practice and report upon the progress of the children they teach. The FEP PE currently requires evaluation of a child's achievement in such a way that it is 'not a question of the assessment of the child and their performance in relation to a given norm or a question of comparing individual children and their performance' (Research Institute of Education, 2004: 40). Headteachers are also required to use a self-evaluation system to assess their kindergarten's ability to fulfil the objectives of the FEP PE, as well as assessing the quality of its environment and the work of the teachers in supporting children's progress. Evaluation both at a pupil and school level is delegated to the individual school under the terms of the FEP PE, although the outcomes of these exercises must be recorded as part of the SEP.

However, in their Annual Report for 2009–2010, the Czech School Inspectorate (CSI), *Česká školní inspekce*, included an evaluation of the implementation of Frameworks for Educational Provision (FEPs) across all levels of compulsory education. FEPs were identified as not fulfilling their function in accordance with the requirements of educational legislation, while their structure was difficult for schools to understand and provided little support for the professional development of teachers (CSI, 2010). Notably, the report offers international comparative data, which suggests, by analogy with recent developments in the English school system (see Chapter 22), that FEPs at all levels of compulsory education may eventually be made more effective as tools for assessing school performance as well as teaching children.

In addition, a recent review of the quality of ECEC within the Czech Republic (OECD, 2012) made positive comments on many areas of practice (including the FEP PE). However, a number of issues were considered to be 'potential areas for reflection' after comparison with similar provision in New Zealand, Norway, and Scotland. In particular, the need for greater integration for the under-3s and preschool children in terms of ministerial responsibility and curriculum approach was highlighted. Benefits cited were greater opportunities for all staff working with young children to strengthen their caring as well as educational skills and the provision of wider opportunities to stimulate early child development. Furthermore, the report noted that the FEP PE gives little guidance on how to differentiate teaching and learning for young children based upon their age or ability.

The FEP PE is also noticeably quiet on multiculturalism and the need to provide for young children and their families in an increasingly mobile and culturally diverse world. Admittedly, the Czech Republic has a relatively low ethnic minority population and it could be argued that attention to this issue is part of the responsibility delegated to individual kindergartens. However, this issue is one that will become more significant following the country's accession to the EU; the past restrictions on freedom of movement between countries are something most Czechs are pleased to forget.

After decades of little or no change, the Czech nation is now encountering regular change as a post-communist country adjusting to a new way of life and the ideals of a liberal democracy within the EU. Young children today are growing up in a rapidly developing society, compared with their parents and grandparents. It is hoped that they will be well equipped for the future by a system of ECEC that maintains the principles set out in the government White Paper in 2001, which was clearly committed to the development of the individual and sought to encourage a positive disposition towards lifelong learning:

> The concept of education directed towards the individual, culturally and spiritually conditioned, conceived of as a life-long process and built on the principle of a knowledge society brings us to the conclusion that education or learning with an educational purpose is both a path and an instrument in the development of human personality and its value cannot be derived only from economic or other such purposes or conceived of in a narrowly pragmatic way.
>
> (MEYS, 2001: 14)

Find Out More

- How might the high demand for places being filled by the growing private sector influence ECEC provision in the Czech Republic in years to come?
- What might be the likely outcomes for the FEP PE should the recommendations of the OECD publication *Quality Matters in Early Childhood Education and Care: Czech Republic* be taken further?
- Explore the long history of ECEC in the Czech Republic and consider its potential to influence early childhood and family life in the future.

References and recommended reading

Act No. 561 of the Czech Republic (2004) *Education Act on Pre-school, Basic, Secondary, Tertiary Professional and Other Education* [*školský zákon o předškolním, základním, středním, vyšším odborném a jiném vzdělávání*]. Available at: http://www.msmt.cz/uploads/soubory/IMzakon561ponovelach.pdf (accessed 2 February 2012).

Comenius, J.A. (1623) *The School of Infancy (Informatorium)*. Translated by W.S. Monroe, 1896. Boston, MA: D.C. Heath. Available at: http://core.roehampton.ac.uk/digital/froarc/comsch/ (accessed 31 May 2012).

Comenius, J.A. (1638) *The Great Didactic (Didactica Magna)*. Translated by M.W. Keatinge, 1967. New York: Russell & Russell. Available at: http://core.roehampton.ac.uk/digital/froarc/comgre/ (accessed 31 May 2012).

Council of the European Union (2004) *Education and Training 2010*. Available at: http://ec.europa.eu/education/policies/2010/doc/jir_council_final.pdf (accessed 31 May 2012).

Czech School Inspectorate (CSI) (2010) *Annual Report of the Czech School Inspectorate on the School Year 2009/2010*. Prague: CSI.

Education, Audiovisual and Culture Executive Agency (EACEA) (2009) *Early Childhood Education and Care in Europe: Tackling Social and Cultural Inequalities*. Brussels: EACEA P9 Eurydice.

Education, Audiovisual and Culture Executive Agency (EACEA) (2012) *Key Data on Education in Europe 2012*. Brussels: EACEA P9 Eurydice.

European Council (2000) Presidency Conclusions, *Lisbon European Council*. Available at: http://www.consilium.europa.eu/uedocs/cms_data/docs/pressdata/en/ec/00100-r1.en0.htm (accessed 31 May 2012).

Falvey, C. (2012) Czechs more dissatisfied with EU membership than at any time since entry to the union, *Radio Prague News*. Available at: http://www.radio.cz/en/section/news/news-2012-05-31 (accessed 31 May 2012).

Lazarová, D. (2003) Referendum endorses EU membership, *Radio Prague News*. Available at: http://www.radio.cz/en/section/news/news-of-radio-prague-843 (accessed 6 June 2012).

Lazarová, D. (2012) Brno centre for childcare launches 'rent-a-granny' scheme, *Radio Prague News*. Available at: http://www.radio.cz/en/subtopic-archive/society+family (accessed 6 June 2012).

Ministry of Education, Youth and Sports (MEYS) (2000a) *OECD Thematic Review of Early Childhood Education and Care Policy: Background Report for the Czech Republic*. Prague: MEYS.

Ministry of Education, Youth and Sports (MEYS) (2000b) *OECD Country Note: Early Childhood Education and Care Policy in the Czech Republic*. Prague: MEYS.

Available at: http://www.oecd.org/dataoecd/9/39/1915167.pdf (accessed 2 February 2012).

Ministry of Education, Youth and Sports (MEYS) (2001) *National Programme for the Development of Education in the Czech Republic, White Paper* [*Národní program rozvoje vzdělávání v České republice, Bílá kniha*]. Prague: MEYS.

Ministry of Education, Youth and Sports (MEYS) (2005) *National Report on Implementation of the Joint European Programme 'Education and Training 2010'*. Brussels: European Commission. Available at: http://ec.europa.eu/education/lifelong-learning-policy/doc/nationalreport08/cz_en.pdf (accessed 2 February 2012).

Ministry of Education, Youth and Sports (MEYS) (2011) *The Education System in the Czech Republic*. Prague: MEYS.

Oberhuemer, P., Schreyer, I. and Neuman, M. (2010) *Professionals in Early Childhood Education and Care Systems: European Profiles and Perspectives*. Opladen: Barbara Budrich Publishers.

OECD (2012) *Quality Matters in Early Childhood Education and Care: Czech Republic 2012*, OECD Publishing. Available at: http://dx.doi.org/10.1787/9789264176515-en (accessed 6 June 2012).

Opravilová, E., Havlínová, M., Bláhová, A. and Krejčová, V. (1993) *Personality-oriented Model of Preschool Education* [*Osobnostně orientovaný model předškolní výchovy*]. Prague: MEYS.

Rabušicová, M. (2008) New developments in the Czech Republic, *European Early Childhood Education Research Journal*, 16(3): 386–90.

Research Institute of Education (RIE) (2004) *Framework Education Program for Preschool Education (FEP PE)* [*Rámcový vzdělávací program pro předškolní vzdělávání (RVP PV)*]. Prague: RIE.

PART 4

Putting it into practice: curriculum and pedagogy

13

DAY TO DAY IN ITALIAN PRESCHOOLS: ENVIRONMENTS FOR LEARNING AND DEVELOPMENT

Paolo Sorzio

Summary

In this chapter, the culture of early childhood education and care in Italy is analysed based on ethnographic observations about the daily organization of educational activities in three different schools, two in towns in the north-east of Italy and one in Reggio-Emilia. By comparing and contrasting different settings, it is possible to highlight an underlying common structure together with some differences. The organization of space and types of activities are shown to be relevant aspects of practice that affect children's learning opportunities. Educational activities can be constrained by particular institutional circumstances, such as a lack of space, and routines and recitation scripts are activities that do not engage children in complex interactional patterns; project work, however, makes it possible to extend children's contributions. Where communicative exchanges are rich and varied, children can engage in more advanced learning situations.

Introduction

In Italy, ideas originating in the progressive movement have been disseminated to the public pre-primary schools resulting in changes in the conceptualization of early childhood as well as in educational practice. As discussed in Chapter 4, the vision of children as actively constructing their own learning through their engagement in purposeful activities has led to the development of new school arrangements. Over the years, teachers have challenged conditions in their school environments to offer educational opportunities to children in their community. The teaching team consists of two teachers for each class, so as to provide different support strategies to learners. Schools integrate children with special needs into ordinary classes, with a specialized teacher; all the classes are multicultural. Characteristically, in pre-primary schools, there are at least three same-age classes, plus one mixed-age class (3–6 years).

It is useful, however, to highlight the differences in the daily organization of educational activities, to reflect on the effects that different learning conditions have on the children's learning opportunities. The following sections present ethnographic observations about the daily organization of educational activities in three different schools. The first two schools in the towns of Conegliano and Sacile are situated in the north-east of Italy, while the third is located in Reggio-Emilia. By comparing and contrasting different settings, it is possible to highlight an underlying common structure together with some differences (Heath and Street, 2008).

Spending the day in three Italian pre-primary schools

Conegliano

The school was established in the late 1960s in a working-class district. Its architecture was based on the transmissive educational culture: small rectangular classrooms, with desks in front of the teacher's chair. The educational model underlying this early school setting was attuned to what Bruner (1996) calls the 'empty vessel' conception of mind. Since children were not considered individuals with developed intentionality, they were expected to acquire skills and appropriate behaviours by rote learning. The inner logic of the curriculum was memorization procedures: children were instructed to repeat rhymes and simple tunes, to make drawings, and write down letters in their handbooks until they were able to learn basic skills. From the behavioural point of view, the most important values were learning to be quiet, compliant, and tidy. Children's curiosities, hypotheses, and plans were not encouraged, and their home culture not valued.

In 1974, a young school principal, with progressive ideas, arrived in the school. She proposed a radical reorganization of the school setting, and the teachers enthusiastically agreed and collaborated in establishing a new school culture. The desks and the chairs were removed, the classroom spaces reorganized, creating corners for children's self-initiated activities (kitchen, puzzle, and reading and pictorial corners), with a small common space, where children and the teachers could perform whole-class routines, talk about their daily activities and home experiences.

The daily schedule of this school is typical in the State pre-primary system, with minimal variation:

- 7.45 am: The school opens and one teacher per class welcomes the first children to arrive; they are allowed to play freely in the classroom corners.

- 8.15 am: All the children are in their classrooms; they have their breakfast with fruit, listen to stories, share with their classmates some home experiences, and perform whole-class routines.

- 10.00 am: All the children and teachers gather in the meeting room where dance and dramatic plays are performed.

- 10.15 am: The other teacher in the classroom teaching team arrives; each class splits into two small groups and they engage in different activities. During the week, the groups alternate in the 'psychomotricity' room (see below), in the classroom, and in the performing arts room; once a week, the children go to the library, where they are asked to select a book and read it at home with their family.

- 11.30 am: The children join together and go to the toilet, according to an established sequence of turns.

- 12.00 noon: At lunch, the children eat in different places, given the problems of available space; some groups stay in their classroom, others join in the performing arts and meeting rooms. The older children help the younger ones to learn to eat appropriately, each child being responsible for his or her own dish and cutlery. The children collaborate with the assistant team in serving the food.

- 1.00 pm: The children play in small groups in the classroom corners; some have a rest in the psychomotricity rooms.

- 2.00 pm: In each classroom, the children take part in activities, and select and prepare materials for the activities the following day.

- 3.30 pm: The children have their snack.

- 4.00 pm: The school day ends and the children go to the common room to meet their relatives.

An important aspect of the school culture is psychomotor activity (called 'psychomotricity'). It is a method used to break down some motor stereotypes in the children's behaviours, as well as providing the basis for more advanced understandings. Two classrooms have been transformed into psychomotricity rooms, full of 50 cm soft cubes, a Swedish ladder (wall bars), a small slide, and dress material of different colours for symbolic play. At the beginning of the activity, the children are allowed to jump, run, roll, climb, construct towers and walls with the soft cubes as building blocks. They can play alone or in pairs and develop their own different objectives: a child constructs a tower by placing one block onto another in a balanced way; two others construct a wall to separate themselves from their peers. Two children jump from the Swedish ladder. The teacher leaves the children to move freely in the room, monitoring whether a child needs any emotional or physical support. The teacher intervenes in two situations only: when a child is not sufficiently aware that his or her actions may be harmful to others, and when a child disrupts another's construction or activity (e.g. when a child's actions cause a tower to fall down).

When two children have built a small 'house' with the soft cubes as bricks, the activity shifts to symbolic play. The teacher encourages this change to a new stage in the play and promotes the children's competence in organizing a given area into different functional spaces. Starting from the moment that the small house is recognizable, she makes an explicit rule that the inside space of the house should be respected and the outside space should be symbolically represented. Therefore, social play develops with improvisation; the small house is considered a castle where a princess is imprisoned, and a prince makes an adventurous trip to liberate her, engaging in duels with other characters played by classmates.

Finally, the teacher announces the 'detachment stage', by inviting the children to say what they enjoyed during the activity and which feelings they experienced. They have time to relax and then they put the room back, grouping the soft cubes according to their size. According to the teachers, the organization of this activity allows the children to express different feelings in a caring space. By experiencing emotions and representing them symbolically, the children develop their competence in the experiential field called 'The body and movement'.

As part of the requirements of the National Curriculum (Department of Education, 2007), the children spend half of the morning on their project work – that is, an educational process in which multiple activities are developed based on a given theme. The identified topic must be part of the learners' experience and is expected to give consistency to the classroom activities. There is no direct instruction, since the children are allowed to propose ideas, participate in the activity according to their level of competence, listen to others, make contributions, and join together to produce some artefact, such as a drawing, a collective narrative or a collage. Although the teachers propose activities and provide materials, the activities are not strictly planned in advance, since they unfold according to the children's contributions.

In the class of 5- to 6-year-olds, the children are engaged in a project called 'Environments'. It is intended that the objects of children's enquiries and representations are the nature and the characteristics of different settings where life is found. Subtopics are 'The Woodlands', 'The Sea', and 'The Towns' and the varieties of life in the different habitats. Each of these activities lasts about one month.

At the outset of 'The Woodlands' project, the children take a trip to the nearby woodlands, where they gather some interesting items, including fruits, leaves, and the bark of different trees. During the project work, the class is separated into two groups of about ten children each, in order to work on different activities related to the project: this arrangement allows the two teachers to match their educational strategies to the children's actions. One group of children works in the classroom on categorizing the material they have gathered. All the items are categorized through classroom dialogue, and relevant features of shape, colour, and size are identified; finally, they are put into different boxes. The children also make drawings of animals and plants, working in pairs to share and develop ideas, to support each other in a very friendly atmosphere. The teacher does not lead the activity; she moves around the children's tables, making suggestions, asking for improvements, recalling some interesting known facts.

The other group goes into the 'performing arts room' (which is actually also part of the dining room). Each child uses part of the materials they have gathered to create a collage about a woodland. The children work individually on their own composition; however, two children work on each table, in order to create opportunities for collaboration. The teacher moves among the pairs, asking children about their ideas and their procedures. She supports a child who intends to represent a stream; they agree on the use of a piece of blue paper as the most suitable material; the child cuts the paper, the teacher asks him if the cut paper is too large and to find out by himself a way to create a proportionate dimension of the river. Another child is devising the woodland as a highly geometrical and abstract representation: the objects are placed according to their shape and colour, rather than their actual position in the natural site; a log is placed close to large stones, a branch floats above the tree, and the leaves are close to the sun. The collage is very rich and well done, although it diverges from the 'naturalistic model' the teacher values; she thus recommends that the child 'make a tree, otherwise it is not clear that you are representing the woodland'. The child modifies slightly the arrangement of objects in her collage and connects some wooden elements in a 'tree' shape. Although the educationally valued model in the activity is the naturalistic representation, the children work out different layouts of the woodland, according to their mental model, their ability to glue pieces to the backing sheet, and the teacher's and their peers' suggestions. During debriefing time, the teacher asks the children to recall their collages, framing their descriptions in well-formed grammatical sentences and using abstract categories.

There are other activities that engage the learners in very different patterns of activity. Every day in the plenary activity, all 65 children and the teachers meet in the large and unstructured meeting room. By sitting in a circle, a large stage emerges in the middle; all the children sing in unison a simple tune. The teachers initiate and control the unfolding of the activity with little, if any, improvisation or opportunity for children's creative contributions. Next, one teacher narrates a story about a king in the forest looking for a princess made prisoner by a monster. At the centre of the stage, some children are acting out the characters with simple and stereotypical gestures, while the other children sing the refrain. The activity seems unchallenging and therefore does not promote the children's more advanced learning strategies.

During the school day, each change of activity is marked by some routines, well-structured patterns of behaviour that the children are asked to perform in coordinated and expected ways, in order to move to different places, allowing the other classes to move in different directions and giving support staff the required time to rearrange the rooms to another function. These are necessary adaptations to the constraints imposed by lack of space, since there are not enough rooms, the rooms available are too small for the educational activities, the classrooms are noisy, and the children's voices rumble. The teachers manage the limitations of space by asking the children to respect the allotted time for moving from one room to another, coordinating their movements to allow the other groups to perform their activities.

Sacile

The school was built in 1976, respecting advanced educational requirements: the rooms are large, one wall in each classroom comprises a large glass window, and there is a spacious dining room. However, a dedicated space for a library was not planned; this is found in a corner of the meeting room. Fifty-six children attend the school; there are two teachers for each class.

The school day starts at 7.45 a.m., the children play freely in one specialized corner of their classroom, called the 'children's centre of interest'. Progressively, more classmates arrive and at 8.15 a.m. all the classes are filled. There are corners to play with toy bricks, to make drawings, to take part in domestic play. In each class there is also a 'blue box', a large table with sand and natural materials (pebbles, leaves, shells) where the children can work out an idea using malleable materials. The teachers move among the groups asking about their plans, getting the opportunity to extend their competence by what they call 'tossing questions'. For example, some children are playing with colours. The teacher asks each of them the name of the colour they are using. A 3-year-old child names her colour with the wrong term. The teacher gives her the colour she named and asks her to compare the two colours. Then she asks the group to recall some objects that have the colours she names.

This kind of teacher–learner dialogue is based on children-initiated free play activities and lasts until 9.40 am; from the beginning of the school day there have been no recognized routines. Before the break, the children engage in a motor-control exercise. They are invited to listen to the 'voice of silence', and therefore they stay silent for a while, relaxing. Then they are encouraged to imagine a butterfly on their shoulder. Slowly, they are invited to feel the butterfly moving on their body and then flying away. They can follow its flight with their fingers and their eyes. This activity seems different from a routine. Whereas the routine does not require any cognitive engagement for the children, the motor control exercise implies a symbolic mental representation and some eye-motor coordination activity. It looks like an approach close to the theatrical technique of making simple gestures meaningful.

During the free play, the teachers 'tossing questions' are based on the contingencies they get from the children's ongoing activities. However, more integrated activities are conducted in the library during project work. Here one class is developing the topic of 'The Sea', started at the beginning of the school year. A large collage displayed on the wall represents a sea with their invented fish. The children were asked to create their own fantasy fish on an A4 sheet of paper, then to carefully reproduce them on an A2 size sheet. The educational goal is to make the learners aware of different scales of representation as well as of the constant proportion between parts. A fantasy story is narrated about a fish, which lives in a museum and therefore knows the sea only through the paintings. The teacher leads the narrative, showing the children reproductions of some famous artists' paintings. The children insert some details and introduce some turning points in the story. Finally, they reproduce the paintings and select a book to read at home with the help of their family.

A Reggio Emilia infant-toddler centre

In the Reggio Emilia system, schools for children aged from 3 months to 3 years are called 'infant-toddler centres', so as to emphasize the typical design of the school environment that is intended to promote the children's active engagement in their learning activities from an early age.

The recently established infant-toddler centre 'Aguas claras' is led by a cooperative of workers and it is affiliated to the municipal school system. It is composed of large rooms, organized into smaller spaces for children's activities. There are 57 children aged 3–36 months. Ample glass windows all round the perimeter offer a constant view of the outside, as well as a great amount of sunlight. There are displays of children's artefacts, photographs representing their engagement in activities, documentation of their dialogues, and of the teachers' observations.

The classrooms are large, each with an atelier. The atelier is full of natural and recycled materials and the children explore the possibilities of 're-signifying' them – that is, giving them a new life as objects with different functions. For example, natural materials can be coloured and arranged to become an abstract composition; small and flat objects can become part of a tent. Many artistic compositions enrich the living space, either placed on the ground or hung from the ceilings.

Small groups of children are engaged in different activities, supported by the teachers. The atelierist offers an expert point of view that allows the children to develop their own ideas into more advanced compositions, and therefore develop their symbolic competences. The atelierist neither gives instruction nor teaches procedures, but suggests different potentialities of the objects and encourages children to develop their intuitions, by focusing on some specific features they have noticed and working out them in depth. Making a drawing of a tree enables the children to develop their perceptions into graphic language. Each child works out a personal representation, highlighting different elements and properties of the same tree. The teachers and the atelierist encourage a variety of representations; a child can create a representation that gives the sense of the density of the leaves, another the geometric shape of the branches, yet another the actual situation of the tree with children around.

Even routine activities become opportunities for 're-signifying' artefacts creatively, such as children's photographs used as placeholders. The children are encouraged to notice significant personal traits of their peers (a smile, their curly hair, a profile) and are allowed to use the digital camera to take pictures of the features they have noticed. The atelierist suggests 'new ways of looking at the human face', but she neither teaches a technique for its own sake nor as a means to assess children's competence. As the atelierist stated, children are not expected to learn a technique to produce an acceptable outcome according to the teachers' standards, but to develop expressive competence. The learners are excited by recognizing a peer through a photographic detail, and develop more complex forms of representation. Young children are supported to use different symbolic codes to express their feelings and ideas even using abstract representations. This is consistent with one principle of the Reggio Emilia approach, that learning the hundred languages of children is the meditational means to develop a child's potentialities (Edwards et al., 1998).

The concept that synthesizes the school day in the infant-toddler centre is that of the school environment as a living organism (Rinaldi, 2006). Space is not only co-designed at the outset by the architects with the teaching staff in terms of space, furniture, and natural brightness, it also forms a part of and support for the learners' activities. Therefore, it is continuously recreated as the children develop their competence. The pedagogist always takes care of the evolving life of the space by introducing new children's artefacts as an integral part of the environment; the displays are constantly enriched by documentation of the ongoing activities. Although there are many more objects in this infant-toddler centre school than in many other schools in the Italian system, the visitor does not have a sense of crowded spaces, since the object display is harmonious.

All the educational activities are co-taught and fully documented, to support the constant inquiring attitude of the teaching team. The process starts with careful documentation of the everyday activities (the teaching staff have digital photo- and video-cameras at their disposal, take field notes, and gather children's artefacts and record their dialogue). Then the team takes time to analyse the documentation and to reflect on the relationships between the adults and the children, in order to 'learn how the children learn', as the pedagogist stated. Therefore, the teaching staff are always very close to the children's developmental processes and can introduce innovative activities that are sensitive to their learning.

The nature of the educational activities and the children's opportunities to learn

The ethnographic analysis of everyday schooling in three different contexts high-lights differences in the organization of space, in the types of activity the children are engaged in, and in the patterns of interaction that support children's understand-ing of their experiences. Different conditions of participation affect the children's opportunities to learn. In the infant-toddler centre in Reggio Emilia, the space evolves as the children develop and the physical arrangements are in 'dialogue' with the children's experiences, through documenting their talk, activities, and artefacts. In the other settings, the buildings were designed without consideration of the con-ditions for everyday educational activities, since they were conceived as containers and therefore the teachers have to deal with environmental constraints in proposing more complex activities.

Through on-site observations of daily practice, different types of activities are highlighted, many of which are apparent in two or more of the schools, and these have implications for learning opportunities (Cazden, 2001).

Behavioural routines

These are finely scripted sequences of actions that the children perform in moving from one activity to another. The routines make the children attend to the same activity at the same time, with the same level of engagement; therefore, the teacher obtains the greatest group cohesion with the least effort. Given the space constraints in the Conegliano school, routines appear as behavioural patterns that allow the dif-ferent groups of children to move from one place to another, without hindering their schoolmates, respecting the time schedule, and maintaining an acceptable level of noise. However, this pattern of interaction offers limited opportunities for children's learning, since it requires only the correct performance of a rigid sequence of actions.

Free play

This is a typical activity the children engage in, especially when they arrive at school and after lunch. The teachers supervise their play, mediate the emerging conflicts, and take the opportunity of children's experiences to extend their understanding, with a particu-lar focus on vocabulary. Learners are asked to identify the characteristics of given items, to attribute the appropriate names to tokens, and compare similar objects according to their distinctive features. However, the teachers' scaffolding strategies seem contingent upon the playing situation and there is little development of the activity.

Activities based on the 'recitation script'

During the school day, the children perform some educational activities that have recurrent discursive formats, with slots for limited children's participation, usually with little variation from the expected answers (Tharp and Gallimore, 1991), such as rhyme recitation, dramatic play, and tune singing. The interactional pattern is focused on the proper sequence of expected actions. The communicative exchanges during the recitation scripts are repetitive and simplified: the children are asked to recall the correct sequence of words and there is little variability in their performance. Therefore, they are given limited opportunities to explore and communicate their ideas. At the Conegliano school, dramatic play in the plenary sessions requires a few selected children to act out stereotypical characters, with the other learners performing simple gestures of accompaniment. An interesting innovation is the theatrical approach developed in Sacile, since the script allows children to develop finely tuned motor coordination.

Project-work activities

During daily activities, projects are developed from ideas that emerge in classroom discussion or in the teachers' monthly collegiate planning. In their regular monthly meetings, the teachers discuss the potential impact of emerging ideas on the children's learning trajectories. They identify the children's interests, work out the core ideas into feasible educational practices, and prepare tools to document the activities and their outcomes. Relevant topics of interest can be expressed by children or proposed by the teachers and are related to environmental phenomena (such as plant growth, the nature and the different physical states of water) or to social experiences (such as a street market activity, the process of baking bread). In the collegiate planning activities, the teachers represent the overall frame of the intended activities in which the children will be engaged in. Visits to museums, natural parks, and libraries are planned; talks are conducted with the children's relatives to explain the educational objectives and establish some connections with family life experiences.

Each topic is intended as a structured theme for a range of activities, in order to provide a shared contextual basis on which learning is promoted. Therefore, the plans are not worked out in full detail, since changes and improvisations are expected, according to the children's interpretations of the ongoing activities.

In the classroom, during project work, the children are engaged in open and complex activities, they can work out their own plans, share ideas with others, integrate sequences of action, manipulate materials, and produce public artefacts. Their contributions are authentic, since they are based on their own interpretation of the topic; therefore, the outcomes of the activities are varied, according to the children's choices. During project work, the focus of the communicative exchange is child-initiated performance. The teachers encourage the children to propose ideas, explain their motives, justify actions and share strategies, rather than simply repeat, recognize, and reproduce what the teacher expects. Therefore, 'each learner must always be challenged at his or her level of competence' (Cazden, 2001: 7). In project work, the difference between the child's performance and the teachers' valued forms are expressed at the reflective level, rather than that of instruction. The children's contributions are more coordinated, extended, and varied than in free play and in the recitation script activities.

Concluding remarks

The Reggio Emilia experience integrates daily activities in the early years setting and municipal initiatives in a deliberate process of early childhood education. The innovative roles of the atelierist and pedagogist create opportunities for children to be systematically engaged in 'sustained shared activities' (Siraj-Blatchford, 2010a) that extend children's understanding through the creative use of different symbolic languages (for a more in-depth discussion, see Chapter 4, pp. 34–6).

In the other two contexts, the teachers are also well motivated and committed to the children's learning. However, the educational activities seem constrained by particular institutional conditions, such as a lack of space, a lack of support from municipalities or a lack of in-service teacher education. Nowadays, despite financial cuts and staff reductions, the principals and teacher committees in the public pre-primary schools are trying to ensure that there are two teachers for each classroom, in an effort to create an effective supporting environment for the children. The co-teaching team offers an extended daytime schedule and differentiates the classroom curriculum, in order that the learners can benefit from finely tuned strategies to support their performance during their daily educational activities.

Acknowledgements

I would like to thank all the children and the teachers in the schools 'R. Zandonai' in Conegliano, 'G. Rodari' in Sacile, and 'Aguas claras' in Reggio Emilia for their kindness in making their everyday classroom activities available for observation and communication.

Find Out More

- Explain why different patterns of interaction in the pre-primary school give the learners different opportunities to improve their understandings. Give examples of different types of interactions and discuss which elements of children's understanding they promote.
- What institutional conditions might constrain the development of advanced educational activities?
- Design your own educational space that would support complex activities in early childhood education.
- How many different educational activities are organized in the pre-primary school day? Is the shift from one to another clearly marked? What different interactional patterns can be recognized? Do they impact on the children's understanding? If so, how?

Dudek (2006) offers a well-articulated discussion on childcare space design by international contributors. Vecchi (2010) presents a very rich account of the importance of artistic languages in children's development and of the role of the atelierist in the Reggio Emilia approach. A clear conceptualization of the relationship between effective educational settings and children's learning opportunities can be found in Siraj-Blatchford (2010b). Daniels (2007) provides an extended discussion of the concept of 'scaffolding' strategies, as flexible adult guidance of children's learning.

References and recommended reading

Bruner, J.S. (1996) *The Culture of Education*. Cambridge, MA: Harvard University Press.

Cazden, C.B. (2001) *Classroom Discourse: The Language of Teaching and Learning*. Portsmouth, NH: Heinemann.

Daniels, H. (2007) Applications of Vygotsky's work: 12. Pedagogy, in H. Daniels, M. Cole and J.V. Wertsch (eds.) *The Cambridge Companion to Vygotsky*. Cambridge: Cambridge University Press.

Department of Education (2007) *Indicazioni nazionali per il curricolo per la scuola dell'infanzia e per il primo ciclo di istruzione*, D.M. 3 Agosto 2007, n. 68 [*National Guidelines for Pre-primary and for Primary and Middle Schools*]. Available at: http://www.indire.it/indicazioni/templates/monitoraggio/dir_310707.pdf (accessed 16 May 2012).

Dudek, M. (ed.) (2006) *Children's Spaces*. Oxford: Elsevier.

Edwards, C., Gandini, L. and Forman, G. (1998) *The Hundred Languages of Children: The Reggio Emilia Approach. Advanced Reflections* (2nd edn.). Westport, CT: Ablex.

Heath, S.B. and Street, B.V. (2008) *On Ethnography: Approaches to Language and Literacy Research*. New York: Teachers College Press.

Rinaldi, C. (2006) *In Dialogue with Reggio Emilia: Listening, Researching, and Learning*. London: Routledge.

Siraj-Blatchford, I. (2010a) A focus on pedagogy: case studies of effective practice, in K. Sylva, E. Melhuish, P. Sammons, I. Siraj-Blatchford and B. Taggart (eds.) *Early Childhood Matters: Evidence from the Effective Preschool and Primary Education Project*. London: Routledge.

Siraj-Blatchford, I. (2010b) Teaching in early childhood centres: instructional methods and child outcomes, in *International Encyclopaedia of Education* (3rd edn.). Oxford: Elsevier.

Tharp, R.G. and Gallimore, R. (1991) *The Instructional Conversation: Teaching and Learning in Social Activity*. Santa Cruz, CA: National Center for Research on Cultural Diversity and Second Language Learning. Available at: http://escholarship.org/uc/item/5th0939d (accessed 15 December 2011).

Vecchi, V. (2010) *Art and Creativity in Reggio Emilia: Exploring the Role and Potential of Ateliers in Early Childhood Education*. London: Routledge.

14

A DAY IN THE LIFE OF A NEW ZEALAND KINDERGARTEN TEACHER: A CURRICULUM OF OPEN POSSIBILITIES

Carmen Dalli

Summary

This chapter discusses elements of a New Zealand teacher's professional practice. Thematic analysis of a continuous video record of a day in her life, and of a narrative reconstruction of the day during a follow-up interview, yielded a view of early childhood professional practice as focused on a 'curriculum of open possibilities'. Her understanding: that curriculum planning required relational involvement and being part of the children's life within the kindergarten community; that professional practice required teamwork and attunement to one's colleagues; and that acting professionally was about being fully present and 'bringing everything together', all contributed to the curriculum. Behind the apparent 'trivia' of the teacher's day, there were layers of activity that maintained a fabric of connections that sustained the open possibilities. In this way, the teacher's role as a curriculum planner emerges as a finely balanced role that is creative and agentic rather than prescribed by narrow curriculum goals. The findings of the study are located within research on New Zealand's early childhood curriculum, *Te Whāriki*.

Introduction

The last few years have seen an unprecedented interest in issues of professional practice in early childhood education, with many countries introducing curriculum documents and regulatory policies aimed at enhancing the quality of early childhood education for children and their families and professionalism within the sector (OECD, 2004; Laevers, 2005). New Zealand has taken a prominent part in this global trend with two key pedagogical and policy developments attracting international interest: first, the introduction of the innovative curriculum document, *Te Whāriki* (Ministry of Education, 1996), and second, the 2002 launch of a comprehensive ten-year strategic plan for early childhood education – *Pathways to the Future:*

Ngā Huarahi Arataki (e.g. OECD, 2004; Moss, 2007). Policies within the strategic plan to progressively upgrade staff qualifications across all teacher-led early childhood services to a benchmark level of a three-year diploma or degree[1] marked out New Zealand as a leader in professionalizing its early years workforce.

This chapter draws on data from the New Zealand case study within a six-country project that explored early childhood practitioners' views of their practice (Miller et al., 2012). In each of the six countries, researchers collected a continuous video record of a day in the life of one early years practitioner and later interviewed the practitioner to collect a narrative reconstruction of the videoed day and to explore her perceptions of her professional practice.

The primary task of the six-country project was to generate rich descriptions of the 'phenomenon' of early childhood professional practice in specific local contexts with their different socio-historical and policy backgrounds. This was not to create a comparative study but rather to open up a space for shared thinking among a group of researchers who were interested in the notion of professionalism, which, as argued elsewhere (Dalli and Urban, 2010: 151), is increasingly understood 'as a discourse as much as a phenomenon', something that is 'fluid, contentious and constantly under reconstruction' in local contexts. The practitioners in the study were a convenience sample of early childhood professionals who were all previously known to the researchers. In each case study, the practitioner worked with children aged 3–5 years, was qualified at the minimum level required in her context, and had worked for at least three years after gaining her qualification.

This chapter draws a picture of professional practice based on key themes in the interview and a narrative reconstruction of the videoed day offered by Bette, the kindergarten teacher in the New Zealand case study. Starting with an outline of current early childhood curriculum research in New Zealand and an overview of the emergent literature on how professionalism is understood in the local early childhood sector, I argue that the themes in Bette's narratives illustrate that behind the apparent 'trivia' of the teacher's day there were layers of activity and a fabric of connections that sustained a curriculum of 'possibilities' consistent with the open ontology of *Te Whāriki*.

Contextualizing early childhood curriculum research in New Zealand

New Zealand research and commentary on the early childhood curriculum can be traced back to the introduction of *Te Whāriki*, first in draft form in 1993 and its final version in 1996 (e.g. Carr and May, 1993; Cullen, 1996; McNaughton, 1996). Previously, discussions about early childhood programmes used a terminology of 'aims and objectives' with 'curriculum' first appearing in the title of an early childhood official document in 1988 (Department of Education, 1988).

Te Whāriki (Ministry of Education, 1996) swiftly became noted as a 'good practice' curriculum, with analytical critique (e.g. Cullen, 1996, 2003) emerging relatively slowly. In 2003, *Te Whāriki* was chosen as one of four curriculum models discussed at an OECD symposium on 'Curricula and Pedagogies in Early Childhood Education' for national policy coordinators held in Stockholm (OECD, 2004; Laevers, 2005). Together with the Experiential Education model from Flanders (see Chapter 15), the HighScope curriculum from Michigan in the United States (see Chapter 11), and the Reggio Emilia model from Italy (see Chapters 4 and 13), *Te Whāriki* was described as an 'open' curriculum (Pramling et al., 2004: 29). Open curricula provide:

> space for individual initiatives from both teachers and children . . . room for exploring, trying things out, for raising open questions to which there are no fixed and final answers . . . opportunities to think and reflect . . . room for children's questions, exploring, creativity, fantasy and challenging . . . for different learning styles and strategies. In this way each and every child can find a learning space and appropriate activities within a programme.
>
> (Pramling et al., 2004: 29)

Scholarly discussions of the 'open' characteristics of *Te Whāriki* have highlighted both positive and problematic aspects. On the positive side, it has typically been noted that the title of the document – *Te Whāriki*, a Māori word meaning a *woven mat* – is symbolic of the way that each early childhood education setting is able to use the principles and guidelines of the curriculum framework to weave its own centre *whāriki* or curriculum (e.g. Guild et al., 1998; Nuttall and Edwards, 2007; Alvestad et al., 2009). In this way, *Te Whāriki* is seen to enable cross-setting consistency at the level of its four curriculum principles[2] and associated strands and goals, as well as making space for the particular characteristics of each individual centre/setting within a very diverse sector to be expressed (e.g. Mutch, 2003). In an interview study with nine teachers talking about *Te Whāriki*, Alvestad et al. (2009) suggested that the openness of *Te Whāriki* also enabled teachers to focus on supporting children's learning by following their interests 'as individual learners who [bring] their own skills, experiences and interests to the early childhood setting' (p. 10). Stated in these terms, *Te Whāriki* could be seen to have inscribed the traditional *child-centred* approach to early childhood practice with new meaning: from a pedagogy based on a view of children as individual initiators of their own learning, the *Te Whāriki* child-centred approach becomes a pedagogy that is negotiated as a socio-cultural activity within a learning community that respects individual interests and choices.

This new inscription of meaning, however, is neither a guaranteed outcome in day-to-day practice, nor necessarily an unproblematic one. For example, Alvestad et al. (2009) argued that following children's own interests was 'a source of tension for the teachers who had their own professional ideas for both skills and content knowledge that they wished the children to experience in the programme' (p. 11). From a slightly different angle, Brostrom (2003) likewise pointed to tensions that teachers might experience because of *Te Whāriki*'s lack of 'explicit reflections on the relationship between its overall aims and examples of educational content' (p. 237). Brostrom favoured a curriculum that enabled teachers to 'choose content that is related to the document's aims' (p. 237) and advocated for a curriculum that would explicitly 'support children to become citizens of the world, able particularly to act in a future society' (p. 236). Others have suggested that teachers are using *Te Whāriki* to justify pre-existing practices rather than to transform their practice (e.g. Nuttall, 2002; McLachlan et al., 2006).[3] Additionally, Nuttall (2002) has argued that while the openness of *Te Whāriki* was an 'enormous strength, allowing maximum regard for centre contexts in teacher decision-making . . . it may also be *Te Whāriki*'s greatest weakness . . . [because] the structure and language of *Te Whāriki* can be easily appropriated to legitimate practice that is ideologically at odds with the theoretical bases of the document' (p. 101).

These findings and other critiques (e.g. Hedges, 2007; Blaiklock, 2008) provide a provocative background against which to present the analysis in this chapter. The research on which it is based adds to the small body of New Zealand research on early childhood teachers' perceptions of professional practice. Elsewhere (Dalli, 2008) I argued for a definition of professionalism that reflects the lived reality of early childhood teachers' practice. Using data from a 2004 national survey of New Zealand early childhood teachers' views of practice, I proposed a 'ground-up' definition of professionalism structured around the three core components of specialist pedagogical strategies, professional knowledge and practice, and collaborative relationships. Analysis of data from the Day in the Life of an Early Years Practitioner project further contributes a profile of professional practice that is consistent with the underlying ontology of *Te Whāriki* as an 'open' curriculum.

The case study teacher: Bette in local context

The practitioner in the New Zealand case study, Bette, was a kindergarten teacher with eight and a half years' teaching experience. Kindergartens were among the first types of early childhood services established in New Zealand in the late 1880s, and the first to receive government funding support; they remain one of the most affordable early childhood services for families. Traditionally, kindergartens have enrolled children aged 3–5 years, with older children attending daily morning sessions and 3-year-olds present on three afternoon sessions a week. Although many kindergartens have adapted this daily structure in recent years, Bette's kindergarten ran on the traditional timetable; on the two afternoons when no children were present, the teachers engaged in programme planning and professional learning and development activities. During a full two-session day, a total of 86 children attended the kindergarten.

Bette was the headteacher in a three-teacher kindergarten in an ethnically diverse community with a mixed socio-economic background in a semi-industrial suburb. She held a three-year diploma of teaching gained from a teachers' college and was contemplating upgrading her qualification to a degree as part of what she saw as a professional commitment to ongoing learning. Her two colleagues likewise met the New Zealand benchmark qualification of a three-year early childhood teaching degree or diploma. A full-day video record of Bette's day was collated one clear mid-winter day in 2007 by a professional cameraman, while I kept a pen-and-paper record of the day as a non-participant observer.

Bette's professional practice: a curriculum of open possibilities

The phrase 'a curriculum of open possibilities' is a composite phrase from statements made by Bette when explaining her view of professional practice and this view was visible in her practice. For example, responding to my question about whether her day had gone to plan, Bette explicitly described the curriculum in her kindergarten as one of open possibilities:

> I think I didn't have any particular plans . . . what happens in our programme planning cycle is . . . we observe the children and we take photos and we write up what they're interested in doing . . . and then we talk about that maybe on a Friday afternoon or a Wednesday afternoon. So then we have in our head maybe eighteen separate *possibilities* [author's emphasis] of what might be happening with different children or groups of children. So that if the elements come towards you and say, 'will you read this?' [tone indicates that read is an example] you say, 'yes!' Because this is an ongoing interest and you *know* [teacher emphasis] – and you say, 'and maybe you could tell such and such a person because they're really interested in [for example] sharks too'. So you know, you'd have maybe ten or twenty things in your head about what could happen and you're not able to ever do all twenty, but it may be that you can see bits of them happening around the place and you could either just throw a supportive comment towards a child . . . You might say: 'And here, take one for Sam too' . . . so it's actually part of the plan and it's part of an ongoing thing that you have all discussed together and put into your head for development.

This statement also highlights that Bette saw programme planning as deriving from the observation of children's interests, and discussions of them in teacher meetings leading to the identification of 'possibilities' for learning as the basis for later pedagogical/curriculum action by the teacher. Bette's phrase 'if the elements come towards you' captures another important aspect of her view of curriculum: specifically, the idea that the curriculum was enacted in the spaces that the particular 'elements' – or happenings of the day – opened up for teaching and learning. Elaborating her view that the curriculum should be responsive to children's interests – both as they were expressed in the immediacy of any one time, and as they became known to the teachers through the children's and teachers' shared history within the kindergarten, Bette memorably said:

> fortunately plans are not an aligning; I mean plans are much more of a question mark and you have to have an *open mind* [author's emphasis] about where any bit of any interest might go . . . just taking opportunities – it's just a huge, vast amorphous bunch of things that might [happen] – possibilities really. So as you say, did what you planned happen? *Yes.* [Bette's emphasis]

These statements by Bette create a view of the curriculum as emergent and fluid with the image of plans as a 'question mark' reminiscent of Pramling and co-workers' (2004) description of open curricula as leaving 'room for exploring, trying things out . . . creativity, fantasy and challenging' (p. 29). Bette's additional statement that a 'huge, vast amorphous bunch of things' could unexpectedly unfold in the course of a normal day as opportunities for teaching and learning further highlights her view that the teacher's role in the curriculum is, as argued by Sands and Weston (2010:

15), one of 'making decisions *in the moment* poised as provocateur, as listener, as learner, as teacher, ever vigilant for opportunities to widen and deepen knowledge'. This image of curriculum decision-making is consistent with the open ontology of *Te Whāriki*; it constructs the teacher's pedagogical role as creative and agentic, rather than as reactive and prescribed by narrow curriculum goals.

Three key themes were identified as capturing additional aspects of Bette's professional practice and as essential in supporting her curriculum of open possibilities.

Theme 1: Professional practice as relational involvement: 'You are all part of each other's lives'

Arriving at Bette's kindergarten, the overwhelming impression was of a place abuzz with activity. Bette began her day in the book corner from where she was able to greet the children and their parents as they entered the main room after stowing their bags in named trays near the front entrance. Bette spent the next thirty minutes of her morning surrounded by children while she read a story chosen by the first boy to join her in the reading corner. As more children gathered around her, Bette's reading became punctuated with a steady flow of comments – not all related to the story – addressed to the group of children around her, and to others who wandered past on their way to nearby activities.

To an outside observer, Bette's comments could easily appear like trivial distractions from the pedagogical focus of storytelling. However, during the interview Bette provided a perspective that linked the apparently 'trivial conversation' to a much larger pedagogical goal, that of creating – and maintaining – personal connections with the children's lives that referred back to their joint history within the kindergarten and encompassed a wide range of experiences. Bette reflected on her morning as follows:

> I felt, looking back on the morning, that there had been a whole lot of trivial conversation . . . but it's like, with each child you are in a conversation that has taken days and weeks. You know, you are all part of each other's lives . . . to the extent that . . . they notice if we have a new pair of shoes and we notice if they have a new pair of shoes . . . we all have a degree of involvement in [the] entirety of our lives together.

Looking closely at the video data in light of Bette's statements about 'conversations that take days and weeks' revealed a pattern of such conversations sprinkled throughout the day. For example, Bette's greetings to children at the start of sessions often included personal comments such as: 'Have you got earrings on today? Were they for your birthday present?' and 'You've got army pants on; I wonder who else will wear theirs today?' or 'Hello! That's Becky's little baby you've got there' (referring to the doll being carried by one of the girls). These greetings both welcomed the children to the new day at kindergarten and established a link to the shared history that the children had with the teacher and with their peers. Similarly, a discussion about haircuts that developed from a girl's comment about wearing plaits, and Bette's comment that a friend had 'missed you on Friday when you weren't here', were among other examples that revealed that underneath the numerous and often fleeting exchanges between Bette and the children, there was a deeper layer of connections based on intimate knowledge, and shared reference points – Bette's conversations spanned days and weeks.

Also nurtured through these apparently 'trivial' comments were caring relationships and a sense of togetherness within the kindergarten. Thus, Bette's questions – 'Where's your sore thumb? Let me look – is it growing better?'; 'I wonder if Alice is better today. Is she here yet?'; and 'I wonder who else will be wearing their army pants?' – functioned both to acknowledge each child's immediate experience, as well as to direct the children's attention beyond their individual focus to a group one.

The sense of caring and intimate involvement in each other's lives, what Brennan (2007) memorably has called 'a culture of tenderness', had an additional significance within the afternoon session. According to Bette, the younger age of children in the afternoon session meant that the teachers were 'more likely to have more of [their] personal time and space – [their] body – . . . taken up with the comforting of children who are separating from their parents'. Bette explained:

> you're kind of more involved in their personal lives . . . More involved with their bowel habits and undies and . . . it's just so open, you know, you have this lovely talk, 'have you got nappies on today or undies?' – 'Oh, I don't have to have undies today, I've just got my nappy' [Bette changes her voice affectionately to sound like a child]. And they're all quite happy to be on a continuum of learning about toileting …

> different children develop a relationship with you – so as teachers you have to be open to that . . . there's one little guy and if he needs to go to the toilet he gets me. So the other teachers know if they see me and this child running towards the loo to check where I was at, and cover for me. So you don't say, 'no, I'm the outside teacher' in that case. You go to the toilet: it's urgent. There are different matters of urgency in the afternoon.

Bette's focus on professional practice as essentially relational emerged strongly in these statements. Additionally, for Bette being professional is personal: it involves making the teacher's body available to children for comfort; it means being prepared to take care of children's very personal bodily needs; and it requires a preparedness to drop everything and run to the bathroom with a child who needs support, thus privileging the child's wellbeing over other demands.

Theme 2: Professional practice as teamwork and attunement to one's colleagues

While Bette's last statement above highlights the importance of attentive responsiveness to children's wellbeing as a characteristic of teacher professional practice, it also makes clear that attentive responsiveness was reliant on support from colleagues who would 'cover' for Bette. Thus, collegial support was extended out of responsiveness to the child, but also because of what Bette described as 'your consciousness as a team of what is happening with your group'. This draws attention to the importance of teamwork in early childhood practice that is attuned to children's wellbeing – a key strand in New Zealand's early childhood curriculum. For Bette, team consciousness was renewed at the beginning of each day when: 'we set up any things that we didn't set up the night before and check in with each other and grade each other's wellness'. Furthermore, teamwork required regular communication:

> keeping in touch during the day and communicating enough. That's a constant issue in a three teacher team – to make sure that . . . all of you know. You have a personal relationship with your colleagues individually, but then you have a collegial responsibility to share a certain amount of information about the children and about their needs; and when you're making the transition between parts of the day, about how that's going to go . . . Or making sure that the necessary apologies [are made] . . . you know, saying: 'There was a phone call about that, I'm so sorry I didn't get out here in time and communicate that to you' . . . dealing with the consequences of miscommunication is part of it as well.

In this way, teamwork among the teachers was not something that occurred only at the structural level of agreeing responsibilities for the day, but also at the level of day-to-day negotiations of human relationships with implications for the enactment of the curriculum.

Theme 3: Acting professionally: 'Being fully present' and bringing it all together

Responding to my question about how she would describe 'acting professionally' in her interactions with children, Bette said:

> while being fully present with a child you still have to access things you've learnt and things that you have studied and things you've planned and you have to access your conversations with the parents, your conversations with the other team members – and bring it with you. In terms of . . . your being present, there is the concept of what the child, right then, needs as well as this other stuff that's in your head.

This statement draws together many of the threads of Bette's thinking about professional practice: to act professionally means to bring together multiple layers of thinking, understandings, and knowledge from diverse sources. Later in the interview she called the moment of bringing it together, or professional decision-making, a moment of 'balancing':

> So you have your knowledge of that child and you have the knowledge of the other children and then you have to look and see what's happening . . . and work out what you're going to do professionally. That's the whole *balancing* . . . So what needs to happen? . . . Yeah, *balance, balancing* [Bette's emphasis].

The following section provides an insight into 'balancing' as curriculum decision-making. It highlights two examples of opportunities for learning that opened up through professional practice focused on a curriculum of open possibilities.

Curriculum decision-making: opportunities when 'the elements come towards you'

Bette's phrase – 'if the elements come towards you' – was a powerful way of explaining that some curriculum experiences unfolded within her kindergarten through apparently serendipitous happenings that were transformed into opportunities for learning through the professional actions of the teaching team.

Case Study: Learning the *haka* and bringing the outside world into the kindergarten

One notable opportunity for learning 'in the spaces that open up' when 'the elements come towards you' was glimpsed in the first half hour of Bette's day. During this time Bette was in the reading corner surrounded by up to eight children while she read the book *The Fish of Maui*. The book was chosen by Rangi, the first boy who arrived in the reading corner. Rangi settled down to listen to the story with which he was obviously very familiar. He pointed to the pictures and contributed phrases from the story as they came up in Bette's reading of it. When Bette turned the page to a picture of Maui with his father, pointing to each in turn, Rangi said: 'that's me; and that's my dad', promptly opening his eyes wide mimicking how to *pukana*[4] in a *haka*[5]. Noticing Rangi's wide open eyes and the ceremonial body stance he had adopted, Bette complimented him, saying: 'You're quite good at that. We'll have to learn to do the *haka*', whereupon Rangi burst into a performance of a short segment from a *haka*. Later that morning, as Bette was leading a group of children making playdough, two other boys could be observed re-enacting the *haka* moves performed by Rangi.

Both these events were fleetingly captured on the video and, as I observed them on the day, made but a momentary impression on me. However, in discussing Bette's programme planning during the interview four days later, Bette made an unprompted reference to Rangi's interest in the *haka* and used it to explain how she and her colleagues saw it as an opportunity for expanding the curriculum, including looking outside of the kindergarten to resource it:

> one of the things that's been very exciting for us is our little boy who's really fascinated with doing *haka* – he's only three – and he calls . . . the Maui books . . . '*haka* books'. He has just seized onto this interest but . . . because of his energy and enthusiasm there are like eight kids who are interested in that whole group of books now . . . we're now looking at how can we build on it . . . and who can

we bring in? Because the boy, [the] *haka*-practitioner, he knows 'women don't know this stuff' . . . At 3, he knows he needs a man . . . So we've been trying to get in touch with the school to see if we can get a *kapa haka* group[6] down, or if we can go and see one there. It might be that we end up needing to get a video of one if we can't manage it . . . we're going to . . . learn what the words are, we're going to learn . . . about the meanings . . . just to enrich the real interest.

Clearly, Rangi's personal interest had serendipitously opened up a space for valued learning for the whole kindergarten, which also had the potential to bring the outside world – the local school *kapa haka* group – into the kindergarten. From Bette's perspective, what I had observed as a momentary display of interest in a common New Zealand cultural practice – the *haka* – had nothing fleeting about it; rather, it was evidence of a child's ongoing interest which she and her colleagues had already identified, were keen to nurture when it re-surfaced, and planned to extend in the future.

Case Study: The dead bird in the garden

The discovery of a dead bird in the outdoor area of the kindergarten was another of the 'vast, amorphous bunch of things' that unexpectedly became part of the emergent curriculum on the day of the study. A boy found the bird under a bush inside the kindergarten gate. At the suggestion of one of the teachers, the boy placed the bird in a plastic container and took it indoors to show to Bette. After exploring with Bette how the bird might have died ('someone put his hand up and it fell into his hand'), and what he might do with the dead bird ('I'm going to keep it'), the boy took the bird outdoors again and with the help of other children and the outside teacher, dug a hole in the garden to bury it. The children then decided to put up a notice to mark the bird's grave. The notice, hand-printed with felt pens on paper from the collage table and taped to a garden stake, said: 'A bird died'. The notice flapped in the light breeze and attracted attention throughout the day from children and parents alike.

The discovery of the dead bird was an unplanned event similar to Rangi's spontaneous *haka*. In having the freedom to explore these events as they occurred, the children had the opportunity to widen their knowledge in ways that arose naturally within a setting where curriculum decision-making was open enough to allow it.

Conclusion

This chapter has presented a picture of early childhood professional practice in New Zealand by bringing data from a study of a day in the life of a kindergarten teacher, Bette, to bear on current thinking about curriculum and its enactment. Three key elements of the teacher's professional practice were identified as contributing to Bette's enactment of *Te Whāriki* as an open curriculum: a focus on relational involvement in the children's life at the kindergarten; teamwork that went beyond structural planning to include ongoing relational attunement to one's colleagues; and professional decision-making described by the teacher as 'bringing it all together' in an act of 'balancing'. These elements of professional practice operated as layers of activity and consciousness that were often hidden behind the appearance of trivia in the teacher's day, both supporting earlier findings that curriculum decision-making is highly complex and simultaneously throwing light on ways in which teachers can implement *Te Whāriki* in the way it was intended – as an open curriculum.

It is also reasonable to suggest that as Cullen (1996: 123) hoped, working with *Te Whāriki* is contributing 'to the growth of professionalism in the early childhood community and its ability to reflect critically about current practice'. While Bette may not be typical of the early childhood education workforce at large, her professional action during the day of the study, and her thoughtful reflections during the subsequent interview, reveal a level of intentionality of practice that demonstrates that it is possible for teachers to eschew the potential for enormous gaps between curriculum ideals and practice identified by some writers (e.g. Cullen, 1996; Nuttall, 2002; Brostrom, 2003; Alvestad et al., 2009). Although the extent to which critical reflection about current practice was also an embedded aspect of Bette's practice has not been a focus in this chapter, this too was present in her professional reflection about the videoed day.

Find Out More

- Explore the conceptual underpinnings of Te *Whāriki* (see Carr and May, 1993).
- Investigate criticisms of Te *Whāriki* and how it is used by teachers (see Blaicklock, 2008; Alvestad et al., 2009)
- What are New Zealand teachers' views of professional practice (see Dalli, 2008)?

Notes

1   The ten-year strategic plan for early childhood education, *Pathways to the Future – Ngā Huarahi Arataki*, introduced under a Labour-led government in 2002, had a target of achieving a 100% qualified workforce in teacher-led services by 2012. A National-led government elected in November 2008 subsequently removed the 100% target and established a new target of 80% qualified by 2012.

2   The four principles in *Te Whāriki* are: well-being / *mana atua*; holistic development / *kotahitanga*; empowerment / *whakamana*; belonging / *mana whenua*.

3   It is worth noting that this argument does rather presuppose that everything that pre-dated *Te Whāriki* needed to change – and this is by no means a demonstrable proposition.

4   *pukana* is a verb meaning to stare wildly, dilate the eyes – done by both males and females when performing *haka* and *waiata* to emphasize particular words.

5   A *haka* is a Māori traditional dance form performed by men, most famously at the start of national rugby games.

6   Most New Zealand schools have Māori Performing Arts groups called *kapa haka* groups; *kapa* means line or row and refers to the way that *haka* are performed by groups of people arranged in lines.

References and recommended reading

Alvestad, M., Duncan, J. and Berge, A. (2009) New Zealand ECE teachers talk about Te Whaariki, *New Zealand Journal of Teachers' Work*, 6(1): 3–19.

Blaiklock, K. (2008) The invisible alphabet: Te Whāriki, letter knowledge, and the development of reading skills, *Early Education*, 43: 12–15.

Brennan, M. (2007) A culture of tenderness: teachers' socialisation practices in group care settings, *European Early Childhood Education Research Journal*, 15(1): 137–46.

Brostrom, S. (2003) Understanding *Te Whāriki* from a Danish perspective, in J. Nuttall (ed.) *Weaving Te Whāriki: Aotearoa New Zealand's Early Childhood Curriculum Document in Theory and Practice*. Wellington: New Zealand Council for Educational Research.

Carr, M. and May, H. (1993) Choosing a model: reflecting on the development process of Te Whāriki: National early childhood curriculum guidelines in New Zealand. Paper presented at the First Warwick International Early Years Conference, University of Warwick.

Cullen, J. (1996) The challenge of *Te Whāriki* for future developments in early childhood education, *DELTA*, 48(1): 113–26.

Cullen, J. (2003) The challenge of *Te Whāriki:* catalyst for change?, in J. Nuttall (ed.) *Weaving Te Whāriki: Aotearoa New Zealand's Early Childhood Curriculum Document in Theory and Practice*. Wellington: New Zealand Council for Educational Research.

Dalli, C. (2008) Pedagogy, knowledge and collaboration: towards a ground-up perspective on professionalism, *European Early Childhood Education Research Journal*, 16(2): 171–85.

Dalli, C. and Urban, M. (eds.) (2010) *Professionalism in Early Childhood Education and Care: International Perspectives*. London: Routledge.

Department of Education (1988) *The Curriculum: An Early Childhood Statement*. Wellington: Department of Education.

Guild, D.E., Lyons, J. and Whiley, J. (1998) Te Whāriki: New Zealand's national early childhood curriculum guideline, *International Journal of Early Childhood*, 30(1): 65–70.

Hedges, H. (2007) Funds of knowledge in early childhood communities of inquiry. Unpublished PhD thesis, Massey University, Palmerston North. Available at: http://hdl.handle.net/10179/580 (accessed 5 June 2012).

Laevers, F. (2005) The curriculum as means to raise the quality of early childhood education: implications for policy, *European Early Childhood Education Research Journal*, 13(1): 17–29.

McLachlan, C.J., Carvalho, L., Kumar, K. and de Lautour, N. (2006) Emergent literacy in early childhood settings in New Zealand, *Australian Journal of Early Childhood*, 31(2): 31–41.

McNaughton, S. (1996) Co-constructing curricula: a comment on two curricula (*Te Whāriki* and the English Curriculum) and their developmental basis, *New Zealand Journal of Educational Studies*, 31(2): 189–96.

Miller, L., Dalli, C. and Urban, M. (eds.) (2012) *Early Childhood Grows Up: Towards a Critical Ecology of the Profession*. New York: Springer.

Ministry of Education (1996) *Te Whāriki. He Whariki Mātauranga mō ngā Mokopuna o Aotearoa. Early Childhood Curriculum*. Wellington: Learning Media.

Moss, P. (2007) Leading the wave: New Zealand in an international context, in *Travelling Pathways to the Future: Ngā Huarahi Arataki. Early Childhood Education Symposium Proceedings*, 2–3 May. Wellington: Ministry of Education. Available at: http://www.minedu. govt.nz/~/media/MinEdu/Files/EducationSectors/EarlyChildhood/ECESymposium.pdf (accessed 5 June 2012).

Mutch, C. (2003) One context, two outcomes: a comparison of *Te Whāriki* and the *New Zealand Curriculum Framework*, in J. Nuttall (ed.) *Weaving Te Whāriki: Aotearoa New Zealand's Early Childhood Curriculum Document in Theory and Practice*. Wellington: New Zealand Council for Educational Research.

Nuttall, J. (2002) Early childhood curriculum in theory, ideology and practice: using *Te Whāriki*, *DELTA*, 54(1/2): 91–104.

Nuttall, J. and Edwards, S. (2007) Theory, policy and practice: three contexts for the development of Australasia's early childhood curriculum documents, in L. Keesing-Style and H. Hedges (eds.) *Theorising Early Childhood Practice: Emerging Dialogues*. Castle Hill, NSW: Pademelon Press.

OECD (2004) *Starting Strong: Curricula and Pedagogies in Early Childhood Education and Care: Five Curriculum Outlines*. Paris: OECD.

Pramling, I., Sheridan, S. and Williams, P. (2004) Key issues in curriculum development for young children, in *Starting Strong: Curricula and Pedagogies in Early Childhood Education and Care: Five Curriculum Outlines*. Paris: OECD.

Sands, L. and Weston, J. (2010) Slowing down to catch up with infants and toddlers: a reflection on aspects of a questioning culture of practice, *The First Years: Nga Tau Tuatahi/New Zealand Journal of Infant and Toddler Education*, 12(1): 9–15.

15

HIGHSCOPE TODAY: PEDAGOGY FOR LEARNING AND DEVELOPMENT
Beth Marshall

Summary

This chapter highlights the main aspects of HighScope today. It discusses the developmental theory and research underpinnings of HighScope. The HighScope Preschool Wheel of Learning graphically presents each of the aspects of the curriculum. The chapter will address each of these aspects, including active participatory learning, components of the HighScope daily routine, adult–child interaction, the learning environment, and assessment.

Case Study

Anna just turned 4 years of age. For planning time, Carol, the teacher, asks the children to draw what they are going to do at work time. Anna draws a long rectangle and puts two circles on the bottom. She also writes a 'BLK' at the bottom. When Carol comes over, she asks Anna to tell her about her picture. Anna explains that she wants to play fire trucks in the block area. Carol asks her more about her plans. Anna explains that she is going to get the big blocks and make a fire truck that she and Jalessa can sit in. Then, they are going to be firefighters. The teacher acknowledges her work and Anna goes and gets to work.

Anna goes to the block area and gets the large, hollow, wooden blocks. Jalessa joins her and together they lay out a large rectangle on the floor. They have to figure out what sized blocks to use (square or rectangle) to make it just the way they both want. Then, they put two small pillows on the floor of the truck 'to make it comfy to sit on'. They look at their work and realize that they need a steering wheel. Since Kenneth is already using the steering wheel salvaged from an old car, they walk through the classroom looking for something else that might work. Jalessa holds up a long unit block, but Anna decides it's 'the wrong shape'. She then spots a dish from the house area. She gets that and brings it back and shows Jalessa how they can turn it just like the real steering wheel. They both agree this will work. They get into the fire truck and take turns steering. Carol notices their play. She builds a small structure nearby with some unit blocks. She pretends it's on fire. The firefighters (Anna and Jalessa) eagerly come over and offer to put it out for her. They use old neckties for hoses and pretend to squirt out the fire. Other children notice the play. Mikey and Hayden come over and ask if they can play. They also want to be firefighters. After some discussion, the girls decide that they need to make the fire truck bigger, so more blocks are added to the back. Mikey and Hayden climb aboard. The firefighter play continues for most of work time. The firefighters add cell phones so they can get calls from people needing help and pretend to put out fires around the room. Rocks and sticks become food.

With about ten minutes left in work time, Anna remembers that she also wants to make a picture for her Grandma, who is sick. She goes to the art area, and selects crayons. She draws a picture that resembles a butterfly. On the bottom, she writes 'LOV ANNA'. She puts it in her cubby just as Mikey is ringing the bell that signals clean-up. Anna puts away the crayons and goes back to the block area to help the other firefighters disassemble the fire truck.

At recall time, Anna gathers back with her small group. Carol explains that for recall today, they are going to play a guessing game. The children are to show what their hands were doing and the rest of the group have to guess what it was. When it's Anna's turn, she demonstrates how she steered the fire truck and pretended to put out fires. Kenneth, who is also in Anna's group, correctly guessed playing firefighters. Anna nodded and discussed what she did. Other children chimed in when they had a part in the plan (seeing a fire, calling for help).

HighScope is an active participatory learning curriculum. It can be distinguished from others in many ways, especially by its emphasis on adult–child interaction and the process of Plan-Do-Review. The above scenario illustrates the Plan-Do-Review process from a child's experience. You will learn a bit more about these components as you read on, but first let's start at the beginning.

The HighScope Curriculum is grounded in both developmental theory and research. HighScope began as a result of the landmark research study known as the HighScope Perry Preschool Study. Through continuing study and use, the curriculum has evolved to what it is today. We know through evidence from the HighScope Perry Preschool Study (Schweinhart et al., 2005) and several other studies (Schweinhart and Weikart, 1997; Marcon, 2002; Ramey et al., 2004), that high-quality preschool programmes make a difference in children's lives. Throughout their lives, children who participate in such programmes achieve greater success as students and adults. They go further in school, earn more money, commit fewer crimes, and ultimately contribute in a positive way to society. The HighScope curriculum originally drew extensively on the work of Jean Piaget (Piaget and Inhelder, 1969), Erik Erikson (1950/1963), and the progressive educational philosophy of John Dewey (1938/1963). Since then, the curriculum has been revised and updated based on the results of ongoing cognitive, developmental, and brain research (Shore, 1997; National Research Council, 2000a, 2000b; Clements, 2004; Gelman and Brenneman, 2004). The teaching practices, particularly the idea that development occurs within socio-cultural settings where adults scaffold children's learning, was first derived from the work of developmental psychologist and educator Lev Vygotsky (1934/1962). While HighScope continues to evolve, taking into account new research findings on what children learn and how they learn, it continues to stay true to its constructivist educational philosophy and is shaped by the wisdom of experienced classroom teachers. As David Weikart states in his book *How HighScope Grew: A Memoir*:

> The High/Scope approach would draw upon child development theory such as Piaget's, but the application of theory had to be tempered by advice from experienced classroom teachers. We would never be a classic, strictly Piagetian-based program . . . Henceforth, the curriculum was to be pragmatic and applied while still relying heavily on sound theoretical principles. I continue to believe that the use of theory, even well-documented theory, must be tempered by the real-world wisdom of experienced staff. Thus today, the HighScope curriculum is an amalgam of related developmental theories hammered into usefulness by decades of teacher experiences in the classroom and on home visits. I have never regretted this decision nor questioned the results. When I see our approach being used throughout the United States and in over 20 countries by a wide range of ethnic, religious and language groups, I see its broad accessibility as support for my decision to listen carefully to the teachers.
>
> (Weikart, 2004: 67)

The HighScope Preschool 'Wheel of Learning'

Figure 15.1, the 'HighScope Preschool Wheel of Learning', illustrates the curriculum principles that guide practitioners in their daily work with children.

Active participatory learning

The HighScope educational approach is based on the belief that young children build or 'construct' their knowledge of the world. That means learning is not simply a process of adults giving information to children. Rather, children are active learners; they discover things through direct experience with people, objects, events, and ideas. They learn best from pursuing their own interests while being actively supported and challenged by adults. HighScope teachers are as active and involved as children in the classroom. They thoughtfully provide materials, plan activities, and talk with children in ways that both support and challenge what children are experiencing and thinking. HighScope calls this approach *active participatory learning* – a process in which teachers and children are partners in the learning process. Active participatory learning, together with *initiative* and the *key developmental indicators*,

Figure 15.1 The HighScope Preschool Wheel of Learning

is at the centre of the wheel of learning to highlight its importance in every other aspect of the curriculum.

Active learning has five ingredients, each of which must be present:

1. *Materials*: Abundant supplies of interesting materials are readily available to children. Materials are appealing to all the senses and are open-ended – that is, they lend themselves to being used in a variety of ways and help expand children's experiences and stimulate their thought.

2. *Manipulation*: Children handle, examine, combine and transform materials and ideas. They make discoveries through direct hands-on and 'minds-on' contact with these resources.

3. *Choice*: Children choose materials and play partners, change and build on their play ideas, and plan activities according to their interests and needs.

4. *Child language and thought*: Children describe what they are doing and understanding. They communicate verbally and non-verbally as they think about their actions and modify their thinking to take new learning into account.

5. *Adult scaffolding*: 'Scaffolding' means adults both support children's current level of thinking and challenge them. Adults encourage children's efforts and help them extend or build on their work by talking with them about what they are doing, by joining in their play, and by helping them learn to solve problems that arise.

Initiative

Active participatory learning is driven by personal initiative, wanting to do something from within rather than to please someone else. Central to HighScope is the belief that young children have an innate desire to explore, discover, and learn. They approach the world with a sense of curiosity that propels them to act, find answers to their own questions, and solve problems they encounter in play. HighScope encourages children to use their initiative to set their own goals, to plan, to act and to reflect, and to develop their own unique strengths and interests.

Key developmental indicators

The key developmental indicators (KDIs), listed in Table 15.1, are the *content* of the HighScope Preschool curriculum. The word *key* refers to the idea that these are meaningful concepts children should learn and experience. The word *developmental* conveys the idea that learning is gradual and cumulative. Learning follows a sequence, generally from simple to more complex knowledge and skills. Teachers use the key developmental indicators as tools for planning, observing, describing, and supporting children's learning and development as they play and interact with them throughout the programme day.

In the case study at the beginning of this chapter, we see examples of the key developmental indicators as they unfold in a child's play. During planning time, Anna experienced KDI 2 Planning, KDI 40 Art, and KDI 22 Speaking. During her work time play, we see an abundance of key developmental indicators. These include KDI 1 Initiative, KDI 3 Engagement, KDI 4 Problem solving, KDI 12 Building relationships, KDI 13 Cooperative play, KDI 16 Gross-motor skills, KDI 17 Fine-motor skills, KDI 21 Comprehension, KDI 22 Speaking, KDI 24 Phonological awareness, KDI 29 Writing, KDI 34 Shapes, KDI 35 Spatial awareness, KDI 40 Art, KDI 43 Pretend play, and KDI 54 Community roles. During clean-up, we see KDI 11 Community. And finally, during recall time, we see KDI 6 Reflection and KDI 43 Pretend play.

Daily routine

The HighScope daily routine is designed to provide the consistency and predictability that children and adults need, while providing enough flexibility so that the children don't feel rushed or bored as they carry out their activities. The day includes periods of both child-initiated time (time for children to plan, to carry out their plans, to recall and reflect on their actions) and adult-initiated time (small group and

Table 15.1 HighScope Preschool Curriculum content: key developmental indicators

---

A. Approaches to Learning

1. *Initiative*: Children demonstrate initiative as they explore their world.

2. *Planning*: Children make plans and follow through on their intentions.

3. *Engagement*: Children focus on activities that interest them.

4. *Problem-solving*: Children solve problems encountered in play.

5. *Use of resources*: Children gather information and formulate ideas about their world.

6. *Reflection*: Children reflect on their experiences.

B. Social and Emotional Development

7. *Self-identity*: Children have a positive self-identity.

8. *Sense of competence*: Children feel they are competent.

9. *Emotions*: Children recognize, label, and regulate their feelings.

10. *Empathy*: Children demonstrate empathy towards others.

11. *Community*: Children participate in the community of the classroom.

12. *Building relationships*: Children build relationships with other children and adults.

13. *Cooperative play*: Children engage in cooperative play.

14. *Moral development*: Children develop an internal sense of right and wrong.

15. *Conflict resolution*: Children resolve social conflicts.

C. Physical Development and Health

16. *Gross-motor skills*: Children demonstrate strength, flexibility, balance, and timing in using their large muscles.

17. *Fine-motor skills*: Children demonstrate dexterity and hand–eye coordination in using their small muscles.

18. *Body awareness*: Children know about their bodies and how to navigate them in space.

19. *Personal care*: Children carry out personal care routines on their own.

20. *Healthy behaviour*: Children engage in healthy practices.

D. Language, Literacy, and Communication[a]

21. *Comprehension*: Children understand language.

22. *Speaking*: Children express themselves using language.

23. *Vocabulary*: Children understand and use a variety of words and phrases.

24. *Phonological awareness*: Children identify distinct sounds in spoken language.

25. *Alphabetic knowledge*: Children identify letter names and their sounds.

26. *Reading*: Children read for pleasure and information.

27. *Concepts about print*: Children demonstrate knowledge about environmental print.

28. *Book knowledge*: Children demonstrate knowledge about books.

29. *Writing*: Children write for many different purposes.

30. *English language learning*: (If applicable) Children use English and their home language(s) (including sign language).

E. Mathematics

31. *Number words and symbols*: Children recognize and use number words and symbols.

32. *Counting*: Children count things.

33. *Part–whole relationships*: Children combine and separate quantities of objects.

34. *Shapes*: Children identify, name, and describe shapes.

35. *Spatial awareness*: Children recognize spatial relationships among people and objects.

36. *Measuring*: Children measure to describe, compare, and order things.

37. *Unit*: Children understand and use the concept of unit.

38. *Patterns*: Children identify, describe, copy, complete, and create patterns.

39. *Data analysis*: Children use information about quantity to draw conclusions, make decisions, and solve problems.

F. Creative Arts

40. *Art*: Children express and represent what they observe, think, imagine, and feel through two- and three-dimensional art.

41. *Music*: Children express and represent what they observe, think, imagine, and feel through music.

42. *Movement*: Children express and represent what they observe, think, imagine, and feel through movement.

43. *Pretend play*: Children express and represent what they observe, think, imagine, and feel through pretend play.

44. *Appreciating the arts*: Children appreciate the creative arts.

G. Science and Technology

45. *Observing*: Children observe the materials and processes in their environment.

46. *Classifying*: Children classify materials, actions, people, and events.

47. *Experimenting*: Children experiment to test their ideas.

48. *Predicting*: Children predict what they expect will happen.

49. *Drawing conclusions*: Children draw conclusions based on their experiences and observations.

50. *Communicating ideas*: Children communicate their ideas about the characteristics of things and how they work.

51. *Natural and physical world*: Children gather knowledge about the natural and physical world.

52. *Tools and technology*: Children explore and use tools and technology.

H. Social Studies

53. *Diversity*: Children understand that people have diverse characteristics, interests, and abilities.

54. *Community roles*: Children recognize that people have different roles and functions in the community.

(Continued)

Table 15.1 (*Continued*)

H. Social Studies

55. *Decision-making*: Children participate in making classroom decisions.

56. *Geography*: Children recognize and interpret features and locations in their environment.

57. *History*: Children understand past, present, and future.

58. *Ecology*: Children understand the importance of taking care of their environment.

---

[a]Regulations in the United States require adult-to-child ratios to be followed both inside and outside in such a manner that free flow movement between the two is rare in HighScope settings in the USA.

large group activities). The schedule is the same every day, with each component taking a specified amount of time. This gives children a sense of control and helps them to act independently.

The order of the parts of the daily routine may vary, depending on the hours and structure of a particular setting. However, planning time, work time, clean-up time, and recall time *always* occur in that order. In half-day programmes, each part typically happens once. In full-day programmes, one or more parts may be repeated and may also include a rest or nap period.

Components of the HighScope daily routine

The following is a summary of each segment of the HighScope daily routine.

Greeting time (15–20 minutes)

Greeting time (Figure 15.2) provides a smooth transition from home to school. Teachers greet children, connect with parents, and read books in a cosy setting. The last five minutes of greeting time are used to read the message board with the children. The message board gives children and adults a chance to share important information relating to the day. An adult writes the messages ahead of time, using 'written' pictures and words so children of all literacy levels can 'read' them together. Adults share announcements and let children know about upcoming special events, new materials, visitors, and so on. The message board can also be used as a starting point for group problem-solving.

The Plan-Do-Review process

The largest part of the HighScope day, generally over an hour in total, is devoted to *a planning time, work time*, and *recall time* sequence called Plan-Do-Review. This is the child-initiated part of the day. In small groups, each child decides what to do during work time – what area to play in, what materials to use, and who else will be

Figure 15.2 HighScope greeting time (photographer Bob Foran)

involved – and shares this plan with an adult. Work time is when children carry out their plans, alone and/or with others and then clean-up. At recall time, they meet with the same adult and small group of children with whom they planned to share and discuss what they did and learned during work time.

Planning time (10–15 minutes)

Planning time begins the *Plan-Do-Review* process. When young children plan, they begin with an intention or idea. Depending on their age and ability to communicate, they might express their plan in actions (picking up a block), gestures (point to the block area) or words ('I want to make a tall, tall building – like where my mommy works'). Planning is different from simply making a choice because it involves children in developing specific ideas about what they want to do and how they will do it. In other works, planning involves more purpose and intentionality than choosing. It is also important to remember that young children can change their plans. In fact, children often do so as they become interested in what someone else is doing, or notice interesting materials they previously overlooked. In the case study above, Anna did complete her initial plan (to play fire trucks) and then she went on to pursue a second idea, to make a picture for her sick grandmother.

Work time (45–60 minutes)

Work time – the 'do' part of Plan-Do-Review – is when children carry out their plans. Children can work with any of the materials in any of the interest areas. Children decide where they will play, what they will play, and who they will play with. All areas and materials are available for children to use in carrying out their plans. Children use materials creatively at work time, repeating and building upon activities that interest them; there are no preset activities. Materials may be moved from one area of the classroom to another. In the case study, we see Anna create a fire truck from blocks and pillows, use a plate for a steering wheel, and pretend sticks and rocks are firefighter food.

During work time, adults focus on supporting the children, interacting with them in calm and respectful tones. Adults observe and listen to children during this part of the day, conversing in a give-and-take manner and avoiding asking questions with predetermined correct answers. They use this time to recognize and scaffold the key developmental indicators as they occur during children's work and play. Adults participate as partners in children's play; they assume roles suggested by the children and follow the children's cues about the content and direction of play. In the case study, when Carol saw Anna's and Jalessa's play stalling, she joined in as a partner and extended their play by creating a need for the help of firefighters. Adults encourage children to explore and use materials in their own way, encourage children's efforts and ideas, and put children in control of evaluating their own work and efforts. Adults in a HighScope classroom involve children in resolving conflicts.

Clean-up (about 10 minutes)

A clean-up time helps children understand the 'find-use-return' principle. Children and adults work together to return materials and equipment to their storage spaces and, when appropriate, put away or find display space for children's personal creations.

Recall time (10–15 minutes)

Recall brings closure to the Plan-Do-Review process. In their small groups, children are encouraged to reflect on, talk about, and/or show what they have done at work time. Younger preschoolers often recall the last thing they did, since it is freshest in their minds. Older preschoolers are more able to recall the sequence of what they did at work time, or they may even recall their original plans. Recall should always immediately follow the work time/clean-up time sequence. Adults use a variety of strategies to encourage children to share and recall their experiences. They assist children as they reflect on their actions, feelings, and plans, and encourage children to recall in ways that are consistent with their developmental levels. This might include pointing or gesturing, demonstrating, describing, drawing, and/or writing. In the case study, Anna first had to remember what she did, and then figure out what her hands were doing to demonstrate to the rest of the small group. When other children were recalling, her brain was busy taking in their actions and making connections to what she saw them doing (for example, 'He was squishing the play dough', 'She's moving the mouse and clicking it – she was at the computer!').

Small-group time (15–20 minutes)

Small-group time is when a group of eight to ten children meet with an adult to experience active learning in a stable, intimate setting. Small groups meet concurrently; the group size is dependent on the adult-to-child ratio for the class. The adult plans the small-group experience from the curriculum content (key developmental indicators), children's interests, and/or interesting classroom materials. At small-group time, the teacher briefly introduces the activity or materials. Children receive the same set of open-ended materials and then work with them in their own unique ways. They contribute their own ideas, use the materials in ways that they find interesting, and participate at their own development levels. For example, in one small group, children were given short lengths of wide, flat ribbon scraps along with paper and a glue stick. The adult watched to see how children responded to the materials. Some children created patterns, another child arranged the ribbons from shortest to longest, and another child glued their ribbons cross-wise on top of each other, creating what she called 'flowers'. Keeping the key developmental indicators in mind, the adult was able to identify the different content learning, and make comments to support each child's unique response to the materials. Small-group time gives children the opportunity to build on their own interests, have experiences in a variety of curriculum content areas, and explore new, unexplored or underused materials they might not use during work time, all with adult support in a smaller setting.

Adults use many strategies, often drawn from HighScope resource books and training, to support and extend children's small-group activities. They observe what children do, move from child to child, look for children's learning based on the key developmental indicators, imitate and add to children's actions and ideas while using the materials themselves, and scaffold children's learning by using comments and acknowledgments to support children's current level of thinking and occasionally offering a gentle extension to help them consider their work from a new perspective or idea.

Large-group time (10–15 minutes)

Large-group time is when all the children and adults participate in an activity together. Large-group time contributes to the sense of community in the classroom. It is a time when everyone comes together to participate in music and movement activities. Like every other part of the HighScope day, the five ingredients of active participatory learning are present.

As with small-group time, large-group time is planned and initiated by the adults, but children do make choices. For example, children decide how to move their bodies to music – they make suggestions for motions to a favourite song or rhyme. It is also a time of day when children can take turns being leaders.

Outside time (30–40 minutes)

During outside time, children can enjoy physical, noisy, and vigorous play. Rather than standing to the side and just observing, HighScope adults join children in their outdoor play. Being outside also lets children and adults connect to their neighbourhood community and use all their senses to appreciate nature.

The outdoors is a place where young children can run, jump, throw, kick, swing, climb, dig, and ride. Their pretend play takes on new dimensions as they move over a larger area, and incorporate trees, rocks, the slide, and leaves into the play. Children have an abundance of choices about what they can do outside. They can be engaged in pretend play, play with manufactured and natural objects, and play alone or with others. Adults not only supervise children for safety outside, but also become engaged with children, scaffolding their learning and discoveries.

Meal times (15–20 minutes)

In most part-day programmes, children and adults share a snack, while full-day programmes have both meal- and snack-times. It is preferable to eat in small groups, with the same adult and children who gather together for planning, recall, and small-group time. The emphasis during meal times is on social interaction. It is important for adults to sit down and eat with children, both as a natural social situation and as an opportunity to share relaxed conversations and to support children's ideas. Meal times are also occasions for children to develop self-help skills such as pouring their own juice, serving themselves, and wiping up spills.

Adult–child interaction

In the HighScope Curriculum, *shared control* is central to how adults and children interact. The curriculum has many specific strategies for accomplishing this goal. Children are in control of child-sized decisions such as where to play, how to play, and who to play with. Adults are in charge of adult-sized decisions including establishing the daily routine, arranging and equipping the classroom, and keeping children physically and psychologically safe. HighScope has neither a directive nor 'anything-goes' atmosphere. Instead, HighScope promotes a supportive climate in which adults and children are partners throughout the day.

The way adults interact with children plays a very important role in children's learning and development (Moyles et al., 2002). Studies of the relationship between teachers' interaction styles support the importance of a child-oriented interaction style. These studies (e.g. Sylva et al., 1980; Wood et al., 1980) demonstrate that in classrooms where teachers are responsive, guiding, and nurturing, children take more initiative and are more likely to be actively involved and persistent in their work. HighScope stresses the importance of active learning, intrinsic motivation, and the engagement of young children. HighScope encourages adults to use identified *interaction strategies, encouragement* (which builds on children's self-evaluation, rather than external praise), and a *problem-solving approach to conflict* as they play and work with children.

Planning the indoor learning environment

Settings for active learning require thoughtful planning. Careful attention to the arrangement of the *interest areas*, the *types of materials*, and *storage of those materials* help children follow through on their ideas and build on their learning experiences.

Assessment

Assessment includes both assessment of the child's learning and development and of the effectiveness of the programme or classroom. It starts with *teamwork* between all members of the teaching team. It emphasizes honest, open relationships to plan for and then assess children's experiences and classroom practices. Adults use *daily anecdotal notes* to help answer the following important questions:

- What are the children's interests?
- What are the children learning?
- What areas of learning are we currently supporting?
- Are any of the areas of learning overlooked or not supported?
- What materials or experiences might be added?

The questions are discussed during their *daily lesson planning session.* They develop lesson plans for the next day that scaffold children's discoveries and learning based on the anecdotal notes and ongoing assessment of children's development. High-Scope has developed and validated a *child assessment* instrument to measure children's development and growth. The HighScope Preschool Child Observation Record (COR) assesses children's overall development. This assessment system is based on anecdotes made during normal classroom activities. It enables adults to look at the whole child and respects and accommodates cultural differences. The COR can be used with typically developing children and with children with special needs and/or disabilities. *Programme assessment* helps teachers assess the quality of the classroom setting and of their programme. The HighScope Program Quality Assessment (PQA) helps programmes, administrators, and teachers reflect on their practice and guide them as they strive to provide a high-quality programme for the children and families that they serve.

Find Out More

- How does your practice incorporate the ingredients of active learning?
- Do the key developmental indicators reflect your goals for preschool-aged children? How would they strengthen your teaching practices?
- How does your setting include both child- and teacher-initiated parts of the day?
- How might the Plan-Do-Review process impact the children you work with? How do planning and reflection connect to concepts of engagement and self-regulation?
- How are the theoretical underpinnings of HighScope similar or different to other curricula? In what ways do research finding shape aspects of the HighScope curriculum and other curricula?

See www.highscope.org

References and recommended reading

Clements, D.H. (2004) Major themes and recommendations, in D.H. Clements, J. Sarma and A.-M. DiBiase (eds.) *Engaging Young Children in Mathematics: Standards for Early Childhood Mathematics Education.* Mahway, NJ: Lawrence Erlbaum Associates.

Dewey, J. (1938/1963) *Experience and Education.* New York: Macmillan.

Epstein, A.S. (2007) *Essentials of Active Learning in Preschool: Getting to Know the High/Scope Curriculum.* Ypsilanti, MI: HighScope Press.

Erikson, E. (1950/1963) *Childhood and Society.* New York: W.W. Norton.

Gelman, R. and Brenneman, K. (2004) Science learning pathways for young children, *Early Childhood Research Quarterly,* 19(1): 150–8.

Hohmann, M., Weikart, D.P. and Epstein, A. (2008) *Educating Young Children: The Complete Guide to the HighScope Curriculum* (3rd edn.). Ypsilanti, MI: HighScope Press.

Marcon, R.A. (2002) Moving up the grades: relationship between preschool model and later school success, *Early Childhood Research and Practice,* 4(1). Available at: http://ecrp.uiuc.edu/v4n1/marcon.html (accessed 8 June 2012).

Marshall, B. (2007) *HighScope Step by Step: Lesson Plans for the First 30 Days.* Ypsilanti, MI: HighScope Press.

Moyles, J., Adams, S. and Musgrove, A. (2002) *SPEEL Study of Pedagogical Effectiveness.* DfES Research Report 363. London: Department for Education and Skills.

National Research Council (2000a) *Eager to Learn: Educating our Preschoolers.* Washington, DC: National Academy Press.

National Research Council (2000b) *Neurons to Neighborhoods: The Science of Early Childhood Development.* Washington, DC: National Academy Press.

Piaget, J. and Inhelder, B. (1969) *The Psychology of the Child.* New York: Basic Books.

Ramey, C.T., Gallagher, J.J., Campbell, F.A., Wasik, B.H. and Sparling, J.J. (2004) *Carolina Abecedarian Project and the Carolina Approach to Responsive Education (CARE), 1972-1992.* ICPSR04091-v1. Ann Arbor, MI: Inter-university Consortium for Political and Social Research (distributor). DOI: 10.3886/ICPSR04091.v1.

Schweinhart, L.J. and Weikart, D.P. (1997) *Lasting Differences: The High/Scope Preschool Curriculum Comparison Study through Age 27.* Ypsilanti, MI: HighScope Press.

Schweinhart, L.J., Montie, J., Xiang, Z., Barnett, W.S., Belfield, C.R. and Nores, M. (2005) *Lifetime Effects: The High/Scope Perry Preschool Study through Age 40.* Ypsilanti, MI: HighScope Press.

Shore, R. (1997) *Rethinking the Brain: New Insights into Early Development.* New York: Families and Work Institute.

Sylva, K., Roy, C. and Painter, M. (1980) *Childwatching at Playgroup & Nursery School.* Ypsilanti, MI: HighScope Press.

Weikart, D.P. (2004) *How HighScope Grew: A Memoir.* Ypsilanti, MI: HighScope Press.

Wiltshire, M. (2012) *Understanding the HighScope Approach.* Abingdon: Routledge.

Wood, D., McMahon, L. and Cranstoun, Y. (1980) *Working with Under Fives.* Ypsilanti, MI: HighScope Press.

Vygotsky, L.S. (1934/1962) *Thought and Language.* Cambridge, MA: MIT Press.

16

CHINA: PEDAGOGY TODAY AND THE MOVE TOWARDS CREATIVITY
Keang-ieng (Peggy) Vong

Summary

One of the educational issues to be addressed by early childhood educators in China today is how to foster creativity in young children. The government has taken the initiative in encouraging the promotion of creative thinking via official guidelines. Theorists advocate play-based curricula and less structured pedagogies with a child-centred orientation, and this has prompted experiments with Western approaches to allow more room within the curriculum for children to be creative. Nonetheless, given the long tradition of a teacher-centred rather than child-centred approach, the diverse understandings of creativity, the various interpretations of creative teaching, and the clash between formal assessment schemes and progressive curricula and pedagogies, is the Chinese government's initiative 'mission impossible'? This chapter aims to illustrate the complex issues involved in promoting children's creativity in China. It will highlight the importance of recognizing cultural and contextual factors in the field of early childhood education and of searching for a cultural definition or even re-definition of creativity, as well as culturally appropriate pedagogies.

Introduction

My initial attempt to understand the discourse and interpretations of creativity as well as the pedagogies employed to promote creativity in kindergarten classrooms took place in 2001 (Vong, 2008a). At that time, China had just become a member state of the World Trade Organization. It was evident there was a need to foster creative citizens so as to sustain China's competitiveness in the global economy. This message remains loud and clear in one of the latest documents, namely the National Outline for Medium- and Long-Term Education Reform and Development 2010 to 2020 (Ministry of Education, 2010). With increasing attention given to preschool education (serving 3- to 5-year-olds), provincial, regional, and municipal governments across China are expected to draft Three-Year Action Plans that should set out and project the general and annual goals, projects, and budgets for the following three years for the development of local kindergartens (Chinese Society of Early Childhood Education, 2011). However, the general policy is that state-owned and governmental institution-owned kindergartens will be kept to a small number and serve as model kindergartens. Individuals and private entrepreneurs (that is, the private sector) are encouraged to establish kindergartens (Outlook Weekly, 2010). Keeping early childhood education outside the public welfare or service system has at least two implications: first, the government's quality control for most kindergartens is indirect; second, the government's educational ideas might be interpreted with great variability among kindergartens. This chapter aims to illustrate the complex issues involved in promoting children's creativity in China. It will describe how creativity has been conceived and promoted since the publication of the recent official guidelines for kindergarten education. Socio-cultural considerations of possible pedagogies to nurture creative ideas in Chinese kindergarten classrooms will be raised, which might challenge current practices.

Creativity defined with a practical sense

The Guidelines for Kindergarten Curriculum – Trial Version was launched in 2001. This official document stresses the significance of fostering in young children innovative and creative ideas. Nonetheless, a decade later, few kindergartens, public or private, emphasize the promotion of creativity as such. Instead, priority is given to domains of development that are of fundamental importance in Chinese culture, such as children's moral development, which is embedded in Confucianism (Sun, 2011). In today's China, the 'side effects' of the One-Child-Family Policy introduced in 1978 are also of much concern among educators and parents as the 'spoiled-child' phenomenon is clear for all (Hesketh et al., 2005). Generally speaking, fostering creativity is given attention and importance in Chinese early childhood education but little deliberate effort is made to facilitate its promotion, even when creativity continues to be recognized as an ability that should also reflect specific cultural meanings or values (Sawyer, 2006). In Chinese contexts, creativity remains an elusive term, making it susceptible to various interpretations and practices at both scholarly and kindergarten level (Vong, 2008a, 2008b).

There is, however, some consensus among Chinese practitioners about what creativity means. A recent visit to Nanjing, a south-eastern city, reveals some of the conceptions of creativity in China, which coincide with the ideas portrayed in my earlier studies conducted in the southern part of the country. These south-easterners' views of creativity and creative pedagogy have been collected from early childhood teacher educators, kindergarten directors and teachers. According to the practitioners, creative ideas are ideas that are novel or unusual for the child and/or the teachers. This also includes problem-solving – that is, having creativity means being able to do something or solve a problem with new ideas. In contrast with Western ideas of creativity, which often carry an affective or psychological sense emphasizing self-expression and features such as originality, imagination, fluency, flexibility, and elaboration (Torrance and Ball, 1984), the concept of creativity in China carries a practical sense and has an almost technical connotation (see also

Vong, 2008a). Chinese teacher educators' interpretations of creativity are similar to the practitioners' views. Interestingly, teacher educators argue that the terms used to explain what creativity means have to be teacher-friendly and conceptually manageable. According to them, words such as 'fluency', 'elaboration', and 'flexibility' found in theories are too intimidating and 'foreign' to teachers. In the early childhood education arena in China, it appears that the 'what' of creativity comes second to 'how' creativity is understood and interpreted by practitioners, and it is this that informs pedagogies to promote creativity in kindergartens.

Pedagogies: carriers of creative elements

As China is a vast country of more than 9 million square kilometres and a population of nearly 1.4 billion made up of fifty-six ethnic groups (Encyclopedia of the Nations, 2012), an understanding of kindergarten practices in different parts of China might help to portray a broad, though still incomplete, picture of the various approaches commonly adopted or somehow associated with fostering creativity in young children. Some of these pedagogies might sound familiar to Western scholars and practitioners in the field of early childhood education, while others are seasoned with Chinese ideas.

The kind of curriculum and pedagogy adopted is associated with at least two factors. One is the openness and economic status of the city, and the other the kindergarten assessment schemes. There is evidence that it is more likely that the government's education policies and ideas are implemented in kindergartens in more affluent cities (Hsueh et al., 2004). Cities with high economic status associated with abundant foreign investments and exposures to Western thinking, such as Shanghai (a mid eastern city) and Shengzhen (a southern city), tend to be more open to foreign ideas, progressive in ideology and practice, and flexible in decision-making. They are seen as 'windows to the world' and, education-wise, more likely to integrate Western ideas into their school systems. The adoption of free-style play in learning corners in the curriculum and Reggio Emilia-inspired practices are more likely to be found in these cities. More structural approaches such as Montessori or Waldorf co-exist with local curricula in inland cities such as Lanzhou and Xian (both are north-western cities). In financially disadvantaged cities such as Guiyang (in the south-west), the kindergarten curricula and pedagogies are relatively traditional and teacher-centred.

Art activities

Various forms of art activities, especially visual arts, are widely considered directly related to the manifestation of creativity. In China, even in rather traditional kindergartens where teacher-led approaches dominate and reading and writing are emphasized, children are given opportunities to work with materials. Some of these are conventional art activities, for example, paper folding, paper cutting, colouring and drawing (to reproduce a picture), and weaving. Other forms of art activities have appeared in Chinese kindergartens in more recent years, probably after encounters with Western approaches, such as using different materials to make collages, construction with junk or used items, free-style drawing and painting. The kinds of visual art activities chosen by a kindergarten depend on the goals and objectives of the programme. In general, more progressive or liberal kindergartens, whether public or private, opt for relatively Western art activities, but all the above-mentioned opportunities for creative ideas are underpinned by a strong belief that basic abilities or skills (*ji ben gong*) should be acquired through imitation and practice. The learner should continue practising until he or she shows competence in the chosen form(s) of art, as these basic skills will eventually allow creativity to emerge (Wong, 2008). In other words, practice does not only make things perfect, it is also the cornerstone for creativity.

Reggio Emilia-inspired project learning

This approach is similar to play-based learning in which young children learn through project work that is play-oriented (de Jonghe, 2001, cited in Pramling Samuelsson and Johansson, 2006: 49, see also Chapter 4 and 13). This Western approach was introduced to kindergartens in China about a decade ago. Enthusiastic advocates aroused heated discussions among scholars and practitioners on issues such as the teacher's role in classrooms, children's autonomy in learning, the building of a sense of community, as well as the effects of different learning environments. Kindergartens that believe in prompting children to learn through project work adopt this pedagogy entirely or as part of their programme. However, the topics or themes of project work are usually chosen or pre-planned by teachers instead of initiated by the children. With the themes in mind, teachers would elicit working ideas from children during class discussions in order to build up their knowledge, skills, and problem-solving abilities. The teaching role of teachers is still prominent amidst the various activities related to the theme. Learning through project work is primarily concerned with knowledge acquisition and development of skills through various activities such as site visits, experiments, and hands-on tasks. Opportunities for creativity are provided in art activities, which involve a lot of three-dimensional object construction as well as novel ideas that emerge from discussion and reflection.

Free-style play in learning corners

One means to benefit children's creative ideas is to stimulate their interactions with the environment. The Reggio Emilia programme, for example, is rich in both the thinking given to classroom set-up as well as the social aspect of learning (Abbott and Nutbrown, 2001; see also Chapters 4 and 13). As the Chinese ideology of early childhood education is further influenced by the constructivist view of children's development and learning, it is increasingly common for both state and private kindergartens to include 'corner time' in their curricula. Under this approach, the classrooms are divided into various learning corners, such as art corner, book corner, block corner, and so on. In each corner, the materials displayed are supposed to stimulate children's interactions with the physical environment, which supposedly benefits concept formation. In some cases, play in the corners is the main focus of the curriculum, with a pedagogy that emphasizes learning objectives realized through playful activities or tasks. In other cases, which represent the majority of kindergarten curricula, play in corners is free-style and regarded as time for children to relax their minds after the core part of the curriculum, say thematic lesson time or project work, is over. In the latter scenario, the underlying idea appears to be that play in learning corners can provide opportunities for creative ideas and creativity to take off because children are free to interact with materials and toys, and little teacher intervention and few rules apply. Nonetheless, corner time is often marginalized and cancelled when children are busy with their primary learning tasks. It is worth noting that, depending on the philosophy and financial situation of a kindergarten, the quality and quantity of free-style play can differ, because time, materials, and the attention devoted to this pedagogy vary greatly (Vong, 2012).

Dramatic play

In more recent years, the role of dramatic play in children's development and learning has been gaining increasing attention in Chinese kindergartens. Such recognition lies in its theatrical features. Children love stories and are often thrilled by opportunities to pretend to be something or someone else. Dramatic play is relatively rule-free and allows children to let their imagination run wild. Children are encouraged to design and make costumes, props and even decorate the stage as needed. They might also tell and act out stories of their own. In certain kindergartens, play or dramatic play might be part of the curriculum and that play is usually acted out in the home corner where materials for creative, pretend, and imaginative play are displayed. In most public and affluent kindergartens, role-play settings have been established by teachers and remain unchanged for a long time. Nonetheless, the value of dramatic play in Chinese kindergartens is considered essential primarily for children's social, moral, and language development.

Realizing the importance of cultural heritage, the content of children's role-play has changed from general themes such as family, clinic, bank, and grocery store to the inclusion of representative members or commercial activities from their communities, such as Chinese pharmacy or well-known local snack store, tea house or restaurant. Children are encouraged to act out the everyday operation of those business activities.

Case Study: Food-store play (see Figure 16.1)

Children dress themselves up and pretend to be the cook or waiters of a food-store, which sells dumplings, Chinese pastries, and soft drinks. Children are encouraged to use their imagination when they role-play, to resolve personal conflicts, to collaborate, and to solve problems collectively. Creativity is interpreted in terms of children's pretend interactions between customers and owners, imagination of the transaction processes, and making items needed in the play. Nevertheless, most of the materials and props are commercial products and ready-made items, which might restrain children's creativity.

Figure 16.1 Children dress up for dramatic play

Dramatic play can also sustain cultural heritage; classical Chinese epics such as the 'Journey to the West', which portrays the Monkey King as the bodyguard for his master, a holy monk, is popular among kindergartens because of the protagonists' personalities. The Monkey King's respect for his master, the clear distinction between good and evil, as well as the significance of perseverance in whatever one does exemplify good personal qualities. As for creativity, it is interpreted in terms of children's pretend interactions between customers and owners, imagination of the transaction processes, and making items needed in the play.

Justifiable perspectives of creativity

The pedagogies described above are underpinned by kindergarten practitioners' conception of creativity, which might not be in full agreement with that of Chinese scholars of early childhood education in terms of effectiveness in promoting children's creativity. There are various issues worth considering.

Theory vs. practice, different perspectives

Chinese scholars' understanding of creativity comes from either Western discussions of the term or is grounded in real-world practice. Scholars who share Western views of creativity might agree that free play in a natural environment, say in a park, is an activity full of possibilities for creative ideas and creative play. They might agree that the playful act of an infant who gives meaning to the shadows of his bib cast on the ceiling is a manifestation of creative ideas (Pramling Samuelsson and Johansson, 2006: 56). For Chinese parents and practitioners, however, this might be beyond their comprehension, as they have different sets or 'registers' for creativity

(Vong, 2008b). As long as parents' and practitioners' concern for learning remains conventional and values the reproduction of knowledge as well as the visible or instant evidence of creativity, the park activity and bib incident will be interpreted from a different angle; that is, for Chinese parents and practitioners, the playful act narrated by Western scholars might simply mean that some funny behaviours were initiated by a child. Furthermore, teachers' ideas and pedagogies to promote creative ideas and creativity are sometimes constrained by class size and administrative concerns (Hegde and Cassidy, 2009). Practitioners' own understanding of and belief in this term have been shaped by their life experiences as learners and practical experiences as preschool teachers, and they tend to justify how creativity should be interpreted to fit in with their own understanding.

Impact of teacher education

It is not controversial to argue that one's conception and interpretation of creativity is much influenced by education. However, according to professors at Nanjing Normal University, a renowned teacher education institute in China, personality plays a significant role in our ability to be creative but unfortunately most Chinese kindergarten teachers do not possess those traits (personal communication, 28 December 2011). Moreover, their creativity, if they are gifted, is highly limited by the education system that they experienced as children. Teacher educators' views of what creativity is and what this implies will have an impact on the ways it is perceived and portrayed by practitioners, and are likely to imprint on student teachers a first impression of what is meant by creative ideas and creativity. One teacher educator commented on a practitioner's creative ideas as follows:

> A teacher would like children to learn about eggs. She fried an egg in front of the whole class who were of course very excited. Firstly, they had never seen that before. It was a fresh experience and also it got their attention; it was a novel strategy. The children witnessed the frying process during which the egg white and egg yolk changed from a semi-liquid to solid state. Then the teacher asked the children to draw an egg. Most children drew a big one and coloured the centre of the egg a bright yellow colour. Some drew several small ones. When a child mixed yellow with white colours, the teacher corrected her. I think it's quite a pity that the drawing part was not handled properly.

This teaching episode exemplifies what creativity means to some Chinese scholars and signifies that there is a distinction between creative teaching and teaching for creativity (Jeffrey and Craft, 2004). The teacher thought creatively to devise a teaching activity, frying an egg, which drew children's attention and curiosity. At the same time, the teacher educator regarded the process as an activity that could also have fostered creativity in children, if the teacher had not restricted children's colouring choices. The example also shows that practitioners have a critical role in eliciting or limiting children's creative ideas. In this teaching activity, even though the opportunity for creative drawing came at the very end of the activity, at least the children were given an opportunity to apply their ideas. Nevertheless, despite the opportunity, the teacher did not encourage the children to think differently or 'out of the box', which was criticized by the teacher educator.

Assessment schemes

In China, education is strongly associated with assessment schemes. One of the means through which quality control of early childhood education is exercised in China is through kindergarten assessment schemes. The schemes vary from province to province but by and large kindergartens are categorized into first-, second-, and third-class institutions; those with poor conditions or which fall short of the stated criteria are outside the categories and have no ranking. It has been found that high-ranking kindergartens encourage play and allocate more time for play and creative activities than low-ranking ones (Vong, 2012). Within a kindergarten, especially in the ones without any ranking, formal or summative assessment involving grading and marking of children's work is common. The philosophy and operation of a summative assessment scheme contradicts the nature of any progressive or play-oriented or creative curriculum and pedagogy, thus constraining the adoption of such approaches.

Further considerations, possible pedagogies

Studies embedded in socio-cultural theory of learning and development have shown the strong impact of culture on human cognition (Wertsch, 1985) and the teaching approaches chosen or adapted (Hegde and Cassidy, 2009), as well as providing an explanation for the appropriateness of diverse preschool practices across countries and groups. The above-mentioned pedagogies, traditional or relatively new, have been applied to advance Chinese children's development in various domains. At the same time, they are also considered to be beneficial for the promotion of children's creative ideas and creativity. Within the Chinese socio-cultural context, however, there could be other means to achieve such goals.

First, influenced by traditional teaching and learning and teacher–learner relationships, the importance of the teacher's role in helping children to advance cognitively and intellectually should be recognized. Nonetheless, if teachers can enhance interactions and dialogues between themselves and children, as well as create opportunities for children's participation during the teaching and learning process, possibilities for creative thinking might be increased (Craft, 2002; Burnard et al., 2006).

Second, parents' philosophical beliefs about education should be taken into account. Chinese educators and parents are highly concerned with children's moral development. Storytelling and reconstruction with role-play activities would be an appropriate pedagogy to instil and reinforce moral behaviours and ethos as well as to elicit creative ideas from young children. Furthermore, practitioners have relied heavily on art as a means to foster creativity and shunned the possibilities associated with other domains of learning. Hence, it seems necessary to explore and expand what other domains might offer to help foster creativity. Creative motor movements would be an option, since the One-Child-Family Policy in China has made both parents and practitioners particularly concerned with young children's health conditions and any activities that could improve children's physical fitness would be welcomed. To further promote creativity in Chinese kindergarten classrooms, one line of thinking would be to set up joint projects between universities and kindergartens, so that theorists and practitioners can learn from each other about children's creativity (Trepanier-Street et al., 1998). Moreover, since assessment of intellectual performance is deeply rooted in Chinese culture, some kinds of formative assessment or process-based assessment should be established within kindergarten programmes. This would help to change the traditional examination and test systems by providing evidence-based information to convince practitioners as well as parents of the effectiveness of pedagogies based on teaching for creativity. The complexities of establishing high-quality early childhood education also deserve much attention and discussion.

Conclusions

Acknowledging the significance of learning in the early years and its long-term effects on later stages of schooling and social benefit (see also Chapters 1 and 10), the Chinese Government has budgeted for developing preschool education across the country. In rural areas where preschool education has to start from 'ground zero', promoting children's creativity will not be the main priority. The primary concerns will be about building proper kindergartens and getting enough practitioners to work in the countryside. Even in the urban districts, there are still many issues to be tackled. Given the low social and economic status of preschool teachers, preschool education is not an option for the majority of high school graduates, especially the top students. The quantity and quality of preschool teachers deserves special attention from both the government and the general public. Teacher education professionals have high expectations of the latest teacher assessment criteria (Ministry of Education of the People's Republic of China – Normal Education, 2011) for quality control of preschool practitioners. There have been eager discussions on setting some sort of standards for teacher preparation programmes. More importantly, professionals in the field are urging the government to bring preschool education into the public service system in order to address the various issues in a systematic manner (Pang and Han, 2010).

Since China opened its doors to the world in the 1970s, the Chinese Government and other sectors have endeavoured to learn from other countries, especially those in the West, on different fronts: technology, ideology, and the means to economic success. Sun (2011) has cautioned that when other educational systems or ideologies are borrowed from foreign countries and other cultures to improve areas within the Chinese context, professionals in the field should be sensible about the 'why' and 'what' to learn from others. In fact, there have been periods of time in Chinese history (Song, 960–1279 to Ming Period, 1368–1644) when teaching methods were inquiry-driven and people had a strong curiosity for knowledge and new ideas (Sun, 2011). This previous avant-garde pedagogy might be appropriate now to promote creative ideas in kindergarten classrooms and should be re-examined for its present-day applicability. Under the impact of globalization, early childhood education in China has inevitably encountered foreign pedagogies and the exchange of ideas is believed to be beneficial for advancement in kindergarten practice. Nevertheless, more effort in searching for culturally and contextually appropriate pedagogies that might involve some fusion of Chinese and foreign ideologies and approaches is needed for Chinese early childhood education to make a statement of its own.

Find Out More

- With rapid changes in the global economy and frequent trans-continental exchanges in many aspects, educational ideas and approaches in the field of early childhood education are being translated from 'foreign to home' practices. Given the different contexts from which those ideas are developed and into which those ideas are adopted, discuss how teacher preparation programmes should respond to the sometimes careless adoption of imported ideas.
- In the teacher education profession, fostering reflective teachers is a lauded goal. Explain the ways in which reflective teaching can facilitate a better understanding of kindergarten education in one's own cultural and historical context.
- Furthermore, as the importance of respect for one's origin, culture, and value system becomes better recognized, in what light should traditional education beliefs be seen in today's preschool education?

References and recommended reading

Abbott, L. and Nutbrown, C. (eds.) (2001) *Experiencing Reggio Emilia: Implications for Pre-school Provision.* Buckingham: Open University Press.

Burnard, P., Craft, A., Cremin, T., Duffy, B., Hanson, R., Keene, J., Haynes, L. and Burns, D. (2006) Documenting 'possibility thinking': a journey of collaborative enquiry, *International Journal of Early Years Education,* 14(3): 243–62.

Chinese Society of Early Childhood Education (2011) *Bulletin about the Three-Year Action Plans.* Available at: http://www.cnsece.com/news/2011831/n488510211.html (accessed 20 January 2012) [in Chinese].

Craft, A. (2002) *Creativity and Early Years Education.* London: Continuum.

Encyclopedia of the Nations (2012) *Country Overview - Location and Size.* Available at: http://www.nationsencvclooedia.com/economies/Asia-and-the-Pacific/China.html. (accessed 20 January 2012).

Hegde, A.V. and Cassidy, D.J. (2009) Teachers' beliefs and practices regarding developmentally appropriate practices: a study conducted in India, *Early Child Development and Care,* 179(7): 837–47.

Hesketh, T., Li, L. and Zhu, W.X. (2005) The effect of China's One-Child-Family Policy after 25 years, *New England Journal of Medicine,* 353: 1171–6.

Hsueh, Y., Tobin, J.J. and Karasawa, M. (2004) The Chinese kindergarten and its adolescence, *Prospects,* 14(4): 457–69.

Jeffrey, B. and Craft, A. (2004) Teaching creatively and teaching for creativity: distinctions and relationships, *Educational Studies,* 30(1): 77–87.

Ministry of Education (2010) *National Outline for Medium- to Long-Term Educational Reform and Development (2010–2020)*. Available at: http://www.edu.cn/zong_he_news_465/20100730/t20100730_501914.shtml (accessed 20 January 2012) [in Chinese].

Ministry of Education of the People's Republic of China – Normal Education (2011) *Qualifying Examination Criteria for Secondary, Primary School and Kindergarten Teachers – Trial Version*. Examination Centre of Ministry of Education [in Chinese].

Outlook Weekly (2010) *National Outline for Medium- to Long-Term Educational Reform and Development (2010–2020) – Expenditures and Budgets for Early Childhood Education*. Available at: http://www.sina.com.cn (accessed 20 January 2012) [in Chinese].

Pang, L. and Han, X. (2010) Legislation of China's pre-school education: reflection and progress, *Journal of Beijing Normal University (Social Science Section)*, 5: 14–20 [in Chinese].

Pramling Samuelsson, I. and Johansson, E. (2006) Play and learning – inseparable dimensions in preschool practice, *Early Child Development and Care*, 176(1): 47–65.

Sawyer, K. (2006) *Explaining Creativity*. Oxford: Oxford University Press.

Sun, M. (2011) Educational research in mainland China: current situation and developmental trends, *Comparative Education*, 47(3): 315–25.

Torrance, E.P. and Ball, O.E. (1984) *Torrance Tests of Creative Thinking: Revised Manual*. Bensenville, IL: Scholastic Testing Services.

Trepanier-Street, M., Gregory, L. and Donegan, M.M. (1998) Collaboration among early childhood teachers and faculty through a Reggio inspired long-term project, *Journal of Early Childhood Teacher Education*, 19(9): 171–9.

Vong, K.I.P. (2008a) *Evolving Creativity: New Pedagogies for Young Children in China*. London: Trentham Books.

Vong, K.I.P. (2008b) Developing creativity and promoting social harmony: the relationship between government, school and parents' perceptions of children's creativity in Macao-SAR in China, *Early Years: An International Journal of Research and Development*, 28(2): 149–58.

Vong, K.I.P. (2012) Play – a multi-modal manifestation in kindergarten education in China, *Early Years: An International Journal of Research and Development*, 32(1): 35–48.

Wertsch, J.V. (ed.) (1985) *Culture, Communication, and Cognition: Vygotskian Perspectives*. Cambridge: Cambridge University Press.

Wong, N.Y. (2008) From 'Chinese learner phenomenon' to 'Hong Kong learner phenomenon', *Journal of Educational Research and Development*, 4(2): 49–62 [in Chinese].

17

CANADA: DEVELOPING AN ETHICAL PEDAGOGY AND CURRICULUM
Anne Hunt

Summary

The New Brunswick Curriculum Framework for Early Learning and Child Care is a co-constructed document. This means that the voices of early childhood educators, children and their families joined actively and in practice with those of the University of New Brunswick Early Childhood Centre Curriculum Development Team and various provincial government departments to create and give local substance to the four values-based, broad goals that are at the heart of the framework. This is an ongoing process requiring continuing conversations and consultations in which no one voice is privileged over another. It is a powerful process engaging all who are involved in shared meaning-making. This chapter tells the story of how, in the initial stages, this process of co-construction helped all of us to build an ethical framework for pedagogical theory and practice and, at the same time, enabled early childhood educators to find a public, professional voice.

Introduction

Our New Brunswick story begins in 2005, when Canadian federal funding was allocated to the provinces for work in the early years. The provincial government made the decision to initiate the production of a curriculum for children from birth to age 5 years, suitable for a wide range of licensed childcare settings, and as a 'source for parents, and for staff in other programs and services designed for young children and their families' (New Brunswick Curriculum Framework [NBCF], 2008: 183). Centres would be required to implement the curriculum and attend the 38 hours of professional learning sessions to maintain their licensed status.

The Early Childhood Centre at the University of New Brunswick was invited to submit a proposal to write the curriculum and implement a related programme of professional learning for the approximately 1350 childcare educators in the English childcare sector. (Note that we are an officially bi-lingual province with one-third of our population speaking French. Educators at the Université de Moncton were invited to write a French document.) Aware of the 'powerful potential' (Moss, 2006) of official curricula for the regulation and surveillance of children and teachers, 'it was with some trepidation that we accepted' (Hunt and Nason, 2012).

A research-based document

Committed to a document that would be based in research, project co-directors Pam Nason and Pam Whitty began with visits to exemplary sites in New Zealand, Australia, Belgium, Sweden, and the UK. This gave us a firm understanding of what various theoretical approaches looked like in practice. We read extensively, attending to Canadian discussions and the work of international scholars regarding appropriate curricula for early learning and care. We produced a series of papers summarizing literature searches on current topics of interest in the field of early childhood education and invited external critiques.

We found the work of John Bennett and his research team particularly valuable, especially their review of practices, policies, and curriculum from more than twenty countries for the OECD (Bennett, 2003). Of note to us was their contrast between the social pedagogical approach with emphasis on broad based goals enacted in a social context that 'recognizes the context of children's learning and the importance of attending to the todayness of children's lives and their diverse personal, social, and cultural experiences', and 'the pre-primary approach [which] focuses on preparing children for school, often neglecting the complexity of children's daily experiences and social interactions' (NBCF, 2008: 183).

We also listened to voices from the past:

enforced learning will not stay in the mind. So avoid compulsion, and let your children's lessons take the form of play.

(Plato, *The Republic*, 427 B.C. to 347 B.C.)

All children do not develop at the same time, some beginning to speak in the first year, some in the second, and some in the third.

(John Comenius, *The School Of Infancy*, 1592–1670)

Childhood has its own way of seeing, thinking and feeling, and nothing is more foolish than to try to substitute ours for them.

(Jean Jacques Rousseau, *Emile*, 1712–1778)

play at this time [childhood] is not trivial, it is highly serious and of deep significance.

(Friederich Froebel, *The Education of Man*, 1782–1852)

The educational value of this play is obvious. It teaches the children about the world they live in. The more they play the more elaborate become their paraphernalia, the whole game being a fairly accurate picture of the daily life of their parents in its setting, clothes, in the language and bearing of the children.

(John Dewey, *Schools of Tomorrow*, 1859–1952)

The practical tasks for each centre are to study the geographic relations in the environment into which the children are born and to watch the children's behaviour in their environment, to note when they first discover relations and what they are. On the basis of these findings each centre will make its own curriculum for small children.

(Lucy Sprague Mitchell, *Young Geographers*, 1878–1967)

What imaginative play does, in the first place, is to create practical situations which may often then be pursued for their own sake and thus lead to actual discovery, or to verbal judgment and reasoning.

(Susan Isaacs, *Intellectual Growth in Young Children*, 1885–1948)

As we continue to search for ways to identify and support each other's differences, we may discover that individuality is and always has been the greatest commonality we share. And some day, when nonconformity itself becomes the tradition, our children and we ourselves will be ready to accept as a matter of course the many images of human kind.

(Vivian Gussin Paley, *Kwanzaa and Me*, 1929–)

Understanding our social context

Committed to the social pedagogical curriculum, we began to explore our social context here in New Brunswick. We brought together educators, directors, coordinators, members of the provincial department of education and social development, and parents and professionals working with young children and their families for a two-day symposium. Together we addressed such tough topics as: what is our vision? What are our beliefs and values about children and educare in the early years? How do beliefs and values inform pedagogies? How do beliefs inform curricular content? How will we set and assess programme standards? We closed this two-day symposium with a plan for an ongoing collaborative process, and a clear mandate to proceed with a social pedagogical approach.

Our vision

The symposium discussions were the basis for a draft of our vision statement:

The uniqueness of each child is implicitly integrated into the philosophy of early learning and child care that underlines the framework. By design, the curriculum will not merely accommodate, but actively honour the diversity of New Brunswick's children and their languages and heritages. This is a challenging and daunting task, one that requires a clear vision and a resourceful, collaborative, and creative approach to providing for our youngest citizens' full participation in the social and cultural life of their communities.

(NBCF, 2008: 2)

Our values

We were also able to arrive at a common set of values extrapolated from our vision statement and driven by the acceptance of the distinctiveness of childhood and the understanding of children's rights based on the United Nations Convention on the Rights of the Child, 1989. We agreed at the outset that making these values specific 'opens them to ongoing negotiation, critique, and change' (NBCF, 2008: 6–7).

- *Inclusiveness and equity*: We value diversities, and honour all individual, social, linguistic, and cultural differences. We uphold the right of every child to participate fully in cultural and artistic life regardless of language, culture, race, religion, socio-economic status, gender, or ability – and encourage the provision of negotiated and equitable opportunities for participation.
- *Compassion and caring*: We value compassion and an ethic of care as essential to nurturing the growth, development, and learning of young children, ensuring the rights of the most vulnerable members of our society and preserving the Earth for future generations.
- *Living democratically*: We value the everyday enactment of democracy that gives children a voice in matters that concern them and provides opportunities to participate in making and questioning collective decisions.
- *Individuality and independence*: We value the unique personalities, talents, and abilities of every person. We value the capacity for independent action, individual accomplishment, and personal responsibility.
- *Social responsibility*: We value respect for fellow human beings and the responsibility of each, according to their ability, to contribute to the enhancement of interdependent communities, cultures, and sustainable futures. We value collective responsibility, solidarity, and collective action.
- *Communication*: We value communication in all its forms, for its capacity to transmit feelings, language, and other cultural knowledge; to advance human thought; to develop human relations; and to enhance the distinctly human ability to reflect critically on the past and plan purposefully for the future.
- *Imagination, creativity, and play*: We value imagination, creativity, and play for their capacity to produce a dynamic and innovative society. We value play and the arts as particularly fruitful ways for children to imagine new possibilities, explore novel ways of doing things, create unique ideas and products, and reinvent culture.
- *Aesthetics*: We value beauty, pleasure, and desire in the growth of knowledge, understanding, judgement, and expression.
- *Spirituality*: We value the child's right to a restorative spiritual space for enhancement of moral and ethical development. [It is important to note that this particular value has prompted deep discussion, critique, and local negotiation as we attempt to separate what we mean by spirituality from what we mean by religion.]
- *Zest for living and learning*: We value the zest for living and learning that embodies curiosity, playfulness, determination, persistence, pleasure in accomplishment, resilience, and the sheer joy of being alive. [This last value was added as we sought further consultation from educators around the province. It captures their day-to-day experiences with the children in their care.]

Translating values into curriculum content

During the two-day symposium, we also looked at the organization of content in exemplary curricula from the USA, Australia, Britain, New Zealand, and Sweden and asked the important questions: What knowledge, skills, dispositions, and feelings are represented in these curricula? How does this compare with what we presently cultivate? What's missing? How will our content reflect our values? Together, we arrived at four broad-based goals: Well Being, Play and Playfulness, Communication and Literacies, and Diversity and Social Responsibility. At the end of our time together, we devised a strategic plan for continued collaboration, consultation, and feedback as we moved forward to begin drafting the framework.

To open this process to the wider community, we travelled throughout the province, arranging to be at central meeting places in each region at 6.30 pm when early childhood educators, directors, elementary school teachers, and other interested people were free to attend. We projected our draft of the values and goals, page by page, onto a screen asking what was missing and what needed changing. As suggestions came forward, we edited the text so that participants could see that the co-constructed nature of the text actually meant that their words and work had consequences for the document as it evolved.

Once we had established the vision, values, and goals, a Curriculum Development Committee was formed with members from Family and Community Services, Early Childhood and School Based Services to assist the University Curriculum Development Team. The committee was engaged in providing strategic advice and counsel, guiding and supporting the development of the framework, as well as the expansion, implementation, and evaluation activities related to it, keeping the team informed about developments in their spheres of knowledge and providing advice and direction on communication strategies to ensure effective linkages between key stakeholders and the UNB Project Team.

The resulting draft was then taken to eight early years sites representing a range of settings. Members of the curriculum development team worked alongside the educators to document the many ways in which the framework was interpreted locally.

The educator as professional

We make a distinction between the 'Official Curriculum' authorized by the government and the 'Lived Curriculum' – what the educator actually does with children. Embedded in our New Brunswick framework is the image of the educator as professional. Our Curriculum Framework implicitly conveys faith in educators to remake the lived curriculum responsive to local contexts. It articulates common goals, values, and learning/teaching principles for early learning and childcare policy and practice. It develops a shared professional language for discussion of early learning and childcare policy and practice. It provides a supportive structure for educators as they co-construct curriculum with children, families, and communities at the local level. It prompts change by directing attention to questions about the ways in which we respect and respond to children's capacities, ideas, and potentials.

The child as meaning-maker

This social paradigm also carries a specific image of the child and all that this image implies for educators.

> In this framework, we acknowledge children as curious and communicative individuals in their own right: young citizens. This image also presupposes children's rights to the basic necessities of life and the inclusion of their cultures and languages in everyday experiences. Children begin learning at birth, and their experiences during the early years have critical consequences both in the present and for their own futures. To thrive as curious, confident, communicative people, they are entitled to nurturing relationships. They also are entitled to engaging and inclusive environments in which well-being is secured, exploration and play supported, home languages and literacies honoured and advanced, and respect for diversity promoted and practised.
>
> (NBCF, 2008: 8)

It also encourages continued professional discussion and local interpretation.

> Beliefs about children and childhood are constructed and interpreted through social, economic, and cultural lenses. As such, expectations and opportunities for children differ from one culture to another, from one place to another, from one time to another.
>
> (NBCF, 2008: 8)

Confronting our trepidation

The uncomfortable part of this process is the fact that it is shaped by the requirement that all licensed childcare centres adopt the New Brunswick Curriculum for Early Learning and Care in which these images of educator and child are encrypted. We, as the curriculum development team, were in a position of power that could easily be interpreted as 'regulate(ing) practice and influence(ing) the way educators construct their identities' (Nason and Hunt, 2011: 83) even though what is regulated, in this case, is a degree of professional discretion, decision-making, voice and control or power.

Needless to say, not all educators were comfortable with this image or the social pedagogical paradigm surrounding it. It is in sharp contrast to the more dominant image of the educator as technician, working towards a prescribed set of outcomes, regulated by children's progress along a predetermined developmental path. Our provincial public school system is situated in this second paradigm and our early childhood educators are well aware that there is pressure placed on them by families and their local schools to see that the children are 'ready for school'.

Finding a professional voice

It was important for the curriculum development team to make explicit the two contrasting paradigms and their implications for professional practice, and to provide opportunities for respectful discussions. Enlisting educators in the curriculum writing process gave voice to their diverse experiences and perspectives across the province and opened up a professional conversation that continues to this day. This conversation shapes and changes interpretations of the document while continuing to adhere to 'our agenda for children and the ways in which we respect children's capacities, ideas and potentials' (NBCF, 2008: 3).

The framework carries photos and sample narratives gathered as we worked alongside educators in a rich variety of settings and uncovered the concerns of educators regarding the language and theoretical base of the document. Further collaborative work in more than a hundred early childhood centres produced a set of support documents designed to give educators a sense of how the lived curriculum looks in other parts of the province and to provide a forum for their professional expression. 'The work presented by educators to their colleagues in the support documents and in institute sessions, gave substance to theory for educators and had a sense of credibility. They were able to see the children with whom they worked in a new perspective, and to express their shifting image of the child' (Hunt and Nason, 2012: 161).

Angela Little, of Passamaquoddy Children's Centre, put it this way:

> As Early Childhood Educators, the compassion, dedication and joy in our profession has multiplied through the new curriculum framework. My mind and heart were always set on program planning through themes until the excitement arose in my three-year-old children on a routine neighbourhood walk. Seeing how this local juggler (encountered as they walked down Water Street) inspired a month long curriculum (focusing on the circus) was my 'A-Ha' moment. I now trust that, through careful observation, determination and getting to know my children better, our curriculum will unfold before us. Though there are many challenges, the excitement of the children telling me what they want to learn is exhilarating.
>
> (Communication and Literacies Support Document, NBCF, 2008: 40)

How does this 'lived curriculum' look?

New Brunswick has a landmass roughly the size of Scotland with about one-sixth of Scotland's population. We are the only officially bi-lingual province in Canada with 40% of us speaking French and 60% English. There are three First Nations groups: Mi'kmaq, Passamoquody, and Maliseet, making up about 5% of the population. There is a growing emphasis on the importance of education in these languages in the early years. We are also welcoming many more immigrant families in recent years, particularly from the Far East. Our sparse but diverse population lives in very diverse settings as well. We have a large forestry industry, an active fisheries workforce, major farming areas and mining communities, as well as three relatively large cities. It is clear that local curricular interpretations will be unique.

Our four broad-based, and overlapping, goals provide a framework for the lived curriculum. They are the basis for observation, planning, and assessment.

Well Being
- Emotional health and positive identities
- Belonging
- Physical health

Play and playfulness
- Imagination and creativity
- Playful exploration and problem-solving
- Dizzy play (*in this form of play, usually initiated by the children, they take pleasure in being on the edge and in sharing the joy of laughter*)

Communication and literacies
- Communicative practices
- Multimodal literacies
- Literate identities with/in communities

Diversity and social responsibility
- Inclusiveness and equity
- Democratic practices
- Sustainable futures

Assessing the learning process

The framework explicitly encourages educators to document learning using narrative assessment techniques:

> Narrative assessment illustrates, describes, and interprets the learning of individual children or groups of children through careful listening, photographs, observations, anecdotal records, and multimodal learning stories such as those developed in conjunction with Te Whāriki the New Zealand Curriculum. The purpose of this kind of assessment is to focus the educator's, children's and parents' attention on what individual children and groups of children are learning within a particular setting.
>
> (NBCF, 2008: 63)

Narrative assessment continues to be an important topic of professional conversations. This is because it requires a major shift in thinking for educators who have been used to using primarily normative assessment – the practice of measuring children's progress in terms of a set of prescribed outcomes and skills. The framework reminds educators that this form of assessment 'must be used carefully and thoughtfully, keeping in mind that all norms are socially and culturally based' (NBCF, 2008: 63).

Educators' narrative assessments, taken from the published support documents, give some sense of the scope of experiences children have as the lived curriculum unfolds in their particular settings. They are wonderful examples of co-constructing and meaning-making involving educators, children, families, and the wider community. How does the educator's image of the children in these narratives shape the learning of those children? How does the children's learning shape the educator? How do the contributions of each child shape and reshape the learning of other children?

Here, for example, is documentation of a learning experience with a group of 4-year-olds, developed after a conversation in which a parent expressed a concern regarding her daughter's concept of other children, particularly those of colour. The educator linked the learning to Goal 1: Well Being and, in particular, to the facet 'Emotional health and positive identities'. Note that other curricular connections may be made giving the overlapping nature of the broad-based goals.

A moment of insight . . .
Early in the year a parent shared a conversation she had had with her child. As the child had spoken of her new friends at our centre, she had referred to the children of colour as 'different' while the white children were 'normal'. This story prompted me to plan an exploration of what we look like. How do we see ourselves? How do we represent ourselves? How do we talk about visual differences?

Planning and process . . .
Setting up the environment: We worked in our usual drawing centre but I added specific tools to aid in drawing self portraits.

Materials: I provided paper, small standing mirrors, and markers, including multicultural markers to more closely match a variety of skin tones.

Support: I invited children to draw themselves and I sat with them at the drawing table, posing questions such as 'What colour marker do you think matches your skin?' or 'What colour are your eyes?' and suggested children revisit their image in the mirror.

Documenting . . .
When the children were finished we mounted the portraits on a construction paper background and displayed a range of process photographs with captions on a bulletin board for families and visitors to see.

Learning . . .
Children made careful observations about themselves and made decisions about best fit (as they chose a marker to represent their skin colour). They were able to use and gain language to talk about differences and similarities as they worked alongside each other constructing their self-images. The children's work shows how they actively represent themselves artistically and they transform their vision from one form to another.

Why this matters:
As children take a closer look at themselves they begin to see what makes them unique. The task of representing themselves provides opportunities to see their individual features. By mounting a display I gave them a place to see themselves in relation to others and to talk together about how they are alike and how they are different. Skin colour is now represented by a range of tones not just white and other.

Leigh White, UNB Children's Learning Centre
(Well Being Support Document, NBCF: 2008: 8–9)

The lived curriculum requires the educator to be observant and responsive to children, families, and community. In some situations, like the one above, curriculum develops from a particular event, issue or challenge. On other occasions, the educator plans experiences based on community connections. The following narrative is from the Play and Playfulness Support Document. The educators involved had assessed their dramatic play area in their multi-age setting and made a decision to include objects to reflect the work of the community.

Case Study: Hauling in the traps

Since lobster fishing is such an important part of our community, we thought it would be fun to set up a dramatic play area depicting lobster fishing. Our planning included bringing in lobster traps, fish crates, ropes and buoys. We also put boats in the water table. As the children engaged in play we observed and learned. The children filled bait-pockets with lego [sic] and other small toys that would fit.

The children had so much fun we thought we would take it one step further and planned a visit to the local lobster plant. The children were fascinated with all the different sizes of lobsters. We learned that the blood sugar of the lobster is taken using a needle to see if the lobsters are fat enough to crate, and that lobster blood is clear, like water.

Back at the centre, we used photos of the adventure to make a book together so we could read about and remember everything that happened.

Judith Bass, Tonia Leavitts, and Darlene Clinch,
Grand Manan Children's Centre
(Play and Playfulness Support Document, NBCF, 2008: 52)

Although the initial intent was to enrich the dramatic play, this documentation may also have been about the world to word connections that were made when a book was created about the trip (Goal 3: Communication and Literacies, multimodal meaning making), or what was discovered about local manufacture and sustainable resources (Goal 4: Diversity and Social Responsibility, sustainable futures). Again we see the interrelatedness of those four goals.

How does the lived curriculum look with our youngest children? The following is a narrative from Monique Doucet, of the Saint John Early Childhood Centre. Monique shares selections from a larger series of documentations about her infants' ball project. Her work makes visible the power of observation and documentation to guide planning as well as the rich learning possibilities of play. Note how often Monique uses the word 'wonder'. What happens when we wonder professionally? How does Monique respect and respond to the capacities, ideas, and potentials of her children?

Case Study: Infants' ball project

Nolan was rolling a ball that made giggling noises and he began laughing as the ball made sounds. As I watched him I wondered what it was about this adventure that made him smile and laugh. Was it the movement of the ball as it rolled across the floor? Was it the sound the ball made? Was it the bright neon colour of the ball that attracted him?

I also observed Nevaeh as she was rolling a textured ball across the floor. She appeared so consumed in the movement of the ball. She would roll it a little and watch as the different bumps of the ball hit the floor. I wondered what she was wondering about. Again, I asked myself what might it be about balls that maintains the interest of these infants?

In the gym we put out a large exercise ball. Jarvis smiled and ran over to it. He began rolling the ball around the gym. Activities like these will be great for Jarvis as he uses the large muscles in his arms and legs. He's also working his hand eye coordination as he moves the ball around other objects and children. Jarvis is learning social skills too. He learns turn-taking with the other children as they share the balls.

Nolan is learning to throw a ball. We encourage him to toss the ball to us and we toss it back to him. He is also discovering how to kick the ball. I have been showing him how with a soccer ball. Nolan is working on balance and coordination as he learns to kick the ball with one foot.

The children explored with clay formed into balls. I wondered if they would treat the clay in the same manner as the other balls. Would they try to toss the clay? Would they notice the texture of the clay and the fact that they can change the shape of these balls?

Having watched the children explore the clay I think that Jarvis did in fact treat them like the other balls. He repeatedly rolled the clay cross the table. Nolan seemed to notice a difference in the texture of the clay compared to other balls he's been exploring. He squeezed the clay balls to change their shape and stacked them on top of each other.

Nevaeh treated the clay as food and was only interested in trying to eat it. Was this because she was seated at the dining table while playing with the clay? Maybe she would have reacted differently if the clay had been placed on the floor with her instead.

(Our Youngest Children Support Document, NBCF, 2008: 32–3)

Children love to read, or have read to them, their own and other children's narrative assessment. This next narrative assessment is written to 4-year-old Gabrielle, who arrived at the UNB Children's Centre one day dressed as Dorothy from the Wizard of Oz. How might this personal tone affect Gabrielle's sense of herself and her capabilities? What about the other children included in the account?

Case Study: Somewhere over the rainbow

Gabrielle, you surprised us when you arrived dressed as Dorothy from The Wizard of Oz! From your ruby slippers, to Toto in a basket, to the perfect braids, you looked just like Dorothy and even signed in as her. When I asked you if you wanted to write the play about your character you didn't hesitate for a moment. You dictated the whole story to me from the part where you sing 'Somewhere over the Rainbow' to your chant of 'There's no place like home.'

Soon other children wanted to be a part of your play. You were busy, with the clipboard in one hand and Toto in his basket, in signing up children for parts in the play, helping decide costumes and finding a yellow brick road.

Paige knew she wanted to be a witch. When she heard that there was a good witch and a bad witch she decided to be the good one. Ava asked to be the bad witch. Paige made a witch's hat but couldn't decide how to make it stay on her head. I suggested a band to staple it on similar to our birthday crown and she decided to use a birthday crown instead. The beautiful yellow dress that she found in the dress up clothes was a perfect costume. Ava wanted a mask. She drew a face on black paper that was quite scary. Tonya helped her cut out eyeholes and put pipe cleaners on the sides to hold it onto her head.

It was obvious that Spencer was to be the lion as he loves to play lions. Braedon put his name down as the Tin Man and in the meantime wrote a play of his own about the dog he had brought from home. Trent agreed to be the Scarecrow and Jibril, Grace, Alexandra and Tonya were to play the Munchkins.

You became concerned at one point that you would need a yellow brick road. Luckily Kim noticed the large sheet of painted cardboard in the hallway. You and your friends paraded it around the room until you decided that the play was to be on the large steps so the yellow brick road was to be below it.

Before the play was performed you felt it necessary to warn the class about the scary scenes and suggest that children could cover their eyes if they get scared. You started the show by descending the stairs and singing your song so beautifully. From then on, you acted, directed and organized this amazing performance. You had a definite idea of how the show was to be performed and encouraged each actor to fulfill his or her role in the way you saw it.

Why this matters:
Gabrielle brought this powerful story that she knows so well to life in her pretending and performing. She was charismatic in her enthusiasm and attracted many other actors, eager to perform in her play. She was challenged to think of ways to act out her story in the environment. Other children used their imaginations as well to create the costumes they needed.

Jill Bateman, UNB Children's Centre
(Communication and Literacies Support Document, NBCF, 2008: 55)

Conclusion

This process of co-construction, of making meaning together, remains both challenging and exciting. It is not a process with an ending and it thrives on conflict. It is hoped that through 'valuing each other's wisdom' and 'viewing that conflict as a pathway to possible alternatives' (NBCF, 2008: 13), 'our children will grow to their fullest potential with dignity, a sense of self-worth, and a zest for living and learning' (NBCF, 2008: 1).

Find Out More

Research the following:

- Narrative assessment as a way of documenting children's thinking as they actively construct, co-construct, and reconstruct their understanding of the world.
- Values-based curricula and how what we believe and value informs curricular content.
- Ethical pedagogy and the role of power relationships in early childhood settings.

References and recommended reading

Bennett, J. (2003) Starting strong: the persistent division between care and education. *Journal of Early Childhood Research*, 1: 21–46.

Comenius, J.A. (1632/1896) *School of Infancy* (edited with an Introduction and notes by W.S. Monroe). Boston, MA: D.C. Heath.

Dewey, J. and Dewey, E. (1915) *Schools of Tomorrow*. New York: E.P. Dutton & Co.

Froebel, F. (1887) *The Education of Man* (translated by W.N. Hailmann). New York: D. Appleton Century.

Hunt, A. and Nason, P. (2012) Navigating between colliding discourses in cross-cultural perspectives on early childhood, in J. Moyles and T. Papatheodorou (eds.) *International Perspectives on Early Childhood Education and Care*. London: Sage.

Isaacs, S. (1930) *Intellectual Growth in Young Children*. London: Kegan Paul, Trench, Trubner & Co.

Mitchell, L.S. (1916) *Young Geographers*. New York: Bank Street College of Education.

Moss, P. (2006) Early childhood institutions as loci of ethical and political practice, *International Journal of Educational Policy, Research and Practice: Reconceptualizing Childhood Studies*, 7: 127–37.

Nason, P. and Hunt, A. (2011) Pedagogy as an ethical encounter: how does it look in our professional practice?, in A. Campbell and P. Broadhead (eds.) *New International Studies in Applied Ethics, Vol. 5. Working with Children and Young People: Ethical Debates and Practices Across Disciplines and Continents.* **Bonn: Peter Lang.**

New Brunswick Curriculum Framework (NBCF) (2008) *The New Brunswick Curriculum Framework for Early Learning and Child Care*. Fredericton, NB: Department of Social Development. Available at: http://www.gnb.ca/0000/ECHDPE/curriculum-e.asp (accessed 9 February 2012).

Paley, V.G. (1995) *Kwanzaa and Me: A Teacher's Story*. Cambridge, MA: Harvard University Press.

Plato (360 B.C./1987) *The Republic* (translated with an Introduction by D. Lee). London: Penguin Books.

Rousseau, J.-J. (1762/1921) *Emile, or Education* (translated by B. Foxley). London: J.M. Dent & Sons.

18

DIVERSE THEORIES FOR DIVERSE LEARNERS? THE AUSTRALIAN EARLY YEARS LEARNING FRAMEWORK

Joce Nuttall and Susan Edwards

Summary

Australia's Early Years Learning Framework (EYLF) draws on multiple theoretical perspectives to inform curriculum planning and implementation in prior-to-school services. In this chapter, we reflect on whether this feature of the EYLF provides a basis for responding to the diverse social and cultural contexts in which young children learn across Australia. We include two examples of educators talking about their engagement with the framework to illustrate how educators are using the EYLF, and to highlight some of the affordances and constraints that educators face in implementing the framework.

Introduction

Writing curriculum documents is demanding work. Curriculum writers have to accommodate a wide variety of variables when thinking about what curriculum documents should say, and are often subject to professional and political expectations that are beyond their control. One of the most recent curriculum documents developed in early childhood education (ECE) is Australia's *Belonging, Being and Becoming: The Early Years Learning Framework for Australia* [EYLF] (Department of Education, Employment and Workplace Relations, 2009), referred to across Australia as 'the Elf' or simply 'the Framework' (Goodfellow, 2009). In this chapter, we examine how the EYLF responds to the challenges of curriculum formation, with a particular focus on how its writers have incorporated a wide range of theories available to early childhood educators in Australia. We are interested in this because we want to examine how an inclusive approach to theory might (or might not) assist educators to respond to the rich variations within and between the children, families, social groups, and contexts they encounter in their work.

The writers of the EYLF had an unenviable task in responding to diversity. First, Australia is geographically huge – larger than continental Europe – and governed on a state-by-state basis as well as centrally by a federal government, based in Canberra. Some states had previously developed curriculum guidelines or frameworks to inform ECE provision (for example, Queensland, South Australia, Western Australia, and Tasmania) but one state (Victoria) provided no curriculum guidance for ECE before 2009. Second, ECE provision in Australia is extremely complex. Its history is of: unplanned and piecemeal provision by a range of state, local government, community, and private providers; diverse services arising in response to local needs; an uneven mix of federal, state, and parental funding; variation in regulatory expectations from state to state; and limited or no provision for indigenous families. Third, during the post-war period Australia has become one of the most culturally diverse nations in the Western world, in addition to over 40,000 years of habitation by over 250 distinct Aboriginal language groups. Although around 80% of Australia's population of approximately 22 million live on the eastern seaboard or on the thin strip of coast around the edge of the continent, many children and families live in rural and remote parts of the country, and both city and country families are subject to the wide variations in class, status, and income found in most contemporary Western societies. And, of course, each of these services and settings includes children with physical or intellectual disabilities, or who are living in troubled circumstances.

However, each of these challenges confronts curriculum writers everywhere. What, then, is distinctive about the EYLF? We argue that one of the most distinctive features of the EYLF is the diverse range of theories evident (both explicitly and implicitly) in the document. The use of multiple theories was a deliberate decision by the writers because they saw acknowledging multiple theoretical perspectives as a way of achieving social justice by respecting diverse worldviews. One of the key writers of the framework, Jennifer Sumsion, says:

> The curriculum writers were committed to demonstrating respect for diversity and difference in standpoints and perspectives, which they considered crucial to imbue in the Framework, while working to a common purpose and shared goal of advancing social justice.
>
> (Milleli and Sumsion, 2011: 74)

We begin this chapter with a brief summary of the EYLF before considering its theoretical underpinnings. We conclude by reflecting whether the 'multi-theoretical' basis of the EYLF makes it a useful resource for professionals working with diverse families and in diverse contexts.

Australia's Early Years Learning Framework

The central focus of the EYLF is 'children's learning', which is seen as being driven by 'three inter-related elements: Principles, Practice and Learning Outcomes' (Department of Education, Employment and Workplace Relations, 2009: 9). The five principles are:

1. Secure, respectful and reciprocal relationships
2. Partnerships
3. High expectations and equity
4. Respect for diversity
5. Ongoing learning and reflective practice (pp. 12-13).

These Principles are viewed as 'underpin[ning] practice that is focused on assisting all children to make progress in relation to the Learning Outcomes' (p. 12).

The second major section of the document outlines five Practices, described as 'principles of early childhood pedagogy' (p. 14). These comprise: Holistic approaches; Responsiveness to children; Learning through play; Intentional teaching; and Learning environments (pp. 14–15).

The third and largest section of the EYLF describes the five Learning Outcomes:

- Outcome 1: Children have a strong sense of identity
- Outcome 2: Children are connected with and contribute to their world
- Outcome 3: Children have a strong sense of wellbeing
- Outcome 4: Children are confident and involved learners
- Outcome 5: Children are effective communicators (p. 19).

Each sub-outcome is then elaborated under two descriptors. The first descriptor says 'This [outcome] is evident when children . . .', and is followed by a list of potential behaviours that educators could look for in the children's learning and development. The second descriptor says, 'Educators promote this learning when they . . .', and provides a list of strategies educators can use to foster the desired behaviours. Figure 18.1 illustrates how the Principles lead to the Practices that inform the Learning Outcomes, and how the sub-outcomes suggest particular descriptors for the child and teacher activities. We have selected to show in more detail 'Learning Outcome 2: Children are connected with and contribute to their world' because this is the Learning Outcome that lists 'children respond to diversity with respect' as a sub-outcome, with its consequent descriptors.

The second descriptor, which focuses on what educators will do to promote learning, is of particular interest because it points to the way the EYLF attempts not only to be a curriculum framework but also a *pedagogical* framework. This is further emphasized by the way the writers locate the theoretical underpinnings of the EYLF under the heading of 'Pedagogy'. In the EYLF, 'Pedagogy' encompasses educators' 'professional practice, curriculum decision-making, teaching and learning' (p. 11). This means that theoretical perspectives are intended to inform not just curriculum *formation* but curriculum *enactment* – in other words, what teachers will actually *do* with children and families. This is not a typical feature of curriculum frameworks, which tend to assume teachers will make curricular decisions as a response to curriculum *content*. However, the writers of the EYLF are acknowledging a distinctive feature of early childhood curriculum by focusing on enactment as well as formation. This is because the curriculum for young children largely consists

Principles	Practices	Learning Outcomes
1 Secure, respectful and reciprocal relationships	Holistic approaches	Children have a strong sense of identity
2 Partnerships	Responsiveness to children	Children are connected with and contribute to their world
3 High expectations and equity	Learning through play	Children have a strong sense of wellbeing
4 Respect for diversity	Intentional teaching	Children are confident and involved learners
5 Ongoing learning and reflective practice	Learning environments	Children are effective communicators

Sub-outcomes

Children develop a sense of belonging to groups and communities and an understanding of the reciprocal rights and responsibilities necessary for active community participation

Children respond to diversity with respect

Children become aware of fairness

Children become socially responsible and show respect for the environment

Descriptors for Child & Teacher activities

This is evident when children:

Begin to show concern for others

Explore the diversity of cultural, heritage background and tradition and the diversity presents opportunities for choices and new understandings

Become aware of connections, similarities and differences between people

This is evident when educators:

Reflect on their own responses to diversity

Plan experiences and provide resources that broaden children's perspectives and encourage appreciation of diversity

Expose children to different languages and dialects and encourage appreciation of linguistic diversity

Figure 18.1 Relationships between Principles, Practices, and Learning Outcomes in the EYLF, leading to sub-outcomes and descriptors for Learning Outcome 2

of how others around them *behave*, not just what other people know (Nuttall and Edwards, 2004; Edwards and Nuttall, 2005). In other words, pedagogy is part of the curriculum and not separate from what teachers do and children experience. In the EYLF, it is interesting to see how the multiple theoretical perspectives are used in the document to support the idea that pedagogy is central to curriculum.

Theories underpinning the EYLF

The writers of the EYLF are explicit about their decision to draw on a range of theoretical perspectives. They argue that using multiple theoretical perspectives was central to achieving their aim of creating a framework that 'provided a catalyst for reflection, dialogue, critique, debate and discussion without advocating or assuming adherence to any one theoretical stance' (Sumsion et al., 2009: 10). The document includes five main theoretical perspectives that the curriculum writers believed to be in common use across Australia prior to the publication of the EYLF. In the EYLF, these perspectives are summarized as:

1. *Developmental theories*: focused on describing and understanding the process of change in children's learning and development over time.
2. *Socio-cultural*: emphasizing the central role that families and cultural groups play in children's learning and the importance of respectful relationships and providing insight into social and cultural contexts of learning and development.
3. *Socio-behaviourist*: focused on the role of experience in shaping children's behaviour.
4. *Critical*: inviting early childhood educators to challenge assumptions about curriculum, and consider how their decisions may affect children differently.
5. *Post-structural*: offering insights into issues of power, equity and social justice in early childhood settings.

(Department of Education, Employment and Workplace Relations, 2009: 11)

In our consideration of the EYLF, we have traced the way these theories inform a key dimension of the document, the Principles, which are a series of statements about what matters to the provision of early childhood education. Broadly summarized, the Principles are:

1. *Secure, respectful and reciprocal relationships*: this principle is about the importance of children being connected with important people in their lives and how this supports children to develop the interdependence that allows learning to occur.
2. *Partnerships*: this principle emphasizes relationships between educators and families. It focuses on valuing cultural experiences and knowledge.
3. *High expectations and equity*: this principle highlights the achievement possibilities of all children regardless of circumstance and emphasizes the educator's role in promoting social justice.

Table 18.1 Relationship between EYLF principles and theoretical perspectives

Principles	Developmental	Socio-behaviourist	Socio-cultural	Critical	Post-structural
Relationships	✓	✓	✓		✓
Partnerships		✓	✓	✓	
High expectations				✓	✓
Respect for diversity			✓	✓	✓
Reflective practice				✓	✓

4. *Respect for diversity*: this principle is about acknowledging the cultural strengths and capacities of all children and families and using these as a basis for curriculum provision.

5. *Ongoing learning and reflective practice*: this principle focuses on how professional learning and reflective practice help educators to engage in meaningful ways with the children, families, and context with whom they work.

Elements of the five theoretical perspectives that the EYLF describes as useful for informing pedagogy also appear in these Principles, with some of the Principles drawing on ideas from more than one theoretical perspective. Table 18.1 shows how the five theoretical perspectives identified by the writers of the EYLF map onto the five Principles.

It is beyond the scope of this chapter to tease out the similarities and contradictions between these perspectives. As a brief illustration, educators who draw on developmental theories will look for particular patterns in children's development (Berk, 2012), and use these to make decisions about what experiences they will provide. Socio-cultural theory, by contrast, emphasizes the importance of adult and child interactions in fostering learning (Edwards, 2009), while critical and post-structural perspectives challenge teachers to think about their beliefs and values (Kilderry, 2004), and how the experiences they provide for children and families address traditional injustices of class, race, gender, and power (Mac Naughton, 2005; Blaise and Ryan, 2012). Suffice to say, the theoretical perspectives underpinning the EYLF represent a diverse range of differing ideas about children, learning, and development, and imply an equally diverse range of approaches and starting points for thinking about how teachers can work with children and families. This was important to the curriculum writers because they hoped that the EYLF would help educators to engage with issues of social equity and justice (Sumsion et al., 2009: 9).

The relationship between pedagogy and theories of learning and development

The inclusion of a diverse range of theories about teaching and learning was an attempt to reflect and promote a respect for diversity within the EYLF itself.

Furthermore, using multi-theoretical perspectives reflected the writers' belief that Australian early childhood educators were already drawing on different theoretical frameworks (Sumsion et al., 2009: 9). A potential problem with using a multi-theoretical framework (rather than more supposedly 'teacher-proof' documents such as pre-determined programmes, plans or checklists) is that it demands that educators are able to observe children's learning and development systematically (employing one or more theoretical perspectives), interpret these observations in valid ways, and plan, implement, and evaluate pedagogy to foster children's learning in response to these observations. However, the writers have argued that they do not see this as a problem. Instead, they suggest that adherence to one theoretical position would have meant that teachers had to work 'unquestioningly' within the parameters of that perspective (Sumsion et al., 2009: 9).

The authors of the EYLF argue that drawing on multi-theoretical perspectives would increase opportunities for discussion, debate, and critique about pedagogy because each theoretical perspective would lead to understanding and describing learning and development in different ways. This would be potentially useful for teachers working with diverse communities because teachers would not have to 'see' children according to one theoretical worldview. This position emphasizes the idea of enacting curriculum through pedagogy as 'interpretive work'. The writers of the EYLF have described pedagogy as a form of 'professional artistry', requiring 'a blend of practical knowledge; skilful performance characterized by intuition, improvisation, imagination and going beyond the known; and an ability to make judgements based on professional knowledge and an understanding of the context' (Fish, 1998, cited in Sumsion et al., 2009: 10). This definition of pedagogy suggests that relying on one theoretical perspective to inform the EYLF would make it difficult for teachers to understand their contexts and 'go beyond the known' in their work.

Critical reflection: the EYLF as a response to diversity

Our argument so far is that the theoretical diversity of the EYLF is an attempt to model professional inclusivity as a way of supporting teachers to think about engaging with diversity in practice. Furthermore, as the curriculum writers themselves have argued, the theoretical basis of the EYLF also recognizes the range of theories already familiar to early childhood educators in Australia. We have also argued that the EYLF is a pedagogical framework, providing advice to educators about how they should respond to a wide range of children, families, and learning contexts. But the writers of the EYLF were, of course, aware of the uneven capacity of early childhood educators across Australia to interpret the framework (Sumsion et al., 2009: 8). However, rather than assume that all educators will recognize, and know how to mobilize, the range of theories in the document when thinking about diversity, the EYLF provides a safeguard by explicitly addressing the issue of diversity at multiple points in the document.

In the document's Principles section, there is specific direction about how educators should *respond* to diversity:

Respecting diversity means within the curriculum valuing and reflecting the practices, values and beliefs of families. Educators honour the histories, cultures, languages, traditions, child rearing practices and lifestyle choices of families. They value children's different capacities and abilities and respect differences in families' home lives.

(Department of Education, Employment and Workplace Relations, 2009: 13)

Then, in Learning Outcome 2, 'Children are connected with and contribute to their world', advice is provided about how educators should *identify children's learning* about diversity, through the sub-outcome 'Children respond to diversity with respect' (see Figure 18.1).

Again, we see here the way in which the EYLF functions both to guide pedagogy (that is, the 'professional artistry' of interpreting situations and contexts) *and* as a curriculum framework, for planning and assessing children's learning and development. So how are early childhood educators responding to the EYLF as a resource for working with diversity? This is the focus of the last part of this chapter.

How are educators employing the EYLF in thinking about diversity?

Case Study: Jo

Jo is an early childhood teacher working in a sessional kindergarten in a middle-to-low socio-economic area in Melbourne, Australia. The children she teaches have a wide range of developmental skills and learning experiences and her centre is characterized by a high degree of cultural and social diversity.

Jo says that the way the Learning Outcomes are framed is important for helping her address this degree of diversity because she can show families where and how children are learning:

We have very diverse families in our centre. We have 17 children born overseas out of 27 in the group. Ten were born in Australia, and there is a whole range of developmental diversity. Because the EYLF Learning Outcomes are very broad, the children always meet some of the outcomes. So it is not like it is unachievable for the children – they can always meet some of the outcomes. This is important for the families because they can see their children are learning at kindergarten and for many multicultural families learning is a very important thing.

Jo talks about how the EYLF provides a platform for supporting families to learn about what their children are doing at kindergarten:

> I like the EYLF because of the simple words, and we can use the words over and over again during the year and in our observations and assessments. This means the families learn the framework too.

For Jo, the EYLF provides a way for her to make meaning with diverse families about what the children are doing in kindergarten. She is able to connect families and children through the learning outcomes that show many ways of being a 'successful' or competent learner. The multi-theoretical base of the EYLF is also important to Jo. She is interested in how the different theoretical perspectives suggest a range of ways of thinking about learning and development. She doesn't see herself as being restricted to one way of thinking:

> The different theories in EYLF help me think more widely because I see learning more broadly rather than being specific to how one theory sees learning.

Jo's interpretation of the multi-theoretical perspectives in the EYLF aligns with the standpoint of the writers of the framework. They were interested in allowing educators to think about many ways of understanding learning and development. For Jo, the possibility of seeing learning and development in multiple ways helps her work with the range of social, cultural, and developmental experiences that constitute her classroom. The multiple theories in the EYLF are important to her for responding to diversity and diverse families because:

> The families are living broadly and so I need diverse ideas about children and their learning. The different theories help me respond to the parents so that I can be more in tune with where they are coming from about their children and learning.

Jo's experience of the framework suggests that the multi-theoretical basis of the EYLF can help teachers work with the diverse social and cultural experiences that characterize children's learning and development. She is able to draw on what the curriculum has to offer in terms of the Learning Outcomes and theoretical perspectives and use (or interpret) these in her setting to make learning meaningful and visible for children and families. Jo is an example of a highly qualified teacher who has had exposure to a range of theories during her teacher education. It is possible that her familiarity with these theories is what helps her use the EYLF in a way that aligns with the intentions of the curriculum writers.

Case Study: Shanti

Shanti, who coordinates a large long-day child care centre in the same part of Melbourne, is struggling to support her staff in engaging with the EYLF. Although Shanti is well qualified and has been able to attend professional development about the EYLF, she faces the challenge of passing these new understandings on to staff with a range of expertise, including some who have no formal qualifications.

In contrast to Jo's experience, Shanti says:

> I mean it was great going [to outside workshops] because, yes, as you said they give you all that knowledge, that content and they're saying that there's no right or wrong way to do this. That's fine, okay, I get that and you're looking at the framework, but yeah you need to take that and actually bring that back to the group and work with them.

The challenge facing Shanti is intensified not only by staff expectations but the high expectations she places on herself:

> Yes and I think because you think that you should know all the answers, when the educators come and ask you about something about the Early Learning Framework, you think you should have all the answers and when you don't, that's when I'm getting really stressed out about it. That I don't want them to think that I'm not knowledgeable . . . So I feel like its constant learning at the moment. I'm in the middle of these massive changes and I'm very quickly trying to just keep up with it all.

Shanti is eager to learn about and 'keep up' with the curriculum framework that is asking her to interpret learning and development according to the context in which she works. Part of this context is the capacity among Shanti's staff to engage with the range of options for its use. The EYLF can be successful in providing a multi-theoretical approach but working in this way relies on teachers understanding how the many theories in the document can support them to develop multiple curriculum and pedagogical pathways with and for children. Despite this challenge, Shanti remains positive about the document and wishes it had been in place when her family migrated to Australia:

> Now when we look at earlier learning frameworks we think wow, that's good. This is how it should be. Of course coming from India, my background and the way I brought up my children, I think I wish I had this before I had my children. And it's just such a wonderful tool.

Shanti's struggles to support her staff in engaging with the EYLF have not turned her away from the document and the way the Principles, Practices, and Learning Outcomes are intended to support children and families. Like Jo, Shanti understands the EYLF as a tool to assist her in *interpreting* rather than *implementing* curriculum: this is the 'professional artistry' that these teachers, despite their different contexts, share with each other.

Conclusion

The EYLF is an important document for Australian early childhood education. It has generated a great deal of interest in issues associated with curriculum and pedagogy in early childhood education. In particular, the multi-theoretical framing on the EYLF has provided many ways of thinking about children, learning and development, and consideration of what diversity actually means. As the EYLF continues to inform early childhood education in Australia, these conversations will be important in helping all educators understand the potential of the framework as a curriculum tool.

Acknowledgements

The authors wish to thank the teachers quoted in this chapter for permission to share their experiences and interpretations of the EYLF in practice.

Find Out More

- Resources are being developed to support implementation of the EYLF. For a copy of the EYLF go to: http://www.deewr.gov.au/earlychildhood/policy_agenda/quality/pages/earlyyearslearningframework.aspx. Scroll down to the heading Supporting Documents to locate a version you can download. For a discussion on the development of the EYLF, go to: http://www.youtube.com/watch?v=vS5VO9C-ICk. This video is hosted by Gowrie Training Australia, a major provider of professional learning in early childhood education. For information on the implementation of the EYLF, go to: http://www.earlychildhoodaustralia.org.au/pdf/rips/RIP0904_sample.pdf. Here you will find a practitioner booklet by Joy Goodfellow, a member of the team that developed the EYLF.
- Approaches to curriculum implementation in early childhood education in Australia and New Zealand, including planning in response to diversity, are described in Arthur et al. (2011) and MacLachlan et al. (2010).
- For an introduction to the history of theorizing about curriculum writing and implementation, and the ways these processes have worked for or against diverse learners, see Apple (2004) and Eisner (1982).
- See Kessler and Swadener (1992), Vandenbroeck (2007), and Langford (2011) for discussions of the relationship between curriculum and diversity in early childhood education.

References and recommended reading

Apple, M. (2004) *Ideology and Curriculum* (3rd edn). New York: RoutledgeFalmer.

Arthur, L., Beecher, B., Death, E., Dockett, S. and Farmer, S. (2011) *Programming and Planning in Early Childhood Settings* (5th edn.). Melbourne, VIC: Cengage Learning.

Berk, L. (2012) *Infants, Children and Adolescents* (7th edn.). Boston, MA: Pearson.

Blaise, M. and Ryan, S. (2012) Using critical theory to trouble the early childhood curriculum: is it enough?, in N. File, J. Mueller and D. Wisneski (eds.) *Curriculum in Early Childhood Education: Re-examined, Rediscovered, Renewed*. New York: Routledge.

Department of Education, Employment and Workplace Relations (2009) *Belonging, Being and Becoming: The Early Years Learning Framework for Australia.* Canberra, ACT: Commonwealth of Australia.

Edwards, S. (2009) *Early Childhood Education and Care: A Sociocultural Approach.* Castle Hill, NSW: Pademelon Press.

Edwards, S. and Nuttall, J. (2005) Getting beyond the 'what' and the 'how': problematising pedagogy in early childhood education, *Early Childhood Folio*, 9: 14–18.

Eisner, E.W. (1982) *Cognition and Curriculum: A Basis for Deciding What to Teach.* New York: Longman.

Fish, D. (1998) *Appreciating Practice in the Caring Professions: Refocusing Professional Development and Practitioner Research.* Oxford: Butterworth Heinemann.

Goodfellow, J. (2009) *The Early Years Learning Framework: Getting Started.* Canberra, ACT: Early Childhood Australia.

Kessler, S. and Swadener, B.B. (eds.) (1992) *Reconceptualizing the Early Childhood Curriculum: Beginning the Dialogue.* New York: Teachers College Press.

Kilderry, A. (2004) Critical pedagogy: a useful framework for thinking about early childhood curriculum, *Australian Journal of Early Childhood*, 29(4): 33–7.

Langford, R. (2011) Critiquing child-centred pedagogy to bring children and early childhood educators into the centre of a democratic pedagogy, *Contemporary Issues in Early Childhood*, 11(1): 113–27.

MacLachlan, C., Fleer, M. and Edwards, S. (2010) *Early Childhood Curriculum: Planning, Assessment and Implementation.* Melbourne, VIC: Cambridge University Press.

Mac Naughton, G. (2005) *Doing Foucault in Early Childhood Studies: Applying Poststructuralist Ideas.* New York: Routledge.

Milleli, Z. and Sumsion, J. (2011) The 'work' of community in belonging, being and becoming: the Early Years Learning Framework for Australia, *Contemporary Issues in Early Childhood*, 12(1): 71–85.

Nuttall, J. and Edwards, S. (2004) Theory, context, and practice: exploring the curriculum decision-making of early childhood teachers, *Early Childhood Folio*, 8: 14–18.

Sumsion, J., Barnes, S., Cheeseman, S., Harrison, L., Kennedy, A. and Stonehouse, A. (2009) Insider perspectives on developing Belonging, Being and Becoming: The Early Years Learning Framework for Australia, *Australian Journal of Early Childhood*, 34(4): 4–13.

Vandenbroeck, M. (2007) Beyond anti-bias education: changing conceptions of diversity and equity in European early childhood education, *European Early Childhood Education Research Journal*, 15(1): 21–35.

19

USING LEUVEN OBSERVATION AND ASSESSMENT TOOLS TO INVESTIGATE OUTDOOR PROVISION

Annie Davy

Summary

This chapter describes a practitioner-led action research project exploring the use of a Process-oriented **S**elf-evaluation **I**nstrument for **C**are **S**ettings (SICS) developed by Professor Ferre Laevers (2005b) and his team from the Centre for Experiential Education, University of Leuven in Belgium. The participants were drawn from two areas of England and the project was initiated, led, and managed by the UK national school grounds charity, Learning through Landscapes. The aim was to improve outdoor learning and the starting point was observation of the children's experiences and assessment of their levels of wellbeing and involvement in the activities and environment on offer. Following observation and assessment by practitioners using the Wellbeing and Involvement (WB&I) scales, factors investigated by the project included the physical space, resources, adult–child interactions, organization and routines in order to develop more enabling and enjoyable environments for deep level learning to take place. Staff from the University of Leuven supported the project throughout, as well as Oxfordshire and Surrey County Councils' Early Years Advisory teams.

Case Study: Observation

STEP 1: Cherry Blossom Nursery: Observations

Note: Steps 1–3 are explained later in the chapter, as are the Leuven Scales of Well-being and Involvement.

Today, I am visiting Cherry Blossom Nursery to practise using the observation and assessment tools developed by Professor Ferre Laevers and team from Leuven University. The visit this morning is part of a new practitioner action research project exploring how to use the Process-oriented Self-evaluation Instrument for Care Settings (SICS) to support children's learning and development in outdoor provision. The starting point is observations of the children's experiences and their levels of wellbeing and involvement in the outdoor area of their early education setting. Several observers are choosing ten children at random to observe for periods of three minutes. We are using the Leuven 5-point scale for Well-being and Involvement to make our assessments.

Our visit is on a beautiful but cold day and there is plenty to watch:

- A 4-year-old girl in a pink sequined dress and plimsolls with white tights is flitting around the outdoor area. She is watching what the others are doing – moving from one area to another, mostly just watching, shifting her weight from one foot to the other in constant motion.
- Three boys are driving around on trucks and bikes. The space is small and they often bash into various obstacles, such as other bikes lying on the ground and the fence of crates separating the preschool from the vast and unused main school playground. Conkers are in the basket of one of the bikes, which sometimes spill over and roll across the ground.
- A group of children are making a collage with a teacher at a table. Other children approach often and look over the shoulders of the little crowd gathered round the table and then run off again. There is little space for them to join in.
- There is a pulley fixed to the beam of the canopy. Several times children approach it and pull it up and down before running off again.
- In the far corner there is a little den in the bushes. Approach and you hear a hum of happy conversation coming out of the foliage. Occasionally a child emerges and runs off, only to reappear shortly after with something else to take back into the den: play cups, conkers, a cushion.

The above scenario is taken from an action research project initiated by Learning through Landscapes, the UK national school grounds charity, working with the research team from the University of Leuven led by Professor Ferre Laevers. The project involved using a process of observation and assessment to improve the quality of outdoor learning experiences in early years settings, and gauging the impact of changes made on the children's overall learning and development.

Formed in 1990, Learning through Landscapes has strong credentials and experience in supporting practitioners in schools and early years settings to improve the quality of the educational provision outdoors. As a pioneering organization, it is always looking to the latest research evidence to refine and improve what it can offer (see http://www.ltl.org.uk/childhood/research.php). Inspired by the work of Professor Ferre Laevers, we wanted to find out how best to use the Leuven approach to improve the quality of early years education outdoors.

International research evidence (Lester and Maudsley, 2006; Gill, 2011; Louv, 2011) shows how access to the outdoors, and natural environments in particular, can improve children's mental health, wellbeing, and learning. There is little research and guidance, however, that explicitly demonstrates how the *quality* of the provision outdoors affects experiences and outcomes for children.

Through this project we wanted to support early years practitioners to meet the increasing pressure to demonstrate the impact of the work they are doing on outcomes for children. Over the course of a year, practitioners were able to document their observations, any changes made to provision and practice, and the effect the changes had on the children's learning and development. We used Learning through Landscapes' cycle of change and materials from the Playout Early Years Toolkit (Learning through Landscapes, 2009).

Our key principles of looking at the use, design, and management of the outdoor areas would remain central, but work with the Leuven team helped ensure our starting point in each case was the direct experience of the children in the setting and their learning journeys. At the time, the practitioners in schools in England were busy grappling with the Early Years Foundation Stage Profile (Department for Children Schools and Families, 2008) and starting to use standardized measures to assess summative learning at the end of the Early Years Foundation Stage (Qualifications and Curriculum Authority, 2008). While this provided useful benchmarking in the summer in which children officially ended their entitlement to 'early years' education, it did not always support practitioners to make evidence-based judgements about the learning journeys of individual children or give indicators as to how they should plan for each cohort of children in terms of the learning environment outdoors.

The Leuven scales for Well-being and Involvement have been widely used across many countries including the UK, particularly by local authority advisory teams and for research and development (see, for example, Pascal et al., 1998). In addition to the Learning through Landscape materials, our key tool was the guidance manual known in the UK as SICS, 'A processes oriented self-evaluation instrument' (Laevers, 2005b). The process includes three simple steps:

- STEP 1: assessment of the actual levels of wellbeing and involvement (scanning of the groups)
- STEP 2: analysis of the observations (explanation of the levels observed)
- STEP 3: selection and implementation of actions to improve quality.

The Learning through Landscapes (LTL) cycle of change (Figure 19.1) is a reflective instrument, which draws on David Kolb's (1984) theories of cyclical experiential learning, Plan-Do-Review, as also used in HighScope early years programmes (Epstein, 2007; see Chapter 15)

Using the Well-being and Involvement scales

The practitioners were first taught to use the observation tools and to look for indicators of high levels of wellbeing and involvement. The more engaged the children are, the deeper the learning that takes place (Laevers, 1994). The SICS manual describes Well-being and Involvement as follows:

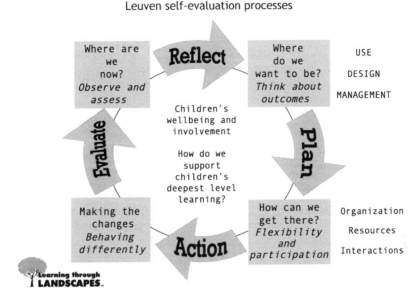

Figure 19.1 Learning through Landscapes cycle of change (adapted)

Well-being

Children with a high level of Well-being feel great. They **enjoy** life to the full.

They have fun, take joy in each other and in their surroundings.

They radiate **vitality** as well as relaxation and **inner peace**.

They adopt an **open and receptive** attitude towards their environment.

They are **spontaneous** and can fully be themselves.

Well-being is linked to **self-confidence**, a good degree of self-esteem and resilience.

All this is based on **being in touch with themselves**, with their own feelings and experiences.

(Laevers, 2005b: 8)

Involvement

Children with a high level of involvement are highly **concentrated and absorbed** by their activity. They **show interest**, **motivation** and even fascination. That is why they tend to **persevere**.

Their mimic and posture indicate **intense mental activity**. They fully experience sensations and meanings.

A strong sense of **satisfaction** results from the fulfilment of their **exploratory** drive.

When there is involvement we know children are operating at the very **limits of their capabilities**.

Because of all these qualities involvement is the condition that brings about **deep level learning**.

(Laevers, 2005b: 10)

We practised using the tools under the guidance of Bart Declercq and Gerlinde Snoeck from Leuven, first through the use of video footage of young children and then in the settings themselves.

It was not easy at first for practitioners to agree on their assessments. Most experienced practitioners know instinctively and can recognize immediately when children are fully engrossed or 'in a state of flow' (Csikszentmihalyi, 1979). The Well-being and Involvement (WB&I) scales help experienced and less experienced early educators to focus more precisely on what they observe in the children. They notice body language, facial expression, and interactions with materials, with staff and with other children. They use the WB&I scales to attribute a number from 1 to 5 in either scale to what they have observed (see Figures 19.2 and 19.3).

THE SCALE FOR WELL-BEING		
LEVEL	WELL-BEING	SIGNALS
1	**Extremely low**	The child clearly shows signals of discomfort: • whines, sobs, cries, screams; • looks dejected, sad or frightened, is in panic; • is angry or furious; • shows signs [wriggles, feet], throws objects, hurts others; • sucks its [thumb], rubs its eyes; • doesn't respond to the environment, avoids contact, withdraws; • hurts him/herself: bangs its head, throws him/herself on the floor.
2	**Low**	The posture, facial expression and actions indicate that the child does not feel at ease. However, the signals are less explicit than under level 1 or the sense of discomfort is not expressed the whole time.
3	**Moderate**	The child has a neutral posture. Facial expression and posture show little or no emotion. There are no signals indicating sadness or pleasure, comfort or discomfort.
4	**High**	The child shows obvious signs of satisfaction (as listed under level 5). However, these signals are not constantly present with the same intensity.
5	**Extremely high**	During the observation episode, the child enjoys, in fact it feels great: • it looks happy and cheerful, smiles, beams, cries out of fun; • is spontaneous, expressive and is really him/herself; • talks to itself, plays with sounds, hums, sings; • is relaxed, does not show any signs of stress or tension; • is open and accessible to the environment; • is lively, full of energy, radiates; • expresses self-confidence and self-assurance.

Figure 19.2 The SICS Scale for Well-being (Laevers, 2005b: 13)

THE SCALE FOR INVOLVEMENT

Level	Involvement	Examples
1	**Extremely low**	The child hardly shows any activity: • no concentration: staring, daydreaming; • an absent, passive attitude; • no goal-oriented activity, aimless actions, not producing anything; • no signs of exploration and interest; • not taking anything in, no mental activity.
2	**Low**	The child shows some degree of activity but which is often interrupted: • limited concentration: looks away during the activity, fiddles, dreams; • is easily distracted; • action only leads to limited results.
3	**Moderate**	The child is busy the whole time, but without real concentration: • routine actions, attention is superficial; • is not absorbed in the activity, activities are short lived; • limited motivation, no real dedication, does not feel challenged; • the child does not gain deep-level experiences; • does not use his/her capabilities to full extent; • the activity does not address the child's imagination.
4	**High**	There are clear signs of involvement, but these are not always present to their full extent: • the child is engaged in the activity without interruption; • most of the time there is real concentration, but during some brief moments the attention is more superficial; • the child feels challenged, there is a certain degree of motivation; • the child's capabilities and its imagination to a certain extent are addressed in the activity.
5	**Extremely high**	During the episode of observation the child is continuously engaged in the activity and completely absorbed in it: • is absolutely focussed, concentrated without interruption; • is highly motivated, feels strongly appealed by the activity, perseveres; • even strong stimuli cannot distract him/her; • is alert, has attention for details, shows precision; • its mental activity and experience are intense; • the child constantly addresses all its capabilities: imagination and mental capacity are in top gear; • obviously enjoys being engrossed in the activity.

Figure 19.3 The SICS Scale for Involvement (Laevers, 2005b: 14)

Using video footage to practise followed by discussion helped the practitioners to develop precision and accuracy in their observations and moderate their judgements of the 'scores' they gave through discussion with others. A crucial point about using these scales is that the score is not a judgement on the child, but rather on the degree of success of the early years provision in providing the type and quality of experience to enable the child to flourish and achieve deeper level learning. The focus is on the process of learning and the quality of experience for the child rather than the outcome. The numerical indicator on the scale is therefore a message to the early educators themselves as to how 'right' they are getting their provision for that child. If scores are consistently low, they need to look harder at what they are offering to that child and how to improve.

Observations should be precise and accurate; they can follow one child over a period of time or can be used as a 'scanning device' to look at the provision overall. In our project, when first visiting a setting we used the observation tools as a scanning device. We observed a child, an activity or an area of the outdoor provision for a few minutes and used the WB&I scales to gauge the child's or children's experience at that time or in that activity: their level of engagement and the kinds of learning that were going on.

Case Study: Analysis

STEP 2: Analysing Our Observations

After about half an hour of observation time at Cherry Blossom Nursery, we (practitioners and project advisers) go indoors to share the questions raised by what we have seen and to discuss the implications for the individual children we have observed and for the quality of the outside learning environment. We ask ourselves many questions:

- The girl in the pink dress (low wellbeing and involvement scores): Why did she seem unable to engage with the other children or the resources? Were there particular circumstances or developmental needs making this child appear isolated and slightly withdrawn? Were clothing, organization or teacher-engagement factors?
- The boys on bikes, children using the pulley, collage activity all showed low involvement scores: What were the possible factors creating the boys' limited engagement with bikes?
- The children's activity around the den indicated high wellbeing and involvement scores: What was making the den a place of such prolonged and active involvement? What was making this area such a hive of intense activity with bright-faced, happy looking children buzzing in and out?

We compare our scores and are pleased and a bit surprised that there is a high level of agreement in our use of the WB&I scales. Laevers and Heylen (2003) state that, notwithstanding the required observational skills, the inter-scorer reliability between two observers using these scales is usually satisfactory.

An important step in analysing the observations is to reflect both on individual children's needs and how these needs are being met by wider aspects of the provision. Within our outdoor learning project, we discuss individual children – particularly those for whom wellbeing scores are low. Are there particular factors around health or home background on the day of observation that may be contributing to indicators of low wellbeing?

Where involvement scores are not as high as early years educators would like, the SICS model suggests the following areas for possible intervention, modification or change:

1. A rich environment – equipment, infrastructure, variety of play materials.

2. Positive interactions with other children and sense of belonging.

3. Room for initiative, choice, and children's participation in determining their own activities, rules, and agreement.

4. Efficient organization, with clear plan for the day, no 'dead' moment (for example, children hanging around waiting for instructions), appropriate groupings, and planning of resources.

5. An empathic adult style, appropriate interventions taking account of children's feelings.

Case Study: Planning

STEP 3: Planning Interventions and Improvement

After analysing our observations at Cherry Blossom Nursery we begin to think about changes that could be made to increase children's wellbeing and involvement outdoors by looking at individual needs, the learning environment, and interactions with adults and organization.

Individual children's needs

The staff can provide added information to help explain external reasons for low wellbeing scores, for example where children are having a difficult time at home, or have been ill. The observations serve as a reminder to staff to follow up in discussions with parents and to ensure such children are tracked over time and if necessary other agencies are brought in to support with specialist help.

We look at more practical issues such as whether all children had access to appropriate outdoor clothing (for example, the girl in the pink dress).

Enriching the learning environments: 'densification'

The Laevers team talk about 'thickening the soup'; they ask how staff might make the learning environment richer by adding learning materials, provocations, and stimulation.

Practitioners pool their ideas:

- Perhaps painted parking bays and moveable road signs or a make-shift petrol station would increase language and motivation.
- A role-play 'building site' and a 'builder's merchant' would offer a 'real' context for transporting materials in the cars and bikes.
- Could the conkers, sand tray, and other resources be co-located with the pulley, which was obviously popular, but not engaging children in prolonged or more complex activities that stimulated learning?
- Could we make the area more interesting through role-play opportunities, for example, so that children can talk about and express what they are thinking/learning from their practical experiences?

Interactions and organization

We agree the planning of the adult-led collage activity had led to apparent 'dead moments' of the children hanging around and waiting their turn. We talk about how this kind of activity might be developed and organized differently so that more children could engage with it independently.

- Could staff encourage more child-initiated 'entrepreneurship' as we had witnessed when observing activity around the den area?
- Could the bike area be extended into the school grounds when they were not in use to increase physical challenge and the space available?

Practitioners' evaluation

Throughout the year, the practitioners continued with their observations using Learning through Landscapes' materials to assist them in auditing their provision and making changes or interventions to improve the quality of children's engagement and learning outdoors. At the end of the project, the practitioners were asked to summarize what they had learned. They reported that the project had reinforced their awareness of the children's emotional readiness and their involvement. They said that their observations had enabled them to improve their planning. Some reported that the wellbeing and involvement scores were highest when children were involved in initiating and developing their own activities.

By observing the children using the scales, we have been able to really see the children that needed support and help, and those that needed something more challenging and stimulating. It made us stop, think and question the decisions we were making 'for' rather than 'with' the children.

(Practitioner)

As a result of observations showing that children were moving quickly from one activity to another without sustained involvement, practitioners at one setting decided to put out less equipment and found that this required the pupils to use their imagination more, which increased levels of involvement.

Another setting established more flexible learning zones outdoors and extended free flow play. Some settings focused on ease of accessibility to the outdoors by creating transition areas between indoors and outdoors, adding a boot changing area or providing wet weather suits so that children could enjoy the elements in all weathers.

Many found that moving and linking up resources increased the children's involvement. One setting placed a workbench and tub of tools with a pulley system and added some foam bricks to create a building site. In another case, the change was simple: 'We now leave our shed doors open so the children can see the additional resources we have and decide what they want to use that day for themselves'.

When asked what differences these changes made to the children, practitioners reported noticing more cooperative learning and that wellbeing and involvement scores had risen for many children as the project progressed. Some reported improvements in behaviour.

> There is much less charging up and down the paved area, and squabbles over bikes. The boys especially love the hill and the tunnel, and play cooperatively and creatively in the open space. They have become less dominating and competitive and are more willing to listen to each other's ideas.
>
> (Practitioner)

Practitioners reported other improvements, including their perceptions that over the project the children had become more confident and more vocal, that they were engaging in activities for longer periods of time, and that they were developing more independent activities such as mark-making outdoors.

Both practitioners and advisers considered a range of ways of measuring improvements. The study was not large enough or controlled in such a way as to enable the establishment of a direct causal link between the interventions made as a result of the project and quantitative measures such as improvements in the Early Years Foundation Stage Profile. However, the practitioners' reflections and the case studies and photographs they produced were observable evidence. We asked them to tell us how they knew that the project had a made a difference. Cited improvements included:

> 100 per cent of parents in Ofsted's survey stated their children were happy to come to school and that they were happy with the school.

> Attendance figures have improved.

> We can tell that children are so much happier and cannot wait to get outside – even children who never would before.

> So much more communication and problem-solving is taking place.

Finally, we asked practitioners how the action research project had changed practice in their setting. Managers reported that teaching assistants involved in the project increased in confidence and were recording more observations and assessments during child-initiated learning. More opportunities for cross-curricular learning were being developed in the outside learning area. Several of the settings changed their routines, such as the way staff were deployed outdoors, and created more time for observations.

Staff are more motivated when new equipment and routines are introduced.

We now embrace our outside classroom rather than thinking it is just outside play time.

Conclusions

Making changes through practitioner research requires participants to be willing to reflect together on what they have observed, to challenge current practice and assumptions, and to be willing to try out new things in direct response to children's cues. Managers often found it easier to suggest changes to physical space and resources than to challenge adult interactions or suggest changes in routines for the day. Throughout the project, Learning through Landscapes staff acted as 'critical friends', supporting practitioners to observe children and to reflect and challenge their own practice without being judgemental. The team from Leuven helped practitioners think about what they could do to support their children to spend more time working in what Vygotsky (1978) describes as the *zone of proximal development* – working at the limit or just beyond their current stage of knowledge and experience – the optimal 'zone' for new learning to take place.

Practitioners documented progress and changes through photographs, observations, and individual child records. At the end of the project, they also looked at the Early Years Foundations Stage Profile scores for their groups. While statistically the group was not large enough to draw any conclusions, and many of the settings were also participating in other professional development programmes at the same time, we were pleased but not surprised to find that the scores had improved – in some cases dramatically so. A survey of practitioners from year one found that 84% of providers had continued to use the WB&I scales for observation and were continuing their focus on improving the quality of the outdoor provision.

Find Out More

- *Measuring for quality.* Read and consider three articles on different approaches to assessing quality of early years education (e.g. Pascal et al., 1998; Roberts et al., 2010). How are these approaches useful to early years practitioners?

- *Learning and the outdoor environment.* Browse the research section of the Learning through Landscapes website, www.ltl.org.uk/childhood/research. php, and write a short synopsis on why learning outdoors is important to young children's development. Read Maynard and Waters (2007). What are the issues they raise about tensions for early years practitioners teaching in the outdoors?
- *Wellbeing.* Interview three practitioners on what factors affect their own wellbeing and what they would look for in their children that would tell them the child had high or low levels of wellbeing. Read and consider UNICEF (2007).

Acknowledgements

Thanks go to the following: the children and staff of all participating settings in Oxfordshire and Surrey; Anna Brooke (freelance project coordinator); Julie Mountain and Jackie Brewer (Learning through Landscapes); Anne James and Kathy Burr (Surrey County Council); Professor Ferre Laevers, Bart Declercq, and Gerlinde Snoeck (Leuven University).

For more info on the Leuven scales for Well-being and Involvement, go to www. cego.be.

References and recommended reading

Csikszentmihalyi, M. (1979) The concept of flow, in B. Sutton-Smith (ed.) *Play and Learning.* New York: Gardner.

Department for Children Schools and Families (DCSF) (2008) *Early Years Foundation Stage.* London: DCSF. Available at: https://www.education.gov.uk/ publications/standard/ publicationDetail/Page1/DCSF-00261-2008 (accessed 30 May 2012).

Epstein, A.S. (2007) *Essentials of Active Learning in Preschool: Getting to Know the High/Scope Curriculum.* Ypsilanti, MI: HighScope Press.

Gill, T. (2011) *Sowing the Seeds: Reconnecting London's Children with Nature.* London: Sustainable Development Commission.

Kolb, D. (1984) *Experiential Learning: Experience as the Source of Learning and Development.* Englewood Cliffs, NJ: Prentice-Hall.

Laevers, F. (1994) The innovative project Experiential Education and the definition of quality in education, in F. Laevers (ed.) *Defining and Assessing Quality in Early Childhood Education.* Studia Paedagogica. Leuven: Leuven University Press.

Laevers, F. (2000) Forward to baSICS! Deep-level-learning and the experiential approach, *Early Years: An International Journal of Research and Development,* 20(2): 20–9.

Laevers, F. (2005a) The curriculum as means to raise the quality of ECE: implications for policy, *European Early Childhood Education Research Journal,* 13 (1): 17–30.

Laevers, F. (ed.) (2005b) *Well-being and Involvement in Care Settings: A Process-oriented Self-evaluation Instrument.* Leuven: Kind & Gezin and Research Centre for Experiential Education. Available at: http://www.kindengezin.be/img/sics-ziko-manual.pdf (accessed 4 June 2012).

Laevers, F. and Heylen, L. (2003) *Involvement of Children and Teacher Style: Insights from an International Study on Experiential Education*. Studia Paedagogica. Leuven: Leuven University Press.

Learning through Landscapes (2009) *PlayOut – Early Years Toolkit*. Available at: **www.ltl.org.uk.**

Lester, S. and Maudsley, M. (2006) *Play, Naturally: A Review of Children's Natural Play*. Play England (Project). London: National Children's Bureau.

Louv, R. (2011) *The Nature Principle*. **Chapel Hill, NC: Algonquin Books.**

Maynard, T. and Waters, J. (2007) Learning in the outdoor environment: a missed opportunity?, *Early Years: An International Journal of Research and Development*, 27(3): 255–65.

Pascal, C., Bertram, T., Mould, C. and Hall, R. (1998) Exploring the relationship between process and outcome in young children's learning: stage one of a longitudinal study, *International Journal of Educational Research*, **29(1): 51–67.**

Qualifications and Curriculum Authority (2008) *Early Years Foundation Stage Profile Handbook*. London: QCA. Available at: http://webarchive.nationalarchives.gov.uk/20110813032310/http://orderline.qcda.gov.uk/gempdf/1847219438.PDF (accessed 30 May 2012).

Roberts, F., Mathers, S., Joshi, H., Sylva, K. and Jones, E. (2010) Childcare in the pre-school years, in K. Hansen, H. Joshi and S. Dex (eds.) *Children of the 21st Century – The First Five Years*. **Bristol: The Policy Press.**

UNICEF (2007) *Child Poverty in Perspective: An Overview of Child Well-being in Rich Countries*, Innocenti Report Card 7. Florence: UNICEF Innocenti Research Centre. Available at: http://www.unicef-irc.org/publications/pdf/rc7_eng.pdf (accessed 5 June 2012).

Vygotsky, L. (1978) *Mind in Society: The Development of Higher Psychological Processes*. Cambridge, MA: Harvard University Press.

20

HUNGARY: KINDERGARTEN AS A PUBLIC EDUCATION INSTITUTION

Éva Kovácsné Bakosi

Translated by Zsuzsa Megyesiné Varga

Summary

This chapter describes how preschool provision in Hungary is organized to ensure that all children can access appropriate kindergarten education. Building on a tradition of educational pluralism, a national Core Curriculum has been developed which provides the basic framework for each kindergarten to develop its own educational programme suitable for local conditions. Hungarian kindergartens seek to make this process unique and personalized by highlighting play, most importantly free play, as the primary activity of preschool children, with an emphasis on local environmental characteristics and needs.

Setting the Hungarian kindergarten in context

Legal, financial, and organizational context

The network of Hungarian *óvoda* (which we have translated as 'kindergartens') forms the first stage of the comprehensive system of public education, and their establishment, operating rules, and financing are regulated – as is the case with any other educational institution – by public education law. The provision of professionally independent, free, and compulsory primary education is a public service obligation of the Hungarian State. While this study was being completed, preschool education in Hungary reached a new stage in its development, set out in the new Public Education Act (in force from September 2012) and the amendment and supplement of the National Core Curriculum of Preschool Education. The latter is the core document regulating and laying down content for early childhood education and has been in force since 2010.

In Hungary, preschool education is free, with the exception that parents pay a small amount for their children's meals (although families of disadvantaged and severely disadvantaged children pay a reduced fee for the meals, or the children can eat for free). Kindergartens receive multi-channel financing (from the state and the local government, or grants). Fifteen per cent of the national budget devoted to education goes to kindergartens, and this has remained at nearly the same level for the past twenty years. From September 2012, attending kindergarten will be compulsory for a minimum of four hours a day for 3- to 7-year-olds. By law, parents have freedom of choice of kindergarten because they 'are free to choose the kind of education they would like for their children' (Szüdi, 1997: 6). Children attend kindergarten from the age of 3 to 6 or 7 years but following assessment a child may stay in kindergarten for one more year after the age of 7, if it is professionally justified.

Kindergartens may be run by the state, municipalities, registered religious entities or other organizations, such as a foundation, but must be organized in such a way that they are open to all children. The institution must not express any religious or ideological commitment, but may speak about the different points of view regarding these issues; moreover, they must allow for non-compulsory religious education to be organized outside school time. A kindergarten can operate independently, or be integrated into other educational institutions, or be part of a multi-purpose institution that, for example, includes daycare provision for children younger than 3 years, or fulfils public education tasks in addition to cultural, educational, art, and sports-related functions. In 2011, there were nearly 2500 kindergartens, functioning mostly in inclusive organizational form; kindergartens with inclusive education have tripled in number over the last ten years. Special units can also be established within a kindergarten 'for the development of children with disabilities, or for those belonging to national and ethnic minorities' (Szüdi, 1997: 8).

Staff and children

The management of the kindergarten is the role of the headteacher, whose responsibilities include administration, instruction, and control of professional, organizational, personnel, educational, and financial areas. The educational personnel are made up of kindergarten teachers, sometimes together with professional helpers (such as social pedagogue, speech therapist, teaching assistants). Nursery nurses, who create personal ties within the groups, support the work of the teachers. In 2011, the teacher-to-children ratio was on average 11.1, with 23 children in a classroom (Department for Educational Development Policy, 2011). According to Hungarian preschool regulations, children must be organized in groups of no more than 25 children (groups accommodating children with special educational needs have smaller numbers). A panel of professionals is drawn up to improve professional provision, while to represent parents' interests a parent panel may be formed. Institutional education is understood as enhancing children's development in collaboration with the family, as a complement to it; partnership between the kindergarten and families contributes to a good atmosphere and high-quality and well-balanced educational work.

Although because of the falling birth rate the total number of children attending kindergarten has fallen by 18% in the past fifteen years, 92% of all 3- to 6-year-olds benefit from institutional provision in day care, kindergarten or primary school

(Department for Educational Development Policy, 2011). The number of pre-schoolers receiving national or ethnic minority education has shown a slight increase with the largest, 3.5-fold increase in the number of Roma minority children participating in preschool education, highlighting the importance attached to ensuring provision for disadvantaged children. It is noteworthy that although the total number of preschoolers has declined, more are in need of special education and care. The last ten years has seen a 43% increase in the number in need of care, even before the decrease in the population is taken into account. The number of recipients of support from family guidance centres is also quite high, 18.5% of all preschoolers.

Conceptual context

Let us look at the professional philosophy, structure, and content of the core programme, which will help to reveal the educational concepts underpinning Hungarian preschool education, the organization of kindergarten life, the main activities, necessary conditions, and outcomes of education. What is the perspective of the new core education programme? In one of our professional journals, Villányi (1998: 51) notes: 'the current performance-oriented preschool approach will be replaced by an approach looking for ways of development appropriate for each child'. In addition, it is characterized by pluralism, child-centredness, education-centredness, restrictions enforced in the best interest of the child, freedom of methodology, and organizational diversity. The traditions of our educational history are also evident in the way we now think about pedagogy; István Wargha stated, '(t)he whole child should be taken as he is, not as he should be' (Wargha, 1843, cited by Kövér, 2001). Elsewhere, Béla Pukánszky (2005) writes that we are reaching more and more an image of the child that goes back to Rousseau, based on the assumption that 'the child's task is not primarily a busy preparation for adulthood (or the next life stages) but living the joys of childhood in the most complete and intense way' (p. 15). Childhood has a unique value, and in order for children to unfold their own inner strengths, they need a patient, supportive, and inspiring atmosphere based on trust (Pukánszky, 2005).

Social context

Before looking at preschool education in detail, we will briefly consider the social context. In part, the statistics introduced earlier illustrate various environmental conditions that obviously influence not only preschool education in Hungary but also in other countries. In addition, our relatively recent transition to a democratic society within the last quarter of a century, our historical and educational traditions, the population distribution, the economic characteristics of some regions, innovation and the drive for development are all factors that influence the development of preschool education in Hungary today. A separate study could be devoted to today's family and the changes that increasingly confirm the importance of the role of the kindergarten (value choice dilemmas, uncertainty about how to manage children, changes in family structures, deepening socio-cultural differences, increase in the number of families in need of help and support). In light of this, the kindergarten as an institution emphasizes the compensatory, exemplary, supporting, and advisory role of the teachers.

The organization of kindergarten life is especially influenced by the diversity within preschool groups. Working with groups of children organized in compliance with the principles of inclusion and integrated education, teachers need diverse, inter- and multidisciplinary preparation, and a rich pedagogical toolbox because they simultaneously have to promote the development of talented children, those developing at a normal pace, disadvantaged children, including children with several disadvantages, children with special educational needs, migrants, and children from different age groups (in mixed age-groups). Teachers' attitudes have changed for the better, but sometimes the level of professional competence can cause difficulty. Another difficulty is the perceived lack of supportive professional staff (teaching assistants, psychologists, speech therapists, social pedagogues) or the limited availability of their expertise to meet diverse developmental needs.

Developing the content of preschool education

Hungary's openness to pedagogical pluralism and alternative solutions extends to kindergartens; diversity and freedom of choice allow differences in environment- and child-related factors to be taken into account. The professional autonomy of the kindergarten is reflected in the fact that, in line with the principles and criteria of the National Core Curriculum of Preschool Education, all kindergartens develop their local Educational Programme, their own organizational and operational rules, Code of Conduct and classroom rules, closely following the applicable provisions. The National Core Curriculum of Preschool Education serves only as a framework and with its holistic approach this results in a comprehensive preschool education, with approximately the same standards everywhere in the country. Two further content regulators are the Guidelines for National, Ethnic Minority Preschool Education and the Guidelines for Preschool Education of Children with Disabilities. Based on these documents and the corresponding eighteen optional education programmes, all kindergartens build and then further develop their own educational system, appropriate to local requirements and needs. Optional programmes offer educational approaches with different features that either affect the whole life of the kindergarten, or emphasize one particular area. These programmes include: Complex preventive preschool programme, Epochal preschool educational programme, Preschool education through games and stories, Step-by-Step programme, Action Agenda, Pre-school education through art, Complex system of play activities, Easier with Freinet, Montessori kindergarten, and Waldorf kindergarten.

The image of the preschool child and the preschool approach outlined in the programme form the guiding principles of the curriculum. The function of the kindergarten and its objectives are defined, the set of tasks and activities are built on this, and the desirable educational atmosphere, the structure of the methods and tools are assigned on this basis. The kindergarten is responsible for creating a calm, cheerful, secure, and loving atmosphere, for organizing the set of activities, and for identifying and creating the necessary conditions to promote children's development. The daily schedule and routine ensuring the appropriate proportion, smooth flow, and flexibility of the activities is an essential condition for the children's development (Kovács and Bakosi, 2004). Hungarian kindergartens are trying to make this system unique and personalized by highlighting play, most importantly *free play*, as the primary activity of preschool children, with an emphasis on environmental characteristics and needs. Kindergartens, by utilizing the above-mentioned optional programmes, or building their own independent system, develop their local curriculum.

Basic principles of Hungarian preschool education

The prevailing principle of Hungarian preschool education is therefore *play-centredness*, with the following objectives:

- It promotes the harmonious development of 3- to 6–7-year-old children, meeting their physical and psychological needs in a *mainly play-oriented system of conditions* providing experiences in a specific atmosphere, where children feel comfortable, relaxed, and are active every day.

- It covers the whole personality, while adjusting to individual rates of development and possible uneven development in some areas.

- It enables children to gain activity-based experience, and so promotes the emergence of positive attributes and abilities essential for the next life stage through child's *playful* activities with educational content.

- It develops an equal partnership between educators, a balanced, symmetrical relationship with the family, based on overlapping knowledge derived from education at kindergarten and in the family.

(National Core Curriculum of Preschool Education. Government Regulation, 137/1996, VIII.28)

The *system of playful activities* and its elements are outlined in Figure 20.1, showing the different organizational forms, variety of activities and content in which freedom enjoys priority.

Flexible principles provide a framework for organizing kindergarten life. *Child-centredness* is another such principle and merits closer examination. The question may arise, what else can a kindergarten be if not child centred? Indeed, this is a natural requirement, but there may be differences in the characteristics of the enactment of child-centredness. In our approach, child centredness is a comprehensive principle, which is meaningful in itself, but in fact can be realized in the fulfilment of other principles. We would consider an institution child centred if the following attributes apply:

- unconditional love extended to all children; patience, respect, appreciation of the children; family-like atmosphere providing emotional security and protection;

- accepting, inclusive attitude, which extends to the establishment of an integrated educational environment;

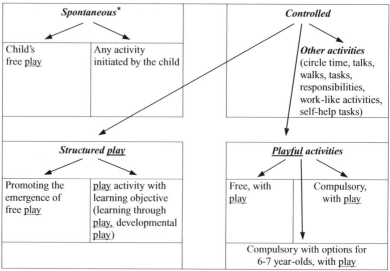

*Under conditions created with pedagogical, developmental intentions.

Figure 20.1 System of playful activities

- keeping in mind the child's best interests, before anything else; the child is the focus of preschool education, where the institution itself is trying to meet the child's physical, emotional, psychological, and social needs to the best of its ability;

- building on the fullest possible understanding of the child, it ensures differentiated treatment of individual characteristics, taking into account what is typical for the child's age and also accommodating different rates of development. To facilitate different patterns of development, the early years educator utilizes a rich set of differentiating tools, personalized treatment, and ways to focus on the individual but influencing the whole of the group, with special emphasis on boosting motivation and active participation (Kovács and Bakosi, 2004; Deliné Fráter, 2010).

- a variety of activities is organized, where *play, especially free play that cannot be replaced with anything else, has a high profile*;

- *play* in the daily schedule within a flexible framework is not only a source of spontaneous joy, but also a context for learning, and the dominant role of play, via the implementation of the *principle of playfulness*, permeates all aspects of preschool life. This makes it possible for the education content (story, rhymes, music, art, movement activities, knowledge of the environment) to be incorporated into the life of the kindergarten in a playful way.

Kindergartens accommodate children with a range of special needs, with help from professionals from outside the kindergarten where necessary. Similarly, special attention is devoted to children with outstanding abilities. Policies dealing with the education of ethnic minority children are laid down in separate regulations. Parents, kindergarten teachers, and even experts, however, have different opinions about integrated education for unimpaired/healthy and disabled children, as well as ethnic and national minorities. Parents are concerned about their children's slower development; teachers refer to the lack of special professional support, and the difficulties of meeting the range of needs. According to those in favour, 'early experience of one another, shared activities and experiences' for challenged and normal children increase the likelihood of them becoming more receptive later; in school, adolescence, and adulthood, *they will demonstrate acceptance, helpfulness* (and will not be 'excluding'). Children with challenges and impairments may be raised in an atmosphere of acceptance, feeling equal, and living a complete life (Kovács and Bakosi, 2004; emphasis added).

Kindergarten life: types of activities

The three basic elements of the activity structure of Hungarian preschool education we identify as follows:

- ✈ play (free play and structured play that is suitable for further development)
- 📖 activities for 'learning by doing'
- 🍽 work-like activity

These three activities are realized through different structural forms, especially because we can observe only a gradual differentiation between them in the child's mind. Sometimes they are completely intertwined, or occur in sequence, while at other times they exist separately. But the teacher is expected to judge these features and relationships appropriately.

An especially critical issue is how to assess the role of play in learning. Here, the approach does not place the learning objective above play. We believe that in this regard spontaneous play, free play, and teacher-initiated play must be separated from each other. *Free play* provides the stage for spontaneous learning, and so does not tolerate any kind of learning objective with a didactic aim. In Hungarian kindergartens, free play is the source of joyful experiences for the children. Free play is supported, aided, and inspired by the teacher as they create the conditions, play together with the children if needed, observe, react, and make remarks in an indirect way (Kovács and Bakosi, 2007). The developmental effects extend to the whole of the psyche, it being the main tool to unleash creativity, resourcefulness, originality, and problem-solving, as each game can be considered a minor creative production on its own (Kovácsné Bakosi, 2011). We create a play environment full of encouragement, experiences, and fun, which triggers emotions, is energetic, allows for self-expression and self-fulfilment – and in which the child's creativity can soar freely. This play environment includes a set of materials and tools, serving as the source of essential experiences and hands-on knowledge, as well as inspiration for creation. For this to become reality, our preschoolers are taken on several field trips. We count on help from parents who are open to welcoming children (for example, in animal and plant care, construction, and other job-related work). These diverse experiences result in an abundance of play themes, and the variety of toys and tools inspires them to create and make up witty ways and ideas during play.

With *initiated play*, teachers always have a well-defined intention. Initiated play always originates from the teacher, and if the child accepts the offer, the game continues in an activity together with the adult. Naturally, throughout, we stay within the frame of play; it must not transform into a didactic activity. In the period in the daily schedule assigned for play, teachers often use this type of play to encourage some children to play, or to make the learning activity more colourful and enjoyable. As emphasized above, *there is a dominance of play* in Hungarian kindergartens. Kindergarten life, surrendered to play, arranged around and enforcing the dominance of play is considered our mission.

This idea leads us to the second group of activities. The definition of *learning taking place in kindergarten activities* is derived from a broad psychological interpretation of long-term changes in the personality, due to experience. In Figure 20.1, we introduced the system of playful activities, but we want to emphasize that kindergarten is not just about making children participate in activities, and learn by doing these; the reader must understand that children *learn in all forms of activity*. Typical continuous playful learning in the kindergarten 'promotes the overall personal development of the child'. Often, parents and kindergarten staff need to be convinced that this is true. Learning takes place in different circumstances throughout the day in a variety of free, optional, initiated, and some compulsory forms of activity.

In the kindergarten, there are playtimes and other scheduled activities in which:

- Free play occurs undisturbed (at least one hour of protected time must be scheduled for free play).

- This can be followed by different optional activities – initiated learning situations to gain experience through play – during any other part of the day.

- Priority is given to 'initiated learning situations' (activities), as children:
  - have a strong desire for freedom (freedom to gain knowledge, satisfy their curiosity, and choose the activity);
  - express determination for what they want to do;
  - are typically driven by curiosity, as an internal motivation determining their stimulation demand.

- The time scheduled for compulsory activities or lessons in kindergarten increases slightly with the child's age. These include physical education, sometimes music, and occasionally environmental and social studies activities involving field trips.

- As well as the classroom, other inside (gym, DIY workshop, visual workshop, music room, art room, etc.) and outside spaces, environmental and social scenarios have a role.

To promote learning, children need a supporting, encouraging, motivating environment, personal involvement, and methodological diversity. These criteria are met as follows:

- freedom of choice of activities rich in experiences;
- colourful, stimulating physical environment;
- variety of learning contexts/scenes (inside, outside; natural/original, created/simulated);
- cooperation between the participants of the learning process and the learning support staff to engage in children's age-appropriate preparation;
- building on the child's prior experience, knowledge – attention to the child, the child's active participation;
- conditions facilitating children's discoveries and exploration, creativity, experience-based learning, active role. Thus, children can discover, find out, watch, observe, notice, find, come across, dig out, excavate, stumble upon, see, see into, scan, detect, feel, experience, pay attention to, sense, perceive, realize, identify, seek, learn, investigate, explore, search, find, all of which are essential to guarantee discovery-like learning based on hands-on experience;
- project design can be adapted to the learning environment outlined above;
- different developmental factors are taken into account. To meet the individual features of diverse development, teachers elaborate the stages of activities and processes. They develop theme units, and break down the knowledge content according to its level of difficulty: easy, more difficult. This is followed by decisions on time frames, the number of practice occasions, and other quantitative indicators. Then comes the selection of methods (common activities, game of 'my turn, your turn', giving help, invitation – attraction, encouragement, appreciation, formulating examples of solutions, requesting proposed solution, negotiating, and so on). We apply personalized positive evaluation.

We can conclude that in 'learning through activities', learning occurs not in strict, didactically ordered teaching but instead:

- by doing it;
- through recognition, discovery, and observation;
- in the procedure of getting to know;
- by trying, experimenting, attempting, and testing;
- while looking at, looking for, finding, and satisfying curiosity;
- by raising interest, increasing and maintaining motivation.

The third type of kindergarten activities to be introduced in this chapter is *work-like activities*. Such activities contribute significantly to the development of children's environmentally conscious behaviour, and responsibility for the work done in the community. Children's work-like activity is a typical yet unique form of kindergarten life rich in activities. It is typical, because it appears in every kindergarten institution, yet it is unique as in several respects it relates to play; however, it is not the same as play, since it has an end result/product, and its voluntary character is limited. It is often intertwined with play, while at other times it appears as a continuation of a different activity, or even an independent activity. As such, it contributes to the satisfaction of children's primary or secondary desires, wishes, and the development of their motivation, abilities, characteristic features, and habits. In kindergarten, it is very important to emphasize the motivational side of this activity. Continuous and systematic activity is a very powerful tool to enhance children's *independence*, and to make community relations stronger.

The aim of children's work-like activities is to help them develop a responsibility for duties, internalize the drive for doing more formal, controlled tasks beyond the freedom of play, establish a positive attitude towards this kind of activity (love of work), and incorporate it into the set of activities promoting self-growth and self-fulfilment.

Case Study: Helping to clear up

While clearing up after visual art activity, water spills on the table. The kindergarten teacher takes a large piece of cloth and begins to mop up the water, occasionally wringing out the cloth over a bowl. The children watch this with interest. One of them holds the bowl for the mopped up water. After stopping the water flow, the children are given a small piece of cloth each, and they also start the activity. The teacher helps them if necessary, especially with wringing out the cloth. Towards the end of the activity the teacher lets them do the task alone. Some of them add individual movements to the activity (one moving in one direction, another makes circular movements, and another wrings out the cloth in a peculiar way).

Children can undertake the following three types of work-like activities: adult acting together with children, child carrying out a task independently, children's joint activities.

An activity carried out together with the adult can be:

- child observes the adult do the task, but makes some contribution to it;
- child actively helps the adult do the task;
- child contributes equally to the task;
- child does its part independently, in joint work-like activity (alone or in group).

A child working independently might include:

- after prior discussion, child carries out task with indirect assistance (occasional duty, i.e. washing toys, small repairs);
- regular work-like activities (self-help tasks, child-on-duty daily jobs);
- chikd takes responsibility on a voluntary basis.

Children's joint activities include:

* procedures that children are already *familiar* with, opportunities to take joint responsibility for duties carried out by several children in collaboration (cleaning up in classroom or in the outside area, taking care of plants and pets);
* novel tasks, responsibilities (welcoming children who are new to kindergarten or younger ones, preparation for a show or an exhibition);
* seeking and initiating independent work-like activities.

Planning flexibly for all children

The planning process of the life of the kindergarten begins with the development and elaboration of the local preschool curriculum by the teaching staff. The education plan (or syllabus) of the group is drawn up with the children and their environment in mind. The structure of the education plan and its content varies by educational programme and institution. It sets the goals for development, determines the tasks to achieve those goals, selects and identifies the necessary activities and content, determines the different stages appropriate to the children's pace of development, organizes it all into a system, and assigns a time frame. There are no levels to be reached, only developmental characteristics described in the preschool Core Curriculum that serve as benchmarks. Teachers can make a thematic plan, project plan (see sample in Figure 20.2), a schedule or network plan, where they can sort tasks into weekly, fortnightly, monthly, and quarterly plans.

The process of establishing routines, with red-letter days and holidays inserted, provides the content of the education plan. The education plan is the flexible framework of the pedagogical processes adjusted to the child. Another planning document is the *daily schedule*. We try to develop a daily schedule that ensures the dominance of free activities, is flexible but predictable, and adapts to the needs of individual children. Play and exercise in the fresh air are very important, and it must not be crowded.

Quality, progress, and transition

As happens elsewhere (see Chapter 10), it has been necessary to elaborate *quality indicators* appropriate to the kindergarten and the preschooler, which through monitoring and evaluation determine whether the programme is operating at a suitable level, and to identify areas for development (using the framework of the Institutional Quality Management Programme). For this purpose, with the guidance of the Education Research Institute, a programme package has been prepared to monitor and examine the rate and course of children's growth and development (Kovácsné Bakosi, 2004). With these measuring tools, together with those compiled by the respective preschool institutions, kindergarten teachers assess progress towards achieving their goals.

BIRDS, TREES

PLAY
- wooden construction blocks
- DIY with wood
- games outside in the woods
- play in the yard on wooden toys
- 'bird hospital' role play

IN PLAY TIME
- looking at picture books with birds, trees

NATURAL AND SOCIAL ENVIRONMENT
- trip to the nearby forest, observing flora and listening to birds' sounds
- collecting fallen leaves, seeds
- role of trees in birds' life (nesting place, camouflage)
- examination of storks' and swallows' nests
- collecting feathers
- observing leaves of bushes and trees in the yard; criteria: change in colour, movement, stains
- trip to a botanical garden
- trip to a tree nursery
- visit to the aviary in the zoo
- trip to garden centre
- trip to the emu farm
- visit to the bird hospital
- visit to pigeon exhibition,
- visit to pheasant breeding station

STORIES, POEMS
- Mora Ferenc: The tit's shoes
- Varró Daniel: madárhatozó Badar (poem anthology)
- Nagybandó András: Seven trees (poem anthology)
  linnet, goldfinch, canary, robin, wren, owl, more than 50 Two-line rhymes on different birds.
- Zelk, Z.: Goldfinch's Nest, poem of the brave bird
  Szutyejev: What bird is that?
- Lazar, Ervin: The ambitious blackbirds
- Egry, György: None of the trees
- Mora, Ferenc: The Swallows
  Csorba, Győző: How far have the sparrows jumped?
  Tree Tales : Egg Tree, World Tree, Golden Apple Tree, White Pear, Bacon Wood, Gem Tree, World-sound tree, Tree as tall as the sky.
  Tale of Creation: e.g. The wise owl.
  Proverbs, riddles
  Language and literacy development
  Vocabulary expansion - species of birds, trees
  Development of articulation, developing speech organs: trees in the wind, bird sounds, sound imitation. Sentences.

MOVEMENT
- Swallows on the wire…
- Hen and chicks…
- Swallow-catcher
- Stork without a chimney
- The hawk and the little chicks

DRAWING, DECORATION, HANDICRAFT
- rubbing image of tree barks
- drawing and paining of leaves and flowers
- leaf prints with tempera
- leaf compositions with glue (collage)
- birds (clay, play dough)
- follow-up, working up experiences (drawing, painting)
- model table (modelling)

MUSIC GAMES WITH SONGS

Rhymes:
ÉNO*
46 We were birds
56 The magpie flies

Children's game songs w/trees & woods:
ÉNO*
138 Cherry tree bends
104 The walnut tree has dried
173 Pear tree
315 Two robins sitting on a
258 Bird is flying
182 The forest rattles
117 Cutting-cutting the tree
290 Three birds
228 Swallow from the roof

136 One cherry-cherry
61 Plum falling
320 What a magnificent tree
304 Outside, in the trees (canon)
104 Tall is the Ruta tree*
32 The walnut tree has bloomed *
98 In Green Forest, walking*
113 In Green Fortress lives*
300 Green leaf, green leaf*
(Romanian folksong)

Music for listening: *T***
140 Twig, twig, little twig
101 Orphan bird is hiding
41 Little dove is sad
340 Csinálosi woods (in two parts)
56 Buds of the rosehip
108 To the green forest
6 Little bird is gone
94 Forest, forest, high is its
96 Forest, forest, forest in M
307 The dances in the l (canon)
169 Skylark darling
335 Blackbirds (Kodály Z.)

Abbreviations:
*ÉNO = Forrai, Katalin: Music in Preschool. Editio Musica, Budapest, 1974.
**T = Törzsök, Béla: Listening to music in Preschool. Zeneműkiadó, Budapest, 1982.
*** folksong

Figure 20.2 Sample project plan (competence-based teaching and learning project in Hajdú-Bihar county)

Kindergartens, just like other public educational institutions, must not ignore the issue of aptitude and suitability necessary for the next stage of life (see also Chapter 7). The national Core Curriculum includes the basic features of children's developmental characteristics at the end of kindergarten. A *progress record* (not compulsory, but widely used) keeps track of children's individual progress, but the child does not take it along to primary school; it remains in the kindergarten. It is a means of getting to know the child in a more objective way, providing facts for better planning of developmental conditions for the child, for more flexible education processes (Bakonyi, 2009).

Kindergarten staff would like to promote children's suitability for school by making sure that the kindergarten fulfils the functions of a kindergarten and protecting preschoolers from tasks and expectations associated with primary schools that are inappropriate for their age. Unfortunately, often in response to parental pressure, the kindergarten cannot remain entirely unaffected by the 'requirement-and-performance-centredness' of the primary school (as indicated by an increase in the proportion of compulsory activities, special workshops, and school-like rules of conduct). As a result, the kindergarten is in a double grip. However, transition to school is gradually becoming smoother and schools are increasingly aware of the fact that the preparation for school lifestyle is actually the task of the primary school (Kovácsné Bakosi, 2010). It should also be acknowledged that the family and the kindergarten, as well as the primary school, have well-defined tasks in the kindergarten-to-school transition.

Conclusions

In Hungarian kindergartens, teachers aim to provide conditions to promote development: a balanced, peaceful, encouraging, loving atmosphere; conscious and systematic observation; constant preparedness and readiness; recognizing spontaneous situations; creating purposeful situations; raising and maintaining children's motivation and interest; setting a model to follow and imitate; allowing for freedom and children's autonomy; providing opportunity for self-expression; and answering children's questions. They use methods to suit children's individual characteristics, to boost self-esteem, by supporting, inspiring, motivating, encouraging, and enhancing children's independence and conveying trust and love.

Find Out More

- Read and find out about the features of the alternative kindergarten programmes mentioned on page 232. Which one can you identify with? Can you explain why?
- How do you interpret the phrase 'individualized socialization'? How could it be applied to Hungarian kindergartens? And to your own context?
- 'Play provides the stage for learning'. How would you enact this principle in your pedagogical practice?

References and recommended reading

Bakonyi, A. (2009) *Az óvodás gyermek fejlődésének nyomon követése [Tracing Children's Progress in Kindergarten]*. Budapest: Educatio Társadalmi Szolgáltató Nonprofit Kft.

Deliné Fráter, K. (2010) *A differenciáló pedagógia alapjai, sajátosságai az óvodai nevelésben: Alkotóműhely 2 [Basic and Specific Features of Differentiating Pedagogy in Kindergarten: Workshop Series 2]*. Series editor: É. Kovácsné Bakosi. Debrecen: DE Faculty of Child and Adult Education.

Department for Educational Development Policy (2011) *Statistical Yearbook of Education 2010/2011*, Vol. 8: 141. Budapest: Ministry of National Resources.

Eurydice (2009) *Organization of the Education System in Hungary 2008/2009*. Brussels: European Commission. Available at: http://eacea.ec.europa.eu/education/eurydice/ documents/eurybase/eurybase_full_reports/HU_EN.pdf (accessed 5 June 2012).

Kotán, A. (2005) Az óvodai nevelés intézményrendszere és finanszírozása [Institutional system and financing of kindergarten education], *Educatio*, 2005 (4): Óvodák. Available at: http://epa.oszk.hu/01500/01551/00034/pdf/ (accessed 5 June 2012).

Kovács, Gy. and Bakosi, É. (2004) *Óvodapedagógia I [Preschool Pedagogy I]*. Debrecen: Authors.

Kovács, Gy. and Bakosi, E. (2007) *Játékpedagógai ismeretek [Pedagogy of Play*, 2nd edn.]. Debrecen: Authors.

Kovácsné Bakosi, É. (2004) *Mérőeszközök az óvodai játék és tanulás méréséhez [Measurement Tools to Assess Play and Learning in Kindergarten]*. Debrecen: Author.

Kovácsné Bakosi, E. (2010) *'Már nem óvodás, de még nem igazi iskolás'; Nézőpontok az óvodások felkészüléséről, az átmenetről* ['Not a preschooler any more, but not yet a schoolchild'; Points of view on kindergartners' preparation for transition], in A. Gábor (ed.) *Képzés és Gyakorlat Konferenciák III. Az óvodapedagógiától az andragógiáig*. Kaposvár: Kaposvári Egyetem Pedagógiai Kara.

Kovácsné Bakosi, É. (2011) 'Szabadon szárnyaló értelem': kreativitás a játékban ['Mind soaring freely': creativity in play], *Óvodai Nevelés (Preschool Education)*, 4: 13–19.

Kovácsné Bakosi, É. (undated) *Játék és tanulás az óvodában [Play and Learning in Kindergarten]*. National Institute for Public Education. Available at: http://www. oki.hu/oldal.php?tipus=cikk&kod=ovodai-bakosi-jatek (accessed 5 June 2012).

Kövér, S. (2001) *Az óvoda légköre* [The atmosphere of kindergartens], *Kisgyermeknevelés*, 3: 13–20.

Oberhuemer, P., Schreyer, I. and Neuman, M. (eds.) (2010) Hungary, in *Professionals in Early Childhood Education and Care Systems: European Profiles and Perspectives*. Opladen and Farmington Mills, MI: Barbara Budrich Publishers.

Pukánszky, B. (2005) *A gyermekről alkotott kép változásai az óvoda történetében* [Changes in the image of the child in the history of kindergarten], *Educatio*, 14(4): 703–15. Available at: http://www.pukanszky.hu/Ovoda.pdf (accessed 13 May 2012).

Szüdi, J. (1997) *Óvoda a közoktatás rendszerében [Kindergarten in the System of Public Education]*. Budapest: Okker Kiadó.

Villányi, G. (1998) *Az Óvodai nevelés országos alapprogramjának implementációja [Implementation of National Core Curriculum of Preschool Education]*. *Új Pedagógiai Szemle*, September. Avaliable at: http://www.oki.hu/oldal.php?tipus=cikk&kod=1998-09-ta-villanyi-ovodai (accessed 13 May 2012).

Wargha, I. (1843) *Terv a kisdedóvó intézetek terjesztése iránt a két magyar hazában [Plan of Dissemination of Child Care Institutions]*, Pest. 20.

21

THE JAPANESE VIEW OF NATURE AND ITS IMPLICATIONS FOR THE TEACHING OF SCIENCE IN THE EARLY CHILDHOOD YEARS
Manabu Sumida

Summary

This chapter looks at one of the content fields (or 'areas of learning') of kindergarten study in Japan (i.e. 'Environment') from the Japanese view of nature. Historical changes in the Japanese kindergarten course of study, including the renaming of the content field 'Nature' to 'Environment' in 1998, are also outlined. Practice in the area of 'Environment' in the Japanese kindergarten is discussed, and differences between the Japanese view and scientific view of nature summarized. The Japanese view of nature tends not to distinguish between nature and art, or between nature and humans. Rich natural environments are provided for young children in Japanese kindergartens; however, very few activities offer opportunities for young children to observe natural things objectively and logically. Drawing on a case study, I discuss how traditional Japanese nature activities could be extended to science to provide enriched opportunities for multifaceted learning.

Introduction

Small animals, such as rabbits and turtles, are often housed in corners of the playground and flowers, such as tulips, are grown in school gardens. Such scenes are quite common in kindergartens in Japan. Through plants and animals viewed both in and out of the kindergarten, children are given opportunities to have contact with natural events and phenomena. This kind of activity is seen throughout early childhood education in Japan.

In many cases, however, the focus is on developing children's sympathy and/or enriching their emotional response to nature through close encounters with natural events and phenomena, rather than on their intellectual growth. Hatano (2007) noted that the most important educational aim in biology activities in kindergarten was to develop an appreciation of, and respect for, life through various interactions with nature. He pointed out that in the process of making *dorodango* (mud balls, a traditional pastime among Japanese children), kindergarten children are able to achieve mental balance and peace of mind, rather than just acquiring knowledge about the size and solidity of stones.

Literature reviews (e.g. Wellman and Gelman, 1998) justify the belief that naive physics and naive biology act as innate constraints, 'domains', in which young children acquire scientific knowledge and change their scientific understanding. Gopnik and colleagues (2001; Gopnik, 2009) noted that young children are like scientists, in that they can create a theory through observation and experimentation. Thus it is no longer justifiable to insist that scientific investigation such as observation and experimentation should not be introduced until the upper grades, or that, based on the developmental characteristics of young children, early childhood education practice should be hands-on only (see, for example, Metz, 1997).

Based on the results of our research, even young children can develop an inquiring mind and curiosity for various topics such as 'Water', 'Movement', and 'Living Things' through the provision of appropriate materials, experiences, and learning environments (Fukada et al., 2005; Sumida et al., 2007). The importance of learning science as a process from the early years has been highlighted (e.g. Saracho and Spodek 2008; National Research Council, 2010), as has the contribution of the scientific process to the development of language ability and social skills (Settlage and Southerland, 2007).

As Settlage and Southerland (2007) pointed out, providing 'experiences' for children is not enough to bridge the gap between naive curiosity and scientific inquiry; explanations based on evidence and appropriate connections between scientific knowledge and experiences are also required. Quality opportunities to encounter science are important for all children starting early years provision in modern industrial, technological, and scientifically oriented societies. This chapter looks at the reconsideration of 'Environment' as one of the content fields in the official course of study for kindergartens in Japan. The discussion focuses on how Japanese kindergarten activities involving nature could be incorporated into science education and enriched to promote diverse learning outcomes.

From 'Nature' to 'Environment' in the Japanese kindergarten curriculum

Japanese *youchien*, usually translated as 'kindergartens' in English, provide pre-primary education for children aged 3–5 years. Since 1956, the Japanese Ministry of Education's 'National Course of Study for Japanese Kindergarten' has provided legally binding educational guidelines for all children aged 3–5 attending public and private *youchien*. The official course of study, first implemented in 1956, was revised in 1964, 1989, 1998, and 2008. In the 1989 revision, the content field (or 'area of learning') 'Environment' was reconstructed, a major turning point for science education in the early years in Japan.

The National Course of Study for Japanese Kindergarten was implemented to provide standards for the contents of instruction in 1956 (Ministry of Education, 1956). For science education in the early years, one of the five educational goals was to cultivate an understanding of, and emotional response to, the surrounding natural and social worlds, events, and phenomena. In the first course of study for kindergarten, there were six content fields: Health, Society, Nature, Language, Musical Rhythm, and Drawing and Handicrafts. The course of study also indicated the 'developmental characteristics of young children' and 'desired experiences' in each of the six fields. The desired experiences in the content field 'Nature' are shown in Table 21.1.

The contents and aims of each field were different from subjects in primary school; however, the content fields were established as part of a sequence leading into the subjects taught in primary school. Indeed, it was mandatory to consider the primary curriculum in the course of instruction at kindergarten (Ministry of Education, 1956).

Upon its first revision in 1964, one of the eleven main principles of the National Course of Study for Japanese Kindergarten was to develop an interest in, and curiosity for, natural and social events and phenomena in order to 'cultivate the germ of the ability to think' (Ministry of Education, 1964). The principles of the content field of 'Nature' included:

1. treating animals and plants in their surrounding environment with care, and becoming familiar with nature;
2. developing an interest in, and curiosity for, the natural events and phenomena of their surroundings, and observing, thinking about, and operating within them by themselves;
3. acquiring simple skills necessary for accommodating to everyday life;
4. developing an interest in, and curiosity for, the concepts of quantity and number, and diagrams.

A specific consideration of Principle 2 was to enable children to notice the basic facts of natural science as the opportunity arose, to develop the inclination to observe and the ability to think correctly about natural events and phenomena, to stimulate their originality and imagination as often as possible, and to enrich consideration and understanding that was developmentally appropriate to young children (Ministry of Education, 1964). This revision could be interpreted as fostering the development of a scientific way of thinking in the Japanese context. Yamauchi (1981) described how educational goals for nature could be achieved only through an interaction between children and nature. Japanese early childhood education had started to have the educational goal of developing a sense of science among children and of cultivating their growing capacity for scientific thinking in the content field 'Nature' as embedded in Japanese language and culture (see Sumida, 2012, for further discussion of the importance of language and culture in shaping ways of thinking about nature and science).

The second revision of the National Course of Study for Japanese Kindergarten in 1989 was crucial in the history of the development of the curriculum. The six contents fields were reconstructed to five: Health, Human Relationships, Environment, Language, and Expression. The overall objective of the field 'Environment' was 'to cultivate enriched emotions and the growing ability to think through developing an interest in, and curiosity for, events and phenomena surrounding them, such as nature' (Ministry of Education, 1989). The content field 'Environment' included

Table 21.1 'Desired experiences' in the content field 'Nature': National Course of Study for Japanese Kindergarten, 1956

---

1. Observing and talking about their surroundings

Observing and talking about flowers, grasses, and trees

Observing, keeping, and talking about goldfish, little birds, insects, hens, and rabbits

Observing butterflies, dragonflies, and ants

Observing the growth of and changes in animals and plants

Observing sunrise, sunset, the moon, and stars

Taking notice of clouds, rain, snow, rainbows, and wind

Viewing mountains, rivers, and the ocean

Listening to the songs of birds and sounds of insects

Recognizing various sounds

Taking notice of the distance, direction, height, position, and speed of objects and making comparisons

2. Taking care of animals and plants

Sowing seeds, planting seedlings, and watering plants

Helping with weeding in a flower garden

Taking care of tadpoles, goldfish, little birds, and insects

Being aware that adult animals take care of their young

Being aware that food appropriate for animals varies from one species to another

Not damaging trees or picking flowers

3. Being aware of changes in and beauty of nature

Observing changes in the seasons

Comparing sunrise and sunset, and sunny places and shady places

Comparing warm days and cold days, and other weather such as sunny days, cloudy days, rainy days, and windy days

Appreciating the beauty of mountains, the sea, rivers, animals and plants, and stars

Observing changes in animals such as the transformation of a tadpole into a frog

Checking the day's weather, be it a sunny day or a rainy day

4. Collecting various objects

Collecting leaves, nuts, shells, and pebbles

Showing various kinds of things collected and talking about them with friends

Comparing the size, weight, number, and shape of things

Displaying things collected

Thinking about how to put collected things away

5. Observing machines and tools

Developing an interest in observing locomotives and cars

Developing an interest in the mechanisms of toys

Being aware of the differences between wood products and metal products

Using magnets and a magnifying glass

---

developing an ability to interact actively with the surrounding environment, natural and social events and phenomena, and to cultivate attitudes for incorporating them into children's lives (Ministry of Education, 1989). The aims, contents, and ways to deal with the contents of 'Environment' are summarized in Table 21.2.

Table 21.2 Aims, elements, and means of addressing the elements of the content field 'Environment': National Course of Study for Japanese Kindergarten, 1989

1. Aims

- To develop an interest in, and curiosity for, various kinds of events and phenomena through familiarity with the children's surrounding environment and interaction with nature.

- To initiate interactions with their surrounding environment, and to incorporate them into their lives and cherish them.

- To enrich children's sense of the nature of things, the concepts of quantity and numbers, etc., through observing, thinking about, and dealing with surrounding events and phenomena.

2. Elements

- Leading a life close to nature and being aware of its grandeur, beauty, and wonder.

- Being aware of changes in nature and in people's lives in accordance with the season.

- Developing and incorporating an interest in surrounding events and phenomena, including nature.

- Acknowledging the importance of life and respecting it by becoming familiar with the surrounding animals and plants.

- Treating their surroundings with care.

- Using their surrounding objects to think about and try things out.

- Developing an interest in the mechanisms of play equipment and tools.

- Developing curiosity for the concepts of quantities and diagrams in everyday life.

- Developing an interest in, and curiosity for, the information and facilities that play important roles in their lives.

- Being familiar with the national flag and all its functions inside and outside the kindergarten.

3. Means to address the elements

- Children should be encouraged to develop a willingness to involve themselves voluntarily with nature through conveying to others and sharing with each other their emotions about events and phenomena, animals and plants surrounding them. This should be done in such a way that through these various relationships, children can foster a feeling of attachment to and sense of awe regarding these things, a respect for life, a spirit of social responsibility and an inquisitive mind.

- Children should be encouraged to place importance on their experiences based on the necessities of their own lives, so that interest in, curiosity for and a sense of the concepts of quantities can be fostered.

The significant changes in the 1989 revision were to integrate children's development with the five new content fields, and to place emphasis on comprehensive play-centred instruction. Mitsunari (2007) noted that the 1989 revision appeared simultaneously with the transition from teacher-centred education to children-centred education in kindergartens in Japan. However, he noted that the 1989 revision of the National Course of Study for Japanese Kindergarten, launched under the slogan 'Educating children through their environment', was misunderstood by teachers. As a result, some teachers did not teach anything to children and just kept monitoring the children's activities (Mitsunari, 2007).

The 1989 revision seemed therefore to have regressed the development of scientific literacy in kindergarten, though this went largely unnoticed by Japanese teachers because the aims and contents involved in 'Environment' had great affinity with the Japanese view of nature. For example, Fujioka (2011) insisted that emotional experiences were necessary to be familiar with nature in the development of a sense of science. The Japanese view of nature will be explained in more detail in the next section.

The Japanese view of nature

To understand the National Course of Study for Japanese Kindergarten better, it would be helpful to examine the Japanese view of nature. For a long period, many prominent Japanese works of literature and art involved nature; however, nature was not itself the object of scientific research. In general, science is identified as a culture that has emerged from the Western Modern Age, especially modern Western Europe (Cobern, 1998, 2000). Sumida (2012) contrasts Japanese and Western worldviews of 'Nature' from their different language-culture cognitions. The different worldviews of nature are well illustrated in the following old Japanese poem by Kino Tomonori (Ito, 1995): 'Cherry blossoms, on this quiet lambent day of spring, why do you scatter with such unquiet hearts?'

Newton might have resolved the concept behind the light from the sun, which is expressed as 'lambent' in the poem, using a prism and developed the theory of colour and light: 'Cherry blossoms scattering' might have inspired Galileo or Newton to discover the law of motion and gravity. Japanese people prefer to empathize with nature and natural phenomena and 'lambent' or 'cherry blossom scattering' have produced outstanding poetry and literature on nature. The Japanese view of nature emphasizes the appearance of the natural phenomenal world.

Kawasaki (2002) states that the Japanese worldview is basically different from the Western scientific worldview. He argues that the Japanese worldview leads Japanese people to search the phenomenal world for what appears to be so. In contrast to the Western worldview, the Japanese worldview does not rely on the world of ideas. It is not possible to describe the Japanese relationship between 'appearance' and 'what is transcendental' in terms of the dichotomy between 'appearance' and 'reality' as expressed in Standard Average European. The English term 'appearance' implies 'mutable and particular' and the English term 'reality' implies 'immutable and universal'. The dichotomy between them is linked with the value upheld by

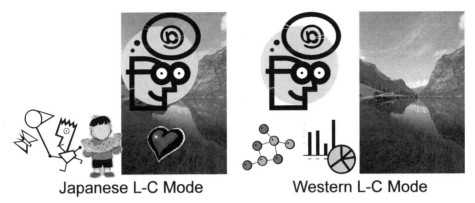

Japanese L-C Mode   Western L-C Mode

Figure 21.1 Japanese and Western Language-Culture (L-C) modes of understanding nature

the mainstream of Western philosophy for what is timeless and immutable (Boas, 1973).

In the Japanese Language-Culture tradition, 'reality' allows for a mutable and particular character, which is found only within appearance. The Japanese Language-Culture tradition has never valued the timeless and immutable and Japanese people take it for granted that they can appreciate the value associated with the mutable and particular. For example, Nakamura (1969: 359) argues 'the Japanese esteem the sensible beauties of nature, in which they seek revelations of the absolute world'. Nakamura's argument may perplex Westerners, because there seems to be a Japanese sameness encompassing the phenomenal world and the world of ideas, with no distinction between the two. These ideas are reflected diagrammatically in Figure 21.1.

Nakayama (1998) surveyed Grade 5 and 8 pupils' view of nature in six countries: Australia, China, Japan, the Philippines, Thailand, and the USA. He reported that there was a strong tendency among Asian pupils not to regard 'nature' as a target for logical explanations and finding things out, and that Asian pupils tended to regard familiarity between 'nature' and 'human' as important and 'nature' as something good for 'humans'. Asian Grade 5 and 8 pupils agreed with the item 'Nature and humans are inseparable' significantly more often than the Western pupils.

Thus the purpose of activities such as collecting and raising insects, which are very popular in Japanese kindergartens, is not to study the body parts and the ecology of insects or to 'observe' them from an immutable and universal point of view. It is to acknowledge life and develop an appreciation and respect for it. Scientific language, on the other hand, has to eschew personal feelings and fancies and aspire to objectivity and universality in line with nature (Crosland, 2006). The Japanese view of nature (*shizen* in Japanese) has more affinity with 'environment' than 'nature' in English, and is thus incommensurate with the Western scientific view of nature.

Case Study: The Ladybird Project – a case study of the content field 'Environment' in a Japanese kindergarten

Context and participants

The course of study for Japanese kindergartens emphasizes child-centred activities, such as spontaneous and integrated play. The project discussed here was implemented over two weeks in a kindergarten class located in Ehime prefecture. The project was introduced to 4-year-old children in the kindergarten by a female teacher and included a range of activities that enabled children to find, collect, feed, and watch ladybirds. The conversations between the teacher and the children were recorded using her own voice recorder.

Specifically, the 4-year-olds in the kindergarten went to 'Zukkoke Land' (a small hill situated on the premises of a nearby primary school). Since they were given time for free play, some children started picking flowers and running around. However, four children, including the focus of this study (Child A, initially considered a timid child), found some ladybirds and started collecting them. Prior to the activity, each child had an insect collecting pot for his or her own use.

Activity flow

'Catch a ladybird for me': 6 May

While other children were trying to catch ladybirds, Child A tugged on the hemline of the teacher's uniform and pleaded, 'Catch me a ladybird. My ladybird, my ladybird, please.' The teacher responded to Child A by saying, 'Let's catch your ladybird together.' Since it was a challenging task, the bell rang before they could catch any. Then the teacher asked, 'Shall we come back here to catch them tomorrow?' Child A replied, 'Yes, yes.' However, they couldn't find any the following day either.

'I caught it!': 9 May

On the third day, Child A was searching for ladybirds beside Child B who was good at catching them. Delighted, Child A beamed and shouted, 'I found one!' Child B kindly said to him, 'Catch it slowly so that it doesn't fall down on to the grass.' Child A scooped it gently and requested the teacher to, 'hurry, hurry, open the lid of my pot, Miss. It will fly away.' Then he placed it in the pot and closed its lid. He proudly showed it to the teacher saying, 'I did it. Here's the ladybird that I caught.'

Before long, Child B, who was looking for ladybirds on the hillside, called out to the children, 'I have found a family of ladybirds. Come, come!' They saw four ladybirds on the leaves of felon herb. Child A was able to catch a second ladybird there as well. 'Place the leaves with the ladybird in the pot,' Child B suggested. Accordingly, Child A picked a leaf from the plant and placed it in the pot. 'Now you have a nice house for them,' the teacher said.

'Yes,' he replied. Child B informed him, 'You may put some greenflies in the cage 'cos ladybirds eat them.' The teacher beside them asked, 'B, where are the greenflies? Please tell us.' Then, Child B pointed in their direction, 'Here, here.' Child A picked up a smooth tare leaf with many greenflies clinging to it and placed it in the pot too. When he returned to the kindergarten room, he proudly said to his peers and teachers in the room, 'I caught them!' while showing the ladybirds in the insect pot.

'Ladybirds fly. They like leaves and eat greenflies': 10 May

Child A came to kindergarten while holding the pot with the ladybirds that he had managed to catch as if they were his treasure. He said to the teacher, 'The ladybirds sometimes fly. They fly in this pot.' 'Huh, they fly? How do they fly?' asked the teacher. Then, he promptly replied, 'Wings come out, and they fly. My ladybirds flew.'

After that, he went out to collect more ladybirds and saw Child C, who was alone at the time, placing ladybirds into his insect pot. Then he initiated a conversation with Child C: 'Ladybirds like leaves and greenflies. Greenflies are yellow green. I caught them just over here.' Upon hearing these words from Child A, Child D started singing an improvised song: 'Greenflies are meals for ladybirds. You can find ladybirds where greenflies are. 'Cos they are meals for ladybirds.' Child A just scoffed at the song and went to start looking for ladybirds again.

'My Ladybirds are seven-spotted ones': 11 May

While staring at the ladybirds in the pot, Child C mumbled, 'They wear different clothes.' 'Are their clothes different?' asked the teacher. 'Well, the patterns are different,' he replied. Then the teacher shared the information with Child A: 'I heard C's ladybirds have different patterns.' Child A compared his with C's and said, 'Their patterns are different from mine.' Then Child B said, 'Yours are seven-spotted ladybirds.' Besides, C's have red spots on their black back. Wondering what kind of ladybirds C's ones were, the children searched for a book about ladybirds. With their heads together, including A's, they peered at the book. Child A pointed to a picture in the book and said, 'This is the same as mine.' Child A found out that his ladybirds are called 'seven-spotted ladybirds', and C's are 'multi-coloured'. The teacher added, 'Yours have seven spots on their back. That's why they are called seven-spotted ladybirds.' After hearing it, Child A confirmed the details by counting the number of spots.

'I found a pupa': 13 May

Child B found a pupa of a ladybird and said, 'Look, a ladybird pupa [*sic*]. A ladybird comes out from this and it grows.' 'Same as crawfish', Child A conjectured. While doing so, Child A gave instructions to Child B, 'Pick up gently together with a leaf. Then, attach the leaf to the pot with tape.' Child A watched him intently.

'I found a pupa too': 16 May

Child A returned to kindergarten with the ladybirds in the pot and a lady-bird's pupa in a cup. 'Look. I went out to catch it with my mother. It's a ladybird pupa [*sic*].' He showed the cup. Inside the cup was a leaf attached with tape. A pupa was on the leaf. The teacher said, 'It doesn't move, does it?' 'A pupa doesn't. It will be a ladybird soon,' Child A replied. Then, he produced two name-cards in the colour and shape of his insects. He held them out to the teacher and requested, 'Please write their names on these, Spotty and Dotty.' He attached the completed name-cards to the cup using clear tape.

'I'll catch it for you': 19 May

Child F was a new recruit to the group collecting ladybirds. 'If I find it, I'll give it to you. A ladybird flies and spatters stinky water,' Child A said while guiding Child F to the place they referred to as 'a house of ladybirds.'

'Ladybird picture-card show': 20 May

Before going home, the teacher gathered the whole class together and told a story by showing picture cards of 'A ladybird with seven stars on its back' (Imamori, 2005). One of the picture cards illustrated a scene in which the ladybird, when attacked by an enemy, spattered orange-coloured liquid. When Child A saw it, he excitedly claimed, 'I've been spattered.' He was eagerly listening to the story, obviously stimulated by various photos of lady-bird eggs and larvae, which were all novel to him.

'I let my ladybirds go away': 23 May

Child A came to kindergarten with an empty insect pot. 'What happened to your ladybirds?', the teacher asked. He answered, 'I let them go. A baby lady-bird, too.' He told her that the pupa had become a ladybird on the weekend, and that he had released all the ladybirds altogether.

Collectively, at first, the children had eagerly collected ladybirds. Then they had experiences in which they fed and raised these insects by themselves. Through those experiences, they seemed to stumble upon the realization that ladybirds are not mere objects to be kept for themselves, but living things that have their own lives, just like they have as children. Moreover, the children began to realize they were giving living greenflies to the ladybirds as their food.

Discussion

The 4-year-olds' activities of finding, collecting, feeding, and watching ladybirds described in the case study above will be discussed from two points of view – scientific awareness and multifaceted learning – to show how these could be developed into diverse and rich learning experiences.

Connections with fundamental scientific concepts

During the two weeks of ladybird activities, Child A developed a lot of scientific awareness. As a result, the following were considered scientific ideas that could form the foundation of children's scientific learning later in their education:

- *Habitat of insects*: Children discovered where the ladybirds' habitat was in order to collect them.
- *Food of insects*: Children wondered and searched for the ladybirds' food in order to feed them.
- *Diversity of insects*: Children noticed the ladybirds' characteristics and distinguished between them according to their different patterns.
- *Metamorphosis of insects*: Children got an idea about the ladybirds' metamorphosis through discovery and observation of ladybird's pupae.
- *Life cycle of insects*: Children came across the ladybirds' life cycle because they wondered about the life cycle stage, 'pupa'.
- *Food chain*: Children learned about the food chain between living things since they knew that a ladybird eats many greenflies.

Multiple and integrated learning

Scientific activities during the integrated play that is a particular feature in early childhood in the natural environment, and which also emphasizes cooperation with others, are well suited to promote children's learning. Children's scientific play can be sustained, extended, and profound when appropriate environmental considerations are set in place. In the Japanese kindergarten, this can include making a viewing case and net available for each child for the purpose of collecting insects. In addition, a magnifying glass, together with drawing paper, is normally laid out for observing insects collected by children. Some picture books are arranged in the animal corner so that children can look at them whenever they have questions.

Child A had been quiet and shy. He had tended to depend on the teacher's help, that is, he required a one-to-one relationship with her. However, this changed through the course of the two weeks of ladybird activities. For instance, he proactively led a friend to the place where they could collect ladybirds. Moreover, he came to speak with confidence about his awareness and experiences in front of others. The integrated diverse learning observed in this case is indicated in Figure 21.2. The figure was arranged on the basis of Gardner's multiple intelligences (Gardner, 1999).

For Child A, the two weeks of activities involved different aspects of learning: 'intrapersonal learning' in which he attained self-fulfilment and learned about caring for small insects like the ladybirds that he managed to collect; 'linguistic learning' in which he learned rich expressions based on his own experiences; and 'interpersonal learning' in which he learned how to share information and cooperate with his friends through collecting and feeding the ladybirds.

Lastly, coordination and cooperation with Child A's family require a mention. They form the background for the intelligent awareness and study which Child A

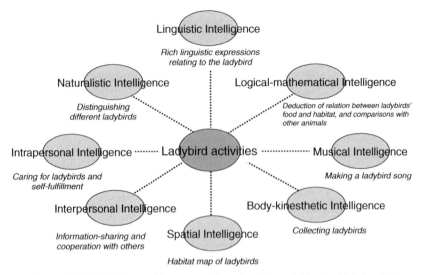

Figure 21.2 Multiple and integrated learning through the Ladybird activities

experienced. He went out to collect a ladybird pupa with his mother. His family, not only the kindergarten teacher, cared about his awareness and consideration towards ladybirds. In addition, a scientific event or exhibition held by a museum or a university could have been utilized to share information. Coordination and cooperation with the family and community will increase the strength of relationship between scientific play in early childhood and everyday life, making scientific play richer and more fruitful.

Conclusion

Since its inception, Japanese science education in early childhood has traditionally given priority to integrated learning, shying away from teaching individual subjects separately, and integrating peer collaboration into children's development. Academic learning, however, was not highly regarded. Specifically, it can be said that in early childhood, Japanese science education has focused on children's own interests and concerns through free play in order to awaken their emotion about natural phenomena rather than develop scientific literacy, as mandated in the 1956 National Course of Study for Japanese Kindergarten. It seemed, however, that children's naive intellectual curiosity was prevented from being fully channelled to scientific exploration and scientific thinking, by over-emphasizing the value of free play and limiting the teacher's role to an overly passive one. This dilemma intensified during the 1989 revision of the National Course of Study for Japanese Kindergarten, particularly when the name of the content field was changed from 'Nature' to 'Environment'.

The Japanese view of nature in kindergarten education results indirectly in a dichotomy between the traditional emphasis on empathy (or experience itself) and the cramming of knowledge about natural events and phenomena as the proper approach in early childhood, provoking controversy over the choice between free play and direct instruction; sometimes giving superficial weight to both also creates discussion. However, the presupposition that young children can only think concretely and not conceptually seems to have been totally refuted by research findings available today. Instead, what perhaps is needed in Japanese early childhood science education is innovative assessment to enhance children's potential for intellectual development through scientific activities but which is, at the same time, based on children's generative learning.

This could become a critical issue in science education in the early childhood years and suggests fruitful areas for research. How might coordination be achieved between the scientific worldview and views acquired elsewhere, while taking note of the contradictions and conflicts between scientific cultures and the cultures embedded in Language-Culture communities? The present discussion will contribute by enriching Japanese teachers' view of kindergarten activities and encouraging them to re-evaluate their diverse possibilities, and might also contribute to discussions in other countries where their own Language-Culture view of nature is incommensurate with that of Western scientific thought. Furthermore, as Sumida (2012) proposed, the concept of science education as a second language education could open the door to discussions in all countries regarding science learning in the early years, as a means of meeting diverse needs in a broader and more practical context in modern science-oriented society.

Find Out More

- What is the view of nature in kindergartens in your country?
- What sort of learning activities about nature occur in kindergartens in your country? In what ways are these particularly appropriate to the Language-Culture context?
- Which experiences would support the understanding and appreciation of different views of nature, and how would you assess them?

References and recommended reading

Boas, G. (1973) Nature, in P.P. Wiener (ed.) *Dictionary of the History of Ideas*, Vol. III. New York: Charles Scribner's Sons.

Cobern, W.W. (ed.) (1998) *Socio-cultural Perspectives on Science Education: An International Dialogue*. Dordrecht: Kluwer Academic.

Cobern, W.W. (2000) *Everyday Thoughts about Nature: A Worldview Investigation of Important Concepts Students Use to Make Sense of Nature with Specific Attention to Science*. Dordrecht: Kluwer Academic.

Crosland, M. (2006) *The Language of Science: From the Vernacular to the Technical*. Cambridge: Lutterworth Press.

Fujioka, H. (2011) Study in the field of the Environment in Kindergarten Course of Study: focus on transition and evaluation, *Annual Report of Researches in Environmental Education*, 19: 1–11 [in Japanese].

Fukada, S., Sumida, M., Masukagami, M. and Sakata, C. (2005) Learning about water in a Japanese kindergarten (*yochien*): two approaches to teaching science, *International Journal of Early Childhood Education*, 11(2): 65–80.

Gardner, H. (1999) *Intelligence Reframed: Multiple Intelligences for the 21st Century*. New York: Basic Books.

Gopnik, A. (2009) *The Philosophical Baby: What Children's Minds Tell Us About Truth, Love, and the Meaning of Life*. New York: Picador.

Gopnik, A., Meltzoff, A.N. and Kuhl, P.K. (2001) *The Scientist in the Crib: What Early Learning Tells Us About the Mind*. New York: HarperCollins.

Hatano, T. (2007) Education for natural science in kindergarten, *Bulletin of the Faculty of Education Mie University*, 58: 198–202 [in Japanese].

Imamori, M. (2005) *A Ladybug with Seven Stars on Its Back*. Tokyo: Kyouikugageki [in Japanese].

Ito, S. (1995) *Japanese View of Nature*. Tokyo: Kawade-shobo-shinsya [in Japanese].

Kawasaki, K. (2002) A cross-cultural comparison of English and Japanese linguistic assumptions influencing pupils' learning of science, *Canadian and International Education*, 31 (1): 19–51.

Metz, K. (1997) On the complex relation between cognitive developmental research and children's science curricula, *Review of Educational Research*, 67(1): 151–63.

Ministry of Education (1956) *Course of Study for Kindergarten*. Available at: www.nier.go.jp/guideline/s31k/index.htm [in Japanese] (accessed 10 April 2012).

Ministry of Education (1964) *Course of Study for Kindergarten*. Available at: www.nier.go.jp/guideline/s38k/index.htm [in Japanese] (accessed 10 April 2012).

Ministry of Education (1989) *Course of Study for Kindergarten*. Available at: www.mext.go.jp/b_menu/shuppan/sonota/890302.htm [in Japanese] (accessed 10 April 2012).

Mitsunari, K. (2007) The significance of education through the environment in early childhood education: based on the transition of kindergarten education guidelines and Dewey's way of thinking about the environment, *Bulletin of Kobe Tokiwa College*, 29: 25–31 [in Japanese].

Nakamura, H. (1969) *Ways of Thinking of Eastern Peoples*. Honolulu: University of Hawaii Press.

Nakayama, H. (1998) Results and implications of children's views of nature across the six countries, in S. Takemura (ed.) *Study on View of Science in Children, School and Society*. Research Project Report of Grant-in-Aid for International Cooperative Scientific Research (Project Number: 07044008).

National Research Council (2010) *Exploring the Intersection of Science Education and 21st Century Skills*. Washington, DC: National Academies Press.

Saracho, O.N. and Spodek, B. (2008) *Contemporary Perspectives on Science and Technology in Early Childhood Education*. Charlotte, NC: Information Age Publishing.

Settlage, J. and Southerland, S.A. (2007). *Teaching Science to Every Child: Using Culture as a Starting Point*. New York: Routledge.

Sumida, M. (2012) The Japanese and Western view of nature: beyond cultural incommensurability, in. T. Papatheodorou (ed.) *Debates on Early Childhood Policies and Practices: Global Snapshots of Pedagogical Thinking and Encounters*. Oxford: Routledge.

Sumida, M., Fukada, S., Nakamura, H., Masukagami, M. and Sakata, C. (2007) Developing young children's scientific, technological, and social competency through 'Pendulum' play activities at Japanese kindergarten, *Asia-Pacific Journal of Research in Early Childhood Education*, 1(1): 83–100.

Wellman, H. and Gelman, S. (1998) Knowledge acquisition in foundational domain, in D. Kuhn and R. Siegler (eds.) *Handbook of Child Psychology*. New York: Wiley.

Yamauchi, S. (1981) *Educating Nature for Young Children*. Tokyo: Meijitosho Suppan.

22

EARLY CHILDHOOD EDUCATION AND CARE IN THE UK: PIECEMEAL DEVELOPMENT THROUGH PHILANTHROPY, PROPAGATION, PLURALISM, AND PRAGMATISM

Jane Payler, Jan Georgeson
and Karen Wickett

Summary

In this final chapter, we briefly review developments in ECEC in the four constituent countries of the UK before closing with a case study of one setting in England as an example of how international ideas can be picked up and assimilated into practice to meet local needs and priorities.

Introduction

For over a century, the development of provision for the care and education of young children in the UK has been characterized by a diversity of approaches and motivations. We have a long history of home-grown programmes (Robert Owen, the MacMillan sisters) but also of propagation through 'grafting' – the enthusiastic adoption of approaches from other countries (Froebel, Montessori and, more recently, HighScope and Reggio Emilia). The motivations behind support for early childhood provision have included the philanthropy and community-mindedness of church and social groups, sometimes in collaboration with the self-help movement of community playgroups, but also a heavy dose of political pragmatism to use ECEC to meet political agendas or serve national needs. Day care nurseries were quickly set up to help women to work in factories during the Second World War (and disappeared just as quickly in the 1950s as women were returned to the home) and more recently provision of quality childcare has been adopted as a major incentive to prompt single parents back into work to reduce welfare dependency. Early years academics and lobbyists have been striving for recognition of the importance of appropriate curricula and pedagogy to support young children's learning and development, interpreted according to specific social, cultural, and historical contexts (Walsh et al., 2010: 55); governments meanwhile have focused on providing access to childcare places for working parents or compensatory education and development for children from disadvantaged families, all with a view to reducing inequalities in life chances and creating successful schoolchildren for a successful work force.

Adding to the complexity is the changing constitutional status of the four countries (England, Wales, Scotland, and Northern Ireland) that make up the UK, amplifying differences in the ways in which early childhood provision is organized in the four countries. At the same time as early years was moving into the centre of policy and funding across the UK, the advent of the Labour government also led to devolution of power to the four home countries in 1999. Although provision in England is often assumed as the default option for the whole of the UK, English practitioners are surprised – and occasionally a little jealous (Thomas, 2005: 75) – when they become aware of the different direction taken by their colleagues in the provinces. The differences between the four countries are complex and there is not enough room here to do more than give a flavour of the different ways in which provision has developed.

Early childhood education and care in England

The age at which children must by law start attending school is – and has been since the Education Act of 1870 (House of Commons, 2001) – the term following their fifth birthday but, since around 2000, most children have tended to start school from the beginning of the school year in which they become 5, joining the 'reception class'; younger children, however, might gradually build up to whole-day attendance during their first term. The reception class provides a bridge between early years provision and entry to Key Stage 1 at 5–6 years of age, when children embark on the National Curriculum. Over the last twenty years, early years provision for children before they start school moved up political agendas as the long promised expansion of nursery education finally became a reality. A series of reports in the early 1990s – The Rumbold Report *Starting with Quality* (DES, 1990) and the Royal Society of Arts Report *Start Right* (Ball, 1994) – had argued the case for quality in early years education. Then in 1996, over twenty years after Thatcher's White Paper (DES, 1972) had proposed that nursery education would be provided for all who wanted it, the Conservative government introduced 'vouchers' for free part-time nursery education for all 4-year-olds. With the change of government the following year, and Labour's mantra of 'education, education, education', funding was gradually extended and, at the time of writing, all 3- and 4-year-olds in England are entitled to 15 hours of free nursery education for 38 weeks a year, and 20% of 2-year-olds (those who are disadvantaged according to the 'free school meals' formula) will be entitled to free nursery provision, with plans to extend this to 40% from September 2014.

Because of the piecemeal way in which provision for early education and care has developed in England (and indeed in the UK in general), 'nursery education' takes place in a very wide range of early years settings (nursery schools and classes, reception classes, private, local authority and workplace day nurseries, children's centres, community playgroups and preschools, and by childminders). These settings have different finance streams (public, private, voluntary, and mixed funding), different session times, different kinds of buildings, and employ staff with a bewildering array of different vocational and academic qualifications (as well as some staff with no qualifications) (DfE, 2010).

Over the last fifteen years, a new kind of setting, the 'children's centre', has developed out of the Sure Start programme and the Labour government's 'Every Child Matters' agenda to provide a local 'one-stop shop' for children's services, with an emphasis on universal services, joined-up working and social inclusion, and usually including daycare provision (DfES, 2003). Nonetheless, all settings that provide government-funded early education are inspected to the same regulatory framework and must help children progress towards the same 'early learning goals'. These were set out in the 2008 Early Years Foundation Stage (EYFS), a comprehensive framework setting out standards for the welfare, care, learning, and development of children from birth to age 5 years (DCSF, 2008).

In September 2008, all registered early years providers and schools were required to use the EYFS, which built on earlier curriculum guidance from the government, and was shaped by changing government agendas. The 'Desirable Outcomes for Children's Learning on Entering Compulsory Education' (DLOs; SCAA, 1996) had accompanied the Conservative government's introduction of nursery vouchers and set out what children were expected to know before they entered Key Stage 1 of the National Curriculum. The DLOs document was criticized for its emphasis on outcomes, which seemed more like subject-specific attainment targets, confirming suspicions that early years provision was becoming shaped by the National Curriculum (Edwards and Knight, 1994: 3). With the advent of the Labour government the following year, new curriculum guidelines were developed 'to address concerns that early years practitioners might be delivering an inappropriate curriculum in their attempts to reach targets' for 3- and 4-year-olds (English, 2001). The Curriculum Guidance for the Foundation Stage (CGFS; QCA, 2000) set out principles and practice to support a play-based curriculum for children aged 3–5 years, which by then was recognized as a distinct educational phase. The CGFS broke development down into defined 'stepping stones' towards thirteen 'early learning goals' in broadly the same six areas as the DLOs: communication, language, and literacy; mathematics; personal, social, and emotional development; knowledge and understanding of the world; physical development; and creative development. At the end of the school year in which they became 5, children were assessed on a 9-point scale for each goal, and this assessment, the Foundation Stage Profile, replaced existing highly variable baseline testing on school entry. The CGFS was supplemented two years later by *Birth to Three Matters* (DfES, 2002), a framework of non-statutory guidance materials and resources to support those working with babies and toddlers, which was generally well received by the workforce.

The introduction of the 2008 EYFS brought together curriculum guidelines (CGFS and *Birth to Three Matters*) and regulatory frameworks (National Standards for Day Care: DfES/DWP, 2003) for the whole age range from birth to age 5 years. Although derided by some as a 'nappy curriculum' enabling the state to prescribe what is taught from birth, the aim was to provide a seamless progression from baby to schoolchild, and reflect the government's Every Child Matters agenda. This is evident in the four guiding principles:

1. *The unique child*: Every child is a competent learner from birth, who can be resilient, capable, confident, and self-assured.
2. *Positive relationships*: Children learn to be strong and independent from a base of loving and secure relationships with parents and/or a key person.
3. *Enabling environments*: The environment plays a key role in supporting and extending children's development and learning.
4. *Learning and development*: Children develop and learn in different ways and at different rates and all areas of learning and development are equally important and inter-connected.

The development and roll out of EYFS to settings was accompanied by well-funded initiatives for workforce development, with the introduction of Early Years Professional Status and the vision of a graduate leader in every setting by 2015, leading a workforce all vocationally qualified to a minimum of Level 3. Training and professional development across the children's workforce were aimed at more 'joined-up working', as part of the government's response in 2003 to the inquiry into the death of Victoria Climbié and the Every Child Matters agenda.

Another change of government and a downturn in the economy has led to another change in direction, from universal to targeted services, and from the Foundation Stage as a stage of learning in it own right, to a time to develop readiness for school. The new government commissioned an independent review of the EYFS, the Tickell Review of the Early Years Foundation Stage (Tickell, 2011), underpinned by the Field and Allen reports (Field, 2010; Allen, 2011), and a revised Early Years Foundation Stage was launched and implemented by all registered early years providers from September 2012. While the four Principles remain, there is a new focus on foundational learning in three *prime* areas of learning and development (physical; communication and language; personal, social, and emotional) with four additional *specific* areas (literacy; mathematics; understanding the world; expressive arts and design). The government's desire to identify inadequate learning and development and put in place targeted interventions is reflected in the new statutory Progress Check for 2-year-olds (Department for Education, 2012: 10), similarly seen in the phonics test in primary schools for 6-year-olds.

Early childhood education and care in Wales

There is a very different flavour in the Welsh educational scene from the English one. This is strengthened by a more marked historical sense of community, where collaboration rather than competition is the watchword for public services, and where co-operative instincts are deeply ingrained in local communities. Wales' distinctive educational heritage has emerged a consequence of a long struggle for its own identity, which many would argue was fought in the teeth of several centuries of opposition from the British (for which read 'English') establishment.

(Hawker, 2009)

Although Professor David Hawker was speaking about the whole of the Welsh education system, what he says applies particularly well to early years education and care. Before 1997, although there was often a different 'flavour' to documents relating to the curriculum in Wales, they fitted within the same overall framework as England. For example, after the Education Reform Act in 1988, Welsh language was added to the National Curriculum in Wales and in 1996 Wales had a different version of the Desirable Learning Outcomes, with the same six areas of learning as England but a different pedagogical emphasis on experiences to promote particular learning outcomes, rather than attainment targets for under-5s to achieve.

In Wales, devolution heralded a divergence from England in many areas of education. As Jane Davidson, Minister for Education and Lifelong Learning, Welsh Assembly Government, wrote in the foreword to *The Learning Country: A Paving Document*:

> We share strategic goals with our colleagues in England – but we often need to take a different route to achieve them. We shall take our own policy direction where necessary, to get the best for Wales. It's right that we put local authorities, local communities and locally determined needs and priorities at the centre of the agenda for schools.
>
> (National Assembly for Wales, 2001)

So it was perhaps not a surprise to see the National Assembly of Wales taking a bold and radically different approach to provision for young children:

> Too often, children are introduced to formal skills before they are ready, with the risk of losing confidence and a love of learning. Children need more opportunities to learn through finding out about things that interest them, rather than focusing solely on what is determined by others.
>
> (Jane Davidson, speaking in the Welsh Assembly, quoted in the
> *Times Educational Supplement, 2003*)

A new Foundation Phase for 3- to 7-year-olds was created, spanning preschool (3–5) and Key Stage 1 (5–7), so that early education formed a continuum with statutory education. In contrast with an apparent move towards increased formality in learning for even the youngest of pupils in England, the Welsh approach, informed by international examples (including Australia, New Zealand, and Reggio Emilia in Italy; see Chapters 18, 14, 13, and 4), explicitly sought to maintain the place of experiential learning through children's first years of schooling:

> The Foundation Phase framework advocates a holistic, experiential and play-based approach to children's learning, with a balance of teacher-led and child-initiated activities (WAG 2008); that is, there is a specific requirement that practitioners allow time for, and find ways of supporting, child-led learning.
>
> (Maynard and Chicken, 2010: 29)

There was strong commitment, and funding, from the National Assembly govern-ment for this development, not least because it offered support for bilingual learning and the chance to shape a specifically Welsh educational identity, with early years education seen as 'crucial to the future of the Welsh language' (House of Commons, 1999).

The assembly found an extra £141 million from education, health, and social services budgets to fund free part-time nursery places for all 3-year-olds in Wales, for integrated centres offering wrap-around childcare and education through play for infants. The money also funded a pilot of a free breakfast scheme and the new Foundation Phase for 3- to 7-year-olds. Although the Foundation Phase was due to be rolled out across Wales in 2006, it was delayed until 2008 to provide more time for staff training and legislative changes. The extension of child-led learning required a generous staff-to-pupil ratio throughout the Foundation Phase; guide-lines stipulated one adult for every eight children, and that at foundation level teach-ers should have a degree in child development. Supported by a statutory framework, 'Framework for Children's Learning for 3- to 7-year-olds in Wales', the new Foun-dation Phase was rolled out over four years, concluding in September 2011 for all 6- to 7-year-olds.

For birth to age 3 years, there is the Flying Start programme, which is targeted at the most disadvantaged communities in Wales, aiming to give them a better start in life. It is made up of free part-time childcare for 2- to 3-year-olds, an enhanced health visiting service (where the health visitor caseload is capped at 110 children), access to parenting programmes and language and play sessions. In the areas in which it runs, these services are universally available to all children from birth to age 3 years and their families. This is linked to the 'Childcare is For Children' initiative, which aims to ensure that childcare supports the developmental needs of children and is widely available and affordable, so that parents can balance work, family, and other commitments. Overall the changes to provision for early education and care have been welcomed by schools and parents, but there are concerns about long-term funding.

Early childhood education and care in Scotland

Reflecting developments across the rest of the UK, one of Scotland's most notable changes in ECEC since the 1990s has been the rapid expansion of preschool edu-cation. From the stated objective in 1998/99 by the Labour government to offer free part-time preschool places to all 3- and 4-year-olds by 2002 (which became a statutory requirement in Scotland in 2002), almost all 3- and 4-year-olds in Scotland now attend preschool part-time, funded for 475 hours per year (equiva-lent to 12.5 hours a week for 38 weeks of the year). Local authorities have ensured the proliferation of early years places through commissions from private and vol-untary providers, known as 'partnership' provision, accounting for around 40% of places in 2010 (Kidner, 2011: 17) and mirroring the variety of settings for nursery education across the UK. More particular to Scotland, however, since the 1980s, is a renewed interest in maintaining and supporting the Gaelic language in Scotland, which has grown (often through parental pressure) following a period in which the language declined (Scottish Government, 2005). In a survey on behalf of the Scottish Government in 2010, it was reported that 127 nurseries in a variety of settings (local authority nursery classes, nursery schools, playgroups) offered some level of Gaelic medium early years education (Scottish Government, 2010). Given the findings of recent research (O'Hanlon et al., 2010) suggesting that far from holding back children's English language competence, Gaelic medium education in fact shows some indication of enhancing it, the expansion of such provision may be likely to receive further support in the future as part of Scotland's distinctive pattern of ECEC.

Since devolution, Scotland has forged its own path in a number of other areas of ECEC, underpinned by clear aspirations to reduce inequalities and focus on preventative measures rather than crisis interventions. As Kidner (2011: 3) explains, the emphasis on local development to engender change was strengthened in 2009 by the Early Years Framework, a strategy that was built on existing developments but also on bringing them together in one policy direction for children from birth to age 8 years. The areas of distinctive development are based around:

- aspirations for integrated services for children across sectors of care and education;
- approaches to curriculum; and
- workforce development.

The implementation of *integrated services* for children was sought through *Getting it Right for Every Child* (Scottish Executive, 2006), described as a delivery mechanism to encourage the coordination of services, reduce bureaucracy, and increase personalization through consistency in assessment and planning for children across services. But this integrated provision is not yet a reality and Children in Scotland (2011) point out the continued divide between education and care: there are no universal funded daycare and education places for children under 3; care settings including day nurseries and childminders are registered with the Scottish Social Services Council, whereas nurseries and schools for children aged over 3 are overseen by Education Scotland. Children in Scotland (2011:13) argues for greater integration and for the benefits of universalism and early entitlement with regard to education and care for the very youngest children, rather than the current complex system of tax credits and nursery vouchers for some, citing the only partial success of Sure Start and Head Start in reaching their intended disadvantaged target group through targeted intervention (Children in Scotland, 2011: 7). Nonetheless, aspects of curriculum development go some way towards encouraging integrated and more seamless provision.

While *curricula developments* again show a divide between the periods up to and after the age of 3 years, integration is visible in the emphasis on holistic development and process-focused curricula, and in the concern for easing transition through – and ensuring coherence between – curricula for infants to older children. The curriculum for the youngest children, Pre-birth to Three, is reflected in the Early Level (from age 3 to the end of Primary 1 at around 5–6 years of age) of the Curriculum for Excellence (introduced August 2010; see Education Scotland, 2011a), spanning ages 3–18 years and aiming to build the capacities of successful learners, confident individuals, responsible citizens, and effective contributors.

Pre-Birth to Three: Positive Outcomes for Scotland's Children and Families (Education Scotland, 2011b), a multimedia resource, provides guidance for practitioners working with the youngest children and their families and implements The Early Years Framework (Kidner, 2011) as part of Scotland's strategy to reduce inequalities and 'build the capacity of individuals, families and communities so that they can secure the best outcomes for themselves' (Education Scotland, 2011b: 12). It aims for an evidence-based, socio-cultural approach founded on research on brain development, attachment and transitions, influenced by *Te Whāriki* (see Chapter 14), incorporating the pre-birth period and reflects the same principles and underpinning philosophy as the Curriculum for Excellence. It is based on four principles:

• rights of the child
• relationships
• responsive care
• respect.

Nine equally important features of effective practice include: the role of staff; attachments; transitions; observation, assessment, and planning; partnership working; health and wellbeing; literacy and numeracy; environments; and play.

From this, children move into the statutory Early Level of the Curriculum for Excellence. This aims to give children a consistent but flexible approach across this 3–6 age range, easing the transition into compulsory schooling and emphasizing a process-focused rather than a subject-content curriculum, echoing some of the aspects from Pre-birth. Its core themes aim to encourage early years practitioners towards a more active-learning and child-centred pedagogy: experiential learning; holistic approach to learning; smooth transitions; and learning through play (Education Scotland, 2011a). But research by Stephen (2010: 25) indicates that while teachers in Primary 1 classrooms all supported such an approach, it was not necessarily reflected in their practice. Experiences and outcomes are defined across the levels, although the intention is that children should move through the levels and parts of the levels at their own pace.

Workforce development has taken a particular route in Scotland. Nursery classes prior to 'partnership' provision were required to employ a teacher for every twenty preschool children (Kidner, 2011: 17), but on removal of this requirement in 2007 and with the expansion of preschool places, fewer teachers were employed, particularly in private and voluntary provision; those who were employed tended to have their hours spread more thinly. There has instead been a move towards up-skilling the partnership early years workforce with practitioners required from January 2010 to have at least a Level 3 qualification, while from December 2011, managers had to hold or be working towards the specified degree in childhood practice (Kidner, 2011: 19).

Early childhood education and care in Northern Ireland

At the time of writing, Northern Ireland, a country whose education system has been identified with conservatism and traditional methods, is facing the prospect of change in early years education and care as it awaits the Early Years Strategy for Northern Ireland (McMillan and Walsh, 2011), following a history of gradual development of ECEC services. In many ways mirroring developments in ECEC across the UK, nursery schools in Northern Ireland developed between the two world wars in areas of social and economic disadvantage with an attendant focus on compensatory support for health and welfare. It was some time later in the 1940s and 1950s before trained early years teachers were employed in nursery schools and were able to obtain a degree qualification to do so. The growth of private and voluntary preschool education, particularly in the form of preschool playgroups during the 1960s and 1970s, led to voluntary training for preschool staff despite the fact that there were no requirements for staff to hold qualifications in this sector of provision (McMillan and Walsh, 2011). However, a new focus on quality improvements in early years provision with the associated raft of policy developments and research evidence since the late 1990s (starting with the Pre-School Education Expansion Programme, PEEP, in 1998), reflecting those in England reported above, led to a requirement for early years leaders to hold a Level 3 qualification and to 'buy in' advice and support from a graduate early years specialist. More recently, in line with developments across the UK, an integrated approach to services for children and families, following Every Child Matters, has been sought.

Up until now, funded preschool education has been limited to children who are aged 3 years, where children generally attend preschool for two and a half hours a day, five days a week for a year before starting Primary 1, which has the earliest compulsory school starting age in Europe (4 years 2 months). Children attend a range of different early years settings, including nursery schools, day nurseries, nursery classes in primary schools, and voluntary or private preschools (Early Education, 2010), again reflecting the piecemeal development of ECEC as in the other UK nations. The early years curriculum followed at present is the Curricular Guidance for Pre-school Education (DENI, 2006a) and aims to encourage a rich play-based approach to activities, influenced by the writing of Malaguzzi (DENI, 2006a: 6; see Chapter 4). An active, experiential, and relational pedagogy is implied with a focus on development in:

- arts
- language
- early mathematical experiences
- personal, social, and emotional development
- physical development and movement
- the world around us.

Assessment is based on observation and aims to involve parents in formulating these assessments and using them to plan children's next steps.

Concern had been expressed in the past in relation to young children aged only 4 years entering school in Northern Ireland from this play-based curriculum and experiencing a curriculum and pedagogy too formalized to meet their learning and development needs (Oberhuemer, 2010). From the year 2000, a more play-based Enriched Curriculum was introduced into 120 pilot schools, culminating in 2007 in the introduction of a new Foundation Stage Curriculum for Primary 1 (4- and 5-year-olds) and 2 (5- and 6-year-olds) (see DENI, 2006b). The aim was to be more responsive to individual children's developmental stages and promote self-confidence and self-esteem (Walsh et al., 2010). Active learning, oral language skills, and the importance of outdoor learning were all emphasized. Evaluation of the Enriched Curriculum showed a move away from a teacher-led formal approach to a more play-based and informal pedagogy (Walsh et al., 2010: 56). Of particular note were the improvements in children's self-discipline, independence, and overall social and emotional development. However, concern was expressed with regard to how far the play-based approach prepared children for literacy and numeracy in later years. Further analysis suggested links between improvements and the level of teachers' competence and understanding in effectively implementing a play-based curriculum, knowing when and how to interact, intervene, prompt and share thinking, and when to instruct.

To address issues arising from having two separate curricula for the early years, which span preschool and the Foundation Stage, there was wide consultation from 2010 to 2011 on an Early Years (0–6) strategy. At the time of writing, the new strategy is still awaited. Its aim is to bring cohesion in curricula and services affecting children from birth to 4 years and their families and the initial years of primary school. This will involve bringing services such as Sure Start, targeted to the 20% most disadvantaged families in the country, into the remit of the Department of Education from The Department of Health, Social Services and Public Safety. The Department of Education's stated priority is to prepare children for learning and to secure parents' support in nurturing and preparing their children, and working with staff in preschool and school (DENI, 2010: 11). It makes it clear that any provision for birth to age 3 years will be 'in a targeted manner' (DENI, 2010: 19) and that the prime responsibility for care and learning for this age group are the parents and family. For children aged 3–4 years, free part-time education will continue to be provided. Connected to this, support for a less formal play-based curriculum for 4- to 6-year-olds is re-emphasized, and the age which children enter compulsory school education is said to be under consideration (DENI, 2010: 20). Additionally, access to Irish-medium preschool provision will be developed following the 2009 Review of Irish-Medium Education, which emphasized 'the benefits that they believe accrue from a high-quality preschool Irish-medium experience' (DENI, 2010: 14).

Reflecting on ECEC: cross-fertilization in action

We end the chapter, and indeed the book, with a case study from one setting in England as an example of how international ideas can be picked up and assimilated into practice to meet local needs and priorities. This process is echoed in many chapters in the book; ideas like play, child-centredness and involvement, as well as specific approaches like Reggio Emilia, *Te Whāriki*, and HighScope (or Step-by Step) now have a global presence, crossing between continents but being adapted to fit local contexts. We invite the reader to trace the links between Karen's story and the ideas and approaches mentioned in the previous chapters – and hope that the book overall has heightened awareness about where ideas have come from and where they can go, in the hands of sensitive, reflective practitioners.

Case Study: Karen's story

In 2003, I was employed as the teacher for a Sure Start Local Programme. My role was to lead and develop the pedagogy across the Sure Start area, particularly in the Neighbourhood Nursery. Practitioners who worked for such programmes had much autonomy when developing practices and services for children and their families (Lewis, 2011), but while I appreciated this luxury I wasn't sure where to begin.

I recalled reading Loris Malaguzzi's work about starting the preschools in Reggio Emilia. One of his guiding principles was that practitioners needed to listen to the children as 'things about children and for children are only learned from children' (cited in Edwards et al., 1998: 51). I also recognized that we can be active participants in families and communities and that it was important to reflect these aspects in our provision, too. I reflected not only on theory, but also on early years practices from other countries to provide different ways of looking at our space (Moss and Petrie, 2002). All in all, the active processes of dialogue and reflection enabled us to interpret and construct practices that met the needs of participants and reflected the particular culture of children, their families, and community.

Reflecting on learning environments

To begin with, as a team we considered our own learning experiences. We realized that when we were involved in an experience in which we were learning and that the learning was fun and meaningful to us, time flew by. Practitioners linked this understanding to the work of Csikszentmihalyi (1979), who identified the state of 'flow'. His theory confirmed practitioners' implicit belief that when a child is busy (in a state of flow) they are having a meaningful learning experience. To support the team in developing a shared understanding of flow and to provide us with tools for fostering it, I drew on Laevers' (1994) five levels of involvement. When learners are experiencing level 5 of involvement, it is similar to Csikszentmihalyi's state of flow.

During a Professional Development day we discussed and reflected on our learning, the children's learning, and levels of involvement. We realized that in order for children to be highly involved we needed to create a learning environment where children really could become highly involved. As a team, we stated our intentions in the Introduction to the Planning File for how involvement would be facilitated through the environment:

Essential elements of the learning environment include –

- open-ended resources/activities
- routines that flow with the learner and enable learners to become engrossed in their learning
- all areas within the setting to be accessible during the whole day, e.g. outside, quiet area, busy area
- practitioners who listen and tune into the children and who will engage with children when it is appropriate

(Introduction to Planning File)

Wellbeing and relationships

Although we were aware that a learner's level of wellbeing would affect his or her levels of involvement, it was not until we explored the key-person role further that we deepened our understanding of the learning environment. Instead of planning mainly for the physical environment, we realized that the learning environment was multi-faceted, all of which need to be planned for in order for learners to reach their full potential. This is particularly true of the emotional environment and links to another important aspect of Laevers' work, levels of wellbeing (Laevers, 2005).

For children to feel secure and able to become highly involved, they need an appropriate relationship with their key-person. An example illustrates: during one practitioner's pedagogic support session, she explained that although a particular child always looked busy, she was unsure of the child's particular interests and how far they were reflected in her play. We went to observe the child together and realized that she did indeed make herself busy, for example playing in the sand and water, pushing them backwards and forwards, but her play was stereotypic and repetitive with little evidence of challenging, playful learning. The practitioner consequently planned to spend more time with the child and establish a deeper relationship with her. In time, the child appeared to feel more secure and showed higher levels of wellbeing. This, the practitioner felt, enabled her to become more highly involved in her play and learning.

Relationships beyond the setting

The practitioner above had taken time to establish a relationship with the child within the setting. But another crucial role of the key-person is to establish relationships with parents/carers and share information. The informal chats as they dropped off and picked up their child from the setting were often times when parents shared valuable information. Duncan et al. (2006) found that parents preferred informal interactions with practitioners rather than formal contacts such as open evenings or parent literacy workshops. Informal chats on a day-to-day basis enabled relationships to develop and information to be shared in an easy yet respectful manner. For instance, a parent mentioned that each weekend he enjoyed going to motor cross races with his son. The key-person used this information to plan for the child. She organized a visit to the motorbike shop and collected old motorbike parts for outside role-play. Such partnerships recognize that children's learning does not only happen in the setting with the practitioners. Indeed, as Easen et al. (1992) argue, 'professional experience and parents' everyday experience are seen as complementary but equally important' (Easen et al., 1992: 285). These relationships enable practitioners to gain a fuller understanding of the child's world and learning beyond the setting and enabled bridges to be built between the child's various learning experiences as well as reflecting the child's culture in the setting.

Recording/documenting learning

To the untrained eye, play can be messy, chaotic, and may superficially show little evidence of learning. External pressures can cause practitioners to compromise their beliefs that young children learn through play. Therefore it was crucial that we evidenced the children's learning during their play. We had moved away from tick sheets when recording children's learning, as we believed these only recorded and valued certain skills. Instead, we wanted to illuminate *how* children were making sense of the world during their playful activities. As a team, we developed our skills at writing narrative observations. We explored *why* we noticed what we saw and why this interested us. This process of 'radically looking' and 'radically listening' (Clough and Nutbrown, 2002) made the familiar strange and enabled us to gain a sense of the child's perspective of the world. The analytical concepts and tools we adopted were schemas (Athey, 1990), levels of involvement and wellbeing (Laevers, 2005), and Lillian Katz's dispositions for learning (Katz, 1993).

Developing this aspect of practice changed our identity and role as early years practitioners. No longer did we plan discrete outcomes to teach the children, but rather we accompanied the children as they made sense of the world. Our role was to plan and provide a rich and challenging environment and to watch, listen, and support their learning. It was still important to fulfil policy requirements to demonstrate to those who were sceptical that in fact the children were learning and so our systems of observation, which were linked to the Development Matters in the EYFS (DCSF, 2008), acted as a bridge between policy expectations and enabling the children to play to learn.

Children as meaning-makers

Although we gathered a range of documentation and used it to evidence children's learning as required by policy, we still felt there were not consistent and rigorous processes to show *how* children were making sense of the world. We looked abroad to consider how others in ECEC documented and analysed children's learning. During a Professional Development day we considered Margaret Carr's Learning Stories from New Zealand, documentation from the preschools in Reggio Emilia, and Pen Green's portfolios of children's learning (see http://www.pengreen.org/pengreenresearch.php). Together we discussed and explored these examples and how they might foster possibilities for us. During this process, we created an analytical framework based on Taking an Interest, Wellbeing, Challenge, and Relationships that suited our philosophies and principles.

Listening to children's voices: the wall comes down

When I started my position in the setting, I often observed toddlers in the baby room looking over the metal gate into the main nursery. Sometimes they would cry and shake the gate. After a while a practitioner would carry the child back into the baby room and distract them until they were settled. I often reflected and wondered if this was what the toddler wanted, realizing how the spaces we provide can silence their voices. In time, when practitioners had an opportunity to consider and develop their understanding of a variety of practices, we wrote the setting's principles. It was striking that all members of the team had felt unheard in the past and were determined to ensure that practices ensured all members were listened to. One of the principles now states the team would:

> Listen to each other and ensure that everyone is able to make themselves understood. We are positive in our responses, providing support and encouragement for the individual.

> (Setting's Principles, 2006)

When reflecting on our principles, we realized the environment and our practices were not allowing children's voices to be heard either. The decision was made to knock down the wall between the rooms so that babies and young children could use the whole space as they chose. That was six years ago. Since then other practices such as mixed aged key-groups have developed, enabling greater flexibility. No one practitioner is responsible for the quiet room (previously baby room). Instead, practitioners are responsible for their key-children. If one of their key-children needs a secure space, the practitioner works in the quiet area until the child feels comfortable enough to use other parts of the setting.

Throughout our journey of developing the learning environment, it has been crucial for us to consider theory and practices from the international ECEC community. This process has supported us to articulate our beliefs and understanding about children and the spaces we create for them to support learning.

References and recommended reading

Allen, G. (2011) *Early Intervention: The Next Steps: An Independent Report to Her Majesty's Government*. London: Cabinet Office. Available at: http://www.dwp.gov.uk/docs/early-intervention-next-steps.pdf (accessed 8 June 2012).

Athey, C. (1990) *Extending Thought in Young Children*. London: Paul Chapman.

Ball, C. (1994) *Start Right: The Importance of Early Learning*. ED 372 833. London: Royal Society of Arts.

Children in Scotland (2011) *Early Childhood Education and Care: Developing a Fully Integrated Early Years System*. Available at: http://www.childreninscotland.org.uk/docs/CIS_ECECSpecialReport2_001.pdf (accessed 6 June 2012).

Clough, P. and Nutbrown, C. (2002) *A Student's Guide to Methodology*. London: Sage.

Csikszentmihalyi, M. (1979) The concept of flow, in B. Sutton-Smith (ed.) *Play and Learning*. New York: Gardner.

Department for Children Schools and Families (DCSF) (2008) *Statutory Framework for the Early Years Foundation Stage*. London: DCSF.

Department for Education (DfE) (2010) *Childcare and Early Years Providers Survey: Research Brief*. Available at: http://www.education.gov.uk/rsgateway/DB/STR/d001024/index.shtml (accessed 10 May 2012).

Department for Education (DfE) (2012) *Statutory Framework for the Early Years Foundation Stage*. Available at: https://www.education.gov.uk/publications/standard/AllPublications/Page1/DFE-00023-2012 (accessed 11 June 2012).

Department for Education Northern Ireland (DENI) (2006a) *Curricular Guidance for Pre-school Education*. Available at: http://www.deni.gov.uk/pre_school_guidance_pdf (accessed 28 April 2012).

Department for Education Northern Ireland (DENI) (2006b) *Understanding the Foundation Stage*. Belfast: An Early Years Interboard Group Publication. Available at: http://www.nicurriculum.org.uk/docs/foundation_stage/UF_web.pdf (accessed 8 June 2012).

Department for Education Northern Ireland (DENI) (2010) *Early Years (0–6) Strategy*. Available at: http://www.deni.gov.uk/english__early_years_strategy_.pdf.pdf (accessed 28 April 2012).

Department for Education and Skills (DfES) (2002) *Birth to Three Matters: A Framework to Support Children in their Earliest Years*. Nottingham: DfES Publications.

Department for Education and Skills (DfES) (2003) *Every Child Matters: Presented to Parliament by the Chief Secretary to the Treasury by Command of Her Majesty, September 2003*, Cm 5860. London: Stationery Office.

Department for Education and Skills (DfES) and Department for Work and Pensions (DWP) (2003) *Full Day Care: National Standards for under 8's Day Care and Child Minding*. Nottingham: DfES Publications.

Department of Education and Science (DES) (1972) *Education: A Framework for Expansion*. London: HMSO.

Department of Education and Science (DES) (1990) *Starting with Quality (The Rumbold Report)*. London: DES.

Duncan, J., Bowden, C. and Smith, A.B. (2006) A gossip or a good yack? Reconceptualizing parent support in New Zealand early childhood centre based programmes, *International Journal of Early Years Education*, 14(1): 1–13.

Early Education (2010) *Early Education Response to the Department of Education Northern Ireland Early Years (0–6) Strategy*. Available at: http://www.early-education.org.uk/sites/default/files/Northern%20Ireland%20Early%20Years%20(0-6)%20Strategy%20-%20Early%20Education%20Response%20-%20November%202010.pdf (accessed 6 June 2012).

Easen, P., Kendall, P. and Shaw, J. (1992) Parents and educators: dialogue and development through partnership, *Children and Society*, 6(4): 282–96.

Education Scotland (2011a) *Curriculum for Excellence: Supporting the Early Level*. Available at: http://www.educationscotland.gov.uk/earlyyears/ curriculum/supportingearlylevel/index. asp (accessed 28 March 2012).

Education Scotland (2011b) *Pre-Birth to 3: Positive Outcomes for Scotland's Children and Families*. Available at: http://www.educationscotland.gov.uk/earlyyears/prebirthtothree/index. asp (accessed 28 March 2012).

Edwards, A. and Knight, P. (1994) *Effective Early Years Education*. Buckingham: Open University Press.

Edwards, C., Forman, G. and Gandini, L. (eds.) (1998) *The Hundred Languages of Children: The Reggio Emilia Approach to Early Childhood Education – Advanced Reflections*. Norwood, NJ: Ablex.

English, E. (2001) Teaching for understanding: curriculum guidance for the foundation stage, *Evaluation and Research in Education*, 15(3): 197–204.

Field, F. (2010) *The Foundation Years: Preventing Poor Children Becoming Poor Adults: The Report of the Independent Review on Poverty and Life Chances*. London: Cabinet Office.

Hawker, D. (2009) *What could England Possibly Learn from Wales?* Inaugural Lecture: The College of Teachers at the Institute of Education, University of London, 14 May 2009. Available at: http://www.collegeofteachers.ac.uk/sites/ default/files/images/David%20 Hawker%20lecture%20pdf.pdf (accessed 15 May, 2012).

Hedges, H. and Cullen, J. (2005) Subject knowledge in early childhood curriculum and pedagogy: beliefs and practices, *Contemporary Issues in Early Childhood*, 6(1): 66–79.

House of Commons (1999) *The Welsh Affairs Committee's Report 'Childcare in Wales' Welsh Affairs – Third Report*, 25 May 1999. London: HMSO.

House of Commons (2001) *Select Committee on Education and Employment First Report: Early Years*. Available at: http://www.publications.parliament.uk/pa/ cm200001/cmselect/cme-duemp/33/3306.htm (accessed 20 May 2012).

Katz, L.G. (1993) Dispositions as educational goals. *ERIC Digest, EDO-PS-93-10*. Champaign, IL: ERIC Clearinghouse on Elementary and Early Childhood Education, University of Illinois.

Kidner, C. (2011) *Early Years – Subject Briefing*. Scottish Parliament Information Centre (SPICe) Briefing 11/51. Available at: http://www.scottish.parliament.uk/ResearchBriefings AndFactsheets/S4/SB_11-51.pdf (accessed 14 May 2012).

Laevers, F. (ed.) (1994) *Defining and Assessing Quality in Early Childhood Education*. Leuven: Leuven University Press.

Laevers, F. (ed.) (2005) *Well-being and Involvement in Care Settings: A Process-oriented Self-evaluation Instrument*. Original Dutch version. Leuven: Kind & Gezin and Research Centre for Experiential Education, University of Leuven.

Lewis, J. (2011) From Sure Start to children's centres: an analysis of policy change in English early years programmes, *Journal of Social Policy*, 40(1): 71–88.

Maynard, T. and Chicken, S. (2010) Through a different lens: exploring Reggio Emilia in a Welsh context, *Early Years: An International Journal of Research and Development*, 30(1): 29–39.

McMillan, D. and Walsh, G. (2011) Early years professionalism: issues, challenges and opportunities, in L. Miller and C. Cable (eds.) *Professionalization, Leadership and Management in the Early Years*. London: Sage.

Moss, P. and Petrie, P. (2002) *From Children's Services to Children's Spaces: Public Policy, Children and Childhood*. New York: RoutledgeFalmer.

National Assembly for Wales (NAfW) (2001) *The Learning Country – A Paving Document: A Comprehensive Education and Lifelong Learning Programme to 2010 in Wales.* Cardiff: NAfW.

Oberhuemer, P. (2010) Editorial, *Early Years: An International Journal of Research and Development*, 30(1): 1–3.

O'Hanlon, F., McLeod, W. and Paterson, L. (2010) *Gaelic-medium Education in Scotland: Choice and Attainment in Primary and Early Secondary School Stages.* Edinburgh: University of Edinburgh. Available at: http://www.soillse.ac.uk/downloads/Gaelic-Medium-Education-In-Scotland.pdf (accessed 20 May 2012).

Organization for Economic Cooperation and Development (OECD) (2001) *Starting Strong I: Early Childhood Education and Care.* Paris: OECD.

Organization for Economic Cooperation and Development (OECD) (2006) *Starting Strong II: Early Childhood Education and Care.* Paris: OECD.

Qualifications and Curriculum Authority (QCA) (2000) *Curriculum Guidance for the Foundation Stage.* London: Department for Education and Employment.

School Curriculum and Assessment Authority (1996) *Nursery Education: Desirable Outcomes for Children's Learning.* London: Department for Education and Employment.

Scottish Executive (2006) *Getting it Right for Every Child: Implementation Plan.* Edinburgh: Scottish Executive. Available at: http://www.scotland.gov.uk/Publications/2006/06/22092413/0 (accessed 24 May 2012).

Scottish Government (2005) *Report of the Gaelic Medium Teachers Action Group.* Available at: http://www.scotland.gov.uk/Publications/2005/11/2483916/39176 (accessed 24 May 2012).

Scottish Government (2010) *Review of Gaelic Medium Early Education and Childcare.* Available at: http://www.scotland.gov.uk/Publications/2010/06/22090128/ (accessed 20 May 2012).

Stephen, C. (2010) Pedagogy: the silent partner in early years learning, *Early Years: An International Journal of Research and Development*, 30(1): 15–28.

Thomas, S. (2005) The Foundation Phase: perceptions, attitudes and expectations. An overview of the ethos and an analysis of the implications of the implementation. Unpublished Master's dissertation, Trinity College, Carmarthen.

Tickell, C. (2011) *The Early Years: Foundations for Life, Health and Learning: An Independent Report on the Early Years Foundation Stage to Her Majesty's Government.* London: Department for Education.

Times Educational Supplement (2003) Formal foundation will be flushed away. Available at: www.tes.co.uk/teaching-resource/Formal-foundation-will-be-flushed-away-375685/ (accessed 8 June 2012).

Walsh, G.M., McGuinness, C., Sproule, L. and Trew, K. (2010) Implementing a play-based and developmentally appropriate curriculum in Northern Ireland primary schools: what lessons have we learned?, *Early Years: An International Journal of Research and Development*, 30(1): 53–66.

Welsh Assembly Government (WAG) (2008) *Framework for Children's Learning for 3–7 year olds.* Cardiff: WAG.

Subject Index

Author Index

OBSERVATION
Origins and Approaches in Early Childhood

Valerie Podmore and Paulette Luff

9780335244249 (Paperback)
2012

eBook also available

"This book is an excellent resource for all those studying or working in the field of early childhood. It deals with key issues of observational processes offering a balance between theory and practical activities. It is written in a critical, engaging and informative way, with scope for interesting discussions with students, and is a useful tool for lecturers and students as in learning about observations for all involved in early childhood education."
Dr. Ioanna Palaiologou, Lecturer, University of Hull, UK

Key features:

- An adaptation of a book that has been successful in New Zealand - updated with UK content
- Rich in examples, drawing on a variety of studies, policies and contexts to illustrate key points
- A range of practical techniques, both qualitative and quantitative for practitioners

www.openup.co.uk

 **OPEN UNIVERSITY PRESS**
McGraw · Hill Education

Printed in Great Britain
by Amazon.co.uk, Ltd.,
Marston Gate.